4th Edition

WORK WITH ENGLISH

von
Shaunessy Ashdown,
Isobel Williams und
Steve Williams

in Zusammenarbeit mit der Verlagsredaktion

Cornelsen

Verfasser: Shaunessy Ashdown, Berlin
Isobel Williams, Berlin
Steve Williams, Corio Bay Media, Melbourne
Berater: Erika Armbrust, Renningen
Philipp Fehrenbach, Nürtingen
Stefanie Gröne, Berlin
Nils Krämer, Düsseldorf
Hannelore Zimmermann, Gutach

Projektleitung: Jim Austin
Verlagsredaktion: Kari-ann Seamark
Redaktionelle Mitarbeit: Oliver Busch (Wörterverzeichnisse) Kieran Breen, Alice Gleeson, Stefanie Heimann, Maxi Kramer

Layout, technische Umsetzung und Umschlaggestaltung: Klein & Halm Grafikdesign, Berlin
Titelfotos: Shutterstock (10) AlamyRF/juice Images (1)
Bildredaktion: Gertha Maly
Illustrationen: Oxford Designers & Illustrators

Die Mediencodes enthalten ausschließlich optionale Unterrichtsmaterialien; sie unterliegen nicht dem staatlichen Zulassungsverfahren.

www.cornelsen.de

1. Auflage, 2. Druck 2012

Druck: Stürz GmbH, Würzburg

ISBN 978-3-06-520517-7

Inhalt gedruckt auf säurefreiem Papier aus nachhaltiger Forstwirtschaft.

Vorwort

Work with English 4th Edition ist die komplette Neubearbeitung des bewährten Lehrwerks für die Berufsfachschule. Der zweijährige Kurs baut auf den Englischkenntnissen eines Hauptschulabschlusses auf und führt zum mittleren Schulabschluss (CEFR-Einstufung: B1).

Das Buch ist wie folgt aufgebaut:

Units 1 bis 15	Jede Unit behandelt ein aktuelles, altersgerechtes Thema, ob beruflich (*options after school* oder *work abroad usw.*) oder persönlich (*social media, risky behaviour* oder *promoting tolerance usw.*). Kommunikation spielt eine wichtige Rolle und Binnendifferenzierung wird durch Zusatzaufgaben für Fortgeschrittene gefördert.
World of Work	In jeder Unit bereitet diese Doppelseite auf das Berufsleben vor und trainiert genau die berufsrelevanten Fertigkeiten, die jeder Berufseinsteiger braucht, wie z. B. das Telefonieren, das Bewerben und Kundengespräche.
How to	Die Units des ersten Lernjahrs (Units 1 bis 8) schließen mit einer Seite zur Entwicklung methodischer Kompetenzen ab. Hier beschäftigen sich die Lernenden anhand von kurzen Tipps und dazu passenden Aufgaben mit verschiedenen Lernstrategien wie Vokabellernen, dem Trainieren von Hörverstehen, Lesen und Schreiben, Mediation, u. a.
Exam practice	Doppelseiten in den Units des zweiten Lernjahrs (Units 9 bis 15) bieten Zusatzübungen zur Vorbereitung auf verschiedene Prüfungsformate.
Revision	Die Units 9 bis 15 schließen mit einem kurzen Test, der den Fortschritt der Lernenden überprüft.
Files	*Pairwork files* für die verschiedenen Aufgaben in den Units sind hier zu finden.
Further reading	Hier gibt es 15 zusätzliche Texte, passend zum Thema und Wortschatz der einzelnen Units mit Aufgabenapparat für stärkere Klassen.
Grammar summary	Alle Regeln und Formen sind hier übersichtlich zum Nachschlagen zusammengefasst.
Wörterverzeichnisse	Das Lehrwerk bietet einen Grundwortschatz, ein chronologisches Wörterverzeichnis nicht nur mit Übersetzungen, sondern auch mit Definitionen, Synonymen, Antonymen, usw. und ein alphabetisches Wörterverzeichnis an.

Work with English 4th Edition ist ein praxisnahes, inhaltlich und gestalterisch modernes Lehrwerk, das einen handlungsorientierten Unterricht ermöglicht, den Horizont der Lernenden erweitert und zur Arbeit mit der englischen Sprache motiviert.

Die Autoren und der Verlag wünschen Ihnen viel Freude und Erfolg bei der Arbeit mit **Work with English**!

Inhalt

Work with English im Internet

Auf den Seiten Ihres Kursbuches finden Sie am Ende jeder Unit einen so genannten „Webcode". Wenn Sie den entsprechenden Code auf der Webseite http://www.cornelsen.de/webcodes/ oben rechts eingeben, gelangen Sie zu weiterführenden Übungen, die die Themen der Unit (Grammatik, Vokabel, nützliche Redewendungen usw.) wiederholt. Sie können damit selbstständig zu Hause arbeiten.

Textquellen

S. 44 adaptiert und abgekürzt: http://finance.yahoo.com/career-work/article/109267/6-career-killing-facebook-mistakes

S. 88 adaptiert und abgekürzt: http://www.guardian.co.uk/society/2010/dec/16/christmas-charity-appeal-unity-gangs

S. 112 adaptiert und abgekürzt: http://www.guardian.co.uk/g2/story/0,,497788,00.html

S. 120 abgekürzt und leicht adaptiert: http://www.bbc.co.uk/news/magazine-15017790

S. 121 adaptiert: http://www.drinkaware.co.uk/facts/binge-drinking

S. 136 adaptiert und abgekürzt: http://news.bbc.co.uk/go/pr/fr/-/2/hi/south_asia/8299780.stm

S. 156 adaptiert: http://www.watoday.com.au/world/outsourcing-homework-to-india-20100409-ryh3.html#ixzz1UQLjg7Hp

S. 157 adaptiert: http://www.bbc.co.uk/news/technology-13012041

S. 160 information and quotes from: http://www.echsonline.org/academic-life.cfm/id/green-ambassadors

S. 166 adaptiert: http://www.careerfaqs.com.au/employment-news/1247/Tips+for+surviving+your+first+day+at+work

S. 180 adaptiert und abgekürzt: Barack Obama: *Dreams from My Father* (New York, 2004)

S. 182 abgekürzt und adaptiert: http://www.theexpressionist.com/2009/01/14/illegal-music-downloads-hurt-america/]

S. 185 adaptiert und abgekürzt: http://www.faz.net/aktuell/gesellschaft/familie/zehn-jahre-girls-day-nach-den-maedchen-kommen-die-jungs-1970132.html

S. 186 adaptiert und abgekürzt: http://www.europass.ie/europass/what.html und http://europass.cedefop.europa.eu/europass/home/hornav/Introduction.csp

S. 189 adaptierte Auszüge: http://www.newsthinking.com/story.cfm?SID=166

S. 191 adaptiert von The Better World Handbook: Small Changes That Make a Big Difference by Ellis Jones, Ross Haenfler, and Brett Johnson (New Society Publishers, 2007) und http://www.care2.com/greenliving/help-the-earth-buy-less-stuff.html#ixzz1fKvhuUGY

S. 193 based on information from www.visitmalta.com

S. 194 based on information from http://www.imdb.com/title/tt1010048/; http://en.wikipedia.org/wiki/Slumdog_Millionaire; http://globalvoicesonline.org/2009/01/26/india-reactions-to-slumdog-millionaire/

S. 195 based on information from http://www.fao.org/newsroom/en/news/2008/1000871/index.html und http://lifestyle.t-online.de/fast-food-statt-mozzarella-mittelmeerdiaet-ist-in-suedeuropa-out/id_15751092/index

Why English?

1

1 Warm-up

Use the phrases in the box and the words on the map to give your partner information about this country in which a lot of people speak English.

Example: *The official language of Germany is German.*

- official language
- main industries
- capital city
- population
- famous for
- national holiday
- second-largest city
- number of people per square kilometre
- number of English speakers

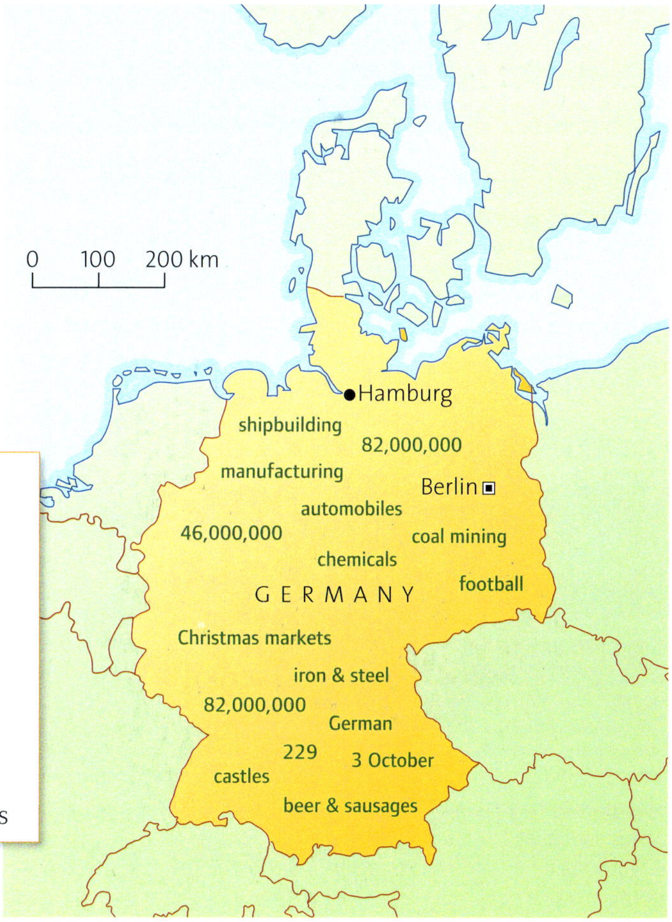

2 Asking questions

a Complete the questions about Germany with question words. Sometimes more than one answer is possible.

a … is the official language?
b … people live there?
c … is the national holiday?
d … is the Chancellor?
e … is English so important there?
f … do the people learn English?

Question words

What …?	*Was …?*	Why …?	*Warum …?*
When …?	*Wann …?*	How …?	*Wie …?*
Where …?	*Wo …?*	Who …?	*Wer …?*
How much …?	*Wie viel …?*	How many …?	*Wie viele …?*

b Now write answers to the questions and discuss them in class.

3 **Understanding the texts**

The map below shows the countries where English is a main language. Match each description (1–9) to one of the countries.

1/2 **4** **Understanding country facts**

a Listen to people from five of the nine countries. Decide which countries they are from.

b Listen again. How many official languages does each country have? What languages do the speakers name?

1 This country has the second largest population in the world – over a billion people live there. It also has the second largest number of English speakers. Many people learn it as a foreign language.

2 This country has more native speakers of English than any other country. English is an important language on the internet because most websites come from this country.

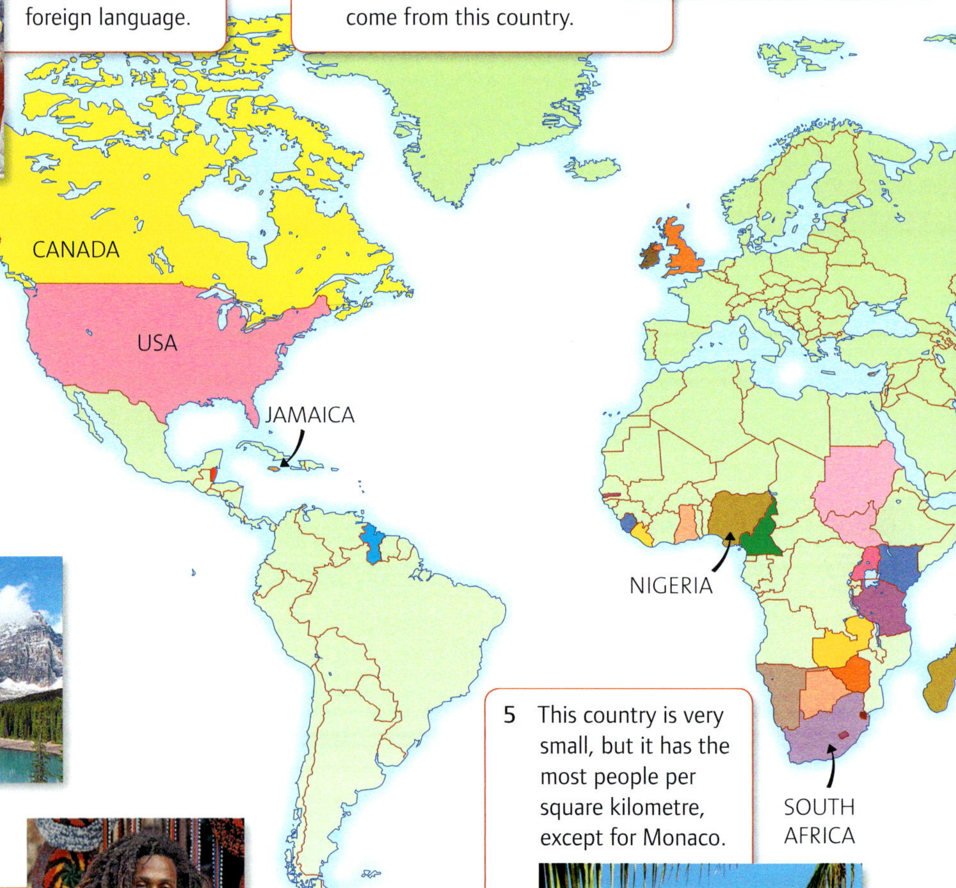

3 This is the second largest country in the world. It is sometimes called 'The Great White North'. Most people live in the south, because the north is very cold.

4 Reggae music and the Rastafarian religion come from this island in the Caribbean.

5 This country is very small, but it has the most people per square kilometre, except for Monaco.

5 Naming countries

Which continent is each of these English-speaking countries in? Make a table.

Africa	Asia	Europe	North America	South America
Botswana	...	...	...	...

I think that country is ...
The blue/orange/green/purple one is ...
I think that country is in Africa/Asia/Europe/North America/South America.

Belize, Botswana, Cameroon, Ghana, Guyana, Ireland, Kenya, Madagascar, Namibia, Pakistan, Papua New Guinea, Sudan, Tanzania, The Philippines, Uganda, The United Kingdom, Zambia, Zimbabwe (► p. 261 for pronunciation)

9 You can see wild leopards, lions, elephants, giraffes and zebras in this country's national parks. It has 11 official languages.

8 This country has a very large film industry called 'Nollywood'. 158 million people live here. That's more than in any other African country.

6 The people of this country live either on North Island or South Island. They are famous for their tattoos.

7 This is a country and a continent. It is often called 'Down Under', because it is so far south.

1/3 **6** **Saying dates**

a Listen to the five speakers from exercise 4 on page 8. They are talking about their national holidays. Copy and complete the table. The language in the box might help you.

first democratic elections • founding of first colony • independence • unification

Name	Country	National holiday	Date	Year	Historic event
Carina	Australia	...	...	...	...
Kim	Canada	...	...	...	...
Sanjay	India	...	...	...	...
Talia	South Africa	...	...	...	...
Rodrigo	USA	...	...	...	...

b Say some dates. Your partner writes them down and guesses why they are important.

Is it your birthday?

Is it German Unification Day?

When were you born?

I was born … on the twentieth of March, two-thousand (and) two (20 March 2002).
on May (the) fifteenth, nineteen-ninety-nine (15 May 1999).
in January / in 1995.

GRAMMAR

to be

simple present		***simple past***	
I **am**	we **are**	I **was**	we **were**
you **are**	you **are**	you **were**	you **were**
he/she/it **is**	they **are**	he/she/it **was**	they **were**

7 ***to be***

Complete the statements with the right form of *to be* and the word *not* where necessary.

Example: *Carina: Nowadays, most Australians are white. But I am not a white Australian.*

1 Carina: I … from Australia. I … from New Zealand.
2 Kim: My family … from Canada. We … from the USA. What nationality … you?
3 Sanjay: I … Indian. My brother and sisters … in India anymore. My brother … in the USA and my sisters … in the UK.
4 Talia: I … in Austria last Christmas. … you from Austria? Oh, you … from Austria, you … from Germany. Where in Germany … you from?
5 Rodrigo: I … from the USA, but my parents … from Puerto Rico. They … in Puerto Rico last year to visit our family.

GRAMMAR

Possessive adjectives

I	my	we	our
you	your	you	your
he/she/it	his/her/its	they	their

TIP

You can say 'you' to me!
Englisch hat nur ein Wort für *du*, *Sie* und *ihr*: ***you***.

Kannst du bitte helfen? — *Can you help, please?*
Könnt ihr bitte helfen? — *Can you help, please?*
Können Sie bitte helfen? — *Can you help, please?*

8 **Possessive adjectives**

Complete these sentences with the correct possessive adjective.

1 I'm from Canada. … two official languages are English and French.
2 You're from Canada, aren't you? You speak English but is … second language French?
3 My parents are from Puerto Rico. … first language is Spanish.
4 I speak a little Spanish. It's … third language.
5 He doesn't speak English. … first language is Arabic.
6 We learn German at school. It's … third language though – we learn French first.

9 **Translating *sie* and *ihr***

a Change *sie* to *she* or *they* and say who it is.

Example: *'Sie' have large jungles in their countries.*
Sie = they = Carina, Sanjay and Talia

1 'Sie' is from New South Wales in Australia.
2 'Sie' live in North America.
3 'Sie' have less than a billion people in their countries.
4 'Sie' speaks English and Afrikaans.
5 'Sie' learns French in school, because it is an official language of her country.
6 'Sie' don't speak American English.

DANGER!

Vergessen Sie nicht:
Im *simple present* –
he/she/it – das 's' muss mit!

b Now do the same with *ihr* (*her* or *their*).

1 'Ihre' family moved from Europe to Africa in the 1600s.
2 'Ihre' countries are home to wild elephants.
3 'Ihre' languages are English and French.
4 'Ihre' school is closed on Freedom Day.

TIP

Sprechen Sie während des Unterrichts so viel Englisch wie möglich.

What does … mean? — *Was heißt … ?*
How do you say … in English? — *Wie sagt man … auf Englisch?*
How do you pronounce that? — *Wie spricht man das aus?*
Can you repeat that, please? — *Können Sie das bitte wiederholen?*

10 **Taking part in the 'global conversation'**

Why do you think English is important? Read the text. Do Jana and Sanjay agree with you?

1/4

EnglishChatIndia.in

Profile: Jana S.

Hi, I'm Jana, from Germany. I'm new on this website and I want to meet people from other countries who speak English. I'm very interested in India and I have a lot of questions about the country. Does everyone really speak English there? Maybe someone from India can answer my questions. Please send me a message!

Messages between Jana S. and Sanjay M.

Sanjay M.

Hi Jana! Nice profile! I'm Sanjay. I can answer your questions about India. India has many languages. There is a region that speaks Hindi, a region that speaks Bengali, a region that speaks Urdu – and that's just the beginning! I'm from the Urdu region in the south, and Urdu is my native language. But I need English to speak with people from the north of India. That's one reason why we learn English at school.

Jana S.

Thanks for your message, Sanjay! It's like Europe, isn't it? Germans need English to communicate with all the other Europeans. This is really important because people come to Germany from all over Europe and do business here. In the past, English was only important for some jobs. Today, it's important for every job. That's why I practise my English every day. Do your parents speak English?

Sanjay M.

That's globalization! Many people come to India to do business because we speak English. This is very good for the Indian economy. I think English is also an advantage for Germany. But soon we will not have this advantage because so many other countries will speak English, too.

No, my parents don't speak very much English. It's mostly young people who speak English here. But India is a very young country. 54% of India's population is under the age of 25 – that's 550 million young people! The very young kids, like my little sister, speak the best English. My first English lessons were in my fifth year at school, but my sister had English in her first year!

Jana S.

It's the same in Europe. Kids start English very young. Some schools want all children to speak fluent English by age 16. Then they will learn all their subjects—maths, music, everything!—in English.

(364 words)

11 **Understanding the text**

Say which of the following facts is about India, Germany or both.

1 Each region in the country speaks a different language.
2 They learn English at school to communicate with other people from the same country.
3 They learn English at school to communicate with people from other countries.
4 English is an advantage for the national economy.
5 Most of the people in the country are young.
6 Children start learning English when they are younger now.

12 **Mediation**

Ihre kleine Schwester macht ein Schulprojekt über Indien. Um ihr zu helfen, fassen Sie die wichtigen Fakten von Übung 10 in Form einer Liste zusammen. Berücksichtigen Sie:

- welche Sprachen es in Indien gibt
- wie wichtig die englische Sprache ist und warum
- das Alter der Bevölkerung

GRAMMAR

Simple present

Aussagen	*Verneinungen*	*Fragen*	*Kurzantworten*
I speak.	I don't speak.	Do I speak …?	Yes, I do. / No, I don't.
You speak.	You don't speak.	Do you speak …?	Yes, you do. / No, you don't.
He/She/It speak**s**.	He do**es**n't speak.	Do**es** he speak …?	Yes, he do**es**. / No, he do**es**n't.
We speak.	We don't speak.	Do we speak …?	Yes, we do. / No, we don't.
They speak.	They don't speak.	Do they speak …?	Yes, they do. / No, they don't.

- In der dritten Person Singular (*he/she/it*) wird ein –s an die Grundform angehängt.
- Außer beim *to be* werden Verneinungen und Fragen mit dem Hilfsverb *do/does* gebildet.
- Das ***simple present*** wird für gleich bleibende Zustände und regelmäßige, wiederholte Handlungen verwendet.

Signalwörter
always · never · often · sometimes · usually

13 **Simple present**

Complete the sentences with the correct form of the verbs in brackets.

1 Sanjay … (not have) good teachers at his school.
2 Jana … (read) manga comic books in English.
3 Jana and her friend … (watch) English films together.
4 They … (not watch) the films with German voices.
5 The English subtitles … (help) them understand the films.
6 Sanjay … (not like) American TV series.

TIP

Um Ihr Englisch zu verbessern, können Sie:

- englischsprachige Filme mit/ohne Untertitel ansehen.
- im Internet auf englischsprachigen Seiten surfen.
- mit Freunden per E-Mail oder Skype auf Englisch kommunizieren.
- englische Bücher oder Zeitschriften lesen.
- ins Ausland gehen.

14 **Questions**

Complete the questions and write short answers for them.

1 … (you have) good teachers at your school?
2 … (your friend like) chatting online?
3 … (your parents speak) English with you?
4 … (I have) a funny accent?

15 **Writing**

Write an email to Sanjay from exercise 10. Tell him about why you are learning English and how you practise it. Write 40 – 60 words.

1/5 **1**

Explaining the way 1

Marion is the receptionist at this company. She is explaining the way to five different people. Listen and follow along on the plan below. Where are the people going?

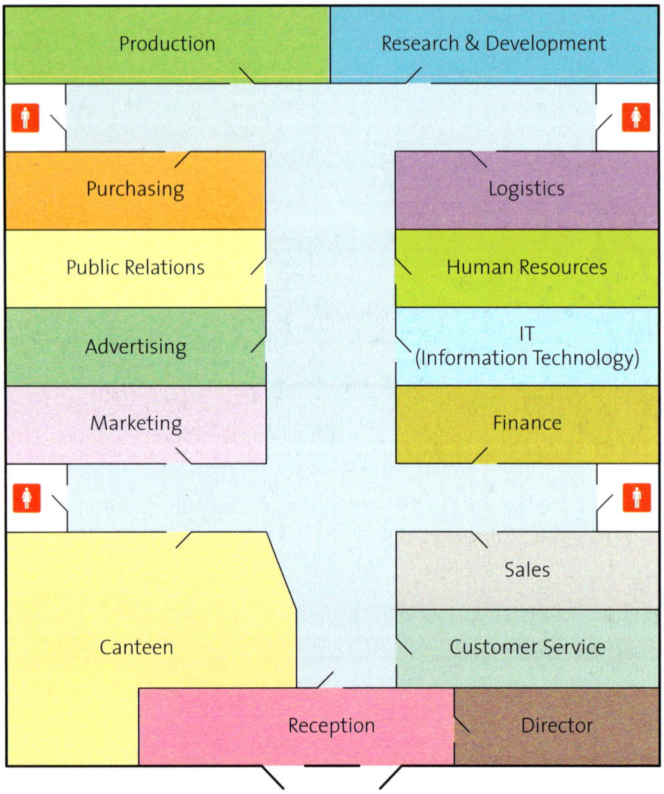

2 **Role-play**

a Marion is having lunch in the canteen now so you have to do her job. Role-play some dialogues with a partner.

Example: *Visitor* *Hello. Could you tell me how to get to the public relations department, please? I have an appointment there.*

Receptionist *Of course. Go straight on down the hall. It's the second door on your left.*

b Now take it in turns with your partner to ask for directions from your classroom to rooms and areas of your school.

Explaining the way

Go straight on down the hall.
Go to the end of the hall and turn right/left.
Take the first/second right/left.
It's on your right/left.
It's the first/second/third/last door on your right/left.
It's at the end of the hall.

3 Explaining the way 2

Partner A, turn to File 1 on page 171. Partner B, turn to File 10 on page 176.

4 Saying the time

a Marion has to call some of her boss's business contacts from different countries. What time is it in Berlin when …

- it's 5 p.m. in Mumbai?
- it's 7.15 a.m. in Johannesburg?

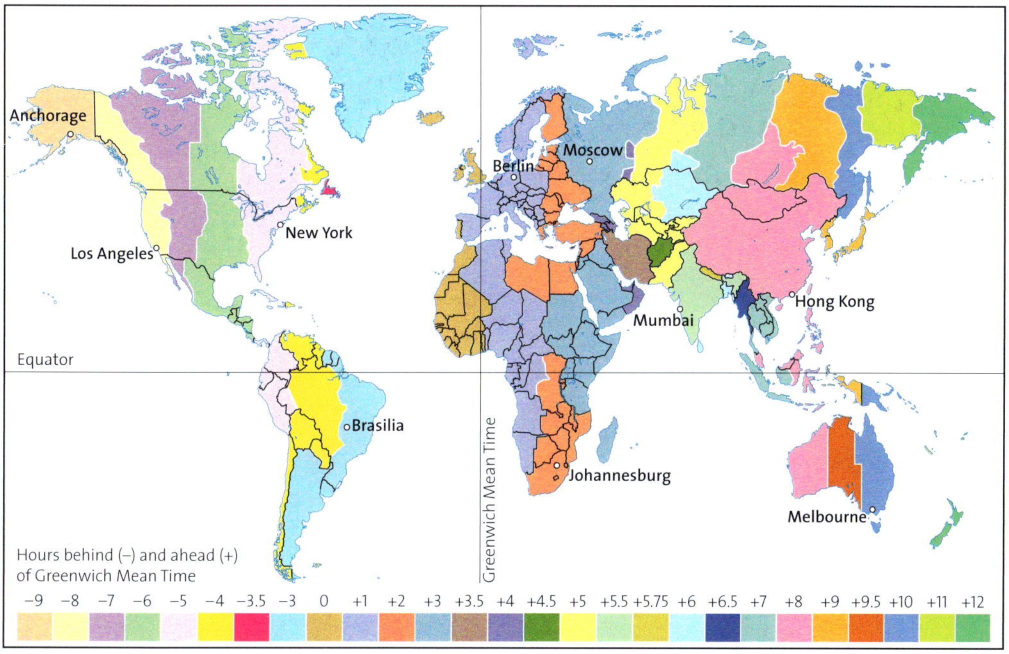

b Write out eight time differences, then ask your partner. Which partner can calculate faster?

What time is it in Sao Paulo when it's 1.15 a.m. in Miami?

Hm… 3.15 a.m.!

Saying the time

12:00	12:05	12:15	12:30	12:40	12:45
12 o'clock noon (*Mittag*) midnight (*Mitternacht*)	five past twelve twelve-oh-five	quarter past twelve twelve-fifteen	half past twelve twelve-thirty	twenty to one twelve forty	quarter to one twelve forty-five

The work day starts at 8 o'clock in the morning / 8 a.m.
It ends at half past 4 in the afternoon / 4.30 p.m.
I go to bed at about quarter past 10 in the evening / 10.15 p.m.

How to … learn new words

1 Warm-up

Tell your partner how you have learned the English words you already know.

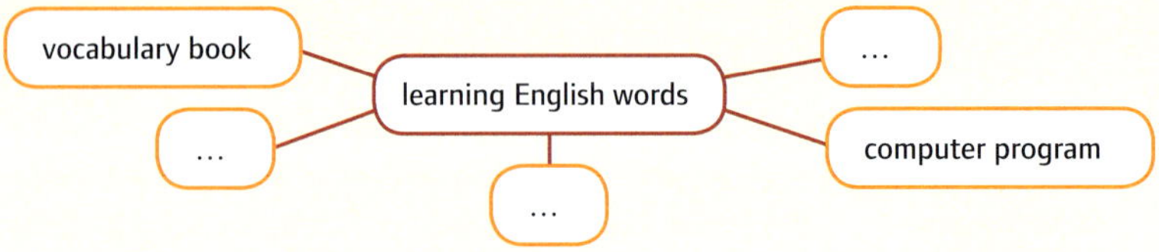

2 Create a vocabulary book

Look at the text on page 12 again and write any new words in your vocabulary book. Don't forget to add a third column to the book where you can add opposites, synonyms and definitions.

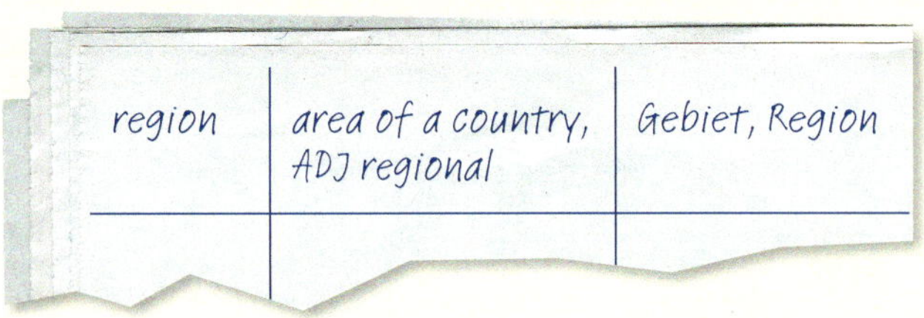

TIP

Vokabeln prägen sich gut ein, wenn man sie aufschreibt. Um Ihr Vokabular zu erweitern, können Sie in Ihrem Vokabelheft auch Definitionen, Synonyme oder Gegensätze und Wortfamilien eintragen. Für Tipps zu Lernkarten siehe S. 23.

3 Use sticky notes

Look up the names of five objects in your classroom. Make sticky notes for these objects. Give the sticky notes to your partner, who has to find the objects and label them with the sticky notes.

TIP

Um zu lernen, wie Gegenstände heißen, sind Klebezettel hilfreich. Beschränken Sie sich nicht auf Hauptwörter. Man kann mit Klebezetteln auch Adjektive lernen, z. B. *pretty*, *dirty* usw.

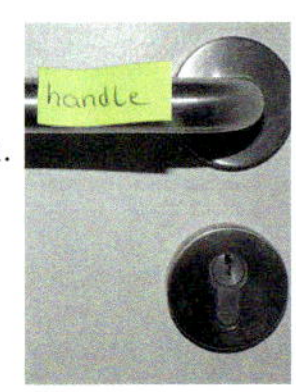

4 Learn words in groups, phrases and sentences

a Match the parts of the expressions from this unit together. Write them in your vocabulary book with the German translation and any extra information such as synonyms.

Example: *1d send a message*

1	send	a	the way
2	answer	b	for directions
3	speak/communicate	c	questions
4	do	d	a message
5	explain	e	business
6	ask	f	with people

TIP

Manchmal ist es wirksamer, Vokabeln im Zusammenhang (als Teil einer Gruppe von Wörtern, einer Redewendung oder im ganzen Satz) zu lernen. So merken Sie sich nicht nur die Bedeutung der Vokabel, sondern auch, wie sie im Alltag gebraucht wird.

b Now think of other expressions using the verbs on the left.

Example: *send a letter, send an email, send a present*

Weitere Tipps zum Vokabeln-Lernen finden Sie auf den Seiten 23, 36 und 101.

Everybody's different

2

1 Warm-up

a Ask your partner questions to complete Barack Obama's family tree. The language in the boxes below may help you.

Partner A: Go to File 2 on page 172.
Partner B: Go to File 14 on page 178.

aunt • brother • daughter • father • grandmother • great-grandmother • half-sister • husband • mother • sister • son • stepmother • uncle • wife

What is his mother's/father's/ name? Where is/was … from? When was … born?

Barack Obama and family – the first non-white family in the US White House

b Use the phrases in the box to describe the families below.

Example: *In this family, three generations live together.*

adopted child/parents • generation • only child • same-sex parents • siblings • single parent

1/6

Germany is our home

Umay, 17, Stuttgart

Some people say I don't look German, but I am German. I am not an immigrant. I'm German with a Turkish ethnic background. My grand-parents come from Turkey. They are still citizens of Turkey, but my parents and I were born here and we have German passports. We are all bilingual. Some of my relatives are from the Kurdish ethnic group. There are a lot of Turkish-Germans in Germany. We are the largest non-German ethnic group in this country. Some Turkish-Germans are very German and some are very traditional Turkish – my family is somewhere in the middle.

Lionel, 15, Dortmund

I only came to Germany a year ago, but I love it here. I'm from the Democratic Republic of Congo. My mother, brother and I are refugees. There are wars and lots of fighting in the DRC. Now we've got asylum here in Germany. Of course we still have a strong connection to Africa and its traditions. It's very far away, so we can't visit our relatives there, but we telephone and email with them. We already have some Congolese friends here and we want to make German friends too. I am making friends at school and I am learning German very quickly. It's my dream to get a good education and then a good job. I hope to become a German citizen and, later, a member of the German Parliament!

Anh, 16, Berlin

My nationality is Italian, but my family background is a bit complicated. My mother was born in China. Her mother is Vietnamese and her father is Chinese. My father was born in Greece. So I am Italian with a Chinese, Vietnamese and Greek ethnic background. We have family traditions from all these places. Right now, my parents and I are living in Germany for a few years because my father is working in a German company. I go to a German-Italian 'Europe School' here. I really don't 'feel' German. I feel Italian. I don't want to give up my life in Italy and I hope to go back there with fluent German.

(349 words)

2 Understanding the text

Answer the folowing questions.

1 Name the three reasons why Umay, Lionel and Anh are living in Germany.
2 Name two ways that Lionel and his family still have strong connections to Africa.
3 Name five things that Lionel and Anh want and hope to do in the future.

3 Family trees

Draw the family trees of Umay, Lionel and Anh. Include the information you have about each family member's nationality and ethnic background.

4 The possessive *'s* or the short form of *is*?

a Read the sentences and decide if *'s* is the possessive *'s* or the short form of *is*.

Example: Lionel's family is from the DRC. — *'s = possessive 's*
Lionel's Congolese. — *'s = is*

1 Anh's country is a member of the EU.
2 Lionel's education is very important to him.
3 Umay's a citizen of Germany.
4 Umay's father is also a German citizen.
5 Some people say Turkey's in Europe, some say it's not.

b Put the words in brackets into the plural or add the possessive *'s*.

Example: Our (passport) are German. — *passports*
This (passport) owner is German. — *passport's*

1 A (refugee) life is not easy.
2 (Umay) family speaks two (language).
3 Different (ethnic group) have different (tradition).
4 One of her (relative) lives in China but this (relative) passport is Vietnamese.
5 Every (country) (citizen) come from many ethnic (background).

5 *a/an*

Complete the text below with the words *a* and *an*.

Life in the Democratic Republic of Congo

The DRC is …[1] country which has been at war for many years. The government has …[2] army which is fighting …[3] rebel army. Many Congolese people are now refugees and live in other countries. The DRC is …[4] very large country with …[5] population of about 60 million. Most of the Congolese live in rural areas; only about 30 % live in …[6] urban area. The land has …[7] enormous amount of natural resources such as gold and diamonds, but the people are very poor because of the conflict. Many do not get …[8] education.
There are over 200 ethnic groups in the DRC, and they speak …[9] unbelievable number of languages. Many speak French. This is …[10] official language because the country once was …[11] colony of Belgium.

6 An email back to the old country

Imagine you are an immigrant to Germany. Write an email to someone in your old country. Tell them what Germany is like and what your life is like here. Write 40 – 60 words.

Think about:
- size of country
- people who live here
- country's culture and traditions

GRAMMAR

Pronouns

subject pronouns		*object pronouns*		*reflexive pronouns*	
I	we	me	us	myself	ourselves
you	you	you	you	yourself	yourselves
he/she/it	they	him/her/it	them	himself/herself/itself	themselves

7 **Object pronouns**

Complete the text below with the right object pronouns.

Diego's Blog

The Carnival of Cultures in Berlin

Berlin is a city with a large international population. 450,000 Berliners do not have German citizenship. Many more of *them* (they) have a mixed ethnic background. The first Carnival of Cultures took place in 1996. This was soon after the Berlin Wall fell when many people from different cultures moved there. Some Berliners criticized this migration, but the carnival organisers wanted to celebrate …[1] (it).
Carnival itself is one of the oldest celebrations in the world. The Europeans started …[2] (it), then it travelled to the Caribbean, South America and Africa. The carnival is a lot of fun for my family and …[3] (I). We love to travel to Berlin and dress ourselves up so that thousands of people can watch …[4] (we). Last year I went with my brother and his wife. I have lots of photos of …[5] (he) dancing with …[6] (she). They looked great and everyone was looking at …[7] (they). Come to the Carnival next year and Berlin will welcome …[8] (you)!

8 **Reflexive pronouns**

Look at the photos from the Carnival of Cultures and complete the sentences with the right reflexive pronouns.

1 The dancers dressed *themselves* up in bright clothes.
2 We are enjoying … dancing.
3 Is that you looking at … in the mirror?
4 She's making … up.
5 I want to go to the Carnival … next year.

9 *there is/there are*

Complete the sentences correctly with the right form of *there is* or *there are*.

1 … a dog at the front of the picture.
2 … normally a lot of people at the carnival?
3 … always so many people here. It's normally very quiet.
4 I hope … some cool bands at the festival this year.
5 … any other Africans at your school, Lionel?
6 … a bus which takes us to the carnival so we have to walk.
7 I hope … a restaurant there so that we can have lunch.
8 … a lot of families with mixed ethnic backgrounds in Germany.

DANGER!
es gibt = ~~it gives~~
there is/are

1/7 10 Understanding descriptions

a Marcus likes to take photographs of his family. Listen to him talk about the pictures below. Decide which ones he describes.

1

2

3

4

b Listen again and complete the phrases you hear.

1 In the background there … some graffiti on the wall.
2 There … some white ducks in the bottom left-hand corner.
3 My parents … sitting on the sofa.
4 My brother … listening to music.
5 He … feeding the ducks.

11 Describing photos

Use the diagram and the words in the box to describe the photo below.

family • are having a birthday party • are wearing funny hats • are having fun • cake • balloons

Bilder beschreiben

in the top left-hand corner
at the top of the picture
in the top right-hand corner
on the left
in the background
on the right
in the middle
on the left-hand side of the picture
in the foreground
on the right-hand side of the picture
in the bottom left-hand corner
at the bottom of the picture
in the bottom right-hand corner

GRAMMAR

Present progressive

Aussagen	*Verneinungen*	*Fragen*	*Kurzantworten*
I**'m looking** at photos. He**'s reading** a book.	You**'re not listening** to me. They**'re not coming** with me.	**Are** you **having** fun? **Is** he **enjoying** the carnival?	Yes, I **am**. – No, I**'m not**. Yes, we **are**. – No, we**'re not**.

- Das ***present progressive*** wird mit *am/is/are* + *-ing*-Form des Verbs gebildet. Ein stummes *e* am Ende des Infinitivs fällt in der *-ing*-Form weg (z. B. make → making). Infinitivendungen wie *-m*, *-n* oder *-t* werden nach kurz gesprochenen Silben verdoppelt (z. B. get → getting).
- Es wird verwendet, wenn man ausdrücken will, dass jemand **jetzt/gerade/im Augenblick** etwas tut oder dass gerade etwas geschieht.
- Das ***present progressive*** steht auch für Handlungen und Vorgänge, die von vorübergehender Dauer und noch nicht abgeschlossen sind, aber nicht unbedingt zum Zeitpunkt des Sprechens geschehen: *I'm doing a course in computer studies.*
- Einige Verben, die Zustände oder Gefühle ausdrücken, werden nicht im ***present progressive*** gebraucht, z. B. *be, believe, forget, hate, have, know, like, love, need, remember, want.*

Signalwörter
at the moment · now · just · still · today

12 Present progressive

a Complete the sentences by putting the verbs in brackets into the present progressive.

Example: His mother … (sit) on the sofa.
His mother *is sitting* on the sofa.

TIP

Wir benutzen oft die Zeitform ***present progressive***, wenn wir Bilder beschreiben, weil Bilder (angehaltene) **Vorgänge** darstellen.

1 I … (get) ready for the carnival in that photo.
2 Can you see my parents in the background? They … (make) dinner.
3 We … (dance) at the concert there.
4 … you still … (listen) to that old CD?
5 He … (not work) just now. He's on holiday.
6 Lionel … (learn) German at the moment.
7 … it … (rain) today? I'd like to go for a walk.
8 They … just … (leave) the house now.

b Replace *am/are/is* with *was/were* to rewrite the sentences in the past progressive. We describe photos this way when the time they were taken is relevant, so add a time clause to each sentence.

Example: *1 His mother was sitting on the sofa when the photo was taken.*

13 Describing photos

Bring some photos to class and describe them for your partner.

TIP

Fertigen Sie Ihre eigenen Lernkarten an.

Schreiben Sie die Wörter auf Kärtchen oder Papierzettel. Auf die eine Seite schreiben Sie das englische Wort. Auf die andere Seite schreiben Sie die Übersetzung, Definition oder einen Beispielsatz. Wenn Sie Kärtchen beidseitig beschreiben, achten Sie darauf, dass Sie den Text auf der Rückseite auf dem Kopf schreiben, weil Sie das Kärtchen so mit nur einer Hand wenden und problemlos Vorder- und Rückseite lesen können.

14 Learning vocabulary

Match the words below and their definitions to make flashcards (see tip box above) for words from the unit.

1	nationality	a	someone who has moved to a coutry
2	immigrant	b	link
3	carnival	c	difficult to understand
4	connection	d	where someone comes from
5	complicated	e	a festival where people dance on the streets

15 Talking about future plans

a You can also use the present progressive to talk about future plans. Complete the text with the present progressive.

I can hardly wait for the weekend to come. On Saturday, I *am meeting* (meet) my friend at her flat and her mum …[1] (cook) dinner for us. We …[2] (not eat) meat because they are vegetarians. Then her dad …[3] (drive) us to a party. He …[4] (not stay) at the party. My mum …[5] (pick us up) at around 10 p.m. and she …[6] (drive) us home. On Sunday I …[7] (go) out of town for the day with my family. We …[8] (take) the train to a big park. Maybe my sisters …[9] (not come) with us – I'm not sure. What …[10] (you do) this weekend?

b Replace *am/are/is* with *will be* to rewrite the text in the future progressive.
Example: *I can hardly wait for the weekend to come. On Saturday, I* ***will be meeting*** *my friend …*

c Tell your partner about your plans for the weekend.

16 Writing

Choose one of the following tasks. Write 40 – 60 words.

1 Write a story based on one of the pictures on pages 20 – 21.
2 You are on holiday with your family. Write an email to a friend. Say what each of your family members is doing.

Booking a hotel room

1 Finding the best hotel

Decide which of the factors below are important in the following situations. Give reasons.

location	**travel times**	**facilities**	**price**	**the opinions of past guests**
in the city centre · near the … · quiet/noisy	how long it takes to get from … to …	conference room · fitness centre · restaurant	reasonable or expensive	'That hotel was wonderful/ terrible!'

1 You want to book a fun holiday for yourself and some friends.
2 You need to hold a meeting in the hotel. People will give presentations at the meeting.
3 You are working in a city for one week and must be at work very early every morning.
4 You need a room in city B for one night because you have to spend the night there to fly from city A to city C.

2 Reserving a hotel room

You are an assistant and it is your job to make travel arrangements for your colleagues. You are searching for a room for Joseph Russell. You call hotels and ask the following questions.

a Match the question to the answers. Each question has two answers.

1 How much does breakfast cost?
2 Is there a private bathroom?
3 What time will the room be ready?
4 Does the room have internet access?
5 How far is the hotel from the train station/airport?

a Yes, it does.
b It's about 10 kilometres, so you will need to take a taxi.
c At 12.00.
d It's free.
e No, I'm afraid not. You have to share a bathroom in the hall with other guests.
f Let us know what time the guest is arriving and we will make sure it's ready.
g Only about a 10 minute walk.
h Eight euros fifty.
i Yes, but it's not free. You have to log in and pay with a credit card.
j Yes, there is.

b You book the hotel room below online. Later, you receive confirmation in an email. Decide if everything is correct in the confirmation and if anything is missing.

* required field

Surname*	Russell		
Other names	Joseph		
Company	Expert Consultants		
Address*	214 High Road		
City*	Wellington		
Country*	New Zealand		
Telephone number*	+64 (0)4 64 65 55		
Email*	Joe@ExpertConsultants.nz		
Check-in date (dd/mm/yy)*	05/12/15	**Check-out date***	06/12/15
No. of rooms required*	1	**Room type**	[ ] single [✗] double
No. of adults*	1	**No. of children***	0

Any additional information or requirements

Mr Russell is flying from Berlin to Istanbul and arriving at 10.30 p.m. He will arrive at your hotel after 11 p.m. He must leave at 6 a.m. the next morning to fly to Tel Aviv. Please confirm that he will be able to check in and out at these times. Thank you.

Dear Mr Russell

It is our pleasure to confirm the reservation of a single room for two nights from 6 December at Airport Hotel. The guest's details are as follows:

Address: Expert Consultants, 214 High Road, Wellington, New Zealand
Telephone: +64 (0)4 64 65 65
Email address: Joe@ExpertConsultants.nz
Guests: 1 adult, 1 child

Thank you for choosing Airport Hotel. We wish you a pleasant stay in Istanbul.

Yours faithfully
The management

3 **Writing an email**

Write an email to the Airport Hotel to tell them about their mistakes.

Dear Sir or Madam
Thank you for confirming the hotel room. I'm afraid …
…
Would you please send me a corrected confirmation? Thank you in advance.
Yours faithfully

1 Before you listen

a You will listen to advertisements for two hotels. Which of the following statements do you think you could hear?

1 Our hotel is high quality/very expensive.
2 Our facilities are brand new/quite old.
3 It's centrally located./It's very noisy.
4 We don't have a swimming pool./We have a conference room.

b What else could you hear in the advertisement?

TIP

Beim Zuhören ist nicht nur Ihr Englisch-Wissen gefragt sondern auch Ihr Konzentrationsvermögen. Bevor Sie mit dem Zuhören anfangen, machen Sie Ihren Kopf frei von Gedanken, in dem Sie eine kurze Zeit Ihre Lieblingsart von Entspannung – z. B. Meditation oder autogenes Training – praktizieren. Überlegen Sie vor dem Hören, worum es in dem Text gehen könnte. Worauf lässt die Anweisung schließen? Gibt es Fotos?

2 Listening for main ideas

1/8

You are searching for a hotel room with the following criteria:

- in Mulhouse, France
- 30 rooms
- a conference room, big enough for 30 people
- located near restaurants and the main train station

TIP

Kümmern Sie sich beim ersten Anhören nicht um Fakten und Details, und schon gar nicht um unbekannte Wörter. Diese Details werden Sie einfacher verstehen können, nach dem Sie die Leitgedanken erfasst haben. Diese funktionieren dann als ein gedankliches Gerüst, an dem Sie beim zweiten Anhören weitere Details aufhängen können.

Listen to the advertisements and decide if one of the hotels might be suitable.

3 Listening for details

1/8 V1

Watch or listen to the advertisement for the more interesting hotel and take detailed notes on the following:

- the five facilities which are mentioned
- the location and the four things nearby which are mentioned
- the two prices which are mentioned
- the web address

TIP

Erst beim zweiten Zuhören sollten Sie auf Einzelheiten achten. Schreiben Sie wenn möglich Abkürzungen. Falls es unbekannte Wörter gibt, versuchen Sie sie aus dem Kontext zu erschließen.

My generation

1 **Warm-up**

When he was younger, Granddad followed every new fashion. Look at the pictures and use the language in the boxes to describe Granddad's life.

Example: *In the Sixties, Granddad was a hippie. He had long hair and wore a floral shirt.*

Granddad – a dedicated follower of fashion

In the	Sixties, Seventies, Eighties, Nineties, Noughties, Twenty Tens,

Granddad is / was	too old for all of that. a hippie. a punk. a rapper. a yuppie. an emo.

TIP

What is the decade called?
1960s – the Sixties
1970s – the Seventies
1980s – the Eighties
1990s – the Nineties
2000s – the Noughties / Two Thousands
2010s – the Twenty Tens

He dyed his hair black and wore tight, black jeans and a hoodie.
He had long hair and wore a floral shirt.
He had purple hair and wore a leather jacket.
He had short hair and wore a suit.
He is bald and wears a cardigan.
He wore sunglasses, a gold chain and a tracksuit.

Talking about my generation

1/9

Baby Boomers

We were born after the end of the Second World War. In 1969 we watched the first Moon landing on our families' small black-and-white TV sets.

When we were young, we didn't have mobile phones or computers. We listened to music on small radios instead of MP3 players. We liked the Beatles or Elvis Presley, Motown or rock and roll.

As young adults, we worked hard, saved money and made comfortable homes to settle down in. A few of us became hippies and 'dropped out' instead.

It was a time of optimism and idealism – Flower Power and the Summer of Love – but we also worried about nuclear war between the USA and the Soviet Union. Many of us wanted to 'Ban the Bomb'.

Generation X

We were born after 1964. Most of our hard-working mums and dads had jobs, so we were independent kids. We played our favourite music, perhaps The Sex Pistols, David Bowie, ACDC or Duran Duran, on our record players in our bedrooms.

Some of us became punks and stuck pins through our ears or lips and dyed our hair pink or purple. Others became skinheads and hated the punks.

Most of us weren't rebels, though. Our parents weren't poor, so many of us went to college or university and got a good education.

As teenagers or young adults, we watched (on our colour TV sets) as the Berlin Wall came down. In those days, smart business people had mobile phones which were big and expensive. We were the first generation to use email and the internet.

Generation Y

We were born after 1981. Few of us remember what it was like to live in a Communist country.

As teenagers, most of us had PCs or Playstations at home and played computer games for hours. Many of us owned a mobile phone.

CDs replaced records and cassettes in our music collections, perhaps including Oasis, Eminem or Britney Spears (who was young and sexy in those days). We also watched endless pop videos on MTV: that earned us the nickname 'the MTV generation'.

However, other people call us 'the Peter Pan generation', because we don't want to grow up. Many of us stayed at home with our parents until our late 20s. Some of us are still there.

We remember the two Gulf Wars and the shock of 9/11. We also began to worry about climate change. It was difficult to be an optimist as a member of Generation Y.

(409 words)

2 Understanding the text

Copy and complete the table with information from the text on page 28.

Generation	Trends	New technology	Events	Music	Characteristics/Attitudes
Baby Boomers	*hippies*	*black and white TV*	*Moon landing*	...	...
Generation X	...	...	...	...	...
Generation Y	...	...	...	...	...

3 Working with words

Complete the sentences with suitable adjectives from the box. They are all in the text on page 28. Be careful: There is one adjective too many.

difficult • endless • expensive • favourite • hard-working • independent • poor • small • young

1 Granddad is old now, but in the Seventies he was … .
2 This is my … song: I like it more than all the others.
3 Mick works from 8 a.m. to 6 p.m. He is very … .
4 I don't need any help, thanks. I prefer to be … .
5 We have enough money – we aren't … .
6 € 1000? That's too … for a mobile phone.
7 The film was four hours long – it seemed … .
8 Did you find this exercise … ? I found it quite easy.

4 Writing: my generation

a Brainstorm ideas with a partner, then add 'Generation Z' to the table from exercise 2 above.

b Write a short article (40–60 words) for your school magazine about your generation. Start like this:

Generation Z
We were born after 1994 ...

Think about these areas:

books • fashion • film • music • technology • world events

5 Internet research

Choose one of the world events mentioned in the text on page 28 or another one you think is important. Go online to find out more about it. Explain to the class why it was important or how it changed the world. The language in the box may help you.

… took place in (*year*).
It was important/special because …
It was the first/last time that …
It meant the end/beginning of …
It changed people's ideas about …

6 Listening to a song

Listen to the song. Do you like it? How does it make you feel?

Talkin' 'bout my generation

The Who, 1965
Lyrics by Pete Townshend

People try to put us down
Talkin' 'bout my generation
Just because we get around
Talkin' 'bout my generation
Things they do look awful cold
Talkin' 'bout my generation
I hope I die before I get old
Talkin' 'bout my generation

This is my generation
This is my generation, baby

Why don't you all fade away?
Talkin' 'bout my generation
And don't try to dig what we all say
Talkin' 'bout my generation
I'm not trying to cause a big sensation
Talkin' 'bout my generation
I'm just talkin' 'bout my generation
Talkin' 'bout my generation

This is my generation
This is my generation, baby

(2nd verse repeated, then first verse repeated)

7 Understanding new expressions

Read the song text carefully. Which meaning fits in the song best?

1 'Put someone down' means
- a to drop them on the ground.
- b to make them feel small and unimportant.
- c to kill them.

2 'Get around' means
- a to walk in a circle.
- b to travel and mix with other people.
- c to avoid something.

3 If you 'dig' something, you …
- a understand or like it.
- b make a hole in it.
- c put it in the ground.

8 Understanding the song

Choose a, b or c below. Note down words/expressions from the song which support your answer.

1 When Pete Townshend wrote the song 'Talkin' 'bout my generation', he was …
- a happy.
- b angry.
- c in love.

2 The song is about …
- a nuclear war between the USA and Russia.
- b how young people and old people see each other.
- c what it's like to be the father of a baby.

3 In the song, Pete Townshend wants to …
- a earn a lot of money.
- b have a long life.
- c stay young and free.

1/11 9 Listening for specific information

a Listen to the radio DJ. Which of the original members of The Who are still alive? What age did the others die at?

TIP

Preparing to listen
Always read the questions before you start to listen. Listen for words that appear in the questions.

Roger Daltrey

John Entwistle

Keith Moon

Pete Townshend

b Answer the following questions.

1 What did Roger Daltrey do after his time in The Who?
2 How did John Entwistle die?
3 What happened with Pete Townshend's musical career?

10 Discussion and presentation

a Work in a small group. What songs are important for people of your generation? Choose a song that you all think is important. Look up the lyrics (*Songtext*) on the internet.

Discuss the following:
- Why do you like the song?
- What do you think it means?
- What do you know about the singer/band?

b Use your notes to give a presentation to the class about the song. The class should then choose one song to represent your generation.

GRAMMAR

Talking about more than one: plurals

Singular	*Plural*
computer	computer**s**
bus	bus**es**

* aber: **boys**, **keys**, **days**, usw.

Singular	*Plural*
family	famil**ies***
wife	wi**ves**
CD	CD**s**

Irregular plurals

Singular	*Plural*
man/woman	m**e**n/wom**e**n
child	child**ren**
person	**people**

Singular	*Plural*
tooth	**teeth**
foot	**feet**
potato/tomato	potato**es***/tomato**es***

* aber: **discos**, **radios**, usw.

- Die allermeisten Pluralformen werden mit **-s** gebildet.
- Bei Nomen auf **-y** nach einem Konsonant wird **-y** zu **-ies**.
- Nomen auf **-s** und **-x** bilden die Pluralform mit **-es**.
- Einige häufige Nomen haben unregelmäßige Pluralformen.

DANGER!

Folgende Nomen werden immer im Plural verwendet: *glasses, jeans, trousers, scissors*. Oder man sagt: *a pair of jeans*.

11 **Plurals**

Complete the text with the plurals of the nouns in brackets.

You may think the 1960s were strange, but what about earlier decades like the 1920s? In those … (day) [1], … (family) [2] listened to their … (radio) [3] – there were no … (TV) [4]. … (man) [5] went to work while … (woman) [6] looked after the house and … (child) [7]. And … (teenager) [8] ? Well, when … (person) [9] turned 14, they had to behave like … (adult) [10]. … (boy) [11] worked like their … (father) [12] and … (girl) [13] learned to be … (housewife) [14].

GRAMMAR

Saying how much / how many

how much? *wie viel?*	much / a lot of *viel*	little *wenig*
how many? *wie viele?*	many / a lot of *viele*	few *wenige*

12 ***Much / many / a lot of / little / few***

Choose the correct word to complete each sentence. Sometimes both may be right.

1 How *much / many* do you know about teenagers in the late 1970s?
2 In those days, *a lot of / much* young people liked punk rock.
3 However, *little/few* teenagers had long, spiky, coloured hair.
4 Nowadays, there are *a lot of / many* different trends.
5 As a result, there is *little / few* pressure to follow one fashion.

Life online

4

1 Warm-up

a Match the descriptions to the social media.

blog • chatroom • forum • instant messaging • multi-player game • social network

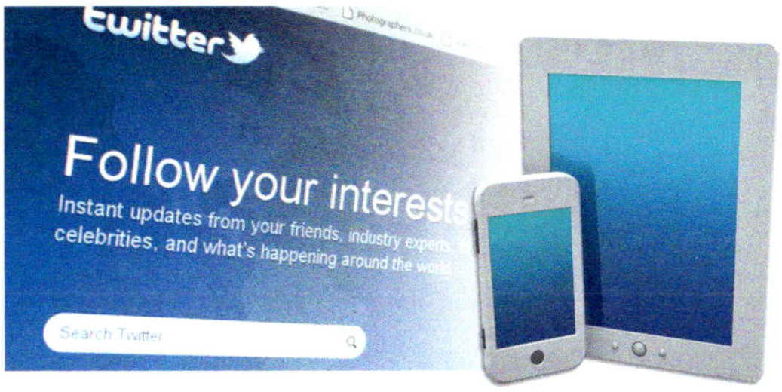

1 You write messages or questions for people to reply to. It may be days before a reply comes.
2 You can use this to send quick messages to one or more people. Strangers cannot easily read your messages.
3 You can exchange messages while you are sitting at the computer. All other users can read the messages.
4 It is a kind of online diary. You upload text and photos and sometimes videos about things that interest you.
5 You have a personal page to tell other people about yourself. People can link your page to theirs if you give them permission (e.g. make them a 'friend').
6 Several people play a game together over the internet.

b Tell your partner how often you use each type of social media.
Example: *I often use a social network.*

I	often sometimes rarely never	write posts for a forum/blog. use a chatroom / instant messaging / a social network.

I	...	all the time. (almost) every day.

TIP

On social networks (Facebook, MySpace, etc.)
to friend someone – *in die Freundesliste eintragen*
to unfriend someone – *aus der Freundesliste löschen*
In real life
to make friends – *sich anfreunden*
to stop being friends – *Freundschaft kündigen*

2 Social network vocabulary

Match these social network concepts with the correct explanations.

1 profile
2 event
3 status update
4 friend
5 apps
6 wall
7 privacy settings
8 link

a This points to another page which you like.
b This says what you are doing or how you feel.
c This is where you tell people about yourself.
d You change these to control who can see your information.
e This is something that is going to happen.
f These are small software programs, e.g. games.
g This is a space where you and your friends can post messages, photos, etc.
h This is a person who you allow to see your information, send you messages, etc.

1/13

A tragedy on Facebook

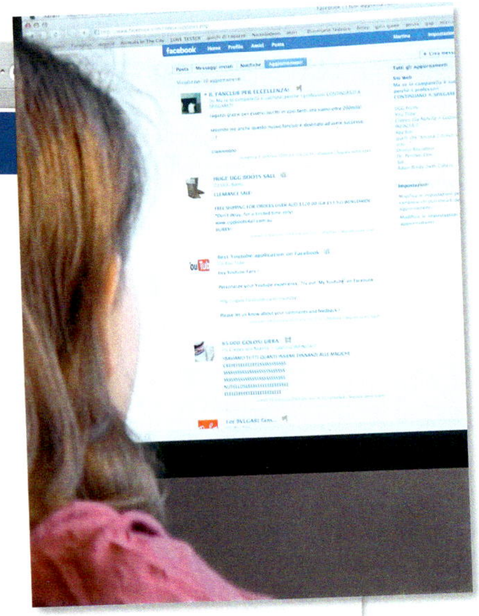

Emma Jaeger lived in St. Louis, Missouri. She liked to use Facebook to keep in touch with her friends. One day she met a new boy online. His name was Brad O'Malley.

Brad contacted Emma through her Facebook page. He wanted to be added as a friend. Emma asked her mother if she could accept.

Tina Jaeger asked her daughter: 'Do you know who he is?'

'No, but look at his profile! He looks nice! Please, please can I add him?'

Mom said yes. For six weeks, Emma and Brad got to know each other on Facebook.

Brad: 'I'm 15. I was born in Florida and have just moved to St. Louis. I play the guitar and drums. When I was seven, Dad left Mom and me. Since then, Mom has looked after me and my two brothers.'

Emma: 'I love swimming, boats, fishing, dogs and rap music. It sounds like you have had some difficulties in your life, Brad. Life has been hard for me too.' Emma was overweight. She was also very depressed.

Every day after school, Emma rushed home to her computer and wrote to Brad.

As she said to Mom: 'Finally I've found a boy who really likes me and thinks that I'm pretty.'

Then, after about six weeks, Emma got a strange message from Brad: 'I don't want to be your friend any more. I've heard that you are not very nice to your friends.'

Puzzled, Emma wrote back: 'What are you talking about?'

Over the next 24 hours, Brad sent more nasty messages to Emma. Other people began to send her messages as well. 'Mom! He's shared my messages with other people,' Emma cried angrily. 'I trusted him and now he hates me, just like all my other friends.' She began to send rude messages back.

Shocked, Tina told Emma to turn off her computer. Emma shouted at her: 'You're supposed to be my mom! You're supposed to be on my side!' She was obviously terribly upset.

Emma ran to her room, crying. Tina and her husband Ron went to the kitchen and made dinner. They talked about the problem with Brad.

Suddenly, Tina had a horrible feeling. She ran upstairs to Emma's room. Emma was in the closet with a belt around her neck. Her face was blue.

Emma Jaeger died the next day in hospital, three weeks before her 14th birthday.

Later that day, Ron opened his daughter's Facebook account and looked at Brad's final message. It said:

'Everybody in St. Louis knows what you're like. You are a bad person and everybody hates you. The world would be a better place without you.'

(443 words)

3 Understanding the text

Decide whether these statements are true or false. Give reasons for your answer in German.
Example: *1 Das ist falsch, weil sie ihn erst im Internet kennen gelernt hat.*

1 Emma knew Brad because they went to the same school.
2 Brad put a photo of himself on his Facebook profile.
3 Brad lived with his father.
4 Emma did not have any problems until she met Brad.
5 Emma was happy because Brad was her online friend.
6 Brad did not show Emma's messages to anyone else.
7 When Emma got upset, her mother wanted her to stop using her computer.
8 When Tina found her, Emma was dead.

4 Discussion

Discuss in a small group why Brad behaved in such a nasty way.

The text opposite is based on a true story, but the names have been changed. Why do you think Brad behaved like this? There are some suggestions below.

He did it when he was angry and felt sorry afterwards.

It was just a joke that went wrong.

Someone told him lies about Emma.

He was a lot older than her.

He wasn't a real person.

He got a new girlfriend.

TIP

Tipps für Diskussionen auf Englisch

Sich zu Wort melden
What I think is this: …
Well, if you ask me …
Jemand anderen ins Gespräch einbringen
What do you think, David?
Höflich widersprechen
You may be right, but …
I don't think that's right, because …

5 Working with words

Use the verbs from the box to complete the text. There are three verbs you do not need. All of the verbs are in the text on page 38.

contact • get • hate • keep • know • look • meet • move • send • ~~share~~ • trust • write

Many people, young and old, use social networks. They are a good way to *share* [1] thoughts and feelings with your friends and …[2] them messages about events like parties, etc. If you …[3] to a new place, social networks are a great way to …[4] in touch with your old friends.

Some people also use them to …[5] new people in cyberspace. Most social networks have ways to …[6] people that you don't know. When you …[7] a message from someone who wants to be your 'friend' online, remember that he/she is a stranger. After some time you may feel that you …[8] the person, but that isn't true.

Remember that online friends are not the same as real-life friends. Also, …[9] after your real-life friends and don't be afraid to tell them if they share too much information online.

6 **Reading for gist**

Read the forum thread. Find someone who:

1 no longer wants online friends.
2 has better friends online than in real life.
3 thinks that online friends are a silly idea.
4 has the same friends online and in real life.
5 likes to make friends with people online.

There may be more than one answer.

What do you think about online friends?

gandalf

My Facebook friends are all people that I have met in real life. Some of them live on the other side of the world, but I see some of them every day at school. I don't want any fake 'friends' who don't know me.

Realist

I don't understand the idea of online friends. What is the point of calling someone your friend if you don't really know them? Maybe it's good for insecure people: 'Oooh, look, I've got 500 friends, I must be really popular!'

konnichiwa

I've met some great people online through my interest in Manga comics. Yes, some of them are definitely friends. I know as much about them as my 'real' friends. Do I want to meet them in real life? Probably not – it might not work.

dora

I have lots of friends on social network sites. It's a great way to get to know new people. You have to be careful, though: people aren't always who they say they are.

JackiB

You won't believe this, but I've just deleted my Facebook page. I don't want to spend hours updating my profile, I want to see my friends face-to-face. Some of my friends think I'm a bit weird, but most of them agree with me.

Twilight

My online friends are important to me. When I've had a hard day at school, I can chat and laugh about things with my friends on the internet. I would be lonely without them. On the internet I can show a side of my personality that I don't show at school. They like who I am, not just how I look.

7 **Your opinion**

What do you think about online friends? Which person in exercise 6 do you agree with most? Write a short post for the forum (about 60–80 words).

Example: *@ dora. I agree with you. I think that ... because ... . That's why I have ...*

1/14 **8** **Listening for detail: cyberbullying**

On Portsmouth Youth Radio there is a programme about cyberbullying.

a Listen to the programme, then decide if the statements below are true or false.

1 Another student made a video of Ben in class.
2 Everyone could see the video on the internet.
3 Ella's boyfriend left her because he did not like her best friend.
4 She put photos of herself and her boyfriend on her Facebook page.
5 Ella sent her boyfriend a lot of text messages.
6 Nathan gets nasty messages from people in chat rooms.
7 A girl sent Nathan an email because of his rude comments.
8 Nathan's family has lost its internet connection.

b Correct the false sentences.

9 **Pair work: you decide**

a Read the definition of cyberbullying and then decide whether you think Ben, Ella and Nathan are cyberbullies. Give reasons for your opinions.

What is cyberbullying?

Cyberbullying is the use of mobile phones, instant messaging, email, chat rooms or social networks such as Facebook and Twitter to annoy, upset or scare someone. Cyberbullying can include making threats, sending insults and posting embarrassing photos of the victim or personal comments about them on a website.

I don't think that he/she is a cyberbully.
After all, he/she didn't mean to hurt anyone.
… was mean to him/her first.
It was a stupid thing to do, but we all make mistakes.
If you … online, then you're a cyberbully. It's as simple as that.
We all have to think about other people's feelings. That isn't an excuse.

b Now report back to the class with your decisions.

10 **Mediation**

Your friend is not always very nice to people on the internet. Write him/her an email in German giving him/her information from the box on cyber-bullying above so that he/she is nicer online. Don't translate word for word.

GRAMMAR

Talking about what has happened: present perfect

Aussagen	*Verneinungen*	*Fragen*	*Kurzantworten*
I**'ve (have) posted** a comment.	I **haven't posted** a comment.	**Have** you **posted** a comment?	Yes, I **have**. No, I **haven't**.
He**'s (has) read** your email.	He **hasn't read** your email.	**Has** he **read** your email?	Yes, he **has**. No, he **hasn't**.
They**'ve (have) seen** the video.	They **haven't seen** the video.	**Have** they **seen** the video?	Yes, they **have**. No, they **haven't**.

- Das ***present perfect*** wird mit ***have/has*** + Partizip Perfekt (3. Form des Verbs) gebildet.
- Man benutzt das ***present perfect***, wenn man sagen will, dass etwas in der Vergangenheit begonnen hat und bis in die Gegenwart andauert, also noch nicht abgeschlossen ist.
  z. B. *I've lived here for three years.*
  (d. h. ich wohne immer noch hier).
- Das ***present perfect*** wird auch für Vorgänge und Handlungen verwendet, die irgendwann einmal – oder noch nie – stattgefunden haben, ohne Angabe des Zeitpunkts.
  z. B. *I've already read that book.*
  (d. h. irgendwann in der Vergangenheit)

Signalwörter
already • always • before • ever …? • for three weeks/months/years • How long …? • just • lately • never • recently • since Monday /2001 • up till now • (not) yet

DANGER!

Since und *for* stehen im Englischen mit dem ***present perfect***. Im Deutschen steht in diesen Fällen meist die Gegenwart:
I've known him for three years. (Zeitspanne)
Ich kenne ihn seit drei Jahren.
He's been on Facebook since 2011. (Zeitpunkt)
Er ist seit 2011 im Facebook.

11 Present perfect

Make complete sentences in the present perfect.

Example: he / send / me a photo
He has sent me a photo.

1 I / finish / my homework
2 my grandma /not use / Facebook yet
3 they / not delete / their profiles
4 Brad / move / to California
5 she / start / a new blog?
6 you / see / the YouTube video yet?

12 Short answers

Give short answers in the present perfect.

Examples: Have you added him as a friend? ✓
Yes, I have.
Has she written to you yet? ✗
No, she hasn't.

1 Have you sent the email? ✓
2 Has Ben invited you to his party? ✓
3 Have your parents seen your photos? ✗
4 Have I shown you the video? ✓
5 Have you changed your profile? ✗
6 Has she used MySpace much? ✗

GRAMMAR

Present perfect progressive

I have been reading emails since 5 p.m. *Ich lese E-Mails seit 17 Uhr.*
- Diese Zeitform wird mit ***have/has*** + ***been*** + **-ing**-Form des Verbs gebildet.
- Es drückt aus, dass eine Tätigkeit in der Vergangenheit begonnen hat und bis in die Gegenwart andauert.

13 Present perfect progressive

Answer the questions using the present perfect progressive.

Example: How long have you been using Facebook? (for five years)
I have been using Facebook for five years.

1 How long have you been reading that email? (for 10 minutes)
2 How long has she been working there? (for five weeks)
3 How long have they been listening to us? (since they came in)
4 How long has Brad been writing to you? (for six months)

GRAMMAR

Some/any

Aussagen	***Verneinungen***	***Fragen***	***Bitten/Angebote***
I downloaded **some** music.	I didn't download **any** videos.	Have you received **any** emails today?	Could you send me **some** information?
Somebody sent me a message.	I don't know **anybody** here.	Has **anybody** seen Emma today?	Can **somebody** help me, please?
Something is worrying you.	He never says **anything** about his problems.	Is there **anything** I can do to help?	Would you like **something** to drink?

- ***Some*** und ***any*** bezeichnen eine unbestimmte Menge oder Zahl.
- Vor nicht zählbaren Substantiven wie *music* und *information* bedeutet ***some*** „etwas", vor zählbaren Substantiven im Plural „einige/ein paar".
- ***not … any*** ist die Verneinung von ***some*** und bedeutet „kein/e".
- ***Some*** wird vor allem in bejahten Aussagesätzen, Angeboten und Bitten verwendet.
- ***Any*** steht meist in verneinten Aussagesätzen und in Fragen.

14 *Some* and *any*

Complete these sentences with *some* or *any*.

1 … of my friends use Twitter every day.
2 Do … of you know how to post videos on Twitter?
3 Steve hasn't written … good Tweets for a long time.
4 I didn't send … Tweets yesterday.
5 There are … good tips for Twitter users on this website.

1 **Mediation**

You find this information on the internet. Use it to write a short article in German for your school magazine. The title: 'Vorsicht vor Unachtsamkeiten beim Umgang mit Facebook: Was werdende Azubis wissen sollten'.

1/15

Six Career-Killing Facebook Mistakes

by Erin Joyce

With more than 750 million users, Facebook is the most popular social networking site. Many users also use it to connect to colleagues, clients and potential employers. In fact, about 30 % of employers use Facebook to check job applicants, so don't make these Facebook mistakes.

1 Unsuitable pictures

Your new employer doesn't want to see pictures of you drinking a bottle of wine or dressed up for a night at the bar. Pictures of your personal life may not create a professional impression.

2 Complaining about your current job

Everybody has done this at least once. While everyone complains about work sometimes, it isn't wise to do it in a public space like Facebook. Though it may seem innocent, it may not impress your potential boss.

3 Information that doesn't match your CV *(Lebenslauf)*

If you say on your CV that your interests are charity work and being captain of the hockey team, but your Facebook profile says your main hobbies are computer games and downloading music, you may not get an interview.

4 Unprofessional status updates

Everyone should know to avoid status updates like 'Thank God it's Friday and time to partyyyyy!!!' However, simple status updates like 'Bob is bored,' can also suggest that you are not a good employee.

5 Not understanding security settings

It is possible to make lists of friends and decide what each list can and cannot see. However, many people do not fully understand these settings, or don't check them. At least make sure that your profile does not allow strangers to see any of your pictures or information.

6 Having embarrassing friends

You can't control what people post to your profile (although you can remove it), nor what they post to their own profiles. Take a look at everything connected to your profile.

If you are looking for a new job, the best advice is to lock your personal profile so that only friends can see it. Then, create a second profile for professional use.

©2010 Chappatte, distributed by Globe Cartoon. More cartoons on Chappatte's web site. Geneva-based Patrick Chappatte works for the International Herald Tribune, for Geneva newspaper Le Temps, and for NZZ am Sonntag. All cartoons reproduced with permission.

2 **Describing a cartoon**

a Describe the cartoon and explain its message. Use the language from the box and your own ideas. Write about 60 – 80 words.

> **Describing a cartoon**
>
> **What you can see**
> The man is probably at a job interview.
> The interviewer is looking at …
> He looks …
>
> **Your opinion**
> Personally, I think that the cartoon is …
> In my view, the cartoonist has made an important point about …
>
> **What it means**
> This is a cartoon about …
> Clearly, the man on the left has …
> The man on the right is probably …
> The message of the cartoon is this: …

b Look at the text on page 44 again. What did the man in the cartoon do wrong? What advice would you give him? Discuss in groups.

1 **Warm-up**

What online tools do you use when you do your English homework or write emails in English?

2 **Online dictionaries**

Visit the online German-English dictionaries in the table. Which of them offers each of the following features?

	LEO	dict.cc	Linguee	BeoLingus
suggests phrases as you type them into the 'search' box				
searches for your word/phrase on websites that have been translated				
gives you a direct link to the word's Wikipedia and Wiktionary articles				
lets you hear the pronunciation				
a vocabulary trainer				
an online forum where you can ask other users for translations				

3 **Using Google**

Use Google to find out which phrase is correct.

Hello
I am (a 15-year-old / a 15-years-old)[1] in Germany. I (have a problem at the home / have a problem at home)[2] which I need help with. I think my mom is (violating my privacy / injuring my privacy)[3]. She (keeps to hack / keeps hacking)[4] into my Facebook account. Every time I (transform my password / alter my password)[5], she figures it out. I (became really sour at her / got really mad at her)[6] and (we argued us / we had an argument)[7]. She says the internet is (dangerus/dangerous)[8] and she (has to me protect / has to protect me)[9]. She also says she pays for the internet and the computer. (She's got a good argument / She's got a good point)[10] there. But how can I (bring her to trust me/ get her to trust me)[11]?
Signed Hacker's Daughter

TIP

Mit Google können Sie herausfinden, wie oft ein Wort oder eine Wortgruppe im Netz erscheint. Google filtert zwar keine Rechtschreibfehler raus, Sie können die Korrektheit einer Wortgruppe aber feststellen, indem Sie bestimmte vertrauenswürdigere Domains absuchen.

.edu – „education" abgekürzt, für akademische Institutionen in den USA reserviert
.ac.uk – akademische Institutionen im UK
.gov – „government" abgekürzt, für staatliche Organisationen in den USA
.gov.uk – staatliche Organisationen im UK

Sie beschränken Ihre Google-Suche auf eine diese Domains, wenn Sie site: eingeben gefolgt von dem Domain-Kürzel. Stellen Sie sich vor, Sie sind nicht sicher wie man sagt „um einen Ratschlag bitten".

Hier können Sie anhand der Anzahl von Ergebnissen sehen, dass die zweite Variante viel gebräuchlicher und deswegen korrekt ist.

The celebrity circus

1 Understanding headlines

a) Complete the headlines with words and phrases from the box below.

> adopt • arrest for drugs • boldly wears • drug scandal • internationally famous • operations • rehab • secretly keeps • violently attacks

1 'Brangelina' … fourth child from third world

2 'Governator' … woman and child in California home

3 Gaga … meat dress to awards show

4 Nielsen: 14 … in 14 days, on TV!

5 Kid becomes … after posting on YouTube

6 Sheen … wife

7 Paris Hilton caught in …

8 Lohan back in … after police …

b) Now write each headline as a complete sentence.
Example: *1 Brad Pitt and Angelina Jolie have adopted a fourth child from the third world.*

c) Write a first sentence for each of the articles. Try to answer the five Ws – who, what, when, where and why – in the sentence. Make up any facts that you don't know.

> **TIP**
> Schlagzeilen sind manchmal schwer zu verstehen. Wörter wie *a* und *the* werden oft weggelassen, und das *simple present* wird oft benutzt, z. B. *adopt* statt ***have** adopted*.

2 Fame at all costs?

a Would you do any of the following things for fame? Tell your partner.

- go on a reality TV show
- get plastic surgery
- take off your clothes for the camera
- do something dangerous

b Now read the text. What other things do people do to become famous?

1/16

So you want to be famous?

The life of a celebrity seems absolutely fabulous. They seem to have everything: media attention, glamorous lives with first-class travel all over the world, countless fans who love them and, of course, money, money, money!

But the reason celebrities seem to be so happy is because they have to look that way. The better they look, the more jobs they get. Nobody wants to work with a celebrity who is 'out'. So celebrities smile for the cameras and do everything they can to appear glamorous, rich and happy, even if they're not. There are so many unhappy celebrities. Just look at the tragic life of Michael Jackson. He was the ultimate pop idol, but he was miserable. He was addicted to drugs and plastic surgery and he died young, like many other superstars.

Unfortunately, there are a lot of people who think that fame means happiness. These people will do everything to become famous and stay famous. They make shocking and obscene comments just to get attention. They insult other people in public. They tell lies about themselves and people in their lives. They hide their sexuality. They undress for the camera. They do dangerous things so that they appear on television. They put terrible pressure on their children. They get as much plastic surgery as they can. Some have even died for fame. We watch these people destroy their lives in the same way we watch bad horror movies – you want to look away, but you can't.

If you make two lists – one of celebrities that you like and one of celebrities that you really dislike – the second list will probably be longer. Most people don't love celebrities, they love to criticize them. Maybe Michael Jackson's biggest problem was that he desperately wanted everyone to love him and that is simply impossible. Love is a good thing, but you don't need the love of talent agents, the media and countless fans to be happy. It's much better to just love yourself as you are.

(335 words)

3 Understanding the text

Decide which statements the author of the article would agree with. Give information from the text to explain your answers.

1 Celebrity status does not mean happiness.
2 We hate celebrities because they are so happy all the time.
3 It is better if fans love you than if you love yourself.
4 There are good and bad aspects to the celebrity lifestyle.

4 **Discussing fame**
Choose one of the following tasks. Work in a group.

1 Make a list of people who have done extreme things for fame. Would you do any of these things? Why (not)?
2 Why do you think famous people often have problems with drugs?
3 Do you agree or disagree with the author's opinion? Find a statement in the article that you agree or disagree with. Think of a celebrity who supports your opinion.

GRAMMAR

Adverbs of manner

Charlie Sheen got married but the marriage ended **quickly**.
Natalie Portman smiled **happily** when she received her Oscar.
Lionel Messi is a **good** player. He plays **well**.
Film directors work **hard**. Their day starts **early** and ends **late**.

- Mit Adverbien beschreibt man, wie etwas geschieht. In der Regel werden Adverbien durch Anhängen von *–ly* an das Adjektiv gebildet.
- Achtung: Bei Adverbien, die von Adjektiven auf *–y* abgeleitet sind, wird das *–y* zu *–i*.
- Das zu *good* gehörende Adverb ist *well*.
- Einige Adverbien (*fast, hard, early, late*) haben die gleiche Form wie das Adjektiv.

5 **Adverbs**
Make an adverb out of the adjective to complete the sentences.

1 Angela is a bad actor. Angela acts *badly*.
2 George is a good singer. George sings ….
3 That was a hard kick. Messi kicked the ball ….
4 Lady Gaga wears strange clothes. She dresses ….
5 That runner is fast. He runs ….
6 Stars are always late. They arrive … to work.
7 Charlie is a heavy drinker. Charlie drinks ….
8 That celebrity should be more careful, and drive more ….

6 **Writing a profile**

a Write a profile of a famous person you like. It can be an entertainer, an author, a scientist, a sportsperson or a businessperson. At the end, say why you like the person.

… is a famous ….	He/She can … and …
He/She is from ….	I like … because he/she is a person who …

b Now read your profile to the class but don't say the name of the celebrity. Can the class guess who it is?

7 **Items in an office**
Bernie Lippschitz is a celebrity talent agent in New York. Find the items in the box in the picture of his office.

chair • door • filing cabinet • floor • keyboard • pin board • plant • printer • shelves • wall • wastebasket • window

8 **Prepositions of place**
Look at the picture and complete the sentences with the words from the box.

behind • between • in front of • near • ~~next to~~ • on top of • opposite • under

1 The window is *next to* a pin board.
2 The filing cabinet is … the shelves.
3 The window is … the desk.
4 The desk is … Bernie's chair and the visitors' chairs.
5 The keyboard is … the monitor.
6 The keyboard and monitor are … the desk.
7 The plant should be … the window, but it's not.
8 The wastebasket is … the pin board.

9 **Mindmapping vocabulary**
Copy and complete the mind map with office vocabulary from the exercises above. Add any other office words that you know.

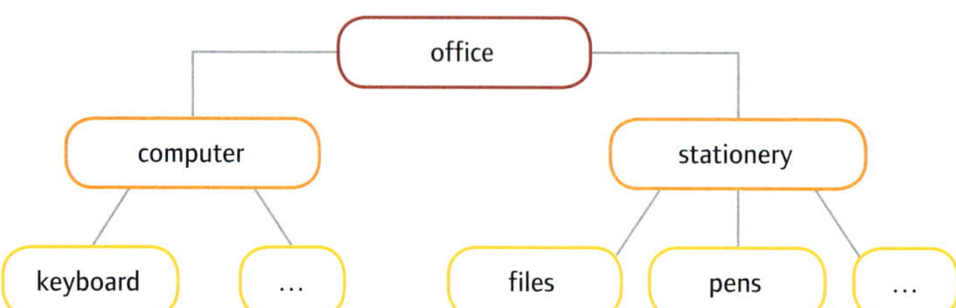

TIP

Mind maps
Erstellen Sie *Mind maps*, um sich Vokabeln und Redewendungen einzuprägen. Beginnen Sie mit einem zentralen Begriff. Dann fügen Sie Nebenkategorien, individuelle Wörter und Redewendungen hinzu.

1/17 **10** **Understanding recorded telephone messages**

a You are Bernie's assistant. Bernie has left some voicemail messages for you. Listen to the first one. What does he want you to do?

b Now listen to all the messages and find the six things he asks for in the picture on page 50.

GRAMMAR

Relative clauses

Relativsätze sind Nebensätze, die ein Nomen näher definieren. Sie werden mit Relativpronomen eingeleitet. Relativsätze werden normalerweise nicht durch Kommas markiert.

Personen näher beschreiben: *who* oder (seltener) *that*
*An entertainer **who/that** arrives late won't get work.*

Dinge, Tiere oder Begriffe näher beschreiben: *which* oder *that*
*An actor needs a quality **which/that** makes him interesting.*

Who, *which* und *that* können entfallen, wenn der Nebensatz ein anderes Subjekt hat:
*The photos are something **(which/that)** Bernie should organize.*
*Margie Charger is one of the singers **(who/that)** Bernie will call.*

11 **Relative clauses**

a Complete each sentence with *which* or *who*.

1 I work for a talent agent … lives in New York.
2 Bernie is the talent agent … I work for.
3 An entertainer … has no skills gets no work.
4 Organisation is a skill … every good manager should have.
5 A filing cabinet is a piece of furniture … can hold photos and files.
6 Talent agents are managers … generally get 10 % of the entertainer's pay.
7 The pay … talent agents get is usually 10 % of the entertainer's pay.
8 One thing … people want is to make a lot of money.

b Sumo wrestling is Japan's national sport and the wrestlers are huge celebrities. Complete the sentences about these Japanese stars with relative clauses.

1 The people … are the Japanese. (love sumo wrestling the most)
The people who love sumo wrestling the most are the Japanese.
2 The wrestlers … are the biggest, the strongest and the smartest. (are the most popular)
3 The foods … are meat and rice. (the wrestlers eat most)
4 The sumo exercises … make their legs strong. (many Japanese people do)
5 The teams … make the most money. (are the most successful)
6 Is sumo wrestling a sport … ? (you would like to try)

c Now decide in which of the above sentences (exercises a and b) you could take out the word *which* or *who*.

12 Reality TV

Read the text about reality TV shows around the world and decide which elements they have in common. Do you know any similar shows in Germany?

1/18

Reality game shows from around the world

RuPaul's Drag Race, USA

RuPaul is a big star in the USA. When he dresses up in drag, he is prettier and more feminine than most real women. He hosts a show where men compete to be America's drag superstar. The challenges usually involve making spectacular outfits in a very short time so they have to work quickly. At the end of every show, a jury tells each performer what they did well and how they could be better. RuPaul then chooses the week's loser, who has to go home.

Young Imam, Malaysia

In this enormously popular show, nine trainee imams compete to become Malaysia's next big religious star. Every week, they have religious tests and challenges such as counselling a married couple. They live in a mosque and are not allowed to use telephones, the internet or television. The Grand Mufti of Malaysia's national mosque judges their performance and eliminates a contestant every week. The winner gets a trip to Mecca, a scholarship to a University in Saudi Arabia and a job in a mosque.

Ladette to Lady, UK

A 'ladette' is a girl who acts like a boy, and there's nothing wrong with that! But the ladettes in this show are rude, aggressive and often drink a lot of alcohol. *Ladette to Lady* puts 8–10 extremely problematic girls in an old-fashioned 'finishing school' (*Mädchenpensionat*) for young ladies. The girls must dress very conservatively and learn things about flowers, cooking and etiquette. There are even bigger challenges, like going to balls with real British aristocrats. The teachers send a girl home every week and the winner is the 'most improved' girl. In season one, she received a sports car.

(281 words)

13 Understanding the text

Answer the following questions about the text.

1 Name four prizes that are mentioned in the text.
2 Name three tasks that the contestants have to complete.
3 Name two places where the contestants live.

GRAMMAR

Comparatives and superlatives of adjectives

	Adjektiv	*Komparativ*	*Superlativ*
Einsilbige Adjektive	long big	longer bi**gg**er	(the) longest (the) bi**gg**est
Zweisilbige Adjektive, die auf –y enden	pretty	pretti**e**r	pretti**e**st
Adjektive mit zwei und mehr Silben	famous important	more famous more important	(the) most famous (the) most important
Unregelmäßige Adjektive	good bad	better worse	(the) best (the) worst

- Auf *–er/–est* werden gewöhnlich einsilbige Adjektive sowie zweisilbige, die auf *–y* enden, gesteigert. Achtung: bei den zweisilbigen auf *–y* wird das *–y* zu *–i*.
- Wenn ein einsilbiges Adjektiv mit einem einfachen Konsonanten endet, z. B. *big*, wird dieser verdoppelt.
- Mit *more/most* werden zweisilbigen Adjektive, die nicht auf *–y* enden, sowie alle Adjektive mit mehr als zwei Silben gesteigert.
- Vergleiche können mit *–er/more … than* oder *(not) as … as* gebildet werden:
  I think *RuPaul's Drag Race* is **more** interesting **than** *Ladette to Lady*.

14 **Adjectives**

Copy this table and complete it with the adjectives from the description of *RuPaul's Drag Race*.

adjective	comparative	superlative
big	bigger	biggest
…	…	…

15 **Making comparisons**

Compare the following three German reality TV shows.
Write four sentences and use different forms.
Example: *Let's Dance is the most popular show.*

Sendung	Beliebtheit (TV-Quoten vom Finale)	Länge des Wettbewerbs	Jurymitglieder
Let's Dance	ca. 6 Mio Zuschauer	9 Wochen	4
X Factor	ca. 3 Mio Zuschauer	12 Wochen	3
Big Brother	ca. 1 Mio Zuschauer	19 Wochen	keine

*(Zahlen von 2011)

16 **Create an original reality game show**

Work in a group to create a concept for a new show. Present your idea to the class.

- Who are the contestants and what title are they competing for?
- What tasks/challenges/tests do they have to perform?
- Does a jury send people home every week? If so, how?

1 Choosing an itinerary

1/19

Rainer Kramer works for a company in Dessau. SooJin Anjou, a Korean business associate of his, has to take the train from Dessau to Kladno in the Czech Republic.

a Listen to their telephone call and fill in the table below.

Option	Length of trip	Price (€)	Departure time	Change trains?
1	...	...		...
2	...	...	...	...
3	...	...	...	...

b Now decide which itinerary SooJin chooses and why. The language in the box may help you.

cheaper/the cheapest • earlier/the earliest • more convenient/the most convenient
takes more/less time • takes the most/least time

2 Working with words

Complete these sentences with words from the box. There is one word too many.

change • costs • itinerary • leave • leaving • platform • takes

1 Do I have to … trains?
2 There's a train … at 5.30.
3 The trip … a little over six hours.
4 The ticket … 50 euros if you … at 16.00.
5 I'll give you the … when I see you next week.

3 The train station

Name the items a-j in the picture.

bench • car number • conductor • first-class car • passenger • platform •
platform area • restaurant car • ticket machine • track

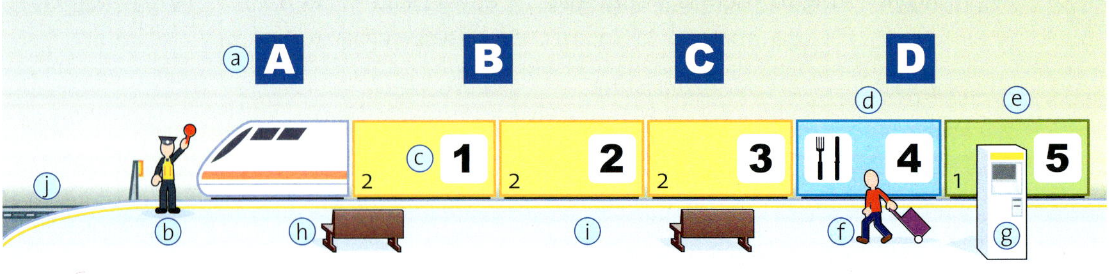

1/20 **4** **Describing the way**

a Listen to Rainer explaining SooJin's itinerary to her. Which of the sentences below do you hear?

1 You need to change trains three times, in Leipzig, in Cottbus and in Prague.
2 You arrive in Leipzig at 6.58. You will be on platform 13.
3 Well, then you need to go to platform 10 to change trains.
4 Your seat is in car 5. You can look on the board on the platform to see where that is.
5 The train leaves Prague at 11.41.
6 There's no reservation for this train so you can sit anywhere.

b Now work with a partner. Use the information below to describe the way from Dessau to Dresden.

Your travel information and reservation, 23.06

Stop	Time		Platform	Reservation
Dessau	depart at	09.21	7	Car 5, seat 6, window, no smoking
Leipzig	arrive at	10.06	12	
Leipzig	depart at	10.28	9	No reservation
Dresden	arrive at	12.33	1b	

5 **Buying a ticket**

a SooJin arrived safely in Kladno. She now needs to buy a ticket from Kladno to Prague. Complete the dialogue with words from the box.

arrives • car • change • conductor • leaves • main • reservation • seat • take • ticket machine • track

SooJin Hello. Do you speak English?
Ticket agent Yes, I do. How can I help you?
SooJin I would like to go to Prague airport tomorrow morning.
Agent Did you try the …[1]?
SooJin Yes, but I couldn't get it to work. I would prefer to buy the ticket from you.
Agent Alright. There is a train that …[2] at 7.11 and …[3] at 8.15.
SooJin Oh, that doesn't …[4] long. It's very fast. Do I have to change trains?
Agent Yes. When you get to the …[5] station in Prague, you need to …[6] trains. If you're not sure which station is the main station, ask the …[7]. The train to the airport leaves from …[8] 6.
SooJin And how much does it cost?
Agent It costs 200 koruny.
SooJin I'll take it, please.
Agent Alright. Here's your ticket. You don't need a …[9] for either of these trains. You can just get on any …[10] and sit in any …[11].

b In pairs role-play buying a ticket. Partner A turn to File 4 on page 173, partner B turn to File 12 on page 177.

1 Improving a text

Look at the two texts below. The text on the left is grammatically correct but would not get a very good mark. The text on the right is better stylistically. (Don't think about the middle column yet.)

mittelmäßige Version	Tipps	sehr gute Version
Why I think TV is bad Television is really bad. It's bad for the body. It's bad for the mind. People need to do more sport. People are fat. Television advertisements are bad. Television shows bad foods. TV shows are bad for your mind. TV is dangerous. I think television, the way it is today, is terrible. It needs to be reformed. Until the TV channels show better programmes, people shouldn't watch it.	a b c d e	**Why I think TV is bad** In my opinion, television is really bad. Firstly, I think it is bad for your body. Secondly, I think it is bad for your mind. Television is bad for the body because people need to exercise. When you watch TV you are just sitting. As a result, people become obese. In addition, television shows advertisements for unhealthy foods, and people buy them and eat them after they see the ads. Most television shows are bad for your mind. They show a lot of people who kill other people and do many stupid and criminal things. When you watch this every day on television, it becomes normal, and this is very dangerous. To conclude, I think television, the way it is today, is terrible. It needs to be reformed. Until the TV channels show better programmes, people should not watch it.

Now look at the middle column and match the arrows a–e to the tips 1–5 below to find out what makes the text on the right better than the one on the left.

1 Ein großer Wortschatz ist das Wichtigste, um gut zu schreiben. Lernen Sie immer wieder neue Vokabeln.

2 Beginnen Sie mit einem einleitenden Absatz, in dem Sie Ihre Meinung und Ihre Hauptargumente kurz erwähnen.

3 Organisieren Sie Ihren Text in mehreren Absätzen. Wenn der Text nur in einem einzigen Absatz geschrieben wird, hat der Leser bereits die Lust zu lesen verloren, bevor er damit begonnen hat, weil ein nicht gegliederter Textblock anstrengend zu lesen ist.
Eine Stellungnahme hat oft die folgenden vier Absätze: Einleitung – Argument 1 – Argument 2 – Schlussfolgerung.

4 Benutzen Sie Konnektoren und andere Ausdrücke, die auf der hinteren Umschlagklappe unter *'Language for Writing'* finden.

5 Begründen Sie Ihre Argumente. Die Aussage *'Television is bad for your mind'* allein reicht nicht. Sie müssen erklären, warum!

2 Writing a comment

Write an article about celebrities for your school magazine. Write 80–100 words.

Many people try to become celebrities—are they making a mistake?

Be what you want to be 6

1 Warm-up

a What lifetime goals might these people have? Use the language in the box to make a statement that fits each person.

Example: *1 A lifetime goal for me is to be a good parent.*

I would really like to A lifetime goal for me is to What I want most of all is to	protect people. push myself to the limit. be a good parent. save lives. change someone's life. be popular. entertain people. solve technical problems. make a lot of money. be my own boss. do something creative. work with a great team.

b Now discuss with a partner which lifetime goals you have.

1/21

Success against the odds

Richard Branson (born 1950)

He came from a wealthy family and went to an expensive private school, but Richard Branson didn't do well as a student. He found it difficult to learn because of dyslexia. When he was 16, he left school. Three years later, in 1970, Richard started the music company Virgin Records. Then he built a recording studio. When punk started, Virgin Records signed the shocking Sex Pistols when other record companies were not interested.

Richard Branson has continued to take risks and start new companies. He has started an airline, a railway company, a mobile phone network and his own brand of cola. In 2004 he started the space tourism company Virgin Galactic. He is also an adventurer: he has broken world records, flown around the world in a hot air balloon and crossed the Atlantic in a powerboat.

Richard Branson on his lifetime goals: 'My interest in life comes from setting myself huge challenges and trying to rise above them.'

William Kamkwamba (born 1987)

William Kamkwamba from Malawi left school at the age of 14 because his family could no longer afford the $80-a-year (€70) fees. When he returned to his parents' small farm, his future seemed limited. However, the teenager had a dream: he wanted to bring electricity and running water to his village. He used a local library to continue his education. One day he picked up an old school book and saw a picture of a windmill. William said: 'I was very interested when I saw the windmill could make electricity and pump water. I thought: "Maybe I should build one myself." He put together a turbine from bicycle and tractor parts and plastic pipes. Soon his windmill generated power and light for the village.

Since then, William's projects have become famous all over the world. He is now at university in South Africa and plans to bring power to all Malawians, only 2% of whom have electricity. 'I want to help my country,' he says. 'There's a lot of work to be done.'

Oprah Winfrey (born 1954)

Oprah Winfrey was born into a poor family in Kosciusko, Mississippi. When she was a little girl, her parents separated. She lived with her grandparents, then her mother, then her father. It was a hard life as her family was poor and by the time she was a teenager, Oprah was a rebel who took drugs. She became pregnant but lost the baby when it was born early.

Despite these problems she did well at school and went to university. She then became a TV reporter at 19, the first black woman in Nashville, Tennessee to do this. In 1978 she moved to an early morning talk show, 'People are Talking'. There, she was able to be herself and express her own opinions and feelings.

Since then, Oprah Winfrey has become one of the most successful TV personalities in the world. In 2010 she was worth over $2.7 billion. She has done a lot to help young people from poor backgrounds to become successful, for example, she set up a $40 million school for girls in South Africa. She gives away more money than any other US celebrity. 'Money gives you the ability to make a difference in other people's lives,' says Oprah.

(551 words)

2 Understanding the text

Match the statements to the people from the text.

A Richard Branson B William Kamkwamba C Oprah Winfrey

1 He/She did not get good marks at school.
2 This person had problems at home.
3 He/She often got into trouble as a teenager.
4 The people in this person's country are very poor.
5 This person owns a lot of companies.
6 He/She likes to solve technical problems.
7 He/She has built a machine.
8 You often see this person on TV.
9 This person has used his/her money to change people's lives.
10 This person wants to help people back home.

3 Working with words

Complete the sentences with verbs from the box. There are more verbs than you need.
You may need to change the form of the verb sometimes.

be • become • break • ~~do~~ • express • give • go • make • put • run • set • start • take

Example: 1 If she *does* well at school, she can get a good job.

1 I work in poor countries because I want to … a difference.
2 She was very rich, but then she … away most of her money to help other people.
3 He … together a sailing boat from bits of wood and plastic.
4 They … risks and nearly lost all of their money.
5 I want a job where I can … myself, not worry about what other people think.
6 It's OK to … your opinions, but you should always think before you speak.
7 We want to … up a youth club for teenagers from different cultures.
8 You don't have to … world records to be a special person.

4 Role-play

Work with a partner. Prepare and role-play an interview with one of the people on page 58.

Preparation

Interviewer
Write questions about the following subjects:
• family background • school • first success
• main achievements • lifetime goals

Interviewee
Use the text to make notes about your answers.

Interviewer
Tell me about your …
What about your … ?
What are your … , would you say?

Interviewee
Well, … Actually, …
In fact, … … , you see.

Example:

William Kamkwamba, tell me about your family background.

Well, I come from a poor family in Malawi. My family has a small farm, you see.

GRAMMAR

Should I use the simple past or the present perfect?

Simple past

1 In 1970, Richard **started** the music company Virgin Records.
2 When **did** Oprah **record** her first talk show?

Wie Sie in Unit 3 gelernt haben, beschreibt das ***simple past*** abgeschlossene Ereignisse und Zustände.

Signalwörter
yesterday · last week/year · three days ago · in 2001 · When …?

Present perfect

1 Since then, William's projects **have become** famous.
2 How long **has** he **been** at university?

Wie Sie in Unit 4 gelernt haben, wird das ***present perfect*** für Vorgänge und Handlungen verwendet, die irgendwann einmal stattgefunden haben, und für solche, die in der Vergangenheit begonnen haben und noch nicht abgeschlossen sind.

Signalwörter
already · always · before · ever … ? · for three weeks / months / years (*Zeitpunkt*) · How long …? · just · lately · never · since Monday / 2001 (*Zeitspanne*) · up till now · (not) yet

5 Signal words

a Choose the correct verb form (simple past or present perfect) and note down the signal words.

Example: Oprah *gave / has given* an interview on TV last week.
– *gave (simple past), last week*

1 I *saw / have seen* an interesting film about Richard Branson yesterday.
2 He *just started / has just started* another company.
3 We *never heard / have never heard* of William Kamkwamba.
4 *Did you read / Have you read* Oprah's autobiography yet?
5 She *started / has started* that talk show in 2005.

b Complete the sentences with the correct tense.

1 How long (you / live) here?
2 When (you / leave) your home country?
3 Our family (leave) Somalia ten years ago.
4 I (just read) an article about Bill Gates, the Microsoft founder.
5 Apparently he (give away) $ 1 billion last year.
6 (you/see) Oprah's new TV show already?
7 We (book) a flight on Richard Branson's airline yesterday.
8 We (want) to fly with Virgin for years.

6 For/since/ago

Complete the sentences with *for*, *since* or *ago*.

Example: Oprah has been a talk show host *since* 1978.

1 He has only lived here … three years, but he speaks perfect German.
2 I've been interested in wind turbines … I was young.
3 They built their first wind turbine two years … .
4 She's flown around the world many times … then.
5 Forty years … , very few black people were TV reporters in Tennessee.
6 I first heard about Virgin Galactic a few days … .
7 My dad has been a fan of the Sex Pistols … he was 16.
8 I haven't watched a talk show … months.

TIP

Eselsbrücken beim Grammatiklernen
Eselsbrücken helfen Ihnen bei kniffligen Stellen.

Beispiele:
„*Did* + Grundform ist die Norm, nach *did* steht nie die *past tense form*."
Did *you* ***go*** *shopping?*

'*Yesterday*, *ago* and *last* always need the simple past.'
We ***went*** *shopping* ***yesterday***.

7 Biographical information

How would you say these things in English?

Example: Ich wurde 1996 geboren. – *I was born in 1996.*

1 Ich wohne seit 10 Jahren in Tübingen.
2 Vor sechs Jahren habe ich Ski fahren gelernt. (*learn to ski*)
3 Letzten Winter bin ich in den Alpen Ski gefahren. (*go skiing*)
4 Ich habe nie an einem Skirennen teilgenommen. (*take part in a ski race*)
5 Wann bist du zum ersten Mal Ski gefahren?
6 Hast du je Snowboarden probiert? (*try snowboarding*)

8 All about me

Now write eight sentences about yourself using the simple past and the present perfect.

9 A remarkable athlete

Read the information about Jothy Rosenberg. Write about Jothy's life in English. Be careful to use the correct tense (simple past, present perfect or simple present) in each sentence.

Example: *Jothy Rosenberg was born in 1957.*

- 1957 geboren
- 1973 wegen Krebs (*cancer*) ein Bein verloren
- 3 Jahre später wieder Krebs
- eine Lunge (*lung*) verloren
- danach Ski fahren gelernt
- seitdem mit einem Bein schwimmen und Rad fahren gelernt
- nimmt jedes Jahr am 1,5-Meilen Alcatraz Sharkfest Swimming Race teil
- dadurch $ 40.000 für Obdachlose gesammelt

1/22 **10** **Listening to a song**

a Listen to the song twice:

1 First time: close your book and just listen.
2 Now follow the lyrics (*Songtext*) as you listen.

Be What You Wanna Be
Darin Zanyar, 2005

Doctor, actor, lawyer or a singer.
Why not president? Be a dreamer!
You can be just the one you want to be.
Policeman, firefighter or a postman –
Why not something like your old man?
You can be just the one you want to be.

Doctor, actor, lawyer or a singer.
Why not president? Be a dreamer!
You can be just the one you want to be.

I know that we've all got one thing
That we all share together.
We've got that one nice dream we live for.
You never know what life could bring,
'Cause nothing lasts forever.
Just hold on to the team you play for.

I know you could reach the top,
Make sure that you won't stop,
Be the one that you want to be.
Now sing this with me:

Doctor, actor, lawyer or a singer, etc.

We may have different ways to think,
But it doesn't really matter.
We're all caught up in the stream of this life.
Focus on every little thing,
That's what does really matter.
Luxury cars and bling, that's not real life.

I know you could reach the top,
Make sure that you won't stop,
Be the one that you want to be.
Now sing this with me:

Doctor, actor, lawyer or a singer, etc.

Last year I used to dream about this day,
Now I'm here, I'm singing for you.
I hope I could inspire you,
'Cause I've got all the love,
'Cause I've got all love for you.

Doctor, actor, lawyer or a singer, etc.

b Now read the opinions about the song and decide which is closest to your own.

1 *It's just a silly pop song with naive, idealistic lyrics.*

2 *I think the message is really cool, but I don't like the music much.*

3 *I like it: It's a catchy song and it makes you think.*

11 Understanding the meaning

Put these ideas into the same order as the lyrics.

Example: *2, …*

1 We're all different.
2 We all need to have a dream.
3 In one way we're all the same.
4 My dream has come true.
5 Money isn't important.
6 Don't expect everything to stay the same.
7 Don't let anything stop you from reaching your dream.

12 Building vocabulary

Work with a partner.

1 Find eight jobs in the chorus (*Refrain*) of the song. Check their meanings in German and write a list.
Example: *doctor – Arzt/Ärztin*

2 Now make a mind map with different jobs that people in your class would like to do. You can use the internet to help you with the English translations.

13 Writing

Do you agree with the singer that it is good to 'be a dreamer'? Is it better to have realistic plans? Write a text which considers both sides of the argument. The tip box and the diagram may help you. Write 60–80 words.

Start like this:
In his song 'Be what you wanna be', Swedish singer Darin Zanyar claims that …

TIP

Einen argumentativen Aufsatz gliedern

Das Thema vorstellen
In this essay I would like to consider …

Discussing both sides
On the one hand, …
On the other hand, …
It is true to say that …
However, …

Stating your opinion
In my opinion, …
In my view, …

Giving reasons
This is because …
The reason for that is …

Summarizing and closing
To sum up, …
All in all, …

realist
- don't waste energy
- focus your efforts
- be satisfied with what you can do
- live in the real world

dreamer
- push yourself
- don't let others hold you back
- you won't achieve much if you don't aim high
- see the possibilities

Writing a CV/résumé

Jessica Krause is applying for voluntary work in the Cairngorms National Park in Scotland. She has written an English CV.

CV

Name:	Jessica Krause
Address:	Mozartstraße 22 a 72341 Altstadt Germany
Telephone:	+49 (0) 7012 519722
Date of birth:	26 February 1997

Education

2003–2007	Altstadt Primary School
2007–2011	Altstadt Secondary School
2011–	Neukirchen Vocational College

Work experience

2011	Work placement, salesperson at Elektro-Markt, Neukirchen
Easter 2012	Voluntary work, conservation worker at Naturpark, Altstadt-Ost
Summer 2012	Holiday job, assistant at Hochdorf Veterinary Clinic

Skills

Languages	English (fluent), Italian (basic)
IT	MS Office, Photoshop

Other

European First Aid Certificate

Interests and hobbies

Conservation
Animal health
Hiking and camping

References available on request

TIP

In Englisch, ein Lebenslauf is called a 'curriculum vitae' or 'CV' for short. That's Latin for 'track/race of life'.
In American English, a CV is called a 'résumé'. That's French for 'summary'.

1 Understanding the text

Use information from Jessica's CV to answer the interviewer's questions.

1 This job involves working with animals. Do you have any relevant experience?
2 How good is your English?
3 Do you enjoy being outdoors a lot?
4 Will you need to do a first aid course?
5 Are you sure that you will like conservation work?
6 Do you speak any languages other than English and German?
7 Please tell me about your studies.
8 What work experience do you have?

TIP

Lebensläufe auf Englisch schreiben

Lebensläufe in englischsprachigen Ländern unterscheiden sich in manchen Punkten von deutschen:
- Es gibt kein Foto.
- Zeugnisse werden nicht beigelegt.
- Manchmal werden Ansprechpartner genannt, die Auskunft über den/die Bewerber/in geben können.

Achtung bei der Übersetzung deutscher Schultypen und Schulabschlüsse:
- Hauptschule/Realschule – *secondary school (GB), high school (US)*
- Berufsfachschule – *vocational college/school*
- Duales System – *apprenticeship scheme*
- Mittlerer Schulabschluss – *GCSE (GB)*
- Fachhochschulreife – *National Vocational Qualification/Certificate*
- Abitur – *A Levels (GB), high school diploma (US)*

2 Working with words

Find the equivalents of these German expressions in Jessica's CV.

1 Lebenslauf
2 Adresse
3 Geburtsdatum
4 Schulbildung
5 Grundschule
6 Hauptschule/Realschule
7 Berufsfachschule
8 Berufserfahrung
9 Praktikum
10 Freiwilligentätigkeit
11 Fertigkeiten
12 fließend
13 Erste-Hilfe-Zertifikat
14 Empfehlungsschreiben

3 Discussion

Discuss in a group: what are the advantages of doing voluntary work? Are there any disadvantages? Are you interested in doing voluntary work when you leave school?

The ideas in the box may help you.

For	Against
wider experience	don't earn money
new skills	delay start of career
make new friends	get out of touch with friends at home

4 It's your turn

Write your own CV. Use Jessica's CV as a model.

1 Prediction

Work with a partner and turn to File 6 on page 174. Look at the heading, introduction and picture and make notes about what you think the text could be about.

TIP

Bevor Sie mit dem Lesen eines Textes beginnen, sollten Sie sich ein paar Gedanken machen, wovon der Text handeln könnte. Lesen Sie zuerst die **Überschrift** und überlegen Sie, was wohl das zentrale Thema des Textes ist. Folgt der Überschrift eine **Einleitung**, lesen Sie auch diese. Einleitungen sind meist einfacher gehalten als der nachfolgende Text und sollen den Zugang erleichtern. Visuelle Hilfen erleichtern das Verständnis. Nutzen Sie die **Abbildungen**, um Zugang zum Text zu finden.

2 Skimming

Now skim the text to find out what the text is about. Were your ideas right? Note down key words to support your ideas.

TIP

Manchmal werden Sie aufgefordert, einen Text nur kurz zu überfliegen (*skim the text*), um das Thema zu erfassen. Lesen Sie den Text zügig durch. Konzentrieren Sie sich auf **Schlüsselwörter** (meist Substantive und Verben), um den Text im Groben zu erfassen. Sollten Sie ein Schlüsselwort nicht verstehen, lesen Sie weiter. Die Bedeutung vieler Wörter wird oft aus dem Kontext deutlich oder später durch ein Synonym erklärt.

3 Scanning

Now scan the text. What significance do the following dates and numbers have in the biography: 1974, 13, 10 in 11, 36 Boys, 4 –?

TIP

Bei der Suche nach spezifischen Inhalten sollte man sich nicht von der Fülle der übrigen Informationen ablenken lassen. Wenn wir z. B. eine Bestsellerliste schnell durchsuchen (*scan*), um die Platzierung eines ganz bestimmten Titels herauszufinden, blenden wir alle anderen Informationen aus.

4 Reading for detail

Say which of these statements is correct and then correct the incorrect information.

1 Tim Raue grew up in one of the richest parts of Berlin.
2 He enjoyed school.
3 His gang was made up of German boys.
4 He learned to cook in a Greek restaurant
5 He believes that his difficult childhood and his experiences help him cope in the kitchen.

TIP

Für das gründliche Erfassen eines Textes kann es hilfreich sein, sich noch einmal dessen Aufbau zu verdeutlichen. Eventuell vorhandene **Zwischenüberschriften** sind dabei von Nutzen. Jetzt sollten Sie auch unbekannte Wörter nachschlagen. Danach können Sie die wichtigsten Textstellen unterstreichen oder klar strukturiert in eigenen Worten aufschreiben. Achten Sie auch auf interessante Details.

Life after school

7

1 Questionnaire

Complete the questionnaire about leaving school and then discuss your answers in pairs.

1 How prepared are you to do the following things?
(1 = totally prepared -> 5 = not at all prepared)

a manage your money
b prepare your own food
c find and keep a job
d deal with older colleagues and bosses
e say goodbye to some friends

2 Which of the following are you looking forward to the most?

a having more choices and responsibility
b not having any more classes at school
c moving ahead in your career
d earning your own money
e making new friends

3 What else are you looking forward to? Name at least one thing.

4 What will you be doing in five years? Will you …

a … have a job?
b … live in the same area?
c … be married?
d … have a pet?

2 Life after school

a Read the following statements about life after school. Which statements do you think most of your classmates would agree with? Rank them from 'most people' to 'fewest people'.

I will love not having to come to school. No more subjects I'm not interested in!

I have no idea what I'm going to do after school ends.

I'm a little bit nervous about my life after school.

I can't wait to start my job/training.

b Now take a poll in class and find out if you were right.

3 After school options

Read the text. With a partner decide who (Kim, Etienne, Jerald or Lisa) is going to develop the skills in the box after school.

artistic • childminding • communication • computer • construction • dealing with people • foreign language • selling • technical

Example: *Kim is going to develop childminding skills.*

1/23

School's out! Now what?

Almost everyone looks forward to the end of school, but what do they do afterwards? Most people get further education or start jobs. However, a small number of people do very original things. Here are a few examples.

Case no. 1: Kim

It took Kim a long time to decide what to do after school. Finally, she decided to spend a year volunteering with a religious organisation. 'I'm actually not very religious, but the organisation I found does good work. They're going to send me to an orphanage somewhere. I don't know where I'll be. Maybe Russia. I'm looking forward to working with the children. There are so many of them that need love and attention.'

Case no. 2: Etienne

When his uncle announced he wanted to build his own house in the country, Etienne asked if he could join him. 'We're going to build the whole thing ourselves. I can't wait!' While his uncle works during the day as a school bus driver, Etienne will work hard on the house. In the evenings and on weekends, the two will work on the project together. When they've finished, maybe the uncle will help Etienne build his own house. It would be a great financial investment.

Case nos. 3 and 4: Jerald and Lisa

These two school-leavers want to work in common professions (graphic artist and automobile salesperson), but their way of doing it is unusual and innovative. They both searched long and hard for relevant jobs or internships. They didn't find anything, so they decided to create their own internships! They searched for people who were doing the jobs they wanted to do and asked to be their assistants. 'I called a graphic artist and asked if I could work for her for free, and she said yes, so I'm going to be her assistant,' says Jerald. Lisa called every car, lorry and motorcycle dealership in the area until she was successful. Her internship starts as soon as she finishes school.

(340 words)

4 Who is it?

Read the statements below and decide who from the text could give these people the best advice about life after school. Give reasons for your answers.

1 Ann: "I really want to help people. There are so many people in need in the world."
2 Joe: "I am saving some money and would like to use it wisely for the future."
3 Bob: "I've got a free summer and would love to do something useful with my hands."
4 Faith: "I can't believe I can't find a job! Surely somebody needs a mechanic?!"
5 Megan: "I love driving. Maybe I could find a job where I have to drive a lot."

5 Looking ahead

Discuss with a partner. What are you going to do after school?

GRAMMAR

Going to future

Aussagen	*Verneinungen*	*Fragen*	*Kurzantworten*
This **is going to be** a great year!	**I'm not going to worry** about my future.	**Are** you **going to move out** of your parents' flat?	Yes, I **am**./No, I**'m not**. Yes, it **is**./No, it**'s not**. Yes, we **are**./No, we**'re not**.

- Das ***going to future*** wird mit *am/is/are going to* + Grundform gebildet.
- Es wird für Pläne und Absichten verwendet, also z. B. um auszudrücken, was man gerade vorhat. Mit *going to* kann man auch sagen, was höchstwahrscheinlich geschehen wird, weil es Anzeichen dafür gibt.

6 *Going to*

Complete each sentence with a form of *going to* or *not going to*.

1 Grace *is going to take* a computer course. (take)
2 What … you … after school? Get a job? Get job training? (do)
3 We … married until we are at least 30. (get)
4 I … a year here in this town, then I want to move somewhere new. (spend)
5 He … successful in his job because he's very arrogant. (be)
6 … your parents … you financially? (help)
7 Don't worry that you … a job. You have to think positively! (find)
8 I know I … further education but the question is 'When?' (finish)

7 A different coming of age

a Complete the text with a verb from the box and the correct form of the *going to* future.

be • buy • not control • ~~experience~~ • not try • stay (2x) • wear

These are not actors in a historical film, they are real Amish people – me and my friends, in fact! About 250,000 Amish live in North America in isolated communities. We are very religious and have strict rules about dress and technology. We're 16 years old now, and soon we *are going to experience* a period of time called *Rumspringa*. During this time, our parents …[1] us as much anymore. I know I …[2] modern clothes and go to the movies. A friend …[3] a car. Some people try alcohol and cigarettes during *Rumspringa* but I …[4] cigarettes.
It …[5] a lot of fun but we have to decide if we …[6] in the Amish community. I like our Amish ways, so I'm quite sure I …[7] Amish. About 85 % of us do.

b Do you think you would like to come of age in this culture? Why (not)?

8 (CD 1/24)

Meeting a careers counsellor

a Nathan is unsure what he wants to do after school. Listen to his discussion with a careers counsellor and then answer the following questions.

1 Why is Nathan meeting Gail?
2 What 'experiment' does Gail try?
3 Which picture does Nathan choose?
4 What will Nathan do next?

b (CD 1/25) Now listen to Nathan's second meeting with Gail and complete the sentences below.

1 Nathan likes the skyscraper picture because …
2 At first Nathan thinks he can't just wander around the city because …
3 He thinks he might like to work as …
4 Gail suggests that Nathan …
5 Nathan doesn't know if …

9

Working with words

Complete Gail's advice with words from the box.

advertisements • blogs • contact • employment • experiences • research

Why don't you …[1] the jobs on the internet? Start at the website of the …[2] office. Then, search job …[3] to get more information. And find …[4] by people who have these jobs. Read what they say about their …[5]. You can even …[6] them if you want.

TIP

Paraphrasing

Wenn Sie dabei sind, Englisch im Unterricht zu sprechen, und Sie kennen ein Wort nicht, widerstehen Sie der Versuchung, das Wort gleich auf Deutsch zu sagen, denn das werden Sie mit einem nicht-deutschsprachigen nicht machen können. Stattdessen versuchen Sie das Wort zu umschreiben, in dem Sie es definieren oder in anderen Wörtern erklären. Die folgenden Redewendungen könnten Ihnen dabei helfen:

It's a thing that you use to …
It's a kind of … (that …)
It's like a …
It's a person who …
It's a place where …
It's when you …

10

Dealing with unknown words

Here are the photos that Gail showed Nathan. Describe one of them to a partner. You are not allowed to use the words under the pictures. Use the language from the tip box instead.

skyscraper

crowd

highway

forest

15 Dream jobs

a Below are three common dream jobs. Match each statement to a job and then decide which future form is used and why.

commercial airline pilot

film director

island beach bartender

1 I'll mix that drink for you right away.
2 Ladies and gentlemen, we land in 10 minutes.
3 We start shooting at 6 a.m. tomorrow. Be in your costumes and make-up by then!
4 This is how we're going to do it: Brad picks Angelina up and carries her over the water. Don't drop her, Brad!
5 Tomorrow the special is ice-cold margaritas. Hope to see you then!
6 Next week I'm flying to Paris four times.

b Now write some more statements that these people could say.

16 Describing a dream job

1/27

Listen to Carrie describe her dream job and decide which of the following phrases you hear.

1 work indoors / outdoors
2 work one / two / … hours a day / week
3 in the country / city
4 in a shop / office / industrial setting
5 have lots of / very little responsibility
6 wear smart clothes / dress casually
7 wear a suit / uniform / jeans
8 have one's own office / company car
9 work hard / not work hard
10 get financial / emotional / creative rewards

17 Dream jobs

a Use the phrases from exercise 16 to describe the dream jobs above.

b Now describe your dream job to the class. Can they guess what it is?

18 Research projects

a Research one of the options for life after school mentioned in this unit or your own option and present your findings to the class. An excellent term to search for on the internet is "gap year".

b Ask two older people what they did in the year after school. Report to the class what you found out.

Covering letters

1 Answering a job advertisement

Young people's CVs are all very similar so the covering letter you send with it is very important to help you stand out and get an interview. Read the following letter. It has some good, useful phrases but which important aspects are missing?

Dear Sir or Madam,

I have seen your job advertisement for a celebrity photographer on your website and would like to apply.
As you can see on my CV, I am finishing vocational school in the summer of this year. Please feel free to contact me if you have any questions.

Yours faithfully,
John Boring

2 Job advertisements

a Read the following job advertisements. Complete the mind map with words which describe 1) the characteristics that the applicants need and 2) the duties they will have to carry out.

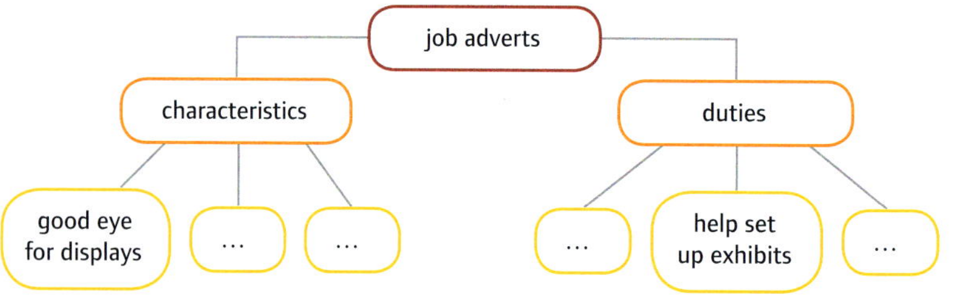

a

Art gallery assistant wanted.
Do you love art?

Our art gallery is looking for someone who can work in our office, sell artwork and help set up exhibits.
You don't have to be an artist, but you should have a good eye for displays. You should also be very organized and good with people.

Send your CV and covering letter to the manager, Phillip Streams, P.Streams@citygallery.com

b

Do you care about human rights?

Our organisation, Middle East Justice, seeks fundraising personnel. Your activities will include planning fundraising campaigns and intensive contact with donors.

c

Large furniture store seeks internet experts to develop and run new online shop.

We need programmers, designers and other IT experts.
Please send CV to HR@Domestico.com

d

Animal caregiver required.

We are a home for wild animals that are injured or orphaned. We need someone who respects animals and knows a lot about them. You should also be interested in wildlife biology.

Your duties will include feeding the animals, giving them medication and cleaning.

Contact: Margorie Epish – info@wildanimalcare.org

b Now match each characteristic with its translation.

1	communicative	a	zuverlässig
2	analytical	b	technikinteressiert
3	a team player	c	kontaktfreudig
4	technically minded	d	kommunikativ
5	outgoing	e	verantwortungsbewusst
6	responsible	f	teamfähig
7	creative	g	analytisch
8	reliable	h	kreativ

3 **Getting the employer interested**

These statements are from covering letters. Read the adverts again and decide which one each sentence is for. Give reasons for your answers.

1 I would like to do this work because wildlife is very important to me and I would really like to help care for it.
2 I am not afraid to ask people for money when I believe that it is for a good cause.
3 I have taken two courses in programming languages and completed all the course work successfully. The programming languages I know are …
4 I organised a cake sale at my school to collect money for charity.
5 I enjoy creative work very much. I have created videos and posters for my friend's band.

4 **Describing your experiences**

Use the words and phrases in the box to complete the sentences. There are more words than you need and sometimes more than one answer is possible.

achieved • been trained in • completed • coordinated • created • developed • founded • led • managed • organized • planned • taken courses in

Example: *I have completed* courses in many programming languages.

1 … a club at my school.
2 … computer science and mathematics.
3 … many events for my youth group.
4 … a shop which sells groceries.
5 … my training as a medical assistant.
6 … tourists through national parks.

5 **Writing a covering letter**

Answer one of the job advertisements from exercise 2. Use the language in the letter in exercise 1 and from the box below.

Writing a covering letter
Dear Sir or Madam, … Yours faithfully, (if you don't know the person's name)
Dear Mr/Ms ___, … Yours sincerely, (if you know the person's name)
I am interested in … because …
I like/love/enjoy …ing
I have created/organized/developed/…

Unter WWEU0701 finden Sie Zusatzübungen zum Thema der Unit.

How to ... give a presentation

1 Typical mistakes

(CD 1/28)

a Listen to the extracts from five bad presentations. Which speaker:

1 ... did not look up important English phrases before the presentation?
2 ... did not take the presentation seriously?
3 ... is unprepared and disorganised?
4 ... does not have a structured presentation?
5 ... sounds bored and doesn't want to give the presentation?

b Can you think of any other mistakes people make when they give a presentation? Make a list.

2 First impressions

(CD 1/29)

You should always have a good first sentence. Listen to these good examples. Which speaker:

a ... gives an impressive statistic?
b ... tells a joke?
c ... tells a story?
d ... asks a question to make the listeners think?
e ... uses a quote to make the listeners think?

3 Structuring a presentation

a Look at the useful phrases below. Match the phrases to the correct part of the presentation.

1 Then, I'm going to talk about / tell you ...
2 First, I'm going to talk about / tell you ...
3 Now, I'm going to talk about / explain ...
4 To conclude, ...
5 Finally, I'm going to talk about / tell you ...
6 Today I'm going to talk about / tell you ...

a Introducing the topic
b Introducing argument 1
c Introducing the next argument
d Introducing the last argument
e Changing the topic
f Finishing the presentation

TIP

Geben Sie Ihrer Präsentation eine Struktur. Eine typische Struktur ist:
- Einleitung des Themas
- Unterthema/Argument 1
- Unterthema/Argument 2
- eventuelle weitere Unterthemen/Argumente
- Abschluss.

Ohne Struktur wirken Sie unprofessionell. Es ist wichtig, dass Sie Ihre Struktur transparent machen, damit Ihre Zuhörer Ihrer Rede folgen können. Diese Klarheit erreichen Sie mit den Signposting-Ausdrücken auf der linken Seite.

b Can you think of any more useful language for presentations? Make a list organized into the categories above.

The biggest complaint was about pay and bosses. In Denmark, 43 % of the employees who took part in the survey said they were unhappy with their pay; in Austria the number rose to 56 %. Meanwhile 65 % of employees in Germany said that their wages were too low. Although more than half of the workers said their boss was OK, almost 40 % don't like their boss. The majority of these people are working in Denmark and Ireland.

Even so, most of these employees working abroad are happy with their jobs and do not regret their decision to move. Although learning the local language has been difficult for most, this hasn't stopped employees from enjoying lunch with their colleagues or having a chat during their coffee breaks, as many share English as a common language.

6 Drawing graphs

Copy and complete the bar chart in your exercise book.

7 Reading for detail

Look at the text again and decide if the statements are true or false.

1 People in the USA took part in a survey about their work.
2 Half of the workers from the original survey answered the questions.
3 Most of the people who took part in the survey said they were happy working abroad.
4 More than half of the employees in Germany are satisfied with their pay.
5 Most of the workers do not like their boss.
6 Most people have learnt the local language.
7 A lot of the employees do not like their co-workers.
8 Employees think that breaks are a waste of time.

8 Discussion

Discuss the following questions in groups. Make notes and report to the class.

1 Would you like to relocate to another EU country? Why/Why not?
2 Which EU country would you like to live and work in? Why?
3 Where would you not like to live and work? Why?
4 What job would you do?
5 What might you need to learn to help you in a new country?

GRAMMAR

Modal verbs and their substitutes

- Hilfsverben (*modal verbs*) sind Wörter wie *may, can, must, should usw*. Sie drücken z. B. eine Fähigkeit, eine Erlaubnis oder ein Verbot aus.
- Hilfsverben haben eine Gegenwartsform, manche auch eine Vergangenheitsform. Ersatzverben (*substitutes*) werden benutzt, um andere Zeiten zu bilden.

***can/be able to* (können)**
- *Can/can't* drücken eine Fähigkeit oder eine Möglichkeit aus.
- *Can/can't* werden nur in der Gegenwart benutzt. Das *simple past* lautet *could/couldn't*; anderen Zeiten werden mit dem Ersatzverb *to be able to* gebildet.

***could/may/might* (könnte/n)**
- *Could, may* und *might* drücken eine Möglichkeit aus.

***must/have to* (müssen); *need not/don't have to* (nicht müssen)**
- *Must* und *have to* drücken eine Verpflichtung oder Notwendigkeit aus.
- *Must* wird nur in der Gegenwart benutzt. *Have* to kann in allen Zeiten verwendet werden.
- Die Verneinung von *must* ist *need not* oder *not have to* (nicht müssen).

DANGER!

must not/mustn't = nicht dürfen
Let's go home now.
We ***mustn't be*** *late.*

***may/be allowed to* (dürfen)**
- *May* und *be allowed to* drücken eine Erlaubnis oder ein Verbot aus. *May* findet man vor allem im formellen Englisch.

***should/shouldn't* (sollen/nicht sollen, sollte/n)**
- *Should/shouldn't* werden benutzt, um Ratschläge zu erteilen bzw. um auf eine Pflicht hinzuweisen.

Hilfsverb	*Ersatzverb*
can	be able to
must	have to
need not	don't have to
may	be allowed to

9 Modal verbs

a) Replace the German words in the sentences below with a modal verb or a suitable substitute.

1 Last year, I *konnte* take part in a practical training course in our subsidiary in Paris. Now my boss says that I *muss* give a presentation about what I learned to my colleagues.
2 He *musste* work hard on his English grammar when he started his training. He's been living in London for three months now and he *kann* write and speak perfect English.
3 You *solltest* set your alarm clock for 7 o'clock. If you arrive late, you *darfst nicht* take the examination.

b Choose one modal verb from the brackets to complete the sentences.

1 She has completed her training so she (*can/could/must*) start looking for work abroad.
2 There are no jobs in my country. (*May/Could/Should*) I look for work abroad?
3 I was born and brought up in Poland. I (*must not/need not/shall*) go to Polish lessons.
4 We are still trainees so we (*can/must/don't have to*) work overtime.
5 I work in an international firm. I got the job because I (*can/could/must*) speak English.
6 You (*could/might/should*) have some questions prepared for the presenter.
7 I don't understand the application form. I (*am allowed to/can/must*) ask someone to help me complete it.
8 You (*ought to/might/must*) try to speak the local language when you are abroad.

c Use the modal verbs *can, could, may, must* or *need not* to rewrite the sentences about Zeynel's experience at work. There might be several possibilities.

Example: He wasn't able to operate all the machines when he started.
He couldn't operate all the machines when he started.

1 He's able to understand what his colleagues are talking about now.
2 He's allowed to have two days off a week.
3 He doesn't have to pay a lot of rent because he lives in company accommodation.
4 He has to share a kitchen with some colleagues though.
5 Perhaps he will stay in Prague for a long time.

d Use modals and the words in the box to make sentences to match the signs. Sometimes there is more than one sentence.

Example: *You must wash your hands before you handle food.*

1

2

3

4

5

as spillages may damage the machinery • as there is a danger of fire • ~~before you handle food~~ • in case something falls on your head • when you are in the quiet part of the train • when you are working with noisy machinery

e Work in a small group. You have five minutes to write questions using modal verbs. Ask your teacher to check the questions, then pass them to another group. Listen to the answers with the rest of the class.

2/4 V2

1 An interview goes wrong

a Watch or listen to the job interview and take notes. What does the applicant do wrong?

b Now brainstorm what tips you would give the applicant to improve the interview.

2 Interview dos and don'ts

Read the text and/or watch the second video and answer the following questions.

1 Which tips are things to do *before* the interview and which are things to do *during* the interview?
2 How many of the tips did you think of in exercise 1b? Do any of the tips surprise you?

Tips for a successful job interview

1 **Prepare for the interview.** Find out as much information as you can about the company. Study their website.

2 **Plan your way to the interview.** Leave home early and allow extra time to get there. You will be more relaxed this way. Never arrive late to a job interview!

3 **Dress up.** It shows you want the job. Don't worry, nobody will think you plan to do it every day.

4 **Prepare answers to the most common interview questions.** Practice your answers with a friend!

Three very common interview questions

Tell me about yourself.
They don't want to know where you were born or what your favourite colour is. They want to know what relevant experience you have. And they want you to tell them you've got some personal qualities that will help the company.

I'm a student at a vocational school.
I've had some training in …
I had a job last summer in an electronics shop.
That went very well/was a good experience.
Look at pp. 74-5 for more phrases.

Why do you want this job?
They want to know that the applicant isn't just looking for *any* job. Even if it's not your dream job, there should be some good reasons for doing it.

I'm looking for a good job/internship in a company where I can get experience in/with …
I like/enjoy …

What are your strengths and weaknesses?
This is a chance for you to tell the interviewer some good things about yourself. When you talk about your weakness, stay positive. Don't talk about things or people you 'hate'. The interviewer wants to hear what you're doing about your weakness. Don't say you have no weaknesses. This only shows that you're not taking the question seriously.

I think my biggest strength is …
… my ability to …
… that I am …
This helps me to …

I think my biggest weakness is…
… my lack of experience. That's why I want to do an internship.
… I tend to …
I'm trying to …
I'm dealing with this by -ing …

Of course, there is a good chance that your interviewer will ask completely different questions. But if you prepare answers to these three questions, you will be well prepared for the interview.

---

5 **Smile and make eye contact.**

6 **Pay attention to your body language.** Keep your hands still. Don't play with your clothes.

7 **Prepare some questions for the interviewer.**
Don't ask about pay right away, though.

What kind of training will I receive?
Who will I work with?
Will I be able to get experience in/with … ?

3 Role-play

a Imagine you have an interview for one of the jobs advertised below. Write good answers to the three most common job interview questions for this person.

Purchasing Assistant

Tasks:
- Sending drawings and documents to suppliers
- Preparing contracts
- Support with administrative tasks

Qualifications:
- School leaving certificate with business training
- Excellent communication skills
- High level of motivation and flexibility
- IT knowledge, including Office software
- Good spoken and written English

Carer

With its 35 care facilities, 3,000 employees and 4,200 patients, Nightingale is one of the leading private care companies in Europe. We are seeking carers for elderly people.

You work
… professionally and think about the needs, desires and habits of the elderly.
… independently and manage the caring process and its documentation.

You are
… professional and able to communicate with people.
… responsible, flexible and reliable.
… able to work in a team.

b Now role-play the interview with a partner.

How to ... deal with mediation tasks

1 **Before you listen**

Sie sind mit einem Freund, der wenig Englisch spricht, in London. Sie möchten zum *London Eye*. Sie sind in der Touristeninformation und fragen, wie man zum *London Eye* kommt.

You	Excuse me, can you tell us how to get to the London Eye from here?
Information	Yes, of course. You can take a bus from the other side of the road or walk to Bank Underground station and take the tube to Waterloo.
You	Just a moment, I'll tell my friend. Also, er meint wir sollten ...[1]
Friend	Ich würde lieber den Bus nehmen, dann können wir vom oberen Deck aus etwas von London sehen. Frag, welchen Bus wir nehmen sollen.
You	...[2]
Information	You can take the 211, the 77 or the 381. All of these buses go past the London Eye but, remember, it will take you about forty minutes to get there by bus.
You	...[3]
Friend	Daran habe ich nicht gedacht. Vielleicht sollten wir doch besser die U-Bahn nehmen. Frag doch bitte, wie wir von hier zum U-Bahnhof „Bank" kommen.
You	...[4]
Information	Walk down this road till you come to the traffic lights, then turn right into Bank Street. The entrance to the underground station is opposite the post office.
You	...[5]
Friend	Welche Linie ist das?
You	...[6]
Information	It's the Waterloo and City Line, travelling towards Waterloo Station. There's a tube every five minutes.
You	...[7]
Friend	Frag bitte, wie lange es mit der U-Bahn zum London Eye dauert.
You	...[8]
Information	It's only 15 minutes by tube, then it's a five-minute walk.
You	...[9]

TIP

Lesen Sie die Vorgaben sorgfältig, um sich über die vorgegebene Gesprächssituation und Ihre Aufgaben klar zu werden. Danach überfliegen Sie den Text der Unterredung, um den Kernpunkt des Themas zu erfassen und machen sich dabei Notizen. Dann übertragen Sie die Informationen auf leicht verständliche Weise, indem Sie vereinfachen. Übersetzen Sie nicht Wort für Wort. Achten Sie darauf, die Pronomen korrekt zu ändern. Fühlen Sie sich bei der Mediation in die Ihnen vorgegebene Rolle hinein.

2 **Written mediation**

Ihr Freund interessiert sich für die Erfahrung anderer Menschen, die in verschiedenen Ländern der EU arbeiten. Lesen Sie die drei Äußerungen von Xaver, Yvonne und Zeynel auf Seite 78. Fassen Sie die Äußerungen auf Deutsch in einer E-Mail an den Freund zusammen.

TIP

Lesen Sie die Aufgabe sorgfältig. Bestimmen Sie, für wen und in welcher Situation Ihre Mediation benötigt wird. Das ist entscheidend für den Informationsgehalt und den Stil Ihrer Übertragung. Achten Sie darauf, welche Form (z. B. Sachbeitrag, E-Mail oder Liste) verlangt wird. Geben Sie nur jene Informationen weiter, die wirklich benötigt werden. Nicht jedes einzelne Wort ist von Bedeutung. Wichtiger ist es, den Sinnzusammenhang zu erfassen. **Denken Sie daran:** Eine Mediation ist keine Übersetzung. Geben Sie auf keinen Fall den kompletten Text Wort für Wort wieder.

Don't judge me

1 **Warm-up**

Why do people form negative opinions about people they don't know? Make a sentence to go with each photo.

		other races/cultures.
	don't understand	alternative lifestyles.
	are suspicious/afraid of	different religious beliefs.
They	don't like	different attitudes to sex.
	are intolerant of	younger/older generations.
	feel uncomfortable about	people with disabilities.
		people who just look different.

2/5

Morris Samuels, second from left, of the Unity charity in Nottingham with Nathan Kelly, Chloe Bingham and Anton Brown.

Photograph: David Sillitoe for the Guardian

Unity through football

It started with a shooting. Fourteen-year-old Danielle Beccan had just left the Goose Fair in Nottingham when a man in a car pointed a gun at her. He fired and the bullet hit her in the stomach. She later died in hospital.

Danielle's only crime was to live in the St Ann's district, the two men in the car came from the nearby Meadows district. They came to St Ann's to find a victim. Danielle was unlucky: wrong time, wrong place.

Danielle's death was just the latest statistic in the drug wars between gangs from the St Ann's, Meadows and Radford areas of Nottingham. There was a shooting almost every week. For Morris Samuels, the murder* of this young girl was the tipping point.

Samuels had lived in St Ann's all his life and he had a reputation as a hard man. The young men respected him. He was also an ex-footballer.

'Nobody did anything about the gang crime problem,' he says. 'Youth clubs and table tennis don't help, and the police just didn't understand. So I came up with a simple plan: to form a football team from members of all three rival gangs. When people play football together, they talk to one another. If these kids talk to each other, anything is possible.'

Samuels called his team Unity and started to recruit players. He went to each district and persuaded gang members to try it. By 2005 he had 24 players. 'I wanted to make it as professional as possible,' says Samuels. 'So I made them all wear shirts and ties to travel. We played our first match against a semi-professional team, Ilkeston Town.'

Nathan Kelly was one of the first to sign up. He was 15 and his school had just thrown him out because he had attacked the head teacher. In his own words he was 'a rebel, a total nightmare'. The only thing that made him happy was football.

'Being in a dressing room with my enemies was hard at first,' he says. 'But Morris was brilliant at keeping it under control. He told us that we were all the same and that we had to work together or the other team would beat us. The rivalry has all gone now and I've got a job I love, teaching sport in school, working one to one with disabled kids and training to be a gym instructor.'

Unity now runs three programmes – seniors aged 17-25, juniors aged 11-16 and girls aged 11-25 – and has more than 800 young people on its books.

Samuel's aim is to break the gang culture and give kids a chance to get qualifications and training.

Before every game there is a compulsory session in the classroom, teaching anything from sex education to maths and English for the younger kids.

For the older age group, there are training courses in sport, car maintenance and security work. 'Our main aims are to prevent crime and to help those who have been in trouble,' says Samuels. Clearly it works: two-thirds of those who were involved in crime have stopped offending since they joined Unity.

DANGER!

murder – *Mord*
murderer – *Mörder/in*

(523 words)

2 Reading for gist

Read this text about gang culture in the English city of Nottingham. Choose the summary which best fits the text.

1 After a young girl died, three gangs decided to stop fighting and set up a football team.
2 A football team in Nottingham decided to end the violence between three gangs.
3 A man in Nottingham set up a football team to solve a problem with gangs.

3 Reading for details

Decide whether the statements below are true or false.

1 The man killed Danielle because she lived in the wrong part of town.
2 Football was the cause of the war between the three gangs.
3 Danielle was the only person who died because of the gang war.
4 The young men listened to Morris because he was a policeman.
5 Morris wanted members of all three gangs to play in one football team.
6 Gang members had to go for an interview to get in the team.
7 Nathan was still at school when he started to play for Unity.
8 Nathan now works in a school.
9 Only boys and men can play for Unity.
10 The players have to do lessons as well as football training.

4 Working with words

Find the word in the box which best fits the explanation. There are more words than you need.

Example: This is when you agree to take part in something. *sign up*

attack • beat • enemy • gang • rebel • reputation • respect • rivalry • ~~sign up~~ • throw out • trouble • victim • war

1 when someone tries to hurt another person
2 what other people think of you
3 a person to whom something bad has happened
4 when two or more large groups, e.g. nations, try to kill each other
5 when two people or groups try to be better than each other
6 a group of people who fight against other groups and may be involved in illegal activities
7 This sort of person does not accept authority, e.g. teachers, parents or police.
8 the opposite of a friend
9 The team which scores more points does this to the other team.
10 If you make someone leave a group, you do this to them.

5 Mediation

On a news website, you read about a city in Germany with a similar gang problem. Write a short summary for the website's forum about how Unity helped the young people of Nottingham in German. Do not translate word for word.

6 Group project

Read this short text about Unity and then complete the exercise.

> Unity is now a victim of its own success. It has done more than any other organisation to reduce gang culture in the city, but it just doesn't have enough mentors. "We desperately need more money to train people," Morris says. The kids put it differently. They say: "We need more Morrises. He has been like a father to us." One even calls him his 'fairy godfather'. Though I doubt he says that to his face.

In groups, think of a fundraising idea to get more money for Unity. Then design and write a flyer to advertise your idea. Follow the instructions in the tip box below.

TIP

Gruppenarbeit
Gruppenarbeit sollten Sie immer auf Englisch machen. Erstens setzen Sie Ihre Englischkenntnisse in die Praxis um und festigen sie dadurch; zweitens wirken die Resultate fließender und authentischer, wenn Sie die ganze Zeit auf Englisch sprechen und denken.

Making suggestions
I've got an idea: why don't we … ?
How about this: …

Inviting opinions
What do you think?
Does that make sense to you?

Suggesting changes
I would rather …
Wouldn't it be better to … ?

Expressing (dis)agreement
Great idea! OK, let's do that.
I don't think it will work.
I can see a few problems with that.

Summarizing
So we're in agreement then. We're going to …

Organizing
Who's going to be responsible for … ?
Would you like to do that, (Sven)?
(Anne), could you write down a list, please?
We've got (15 minutes) left.

GRAMMAR

The past perfect

After Nathan **had left** the gang, he got a job in a school.

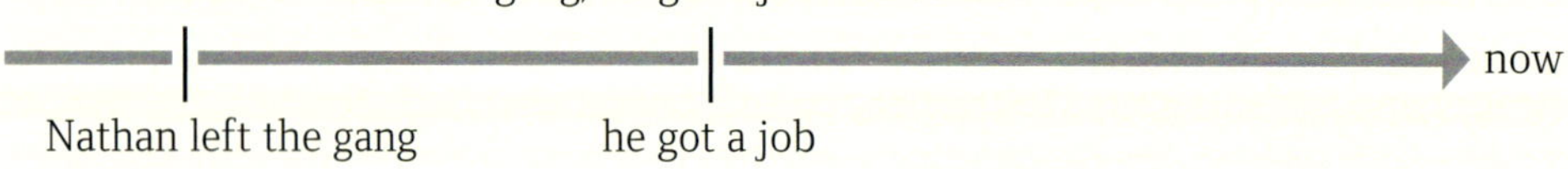

- Das ***past perfect*** wird mit ***had/hadn't*** und dem Partizip Perfekt (3. Form des Verbs) gebildet.
- Die Formen sind für alle Personen gleich.
- Mit dem ***past perfect*** beschreiben wir etwas, das bereits vor einem Zeitpunkt in der Vergangenheit geschah.
- Das ***past perfect*** tritt häufig in Nebensätzen mit ***when***, ***as soon as*** und ***after*** auf.

7 Past perfect

Complete the sentences with the past perfect forms of the verbs in brackets. Be careful about irregular verbs.

Example: After Danielle *had left* the fair, a man shot her. (leave)

1 As soon as Ben … his phone, he called his parents. (find)
2 When Julie … her lunch, she drank a coffee. (finish)
3 Everyone knew Morris after he … there for ten years. (live)
4 As soon as he … the team, Nathan got a new pair of football boots. (join)
5 We turned off the TV when the film … . (finish)
6 After she … school, Kelly began to get into trouble with the police. (leave)
7 As soon as they … the text, the students answered the questions. (read)
8 The teacher was very tired after she … 30 exercise books. (correct)

8 Timelines

Use the timelines to write sentences. Use *when*, *as soon as* or *after*.

Example: Nathan did a training session | he played in his first game | now
After Nathan had done a training session, he played in his first game.

1 Danielle died | Morris decided to stop the gang wars | now
2 the boys played for the same team | they became friends | now
3 Nathan told her about Unity | Ruby signed up | now
4 Unity ran for five years | it had 800 members | now
5 Morris told him about Unity | the journalist decided to write an article | now
6 Joel joined the gang | he soon got involved in drugs | now
7 Nathan left school | he wanted a better education | now
8 Anna read the article | she wanted to become a mentor with Unity | now

9 **Preparing to listen: making predictions**

This rap was written by British teenagers after an attack on a British teenager in Germany. Read the lyrics and complete them with suitable words from the box.

care • clear • equal • Germany • land • places • race • races • skin • vision

Don't judge me

We're all different people, different faces,
From different lives and different …[1],
We've all seen different things,
And to top it all we're different …[2],
But that don't mean* we can't share.
We're different – that don't mean* we can't …[3],
If we make bonds and hold them strong,
That's something that no-one can tear.

We're different, but we're all people,
So even though we're different, we …[4],
You're not better and I'm not better,
So let's stand together and fight this evil!
Let's make a stand, take racism from our …[5].
Don't judge me for my colour,
Or for another – I am what I am.

Don't judge me for the colour of my …[6],
Judge me for what is within.

From England to …[7],
We should all live in harmony,
We shouldn't fight over races,
Or even over places – let me make it …[8],
Stephen Lawrence should still be here,
And **Noel Martin** shouldn't need a wheelchair!

Anthony Walker would be twenty-three,
So many people have died that we've never seen,
So we need to change our ways,
Black and white, we're one human …[9].
Embrace the fact that we're different,
Stop with the ignorance and just listen,
Learn off one another* – that's my …[10]!

Don't judge me, etc.

*that don't mean (Slang) = that doesn't mean
*learn off one another (Slang) = learn from one another

2/6 **10** **Listening for details**

Listen to the rap and check your answers to exercise 9.

11 **Storyboarding a video**

a You decide to make a video to go with the rap. Which verse will you show these images with? Find lines in the rap to justify your choice.

a

b

c

d

b Think of other images to illustrate the meaning of the song. Write a short description of the images you want and then try to find suitable photos on the internet.

> Storyboarding is a way of planning an advertisement, pop video or other short film. Images (photos or drawings) are put into order to give people an idea of the main parts of the film. Advertising agencies often use storyboards to show an idea to a client.

12 **Working with words**

Find the opposites of the underlined expressions in the rap. Use them to complete the sentences.

Example: You say that we're all the same, but I disagree: we're all *different*.

1 As individuals we are weak but as a group we are … .
2 In traditional fairy tales, white represents goodness but black represents … .
3 He was born in a slum but he … a billionaire.
4 Everyone in our school knows that racism is bad, but … has found a solution.
5 Instead of making the situation … , the police made it worse.
6 I can't teach you anything if you don't want to … .

13 **Internet research**

With a partner, go online to find out about one of the three people mentioned in the rap. Find the answers to these questions and any other information that you find interesting. Tell the rest of the class what you found out.

- Who is/was he?
- What happened to him?
- When and where?
- Who was responsible?
- Why did they do it?
- What happened to them?

2/7 1 Listening for details

Thomas Sander is a project leader at the Deutsches Rotes Kreuz in Berlin. He receives a call from a journalist, Erica Andersen, who wants to interview him. Listen to the conversation and complete the text.

Sander Sander.
Andersen Hello, am I speaking to Thomas Sander? It's Erica Andersen here from Associated Press in America.
Sander Yes, this is Thomas Sander. How can I help you, Ms Andersen?
Andersen I'd like to interview you about the work of the German Red Cross. Would it be possible to …[1] to see you at your office?
Sander Yes, of course. Just let me get my diary … Now, when did you have in mind? I'm very …[2], I'm afraid, but I'll do my best to fit you in.
Andersen How about …[3]?
Sander Sorry, I can't do …[4], I'm in …[5]. I can do …[6], though, …[7].
Andersen How about …[8]? Is that too late?
Sander Well, that is a bit late. Could we make it …[9]?
Andersen Yes, …[10] will be fine.
Sander I look forward to seeing you then, Ms Andersen. Bye for now.
Andersen See you tomorrow, Mr Sander. Bye.

2/8 2 Listening for specific information

Thomas Sander realises that he will not be able to keep the appointment with Erica Andersen. He asks his assistant, David Bremer, to contact Ms Andersen and arrange an alternative appointment. Listen to the conversation and write down the date and time of the new appointment.

2/9 3 A voicemail message

The next morning, David Bremer listens to his voicemail messages. Listen to the message and copy and complete the memo.

Telefonnotiz

Nachricht für: ____________________

Uhrzeit: ____________ Datum: ____________

Anrufer: ____________________

Grund des Anrufs: ____________________

____

____

____

Rückruf erwünscht: ja/nein Telefonnr. ____________

Aufgeschrieben von: ____________________

Mediation

4 A friend from Scotland is visiting you when she is caught shoplifting. Mediate between her and the shopkeeper.

Shop owner	Hallo! Warten Sie! Sie haben mich bestohlen!
You (1)	...
Scottish friend	What does he mean? I haven't stolen anything.
You (2)	...
Shop owner	Doch! Ich habe sie gesehen. Sie hat eine Tafel Schokolade in ihre Jackentasche gestopft, dann ist sie ohne zu zahlen aus dem Laden gegangen.
You (3)	...
Scottish friend	*(Looks in her pocket.)* Oh no! I'm terribly sorry – I didn't mean to steal it. My mobile phone rang – I put the chocolate in my pocket and, well, I forgot to pay.
You (4)	...
Shop owner	Das kann jeder sagen, der Sachen aus meinem Laden klaut. Ich glaube es ihr nicht – und wir werden sehen, was die Polizei dazu sagt. Ich rufe sie gleich an.
You (5)	...
Scottish friend	Please don't let him call the police. Look, it really was a mistake, I just forgot. Why can't I pay for the chocolate now?
You (6)	...
Shop owner	Jeden Tag bestehlen mich junge Leute wie sie. Das ist für sie ein Spiel, nicht wahr? Das muss jetzt ein Ende haben, also werde ich sie bei der Polizei anzeigen.
You (7)	...
Scottish friend	I'm just here on holiday and I've never been in his shop before. I really didn't mean to steal the chocolate, it was just a mistake. I've never stolen anything in my life.
You (8)	...
Shop owner	Ach, schon gut, schon gut. Dieses eine Mal werde ich ihr glauben. Kommen Sie beide zurück in den Laden und sie kann zahlen.
You (9)	...
Scottish friend	Please thank him. That's really kind.
You (10)	...
Shop owner	Aber sie soll in Zukunft nicht so vergesslich sein und zahlen, bevor sie den Laden verlässt!
You (11)	...

TIP

In Aufgaben wie dieser sollen Sie beiden Gesprächspartner/-innen die wichtigen Informationen vermitteln: jeweils auf Deutsch oder auf Englisch. Eine wortwörtliche Übersetzung ist nicht nötig. Vergessen Sie nicht, Pronomen usw. sinngemäß zu ändern: z. B. *What does he mean?* → „Sie versteht nicht, was Sie meinen."

Revision

Simple present (▶ S. 13, 199) and present progressive (▶ S. 22, 199)

1 **Correct these false statements.**

Example: Zoe is 16. (17) *Zoe isn't 16, she's 17.*

1 Jack and Harry are in rival gangs. (same gang)
2 Jack has a gang tattoo. (Celtic tattoo)
3 This town needs more police officers. (more social workers)
4 Young people seem optimistic about the future. (pessimistic)
5 The gang situation in this town is getting better. (worse)
6 People are becoming more tolerant of other races. (intolerant)
7 The media are breaking down stereotypes. (make stronger)
8 We're holding an ethnic food picnic this weekend. (music festival)
9 My grandparents are suspicious of foreigners. (afraid)
10 Nathan was at school when he met Morris. (unemployed)

2 **Write questions for these answers.**

Example: Where *do you live*? – I live in New York.

1 When … ? – My birthday is on March 20.
2 … school? – Yes, I go to senior high school.
3 How … ? – I'm 17.
4 … foreign languages? – Yes, I speak German and French.
5 … brothers and sisters? – Yes, I have a sister and two brothers.
6 … younger than you? – No, they are older than me.
7 … to the disco tonight? – No, I'm going to the cinema with my friend.
8 What … on Saturday? – I'm doing an assignment for school.
9 What sports … ? – I don't like any sports.
10 … ? – Yes, you are annoying me. Please go away!

3 **You meet a young Chinese tourist on a bus. What do you say – a or b?**

1 a Do you enjoy your stay in Germany?
  b Are you enjoying your stay in Germany?
2 a Do you speak any German?
  b Are you speaking any German?
3 a What do you do back home in China?
  b What are you doing back home in China?
4 a What part of China are you coming from?
  b What part of China do you come from?
5 a You are speaking very good English.
  b You speak very good English.
6 a Where do you go today?
  b Where are you going today?
7 a What sort of music do you like?
  b What sort of music are you liking?
8 a I'm going to a concert this evening. Would you like to come?
  b I go to a concert this evening. Would you like to come?
9 a Lots of kids from my school are going.
  b Lots of kids from my school go.
10 a I get off now. Have a great day!
  b I'm getting off now. Have a great day!

Risky behaviour

1 Warm-up: questionnaire

a) Are you a risk taker? Complete our questionnaire to find out.
a = I agree; b = I'm not sure; c = I disagree

1 Rules exist to be broken.
2 I like music that is loud and wild.
3 At a funfair, I go on the fastest, wildest rides.
4 It's important to have a plan B in case things go wrong.
5 People tell me that my actions are crazy.
6 I realise that past actions were more dangerous than I thought at the time.
7 I am optimistic during stressful times, e.g. exams.
8 I don't hand in a piece of work until it is perfect.
9 I'm willing to take a risk to get what I want.
10 I know where to go if there is a fire in this building.
11 I wear safety gear when riding a bike.
12 I find speed exciting.
13 I think doing the same job every day would be boring.
14 I will stay in the same career for as long as I can.
15 I often get into trouble with authority (police, teachers, team coach, etc).

How did you score?

more than 20
You are a risk taker. You may be good in a sales job, a creative job or as an entrepreneur.

10–20
You take some risks but you know you need to be responsible sometimes. You may be good in a job which involves some physical danger, e.g. a police officer or security guard.

less than 10
You play it safe. You may be good in a job which requires careful behaviour, e.g. a technical job, manufacturing or health care.

b) Compare results with your partner. Who takes more risks? What advice can you give your partner?

c) With your partner, note down the main points of the 'How to manage risk safely' box in German. Do not translate word for word.

How to manage risk safely

If you never take risks, you will never have any new experiences. You may not develop your full potential, in your career or your private life. Here are some tips:

- Discuss risk with others. That may help you to make a better decision.
- Think before you act. That may stop you from taking foolish risks.
- If it sounds too good to be true, it probably is. Don't be blinded by someone else's enthusiasm.
- Resist peer pressure. Make your own choices, your friends will respect you more.
- Visualize a loved one (e.g. your boy/girlfriend or your parents) taking the same risk. If that worries you, the risk is too big.

Score
1 a 2, b 1, c 0
2 a 2, b 1, c 0
3 a 2, b 1, c 0
4 a 0, b 1, c 2
5 a 2, b 1, c 0
6 a 2, b 1, c 0
7 a 2, b 1, c 0
8 a 0, b 1, c 2
9 a 2, b 1, c 0
10 a 0, b 1, c 2
11 a 0, b 1, c 2
12 a 2, b 1, c 0
13 a 2, b 1, c 0
14 a 0, b 1, c 2
15 a 2, b 1, c 0

2/10

ChatBox – Discussions about life, the universe and everything

Author	Topic
Jack ★★★★ 3 Posts	Posted yesterday 07.30 **Thread: It's my life, why shouldn't I?** Why do adults always want to stop teenagers from taking risks? I found this quote on the internet: 'Take risks: if you win, you will be happy; if you lose, you will be wise.' I love taking risks. For example, it's really fun to do a wheelie on my moped at the traffic lights. You should see the expressions on people's faces! I'm a good rider, so it isn't really dangerous, but it looks cool. If you stop and think, you'll never do anything. At the moment, my favourite risk is writing graffiti tags on bridges and in rail tunnels . If you are too slow, the police could catch you or a train could run you over. It's really exciting! Not all of my risks are illegal, though. This year we're going to the Alps for a winter holiday and I'm going to learn to snowboard. I can't wait!
Gina ★★★★ 5 Posts	Posted yesterday 17.56 **Re: It's my life, why shouldn't I?** Listen to me, kids: Risk taking is addictive – just like alcohol or drugs. If you take too many risks, you will injure yourself. Take extreme sports like bungee jumping or white water kayaking. Thrill seekers love these sports because they get an adrenaline high from them. The level of the thrill must constantly increase to provide the same high. They push themselves to the limit and beyond. I know what I'm talking about. I started skiing as a teenager. In a year I went from beginner to advanced. After three years I was able to ski the most difficult slopes. Then the thrill wasn't enough, so I started to ski off piste. I had a bad accident and nearly died. Now I'm in a wheelchair. There is nothing less exciting than life as a paraplegic*.
Darren ★★★★ 2 Posts	Posted today 10.19 **Re: It's my life, why shouldn't I?** I'm sorry to hear about what happened to you, Gina. Nevertheless, I disagree with you. I'm not saying that all risks are good. Sometimes the risk is too big. For example, if you take heroin or crack, you will probably ruin your life. Or you may endanger someone else's life, for example, by dangerous driving. Where I work, we help youths who take unhealthy risks. (That means kids like you, Jack.) Some are involved in gang fights; others go shoplifting, take drugs or take part in street racing. We teach them skills that they can be proud of and still enjoy the excitement. Yes, they may injure themselves snowboarding, windsurfing, skateboarding or rock climbing, but that's life.

*paraplegic – *Querschnittgelähmte/r*

(437 words)

2 Reading for gist

Read the text and then match the opinions below to the forum members.
Give reasons for your answers.

Example: 'Don't take risks if you might hurt someone else.' – *Darren*

1 'I took risks and now I'm sorry.'
2 'Don't worry – just go ahead and do it!'
3 'You learn by taking risks.'
4 'It's worth doing difficult sports, even if you hurt yourself.'
5 'Risky behaviour is like a drug.'
6 'It's fun to break the law.'
7 'I help people to change their risky behaviour.'
8 'Some risks are too dangerous.'

3 Reading for specific information

Complete the tasks below.

1 Name three risks that Jack takes.
2 Name two reasons why Gina is against risk taking.
3 Name five 'unhealthy risks' and four 'healthy risks' mentioned by Darren.

4 Word families

Copy and complete the table. You can use a dictionary to help you.

verb	noun	adjective
risk	…	*risky*
…	*expression*	…
endanger	…	*dangerous*
…	*excitement*	*exciting (aufregend); excited (aufgeregt)*
	…	*addictive*
injure	…	…
increase	…	…
	accident	…
	skill	…
enjoy	…	…

TIP

Wortfamilien

Vokabeln lassen sich leichter lernen, wenn man sie gruppiert, anstatt wahllos einzelne Wörter auswendig zu lernen. Wortfamilien sind eine Möglichkeit, Vokabeln zu gruppieren.

Wortfamilien bestehen aus Wörtern, die alle den gleichen Stamm haben. Die einfachste Wortfamilie besteht aus Wörtern, die eine sehr enge Form- und Bedeutungsverwandschaft haben. Für viele häufige Wortstämme gibt es ein Nomen, ein Verb und ein Adjektiv. z. B. *live* (leben) – *life* (Leben) – *lively* (lebhaft).

5 Listening for gist

2/11

a Who do these three speakers agree with from the text on page 100 - Jack, Gina or Darren?

b Answer the following questions.

1 What risk does the first speaker take?
2 What example does the second speaker give of a healthy risk? Why does she think it is healthy?
3 What example does the second speaker give of an unhealthy risk? Why does she think it is unhealthy?
4 Why does the third speaker think you should think about your decisions carefully?

6 Discussion

Why do people take risks? In the box there are some reasons that have been mentioned in the unit so far. You can also use your own ideas.

adrenaline high • cool • exciting • fun • new experiences • peer pressure • push oneself to the limit • thrill

7 Too risky!

a Use expressions from the box to describe what people are doing/have done in the photos.

take part in hooliganism • go street racing • binge drink • use drugs • go shoplifting • vandalize property

1

2

3

4

5

6

b Explain possible consequences of the risky behaviour shown in the photos. You can use the expressions from the box or your own ideas.
Example: *If you take drugs, you may …*

become socially isolated / lose your friends	have a serious accident
embarrass your family	have unprotected sex
get a criminal record	ruin your career / lose your job
get into a fight	take an overdose

8 **Try this instead!**
Work in a group. Taking risks is not the only way to have fun. Think of other things you can do in your free time. The mind map below may help you.
Example: *It could be exciting to go rock climbing.*

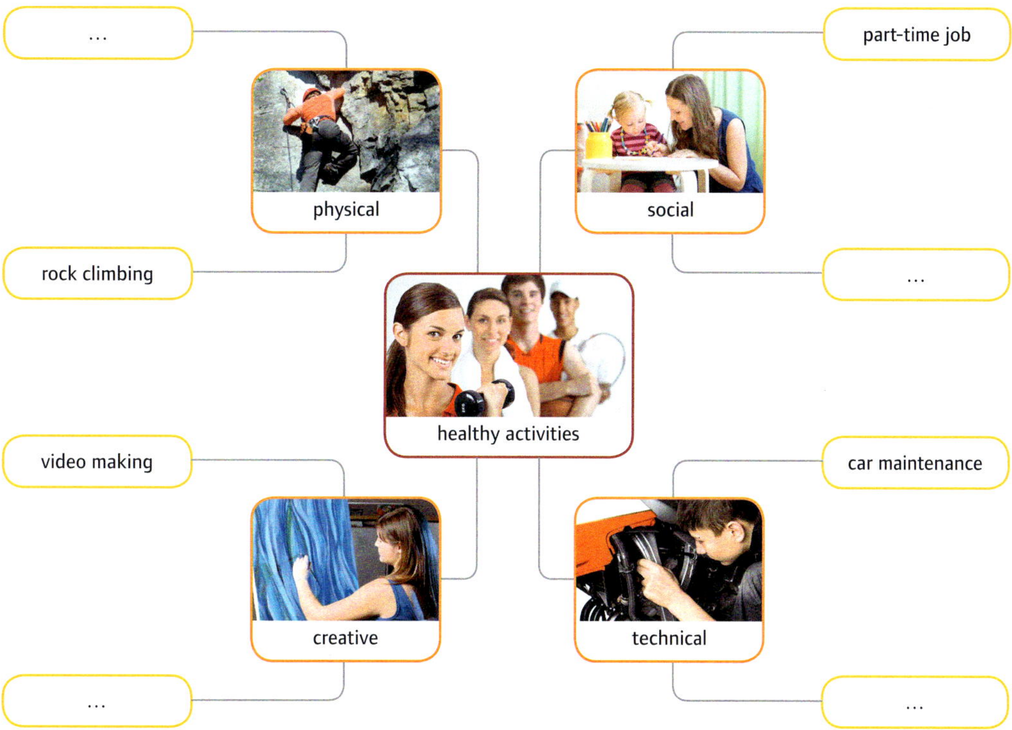

9 **Group project**
Work in a group. Use your answers to exercise 8 to develop a programme for Darren's organization (page 100). Design a poster or web page for your programme. Include the following information:

- Who the programme is for
- What risky behaviour they are involved in
- What activities you offer
- How the programme will help
- Why it will be a success

2/12 **10**

Listening: how to fly a hang glider

a Two students are learning how to fly a hang glider. Their trainer is explaining to them how it works. Listen and complete the notes about the main points.

Example: If you run into the wind, *the glider will take off.*

1 If you shift your weight to the right, …
2 If you shift your weight to the left, …
3 If you pull on the bar and shift your weight forwards, …
4 If you push on the bar and shift your weight backwards, …
5 If the glider stops, …

b Now choose the illustration from the training handbook which matches each point above.

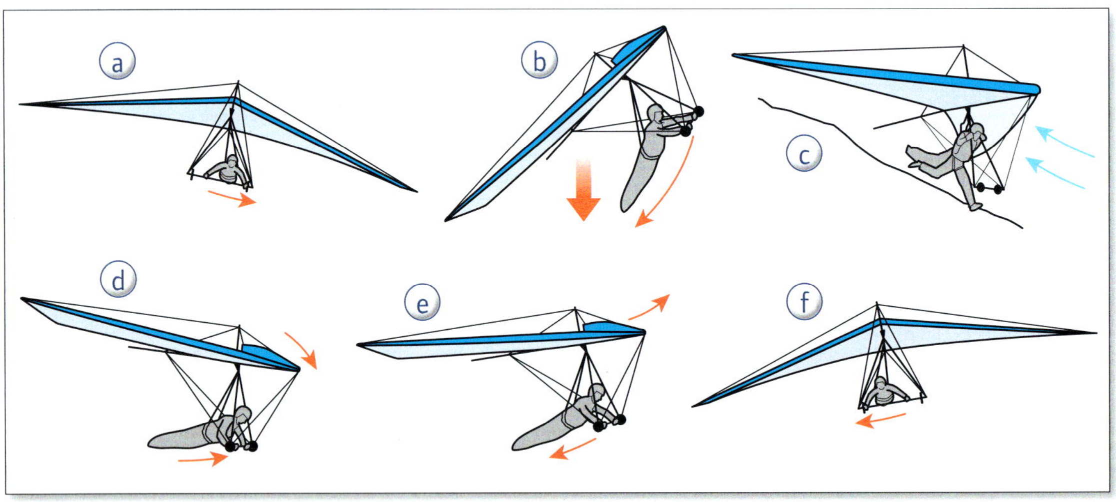

11 **Your turn**

Write simple instructions about how to operate something. There are some suggestions in the box or you can choose your own idea.

ride a bike/moped/jet ski • ride a skateboard/wakeboard • sail a boat/windsurfer • drive a car/go-kart • ski/snowboard/kitesurf

GRAMMAR

Conditional sentences type 1

Ein Bedingungssatz sagt, was unter bestimmten Umständen geschehen wird.
Der Satz hat zwei Teile:

If you **take** too many risks,	you **will hurt** yourself.
If you **don't take** any risks,	you **won't develop** your full potential.
Der *if*-Teil nennt die Bedingung, …	… der andere Teil nennt die Folge.
Der *if*-Teil steht im *simple present*, …	… der Folgeteil steht im *will future*.

- Steht der *if*-Teil zuerst, setzt man danach ein Komma.
- Steht der Folgeteil zuerst, setzt man kein Komma.

DANGER!

Im *if*-Teil steht nie das ***will future***.
Eselsbrücke: *'If' plus 'will' makes me ill!*

12 **Conditional sentences type 1**

Complete the sentences with the correct forms of the verbs in brackets.

Example: If you *take* heroin, you *will ruin* your life. (take) (ruin)

1 If you drink and drive, you … an accident. (have)
2 If she doesn't ski off piste, she …safe. (be)
3 I … well in my exams if I don't feel too stressed. (do)
4 If he … a lot, Marc will soon be an advanced skier. (train)
5 … into trouble with the police if I … a wheelie? (I/get) (do)
6 If you … any risks, you … a boring life. (not/take) (have)
7 Ben… to take drugs if he … to windsurf. (not/want) (learn)
8 If the glider … , it … to the ground. (stop) (fall)
9 … car maintenance if she … the chance? (Alice/learn) (get)
10 If she … on a snowboarding holiday, she … it. (go) (not/regret)

13 **If …, I'll …**

Describe your reaction in the following situations.
Begin your sentences with *if*.

Example: *If my best friend lies to me, I'll be angry.*

What will you do if …

1 … your best friend lies to you?
2 … your teacher gives you a bad mark for this exercise?
3 … the fire alarm rings?
4 … your parents 'ground' you (make you stay home in the evenings)?
5 … someone steals your bike?
6 … you find € 100 in the street?
7 … you lose your mobile phone?
8 … it rains all weekend?
9 … you get your dream job?
10 … your friend wins the lottery?

Dealing with customers

2/13 **1**

Listening for details

David Liebherr is on holiday in Britain. He goes to a doctor because of a pain in his shoulder. Mr Liebherr takes the prescription *(Rezept)* to the nearest pharmacy. Listen to the dialogue and note down the missing information.

DANGER!

prescription – *Rezept*
receipt – *Quittung*
recipe – *Kochrezept*

Pharmacist	Mr Liebherr?
Liebherr	Yes, that's me.
Pharmacist	Here are your tablets, sir.
Liebherr	Thank you. How much is that?
Pharmacist	That will be …¹, please.
Liebherr	Here you are.
Pharmacist	Thank you, sir. Here's your change and your receipt. Have you used this medication before?
Liebherr	No, I haven't. It's the first time I've had this problem.
Pharmacist	OK. These are strong painkillers. It's important to …².
Liebherr	Yes, of course. I'll do that.
Pharmacist	You need to take …³.
Liebherr	Right.
Pharmacist	You should take the tablets …⁴. Drink …⁵ with the tablet. Don't lie down …⁶ after taking a tablet.
Liebherr	OK, I understand.
Pharmacist	Also, don't drive or operate dangerous …⁷ while you are taking these tablets, as they may make you dizzy.
Liebherr	Ah, that could be a problem. I'm here on holiday, you see. I don't live here and …⁸ I have to drive up to Edinburgh in Scotland. So I have to drive.
Pharmacist	Well, see how you feel. This medication doesn't affect everyone in the same way. If you get side-effects like dizziness, you mustn't …⁹ if you have to drive.
Liebherr	OK, thanks very much for your help.
Pharmacist	You're welcome, sir. One more thing: …¹⁰?
Liebherr	Yes, I do. I take these …¹¹. That's all.
Pharmacist	That's fine. Enjoy the rest of your stay in Britain.
Liebherr	Thank you. Bye.
Pharmacist	Goodbye. *(Turns to the next customer)* Can I help you, madam?

2

Working with words

Find useful expressions in the dialogue:

a for dealing with customers in general.
b for dealing with customers in a pharmacy.
c for responding politely to salespeople in a shop.

3

More expressions

Think of more epressions to put in the three categories in exercise 2.

4 **Interpreting: at the pharmacy**

You are doing work experience at a pharmacy when a British tourist comes in. She does not speak German and the sales assistant does not speak English well. Help them to understand each other.

Verkaufsassistent	Sie	Kundin
		Hello, do you speak English?
Nein, leider nicht. Die Apothekerin spricht Englisch, aber sie ist nicht da.		
	Sie bieten Ihre Hilfe an.	
		Thanks. I need some strong painkillers.
	…	
Hat sie ein Rezept von einem Arzt?		
	…	
		No, I'm afraid not. I forgot to bring it. I have a broken arm and I need some painkillers to help me until I go home.
	…	
Starke Schmerzmittel sind rezeptpflichtig *(require a prescription)*. Ich kann ihr diese hier geben.		
	…	
		Yes, those are fine. I take the same brand in England.
	…	
Möchte sie eine 12-er oder eine 24-er Packung?		
	…	
		A pack of 12 is enough, thanks.
	…	
Das macht €4,50.		
	…	
		Here you are. Thanks for your help.

2/14 **1** You are a trainee in an import/export company. You listen to your answer phone messages in the office and hear a message that your American boss has left for you. Listen to the message and answer the questions below. You will listen to the message twice and can make notes while listening.

1 What should you do for your boss?
2 Why is he asking you to do this for him?

2/15 **2** Today's programme 'Youth Matters' on the English radio station 'Waves FM' is about 'kippers' – 'kids in parent's pockets'. This is what the British press call young adults who still live with their parents and get financial support from them. Listen to the programme and complete the sentences below. You will listen to the programme twice and can make notes while listening.

1 In comparison to young British women, …
2 Twenty years ago …
3 The reporter asked Dr Derek Smith …
4 Many young adults can't afford their own house because …
5 In the last decades youth unemployment in Great Britain has …
6 'Boomerang kids' are …
7 University graduates in Britain have …
8 Even when they eventually leave their parents' house …

2/16 **3** You are doing work experience on a building site. People from all over the world are working there, not just from Germany. A colleague from England has been injured in an accident at work and the accident has to be recorded. As you can speak good English and your colleague doesn't know any German, the manager has asked you to help fill in the form. Listen to the dialogue and complete the form.

Arbeitsschutzformular Vorkommnis/Unfall	
Datum und Uhrzeit:	
Ort:	
Hergang:	
Personenschäden:	
Sachbeschädigungen:	
Eingeleitete Maßnahmen:	
Verletzte(r): Name, Vorname	
Geburtsdatum:	
Vorgesetzte(r): Name, Vorname	

TIP

Hier werden zwei ganz unterschiedliche Aufgaben angeboten. Wählen Sie diejenige aus, die Ihren Stärken am ehesten entspricht:

Möglichkeit a ist eine Geschichte. Sie findet in der Vergangenheit statt. Sie werden also Vergangenheitsformen und einen formelleren Stil verwenden müssen. Sie brauchen auch etwas Fantasie.

Möglichkeit b ist eine E-Mail. Sie werden um Rat gebeten. Sie werden also vorwiegend Gegenwarts- und Zukunftsformen und wahrscheinlich auch Modalverben verwenden müssen. Sie brauchen Ortskenntisse und Einfallsreichtum.

4 Choose task a or b. Write at least 150 words.

a Finish the story and give it a title.

Anja woke up just as her train arrived at Oxford. She picked up her rucksack and got off the train. 'That's lucky! I almost missed my stop,' thought Anja as she stood on the platform. Then she remembered that her small bag was still on the train – the train that was now leaving the station. All her friends and family were back home in Germany, and here she was in England with no money, no phone and no passport …

b Your American cousin, whom you have never met, wants to visit Germany at Easter and has written to ask you for advice. Reply to her email and answer her questions.

Hi …

I'm really looking forward to my trip to Germany!
As you know, I'm coming during the Easter holidays. What is the weather like then? Should I pack lots of jumpers and a warm coat or are jeans, T-shirts and a light jacket enough?
What is there to see and do in your part of Germany? I'm interested in sports and I like to be active. I also like to go to the cinema and I like shopping. I find museums a bit boring.
I also want to see other parts of Germany, for example, Munich and Berlin. What's the best way to travel?
I hope you can write back soon. I can't wait to meet you and your family!

Best wishes
Taylor

Revision

Possessive adjectives (▶ S. 11), pronouns (▶ S. 20), *much/many, little/few* (▶ S. 32, 202)

1 Complete the sentences with the most suitable possessive adjective (*my, your,* etc.).

1 It's OK for you to risk … own life, but don't endanger someone else's.
2 Jack is very proud of … snowboarding skills.
3 Gina injured … back in a skiing accident.
4 Many people ruin … lives by becoming addicted to drugs or alcohol.
5 When taking up a dangerous sport, think about … risks carefully.
6 As parents, we have to accept that … children will take risks.
7 Amy and Jules lost … best friend in a hang gliding accident.
8 … friend Brad and I like to do wheelies on … motorbikes.

2 Complete the text with the correct object or reflexive pronouns or possessive adjectives.

In 1999 Australian teenager Jesse Martin became the youngest person to sail round the world solo and without help from others. Another round-the-world sailor, David Dick, was 24 days younger than …[1] (he), but received help. Jesse made the trip in …[2] (he) 10-metre yacht *Lionheart*. The journey took …[3] (he) 11 months. He wrote about …[4] (he) adventures in the book *Lionheart: A Journey of the Human Spirit*. The teenager was modest about …[5] (he) trip: 'I do not consider …[6] (I) to be the world's best sailor … [It's] nothing special.'

What makes young people want to risk …[7] (they) lives in adventures? Do they want to prove …[8] (they), or do …[9] (they) parents sometimes push …[10] (they) into it? Certainly, many people were critical of Jesse's parents and called …[11] (they) irresponsible because they let …[12] (they) 17-year-old son attempt such a dangerous trip. Jesse's mother even had to leave …[13] (she) job because of the criticism …[14] (she) colleagues directed at …[15] (she).

In 2009 another young Australian, 16-year-old Jessica Watson, attempted to break Jesse's record. She had a terrifying accident when a large container ship hit …[16] (she) yacht *Pink Lady*. Fortunately Jessica did not injure …[17] (she) in the accident. However, …[18] (she) trip was not long enough to be a new record.

3 Translate the sentences using *much, many, little* or *few*.

1 Wenige Menschen gehen wirklich an ihre Grenzen *(push o. s. to the limit)*.
2 Wie viel Risiko ist für dich zu viel?
3 Es hat wenig Zweck, vergangene Fehler *(past mistakes)* zu bereuen.
4 Es gibt wenige Sportarten, die wirklich gefährlich sind.
5 Viele von uns wollen mehr Aufregung im Leben *(in our lives)*.
6 Hatten sie viele Probleme in der Schule?
7 Wie viele Unfälle gab es letztes Jahr?
8 Es gibt viele Regeln in der Schule.
9 Viele Jugendliche arbeiten freiwillig fürs Gemeinwesen.
10 Bungyspringen erfordert wenig Geschick, aber viel Mut *(courage)*.

Consumer heaven

11

1 **Warm-up**

Discuss with a partner. Do you think this is a good advertisement for jeans? Say why (not).

I like/don't like the advertisement because …
 it's boring/cool/unusual/stupid/ordinary/artificial.
 it makes you think.
 it doesn't say anything about the product.
 it's selling an image, not just a product.

The advertisers want us to think about … when we see their product.
 nostalgia/independence/freedom/youth/sex appeal

2 **Brand power**

Write your answers to the questions below and then compare answers in a group. Report your findings back to the class.

Example: *The most popular brand in our group is … . When we choose clothes, we think a lot about … and not much about …*

1 What are your favourite clothing brands?
2 When you buy clothes, which of these things are important to you? Number them 1 (most important) to 6 (least important).

- low price
- looks good
- cool brand
- comfortable
- well made
- ethical (made in a way that doesn't harm the environment or people)

2/17

Story of a pair of jeans

There they are, under a big sign saying: 'Famous brands for £19.95 (about €23).' They are just an ordinary pair of blue denim jeans in Cromwell's Bazaar, a cheap retail outlet in Ipswich, England.

'100% cotton. Wash inside out separately,' it says on the label, but it doesn't say where they come from. After all, what would you put on the label? 'Made in Tunisia, Italy, Germany, France, Pakistan, Turkey, Japan, Korea, Namibia, Benin, Australia, Hungary'?

These jeans arrived a few days ago in a van from Lee Cooper's warehouse in North London. Before that, they came through the Channel Tunnel on a lorry from a similar warehouse in Amiens, France. Before that, they came by boat and train from Ras Jebel in Tunisia.

In Ras Jebel, a small town of 3000 people, Lee Cooper clothes are made in three factories. In the factory which made our jeans, 500 women work at sewing machines. Each has a small task to do: zips, pockets, legs. Each works like a robot: bonuses depend on fast work. There are no safety guards on the machines and the women concentrate hard, keeping their fingers away from the sharp needles. Trained machinists make about 58p (around 65–70 cents) an hour.

This factory is not the beginning for our jeans, but in one sense the end. It is the place where all the components come together.

Take that roll of blue denim cloth, for example. It was brought here by land and sea from Italdenim in Milan, Italy. At Italdenim the denim was woven from cotton, then coloured blue using synthetic dye from Germany. At Ras Jebel it will be cut, sewn and washed in huge washing machines with volcanic stone from Turkey to make it soft and comfortable.

Where did the cotton come from? Italdenim buys cotton from several places, but mainly from Benin in West Africa. Some of it comes from Nestor Zinkponon's small farm, where 48 people work in the fields for about 60p (around 65–70 cents) a day. In a bad year, Mr Zinkponon makes just £10 (around €12) profit from 1 tonne of cotton. That's enough to buy one leg of a pair of Lee Cooper jeans.

The only way to make money out of cotton is to have plenty of family members who work for free, says Mr Zinkponon, who has two wives. 'Some farmers have six or eight wives.'

Back in Ras Jebel, the workers use polyester-cotton thread to stitch the jeans together. The polyester was made in Japan, then it was sent to the factories of Coats Viyella in Hungary and Turkey, where it was combined with cotton thread. The thread was dyed orange, white or blue in Spain, then it was sent by ship to Tunisia.

That's not all. The zip was made in France by a Japanese company, YKK, while the buttons were made by a German company, Prym, using zinc and copper from Australia and Namibia.

Back in Ipswich, Cromwell's Bazaar is closing for the night. Inside, in the middle, on a pile under a sign saying 'Famous Brands for £19.95', a pair of jeans lies waiting for its journey to end.

http://www.guardian.co.uk/g2/story/0,,497788,00.html (540 words)

3 Key facts

Find all of the countries mentioned in the text on the world map. What part does each country play in making and selling the jeans? Make notes in English.

Example: *1 England – clothes shop – sell the jeans*

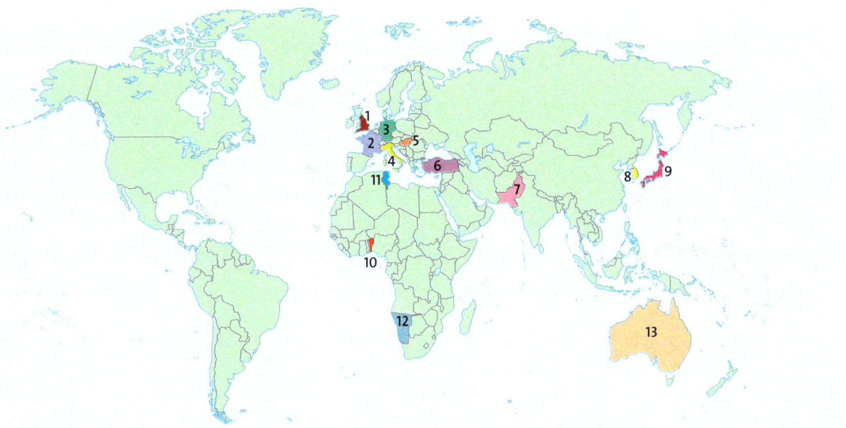

4 Mind map

Copy the mind map onto a large sheet of paper. Complete it with information from the text. Your notes from exercise 3 will help you.

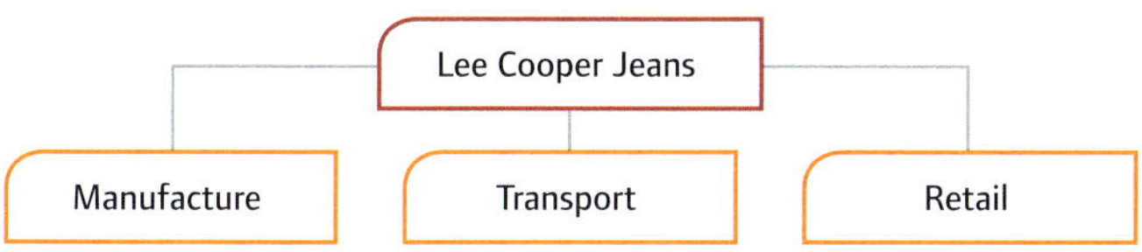

5 Matching

These people all work for Lee Cooper, its suppliers or customers. Do they work in Italy, England, Tunisia or Benin? Give reasons for your answer.

1 'It isn't a bad place to work if you like dealing with customers. We have a wide range of clothes and famous brands are really cheap, so the shop is very busy.'

2 'Last year I injured my hand because the machines don't have safety guards. I couldn't work for three months, so I wasn't paid anything.'

3 'It's difficult to make a profit in this business. If there is a lot of cotton on the market, I only make about $150 a tonne. That's not enough to feed my large family and pay my workers a good wage.'

4 'I work in the warehouse. Over there are rolls of cotton from Africa and here are drums of blue dye from Germany. These rolls of blue denim will be sent to Ras Jebel by lorry and ship.'

6 Summarizing the text

Summarize the text to show how and where the jeans are made.

TIP

Wie man einen Text zusammenfasst
Geben Sie den Sinn soweit wie möglich in Ihren eigenen Worten wieder. Lassen Sie dabei alle unwichtigen Details aus. Dazu sollten Sie keine Meinung zum Text abgeben.

7 **Discussion**

The text on page 112 shows that fashion is a globalized industry. In a group, discuss the advantages/disadvantages of this:

- to the consumer.
- to the environment.
- to the workers in various countries.

Make notes. When you have finished, report back to the class.

8 **Writing an email**

On a social network website you meet Osawe Jonas, a 16-year-old in Benin.
Osawe writes a comment on your page. Write a reply, giving your opinion and reasons.
Write 80–100 words. Your notes from exercise 7 will help you.

My family has a small cotton farm in central Benin. My parents and sisters work very hard every day in the fields to grow cotton. I'm the lucky one in the family because I was able to go to college.

I know that the cotton from our farm goes to Italy, where it is used to make denim for jeans. I like jeans ads because some of them are really cool. However, the prices seem very unfair to me: my whole family's pay for a month couldn't buy one pair of jeans!

What do you think? Is it fair that we get so little money for our hard work?

Example: *Dear Osawe,*
Thanks for your comment. It was really interesting to hear from you.
Obviously you think it's unfair that ...
What I think is this: ...

9 **Preparing to listen**

a These items will be mentioned in the recording. Match the labels to the symbols.
Example: *1 car park*

baby changing room • ~~car park~~ • escalator • information point • lift • medical centre • meeting point • pharmacy • playground • recycling bin • toilets • wheelchair access

b Now write sentences explaining what you can or can't do in these places.
Example: *People in a wheelchair can enter the building here.*

2/18 **10**

Listening for detail

A group of British students is doing a project on shopping centre design. Their teacher tells them about some important points to consider.

a Listen to the recording and decide if the statements below are true or false.

1 The most important question is how to make lots of money.
2 The information point should provide tourist information.
3 There should be an area selling food.
4 All shoppers have the same needs.
5 A playground is a good idea to keep parents happy.
6 If you have an escalator, there is no need for lifts.
7 Every shopping centre should sell a range of food.
8 Teenagers should be shut out.

b Now correct the false statements.

11

Brainstorming

Work in a group. You are a focus group whose job is to plan how to attract young people (15–21) to the shopping centre. First, brainstorm ideas. What things would make a visit to the shopping centre fun? Think of some exciting, unusual ideas.

Here are some suggestions to start with:

rock-climbing wall • skate park • youth drop-in centre

Choose the idea that you like best, and note down some details, e.g.

- Is it indoors or outdoors?
- Is safety equipment needed?
- How many people can use it at one time?
- Why is it needed in your area?

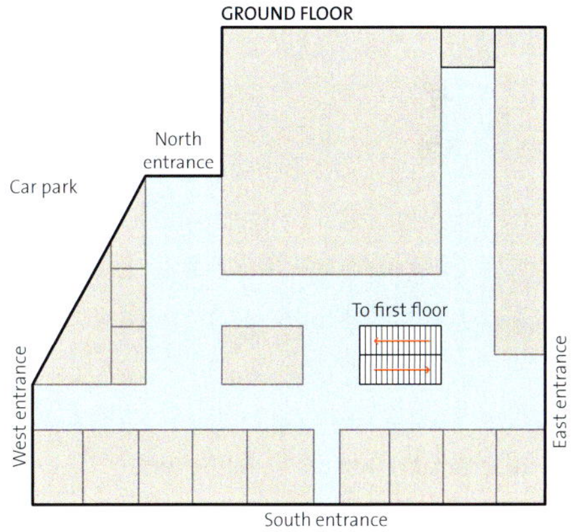

12

Completing the plan

In your group, follow these steps:

1 Copy the plan and decide the best place for each of the facilities from exercise 9. Draw the symbols on the plan.
2 Decide the best place for your idea from exercise 11.
3 Present your shopping centre plan to the class.

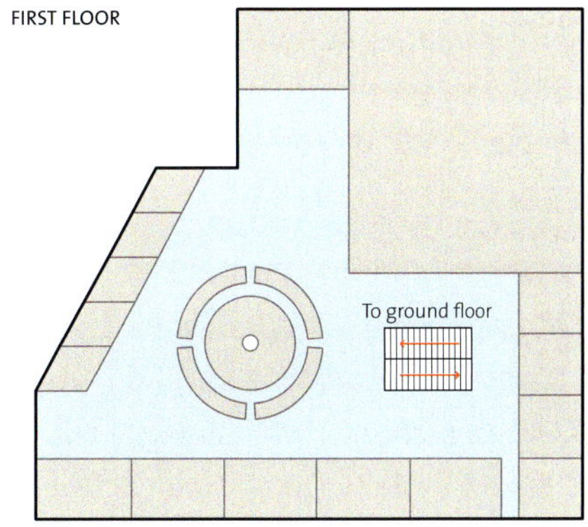

GRAMMAR

The passive

Zeitform	*Aktiv*	*Passiv*
Simple present	They **dye** the cotton. They **wash** the jeans.	The cotton **is dyed**. The jeans **are washed**.
Simple past	They **dyed** the cotton. They **washed** the jeans.	The cotton **was dyed**. The jeans **were washed**.
Present perfect	They **have dyed** the cotton. They **have washed** the jeans.	The cotton **has been dyed**. The jeans **have been washed**.
Will future	They **will dye** the cotton. They **will wash** the jeans.	The cotton **will be dyed**. The jeans **will be washed**.

- Das Passiv wird mit einer Zeitform von *to be* + Partizip Perfekt (3. Verbform) gebildet.
- In einem Aktivsatz sagen wir, wer etwas tut.
- In einem Passivsatz sagen wir, was mit einer Person oder einer Sache getan wird.
- Mit ***by*** können wir sagen, von wem etwas gemacht wird (der ***by-agent***): *The jeans are washed* ***by*** *the workers.*
- Meist verwenden wir jedoch das Passiv, wenn es nicht nötig (oder nicht möglich) ist zu sagen, wer etwas tut oder getan hat.

13 Simple present passive

Complete the sentences with the passive forms of the verbs in brackets.

Example: *Our jeans are made in several factories in Indonesia. (make)*

1 The denim … in big washing machines. (wash)
2 The jeans … to Britain on a large container ship. (send)
3 Many workers … each year because the machines do not have safety guards. (injure)
4 The dye … by us – we buy it from a German company. (not make)
5 Most of our jeans … by people who want cool fashions at a low price. (wear)
6 Shopping centres … by people of all ages. (visit)
7 Nowadays many goods … over the internet. (buy)
8 Often the needs of teenagers … when a shopping centre is built. (not consider)

14 Will future passive

The PR manager at ItalDenim is taking a group of journalists on a tour of the works. Rewrite the sentences in the will future passive. Decide whether you need the *by*-agent.

Example: We will dye this cotton blue. → *This cotton will be dyed blue.*

1 We will turn this cotton into denim.
2 We will send these rolls of cloth to Tunisia.
3 ItalDenim will make an even wider range of cloth next year.
4 Many jeans companies will buy our denim.
5 The new loom (*Webmaschine*) will produce more than 1,000 metres of denim an hour.
6 In a few weeks, people will wear jeans made from this denim.

A week in Malta

12

1 Welcome to Malta!

Find Malta on the map of Europe on page 264. Do you know what languages the people speak there?

TIP

The national language of Malta is Maltese. This is spoken by all natives. The other official language is English and this is spoken by about 88 % of the population. This is because Britain owned the island from 1800 until its independence in 1964.
Another important language is Italian, which was the official language until the 1930s. About 66 % of Maltese people speak Italian. Many people learn it by watching Italian television. Another important language is French, which is spoken by about 17 % of the population.

2 Malta sights and activities

Look at the pictures and complete the names of the sights with words in the box.

beach • cave • church • Grotto • Museum • Palace • ruins • walls

Calypso's …

Classic Car Collection …

Golden Sands …

Grand Master's …

Hagar Qim …

Mdina city …

Ta' Pinu …

The Blue …

3 Research project

The things in the box are important to Malta. Choose one of them or one of the photos above. Find out what it is and why it is important. Then tell the class about it.

The Knights of Malta
Cathedral of St John
Maltese wall lizard
Lampuki Pie

4 **Package holidays**

Look at the following advertisements for one-week package holidays in Malta. Tell your partner which holiday would be best for you and why.

Learn and Leisure Package For Teens

The best way to learn English: lessons in small groups, the opportunity to live with a family plus plenty of social activities with fellow students from all over the world!

€215

Package includes:

- ✓ 20 hours of group English lessons – maximum number of students: 10
- ✓ Student welcome party
- ✓ Water-taxi tour
- ✓ The Malta Experience (audio-visual show)
- ✓ Chamber of Secrets (magic show)
- ✓ Boat party (including DJ, drinks and a Maltese snack)

Ancient Malta

You're passionate about history and the past? Then this holiday is for you!

€230

Package includes:

- ✓ Seven-day Malta-Gozo bus pass
- ✓ Walking tour of Mdina old city
- ✓ Guided tour of Grand Master's Palace
- ✓ Pass to Hagar Qim temple ruins
- ✓ Pass to Middle Ages Museum
- ✓ Plus discounts to many more historical places of interest!

Maltese Adventure!

Tired of sitting on the sofa watching TV? This holiday provides fun and risks for every sport lover!

€310

Package includes:

- ✓ Hiking on Gozo
- ✓ Climbing at the famous Blue Grotto
- ✓ Waterskiing or windsurfing at Golden Sands Beach
- ✓ Horseback riding in the countryside
- ✓ Scuba diving
- ✓ Each activity includes an introduction for beginners

5 Matching

Read the texts written by travellers to Malta. Which holiday from exercise 4 did each traveller choose?

2/20 ①

www.HistoryAddicts.net

Blog entry: Malta

By: MittelAlterFreak

★★★★

Posted yesterday 10.30

This is Anja from Germany. I've often thought it would be cool if I could go back in time to the Middle Ages! Well, of course I can't do that, but this week I'm doing the next best thing: I'm on holiday in Malta.

Malta is an island in the Mediterranean which has historical sites much older than anything I've ever seen in Germany. There are many things to see which are thousands of years old. Today is only my first day here. I will write in this blog every day and tell you all about the historical places I see.

②

Senden | An alle | Anhang | Adressen | Schriften | Farben

To: info@EnglishSchoolMalta.mt
From: Dojin.Park@KMail.kr
Subject: Enquiry

Dear Sir or Madam

I saw your advert online and would like to book your one-week package holiday.

Can you arrange accommodation for me, please? Your website says that it is possible to stay in the home of a Maltese family. This would be ideal for me because I want to speak as much English as possible while I am there.

I look forward to hearing from you.

Yours sincerely

Dojin Park

③

Dear Mum

We are having the best time in Malta! You know how much we love sports and we are trying a new one every day. If we lived here, we would have so much fun all the time! Today is only the second day and we already have a little sunburn. Some of the things we are doing are a bit dangerous, but don't worry!

Love

Cindy and Brad

Linda Johnson
14 Coronation Street
Oxford
OX1 8DP
United Kingdom

TIP

You don't have to travel abroad to practise your English. There are lots of free interactive websites where you can learn new words or test your grammar. There are even free 'language learning communities' where people teach each other languages.

GRAMMAR

Conditional sentences type II

If I **lived** in Malta, I **would speak** English all the time.
I **would speak** English all the time if I **lived** in Malta.

- Bedingungssätze des Typs II werden benutzt, wenn man eine Situation beschreibt, die zwar theoretisch möglich, aber eher unwahrscheinlich ist („Was wäre, wenn…?").
- Im *if*-Teil steht das *simple past*, im Haupteil steht *would* + Grundform.
- Achtung: Im *if*-Satz steht zwar die Vergangenheitsform, der Satz bezieht sich aber auf die Gegenwart oder Zukunft.

DANGER!

Im *if*-Teil steht nie *would*.
Eselsbrücke: *Never ever ever, 'if' and 'would' together!*

6 Conditional sentences type II

a Chose the right answers.

1 Cindy and Brad write 'If we lived here, we would have so much fun all the time!'
- a Cindy and Brad used to live on Malta.
- b Cindy and Brad don't live on Malta.

2 Anja writes 'It would be cool if I could go back in time to the Middle Ages!'
- a Anja was able to go back in time to the Middle Ages.
- b Anja can't go back in time to the Middle Ages but would like to.

b Complete the conditional sentences type II with verbs from the box in the right tense.

(not) eat … be • go … (not) have • ~~(not) have … (not) be~~ •
live … go • love … (not) have to • pay … go

1 If Germany *didn't* have a wet climate, it *wouldn't be* so green.
2 If we … to school from 7.30 a.m. until 9.00 p.m., we … any free time.
3 If we … in the fifth century, most of us … to school.
4 My parents … for half my holiday if I … to a language school.
5 I … to go to Australia if I … fly for 10 hours to get there.
6 Harry … any of the local foods if he … in another country.

c „What if …?" Write sentences in English. Start the sentences with "If …"

Example: Wenn Sie Ihren Pass im Urlaub verlieren würden.
If I lost my passport while on holiday, I would go to the German Embassy.

1 Wenn Ihr Freund Sie anlügen würde.
2 Wenn Sie Ihre Prüfung bestehen würden.
3 Wenn Ihre Eltern ins Ausland ziehen würden.
4 Wenn Sie eine Million Euro gewinnen würden.
5 Wenn Ihre Schwester Ihre Lieblings-CD kaputt machen würde.

7 Preparing for a holiday

a Make a list of things you would do if you went to Malta. Look back at the holidays on page 124 for ideas. For each of these activities, name at least one thing you should do in preparation.

I would like to …	I should …
… go swimming.	*… pack a swimsuit.*

b Now use your list to make type II conditional sentences.
Example: *If I wanted to go swimming, I would pack a swimsuit.*

GRAMMAR

Conditional sentences type III

If he **had planned** his holiday better, he **would have had** more fun.
He **would have had** more fun if he **had planned** his holiday better.

- Mit Bedingungssätzen des Typs III kann man ausdrücken, was in der Vergangenheit hätte geschehen können („Was wäre gewesen, wenn…?"). Dabei stellt man sich etwas vor, was in Wirklichkeit gar nicht geschehen ist.
- Im *if*-Teil steht das *past perfect*, im Hauptteil steht *would have* + Partizip Perfekt.

8 Conditional sentences type III

a Reginald and Wanda didn't prepare very well for their holiday in Malta. Complete the sentences by putting the underlined verbs in the correct form.

Example: Reginald didn't arrive at the airport on time, so he missed his flight and arrived late.
If Reginald *had arrived* at the airport on time, he *wouldn't have missed* his flight and arrived late.

1 Reginald and Wanda didn't bring a map, so they got lost.
If Reginald and Wanda … a map, they … lost.
2 They didn't book a hotel room, so they didn't have a place to sleep.
If they … a hotel room, they … a place to sleep.
3 They didn't change any money to euros, so they weren't able to pay for anything.
If they … some money to euros, they … able to pay for things.
4 Wanda wasn't able to go hiking because she didn't pack any hiking boots.
Wendy … to go hiking if she … some hiking boots.
5 Reginald got sunburn because he forgot to wear a hat.
Reginald … sunburn if he … to wear a hat.

b In fact, Reginald and Wanda made none of the preparations on your list in exercise 8. Continue making type III conditional sentences with your own ideas from that exercise.
Example: *If they had packed swimsuits, they would have been able to go swimming.*

9 Interpreting

a You are staying at the St Constantine Hotel on Malta. The receptionist asks you to interpret for a German hotel guest. What would you say in German and English?

Guest	You	Receptionist
Man hat mir gesagt, die Mitarbeiter in diesem Hotel würden Deutsch sprechen. Sagen Sie ihm das, bitte.		
	Someone told her that …	
		Yes, one of the employees does speak German, but she's got the morning off. Please tell the lady I'm sorry and ask her what I can do for her.
	Er sagt, …	
Sagen Sie ihm mein Name ist Kramer und ich habe ein Zimmer reserviert.		
	…	
		Ah, yes. Kramer. A single room for five nights. Please say her room is ready and ask if she would like breakfast in the morning. It costs nine euros.
	…	
Ja, ich nehme das Frühstück. Wann und wo kann ich frühstücken?		
	…	
		Breakfast is from 7.30 to 10.00 down the hall on your left. You can also eat on the terrace. Would the lady like to go to her room now? It's got a lovely balcony looking out over the sea.
	…	
Das hört sich ja traumhaft an. Ja, ich möchte das Zimmer jetzt beziehen. Vielen Dank fürs Übersetzen. Sind Sie später noch hier? Ich werde noch einige Fragen für den Mitarbeiter haben.		

2/21 **b** When Ms Kramer comes back from her room, she and the receptionist need your help again. Listen to them and interpret what they say. Use the words and phrases given below.

1 … hasn't been cleaned … plates and glasses …
2 *tut ihm leid … kümmert sich sofort …*
3 … get to city centre …
4 … *direkt vor dem Hotel … Minuten*
5 … go swimming … recommend a … get there …
6 … *in der* Ghadira *Bucht … Endstation … kurzer Weg zu Fuß …*
7 … German-speaking employee …
8 … *Englischunterricht …*

10 Writing

Choose one of the following tasks. Write about 120–150 words.

a You are on holiday in Malta. Write a postcard to an English-speaking friend.

b Write an article for your school paper about a holiday or trip that you have been on. Include the following information:

- When you went and why
- What there is to do there
- If you would recommend it

At the airport

1 **Welcome to the airport!**

You want to fly to Malta via Rome. Look at the flight information monitor. Where in the airport should you go first? What other information about your flight is shown?

FLIGHT		DESTINATION	DEP.TIME	COUNTER
QF	085	HONG KONG	7:00	95-97
XA	3675	MADRID	8:40	76-82
CX	104	PEKIN	8:50	45-88
LH	7935	LONDON	9:25	48-65
JK	8257	ROME	10:00	70-88
AC	9538	NEW YORK	11:15	78-88
SR	6482	PARIS	11:37	93-98

2/22 **2** **Checking in**

a Listen to the assistant at the check-in counter. What does the passenger need to say or do?

The passenger has to …
… show … … pay …
… say whether … … go …
… say how many …

b Complete the assistant's statements and questions with words from the box.

aisle seat • bag (2 x) • boarding passes • extra charge • flying • gate • luggage • pieces • ticket and passport • security

1 Hello. May I have your …, please?
2 Where are you … to?
3 Do you have any … to check in? How many …?
4 You'll have to pay an … of 50 euros.
5 Would you like a window seat or an …?
6 Did you pack your … yourself?
7 Has your … been with you at all times?
8 Here are your …. Your … is C 21. Boarding is in 30 minutes, so you should go through …

2/23 **c** Now listen to the full dialogue and note down what the traveller says. Then, improvise a similar dialogue with a partner. Switch roles so both of you get to be the assistant.

3 Going through security

Look at the items confiscated by airport security. How many of them can you name?

4 Airport signs

Look at the airport signs. What does each sign say you can do, have to do or must not do?

2/24 5 Understanding announcements

While waiting at the gate, you hear announcements for different flights. Decide what the passengers on each flight have to do.

a They have to wait an extra 30 minutes.
b They should show their boarding pass and board the plane.
c They should go to a different gate.
d They can go and get a free drink.

6 Boarding the plane

You have two boarding passes. Which one do you need now and which one will you need later?

Airline — Economy Class

Gate C21 | Check In 8:00 | Seat 27B

Flight-no. JK8257
dep. 10:00
arr. Rome (FCO) 11:50

Gate C21
Check In 8:00
Seat 27B

Airline — Economy Class

Gate B16 | Check In 10:45 | Seat 54A

Flight-no. JK7844
dep. 12:45
arr. Malta (MLA) 14:20

Gate B16
Check In 10:45
Seat 54A

1 Your British friend is visiting you and wants to go cycling. Explain to him what is allowed, possible, forbidden or necessary.

- cycling on the left
- cycling on the street, the pavement, the cycle path
- wearing a helmet
- making hand signals when turning

2 What would you do if …

- you lost your mobile phone?
- your school was closed for a week?
- it was your friend's birthday today?

3 Sie lernen im Urlaub einen jungen Iren kennen. Fragen Sie ihn …

- ob er schon einmal in Deutschland war.
- ob er gestern schwimmen gegangen ist.
- was er heute Abend vorhat.
- ob er jetzt mit Ihnen und Ihren Freunden Volleyball spielen möchte.
- ob er auch nächstes Jahr hier Urlaub machen wird.

4 Compare the USA, Canada and Australia. Write four sentences and use different comparative forms.

Country	Area	Population	Length of flight (from Frankfurt/ Main)	Number of German tourists yearly
USA	9.6 million km^2	311 million	9+ hours	2,000,000
Canada	9.9 million km^2	34 million	9+ hours	400,000
Australia	7.6 million km^2	22 million	22+ hours	140,000

5 Sie arbeiten während Ihres Berufspraktikums im Gasthof zum Eber in Tübingen. Der Kellner kann leider kein Englisch. Als eine englische Touristin eine Frage hat, bittet der Kellner Sie zu vermitteln. Was würden Sie im Dialog unten jeweils auf Englisch bzw. auf Deutsch sagen?

Sie	Begrüßen Sie die Kundin und fragen Sie, wie Sie helfen können.
Touristin	I had a cup of coffee here about 20 minutes ago and I left my bag. It has a lot of important things in it. Have you seen it?
Sie (1)	…
Kellner	Niemand hat eine Tasche nachgereicht. An welchem Tisch hat die Dame gesessen?
Sie (2)	…
Touristin	At that one over there in the corner, next to the window.
Sie (3)	…
Kellner	Vielleicht ist die Tasche noch da?
Sie (4)	…
Touristin	No, I've already looked. It isn't there. The bag has my passport and my hotel room key in it. What am I going to do?
Sie (5)	…
Kellner	Ist sie wirklich sicher, dass sie die Tasche hier hinterlassen hat und nicht woanders?
Sie (6)	…
Touristin	Yes, definitely. I took my purse out to pay for the coffee, and luckily I put it in my coat pocket. But I must have left my bag at the table.
Sie (7)	…
Kellner	Als Erstes sollte die Dame vielleicht das Hotel benachrichtigen – für den Fall, dass jemand den Zimmerschlüssel benutzen will, um ins Hotelzimmer zu kommen.
Sie (8)	…
Touristin	I can't, because my mobile phone was in the bag too. Here is the number of the hotel – can you phone for me?
Sie (9)	…
Kellner	Ja, selbstverständlich. Ich mache das gleich. Dann soll die Dame auf die Polizeiwache gehen und den Verlust melden.
Sie (10)	…
Touristin	I have no idea where that is. I've only been in Tübingen for two days.
Sie (11)	…
Kellner	Würden Sie der Dame bitte zur Polizeiwache bringen?
Sie (12)	…
Touristin	Oh, thank you, that would be a great help.

Revision

Relative clauses (▶ S. 51, 204), comparison of adjectives (▶ S. 53, 203)

1 **Complete each sentence with *which* or *who* if necessary.**

1 How much did you pay the guide … went hiking with you?
2 That's the boy … got really bad sunburn.
3 What was the name of the scuba instructor … you met in Malta?
4 We visited an island … had some interesting ancient ruins.
5 This photo shows one of the churches … we visited.
6 Mnarja is an important Maltese festival … is held on 29 June.
7 What's the name of the bar … you went to with your friends?
8 There are only three tourists … want to go waterskiing this afternoon.
9 Tourists … love beautiful old buildings should go to Valetta.
10 Excuse me, is this the bus … goes to Mdina?

2 **Use the comparatives and superlatives of the adjectives and adverbs in brackets to complete the text about the Canary Islands, a popular destination for German and British tourists.**

Gran Canaria is one of the…[1] (popular) islands with tourists: 2 million of them visit every year. However, the island has only one airport, which is the …[2] (busy) airport in Spain. Tenerife is …[3] (big) than Gran Canaria, in fact it is the …[4] (big) of the Canary Islands. Even …[5] (many) tourists visit Tenerife than Gran Canaria – 5 million of them each year. Many people think that La Palma is the …[6] (pretty) of the Canary Islands. On the other hand, it is a lot …[7] (quiet) than the …[8] (large) islands and has much …[9] (little) nightlife, so if you like to party, it would be …[10] (good) to go to Tenerife or Gran Canaria.
Most of the Canary Islands are very mountainous. In fact, the …[11] (high) point in Spain is in Tenerife (3,718 metres). That's …[12] (high) than most of the Austrian Alps. At 670 metres, Lanzarote is the …[13] (flat) of the islands, so that's a good place to go if you don't like hills. Although they are part of Spain, the Canary Islands are much …[14] (close) to Africa than they are to Europe.
Many Britons and Germans retire to the Canary Islands because the climate is much …[15] (pleasant) than …[16] (many) places in Europe: most of the year the daytime temperature is between 20 and 30 °C.

3 **The Channel Islands are English-speaking islands that are close to the coast of France but are not part of France or the United Kingdom. Use the table to compare the three largest islands: Jersey, Guernsey and Alderney. Write at least eight sentences.**
Example: *Guernsey is not as big as Jersey.*

	Area	Population	Position
Jersey	116 km^2	92,500	22 km from France
Guernsey	78 km^2	65,500	48 km from France
Alderney	7.8 km^2	2,400	16 km from France

Role models

1 Warm-up

a Look at the photos and then use adjectives from the box to say whether these people are good role models and why.

Example: *J.K. Rowling is talented and intelligent. She is also generous.*

courageous • gifted • influential • intelligent • generous • kind • optimistic • polite • rich • talented

Prince Harry

Lady Gaga

Vitali and Wladimir Klitschko

J.K. Rowling

Julia Roberts

Martin Luther King

b Tell a partner about one of your role models. Explain why you look up to this person and how the person sets a good example.

My uncle is my role model. He never gives up, even when things are difficult.

TIP

Describing role models

to look up to sb	*jdn bewundern*
to be good at sth	*gut in etw sein*
to set a good example to sb	*jdm als Vorbild dienen*
to try one's hand at sth	*sich in etw versuchen*

2 Talking about people

a Copy the word families table into your notebook. Add the adjectives from the box in exercise 1 and then complete the table.

noun	adjective	adverb
courage	courageous	*courageously*

b Now use words from the table to make six sentences.

3/2

A role model at age 16

Around the world, millions of children are not getting a proper education because their families are too poor to send them to school. In India, one school boy is trying to change that. His education project is changing the lives of hundreds of children.

16-year-old Babar Ali lives in a village in West Bengal, India. His day begins doing work around the house, then he goes to school. To get to school, he has to travel about 10 kilometres with an auto-rickshaw (a tiny, three-wheeled car), then walk the last two kilometres. The school is free, but his family still has to pay for the transportation and his uniform. Unfortunately, most families in Babar Ali's village do not have enough money for these things, so a large number of children there cannot go to school.

"It's not easy for me to come to school because I live so far away," Babar Ali says, "but the teachers are good and I love learning. And my parents believe I must get the best education possible. That's why I am here."

When Babar Ali was nine years old, some friends in the village asked him what he was learning in school, so Babar Ali 'taught' them. It was like a game for them, and it was so much fun and so interesting that they played it every day, and more and more children came to get lessons from Babar Ali. They were hungry for an education and Babar Ali was a natural-born teacher.

Babar Ali at the school he started in his family's yard

Today, about 800 local children, who are too poor to go to school, come to Babar Ali for free lessons. He has started a school in his family's yard where he and 9 other 'teachers' give lessons. Like Babar Ali, these other teachers are students at school or college. They go to their own lessons in the mornings and then they go to Babar Ali's school in the afternoons and teach what they have learned. The teachers give their time voluntarily.

Babar Ali doesn't charge for anything, even books and food are funded by donations and given to the children for free. Children as young as four come for lessons in mathematics, science and Bengali, the local language.

The school is completely outdoors. Children sit on the ground and teachers teach without any board or electrical devices. During monsoon season, lessons are often cancelled because of rain.

It is common for boys in Babar Ali's village to work in fields instead of going to school. The girls mostly work in households. This is what most young people do during the day before coming to Babar Ali's. "Without this school, many children wouldn't get an education," says Babar Ali.

Abridged and adapted from BBC NEWS: http://news.bbc.co.uk/go/pr/fr/-/2/hi/south_asia/8299780.stm

(449 words)

3 Understanding the text

Who says what? Match the statements (1–5) to one of the people (a–d) and give reasons for your answer.

a Babar Ali
b one of his volunteer teachers
c a pupil
d a parent of one of the pupils

1 I want to become a nurse. Babar Ali's school might make that possible.
2 Without his school, our children would not be literate.
3 This young man is a real role model. He is setting a good example to others.
4 I think it is my duty to educate people, to help our country build a better future.
5 I am fortunate because I am able to attend college. I want to share my good fortune with others. That's why I joined the school project.

4 Working with words

Complete the sentences with suitable nouns from the text.

1 Every child in the world should be entitled to an … .
2 Hundreds of boys and girls attend Babar Ali's … .
3 Babar Ali would love to introduce computer-assisted … at his school.
4 A lot of the children at Babar Ali's school dream of going to … .
5 Babar Ali is strict with the pupils, just like a real … .

5 Mediation

As part of a school project you are researching education in different countries. Read the text and write a list in German of 1) problems with education in India and 2) how the government is trying to solve these problems.

Education in India

There are many good schools in India, but there are about 8 million children who cannot go to school and only 40 % attend secondary school. The situation is improving, however. In 2003, there were 25 million children who did not attend school.
Whether or not a child attends school often depends on his or her caste, or social class. Indians are born into the caste of their parents. There are dozens of castes and each one has a name and a profession. It is very difficult for an Indian to live in a way which is not typical for their caste. Another factor is gender: fewer girls attend school than boys. India is dealing with these problems by giving more free education to girls and to members of the lower castes. Discrimination on the basis of caste is officially illegal in India.

6 Completing a story

Finish the story and add a suitable title. Write 120 words.

Amrita is 13 and lives in a village in West Bengal with her family. She always dreamed of becoming a doctor, but there was no money for school. One day, she heard about …

3/3 7

Listening to a song

Listen to the song then discuss in groups. Who is the singer talking to? What is the message of the song?

The Wind beneath my Wings

It must have been cold there in my shadow,
to never have sunlight on your face.
You were content to let me shine, that's your way.
You always walked a step behind.

So I was the one with all the glory,
while you were the one with all the strength.
A beautiful face without a name for so long.
A beautiful smile to hide the pain.

Did you ever know that you're my hero,
and everything I would like to be?
I can fly higher than an eagle,
'cause you are the wind beneath my wings.

It might have appeared to go unnoticed,
but I've got it all here in my heart.
I want you to know I know the truth, of course I know it.
I would be nothing without you.

Did you ever know that you're my hero?
You're everything I wish I could be.
I could fly higher than an eagle,
'cause you are the wind beneath my wings.

Did I ever tell you you're my hero?
You're everything, everything I wish I could be.
Oh, and I, I could fly higher than an eagle,
'cause you are the wind beneath my wings,
'cause you are the wind beneath my wings.

Oh, the wind beneath my wings.
You, you, you, you are the wind beneath my wings.
Fly, fly, fly away. You let me fly so high.
Oh, you, you, you, the wind beneath my wings.
Oh, you, you, you, the wind beneath my wings.

Fly, fly, fly high against the sky,
so high I almost touch the sky.
Thank you, thank you,
thank God for you, the wind beneath my wings.

3/5 V3 **3** **Listening and taking notes**

final count down	final count down	final count down
Barbara Grushka CEO	**Heather Meyers** Project Manager	**Esteban Benitez** Technician

a Watch or listen to the meeting. Work in groups of three. Student A takes notes for the CEO, Student B for the project manager and Student C for the technician. Take notes on the following things:

- Actions the attendee will take after the meeting
- Decisions taken in the meeting
- Reference information the attendee will need to complete their actions

b Now compare your notes with the rest of the class.

4 **Re-writing and re-organising notes**

Most professionals take notes during work meetings. Then, they re-write and re-organise their notes afterwards. This 'forces' them to review what was said at the meeting. Transfer your meeting notes into the following table.

Actions (what *you* will do after the meeting)	Decisions taken	Reference information
…	…	…

3/6 **5** **A trade fair in Germany**

After the successful show Bam! has asked Final Countdown to do the same show at a trade fair in Germany. To do this, Final Countdown have the help of a German intern – you! You are at the next meeting. Copy the form below and then complete it with details from the meeting.

Final Countdown events
Information for venue

Name of event: *Bam! Produkteinführung*
Date of installation: …
Date of show: …
Special notes: …

Date(s) of event: …
Elements to be installed: …
Space needed: …

Listening

3/7 **1** You listen to five people giving their opinion on a radio programme about whether we need role models. Copy the table below and then listen and complete it with information from the text. You will listen to the programme twice and can make notes while listening.

Speaker	Importance of role models	Role model	Reason
Adam	…	…	…
Anna	…	…	…
Brendan	…	…	…
Hollie	…	…	…
Lexi	…	…	…

3/8 **2** You are listening to a programme in which Jack O'Donnell, an Australian from the Outback, is talking about his years at school. Listen to the programme and decide if the statements below are true or false. Correct any false statements. You will listen to the programme twice and can make notes while listening.

1 When Jack was a child, his family lived in a small town in the Outback.
2 You could travel everywhere easily by car.
3 Jack was never lonely because there were a lot of young people in the area.
4 When Jack's father was at school, he had to go to a boarding school on the coast.
5 The School of the Air started because all farmers in the Outback had a telephone connection.
6 Jack had to go without schoolbooks and worksheets.
7 The flying doctor brought Jack's teacher to his house once a year.
8 The School of the Air doesn't exist anymore because all kids in the Outback have an internet connection.

Listening / Writing

3/9 **3** You are doing work experience in a doctor's surgery. Your boss was recently at a conference in London and stayed in a hotel there. You listen to your answer phone messages and have a message from the hotel in London. Copy the memo below and then listen to the message and complete the memo. You will listen to the message twice and can make notes while listening.

Telefonnotiz

Nachricht für:

Aufgeschrieben von:

Anrufer:

Grund des Anrufs:

Telefonnummer für Rückruf:

Writing

4 Choose one of the tasks below. Write at least 150 words.

a Choose a picture and write a story about it.

b Write an article for your school magazine about soap operas.

Can young people learn anything useful from soap operas, or are they just entertainment? Should parents be worried if their teenage children watch a lot of soap operas?

Revision

Some and *any* (▶ S. 43, 203), adverbs (▶ S. 49, 203), plural nouns (▶ S. 32, 202)

1 **Choose the correct alternative: *some* or *any*.**

1 *Some / Any* children in Babar Ali's village are too poor to go to school.
2 Can *somebody / anybody* here think of an inspiring role model?
3 Can pupils sit *somewhere / anywhere*, or does each pupil have his or her own place?
4 Do *some / any* of the boys go to work instead of going to school?
5 Is there *something / anything* you would like to ask the children, Babar?
6 Could I have *some / any* more paper, please? I don't have *some / any* paper to write on.
7 *Some / Any* of these children are in lower castes but there aren't *some / any* who are treated badly.
8 I can't think of *some / any* reason why celebrities should be role models unless they have done *something / anything* really special.
9 *Some / Any* celebrities think they can behave as they like without *some / any* responsibility for their fans.
10 Please tell me *something / anything* about the caste system – I don't know *something / anything* about it.

2 **Complete the sentences with the adverb forms of the adjectives in brackets.**

1 The children looked at the ice cream … (hungry).
2 The ice cream seller … (generous) gave them an ice cream each.
3 The teachers don't get paid, they work here … (voluntary).
4 'Perhaps I'll get a 1 in English,' she thought … (optimistic).
5 The pupils all talk to their teachers very … (polite).
6 '… (official), the school leaving age is 16, but many of our pupils leave school … (early),' explained the principal.
7 The caste system is … (extreme) old and some people still discriminate … (illegal) against members of certain castes.
8 It's important to work … (hard) if you want to do … (good) in your exams.
9 The pupils didn't want to get to school … (late) so they walked very … (fast).
10 'Please finish the revision exercises … (quick) so we can start the next unit,' said the teacher … (impatient).

3 **Find in the box:**

- 2 uncountable nouns.
- 3 plural nouns that do not have a singular form.
- 2 nouns that form their plural with *-es*.
- 7 nouns with completely irregular plurals.
- 2 nouns that turn *-y* to *-i* in the plural.

child • day • disco • family • foot • hobby • information • jeans • man • news • person • potato • radio • scissors • tomato • tooth • trousers • wife • woman

Food and sport

14

1 **Warm-up**

a Look at Harvard University's 'Healthy Eating Pyramid'. Then match the categories in the box below to the right place on the pyramid.

alcohol • dairy • exercise and weight control • fish, poultry and eggs • nutritional supplements • nuts and beans • plant oils • red meat and butter • starchy foods and sweets • fruit and vegetables • whole grain foods

b Now decide which category the words below belong in.

beef • berries • bicycle • brown bread • carrots • chicken • fizzy drinks • green beans • milk • multi-vitamin pill • peanut butter • red wine • salmon • sausage • scales • sunflower oil • white rice • whole grain pasta • yoga mat • yoghurt

c Tell your partner how much you should get from each category to lead a healthy lifestyle.

You should eat / drink very little …

You should get a daily dose of …

2 A nutrition quiz

a Look at the quiz and decide if you think the statements are facts or common myths.

1 Vitamin tablets work.
2 Vegetarians do not get enough protein.
3 You can catch the flu from going out in cold weather without a coat or with wet hair.
4 The best source of calcium is milk.
5 Drinking a glass of red wine with dinner is good for you.
6 Fibre (*Ballaststoff*) gives you gas.
7 Fats are bad for you. They make you fat.
8 You should drink four litres of water a day … or five … or ten.

b Now decide which answer below (a – h) matches which statement (1 – 8).

a How much you need depends on the weather, how much you eat and how active you are. Drinking 3 litres will be enough for some men on some days and 2.2 litres will be enough for some women on some days.

b Myth. Vegetarians can get enough of this nutrient by eating nuts, beans and other plants. Vegans can also get enough calcium and vitamin D from non-dairy foods.

c This nutrient is extremely important. Women should get at least 20 grams of it every day; men at least 30 grams. If you are not getting enough, you should eat more vegetables, fruit, beans and whole-grain foods. However, if you suddenly eat more than normal, you may get gas. To help prevent this, soak beans well before you cook them.

d Taking one of these is a way to make sure you get all the nutrients you need. Of course, you can take too many: too many supplements can be harmful, as can 'mega' supplements which contain huge doses (far more than 100 % of the recommended amount).

e Not for everyone. While a single glass with dinner has shown to help prevent heart disease, it increases the risk of breast cancer.

f Myth. The only way to catch this disease is through contact with the influenza virus. This often happens in the winter when it is cold, so people often think the weather is the cause, but there is no relation. To strengthen your immune system, eat a diet high in fruits and vegetables and whole grains and do not drink too much alcohol.

g Myth. Dairy products can have a lot of saturated fat (*gesättigtes Fett*) and vitamin A, which can actually make bones weaker. The best sources of calcium are plants: dark green leafy vegetables like spinach, broccoli and baked beans.

h It depends. Saturated fat (*gesättigtes Fett*) found in red meat and deep fried foods are generally bad for you. But there are healthy, unsaturated fats that the body needs. Good sources are uncooked olive and vegetable oils, nuts, and fatty fish such as salmon.

Source of information: Harvard University School of Public Health website

3 Understanding the text

a Use your own words to complete the following sentences.

1 To avoid getting the flu, it is more important to … than to ….
2 When buying vitamin supplements, you should ….
3 It's hard to say how much water a person should drink because ….

b Based on information in the text, use the phrases below to make complete sentences.

Vegetables …	… has/have too much …	… saturated fat.
Pork, beef and chips…	… is/are a good source of …	… unsaturated fat.
Plant oils …		… fibre.
Milk and cheese …		… protein.
Nuts and beans …		… calcium.

c Name three reasons why it is important to eat vegetables.

4 Food and nutrition vocabulary

Collect all the food and nutrition vocabulary from the past two pages in a mind map. Add any other words you know.

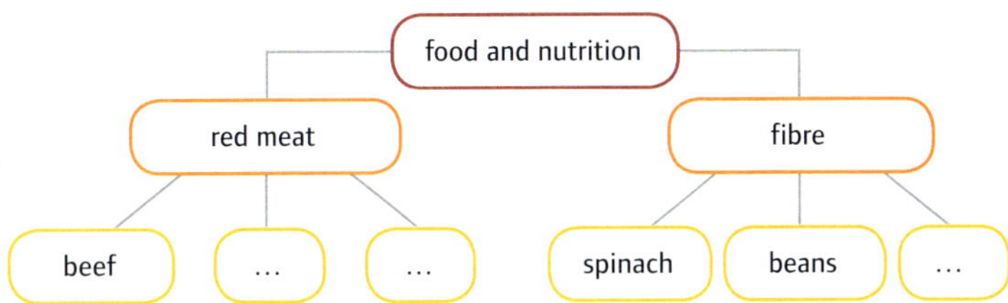

5 Planning a meal

Imagine you work in the kitchen at a health spa. Look at the food pyramid and the nutrition quiz again and plan the menu for a meal. Choose breakfast, lunch or dinner and decide which foods you will use to offer a healthy, balanced meal.

6 Writing a story based on a picture

Choose one of the pictures below and tell the story behind it.
Write 150 words.

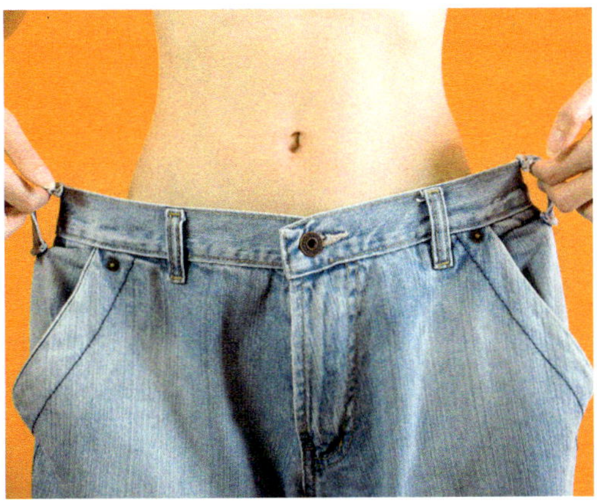

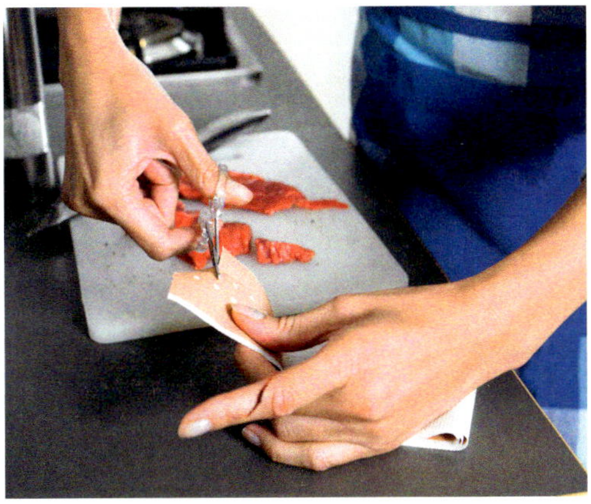

3/10 **7** **Before you read**

How many people in the class do you think eat fast food every week? Do a poll to find out.

Fast food in Asia

In this week's *Food around the world* we visited Ratna Osman who lives in Kuala Lumpur, the capital of Malaysia. She loves traditional food, in fact, her favourite food is Nyonya acar. Malaysian meals often have many dishes and this one is usually served as a side dish. If you're interested in making it, you need approximately 20 different ingredients (including roasted shrimp paste, fresh curcuma and blue ginger) and several hours of preparation time. There are seven vegetables in the dish and they must be fresh. All the vegetables must be chopped and boiled *separately* – that's how 'slow' Asian food can be!

Today Ratna has spent a busy morning shopping with her husband and son. In need of a bit of rest and relaxation, she would like to have lunch in a traditional Malaysian sit-down restaurant, where waiters bring them lots of plates of food, but their little boy prefers eating at McDonald's, so they agree to go there.

Once inside the crowded restaurant, Ratna says how she hates waiting in line and dislikes feeding her child unhealthy food, 'but the boy likes to play in the McDonald's play area, and he wants to have his hamburger, so we're here,' she says. She admits coming here every week, and she is not alone. Fast food is relatively new in Malaysia and one might expect it to be unpopular but the big chains have managed to win lots of customers. 59 % of Malaysian adults admit to eating fast food once a week. This is far more than in Europe, where only 11% have this habit. Even in America, the week involves stopping by a fast-food restaurant for 'only' 35 % of the adult population.

The fast-food trend has continued to hit other Asian countries, too. 41 % percent of Chinese, 61 % of residents of Hong Kong and 54 % of Filipinos choose to go to fast-food places at least once a week. Asians are now more likely to carry their lunch in a bag than anywhere else in the world.

When Western fast-food chains open restaurants in Asia, they have to change their menus a bit. In the past, they made only very small, cosmetic changes to the menus. But now the Asian market has grown so big, companies like McDonald's give each country its own menu. Asian customers want an exotic, 'American' taste from McDonald's, but they also want foods they know well and like eating. For example, the Chinese prefer to top their ice cream with red bean paste than with caramel. The Singaporeans enjoy eating their 'McRice' hamburgers on fried rice patties instead of bread. Wasabi filet of fish is on the menu in Hong Kong.

During our interview, Ratna begins to think about her choices. 'I hate to say this,' says Ratna, 'but if another parent asked me to recommend a restaurant, I probably wouldn't suggest coming here. I think I will try to follow my own advice and avoid eating here too often in the future.'

(505 words)

8 Understanding the text

a Read the text and say whether the following statements are true or false. Correct the false statements.

1 Acar is easy to make.
2 Ratna eats at McDonald's every week.
3 Fast food is less popular in Asia than in America.
4 McDonald's only makes small changes to its Asian menus.
5 Ratna would not tell other parents to bring their children to fast-food restaurants.

b Answer the following questions.

1 Name two reasons why acar is a good example of Asian 'slow food'.
2 Name two reasons why Ratna's son likes McDonald's.
3 Name three examples of differences between Western and Asian fast-food menus.
4 Name three ways fast-food chains attract Asian customers.

9 Mediation

You work for a fast-food company that is considering opening its first Asian restaurant in Kuala Lumpur. You think the article 'Fast food in Asia' could be useful. Write your boss an email in German including information about the following points.

- Reasons why Asian children like McDonald's
- Differences between Western and Asian fast food

10 Create a restaurant

Work with a partner or in a group to create a concept for an original, *healthy* fast-food restaurant. Decide on the following things and then present your concept to the class.

- The name and logo of your restaurant
- The location
- Who your customers will be
- Your menu

11 *-ing* form or the infinitive?

a Sort the following verbs from the text into the right category.

interested in • ~~would like~~ • prefer • agree • hate • ~~dislike~~ • like • want • admit • expect • manage • involve • ~~continue~~ • choose • enjoy • suggest

-ing	*-ing or to*	*to*
dislikes feeding	continue boiling continued to hit	would like to eat

b For each verb, make your own sentence which is easy for you to remember.
Example: *I dislike washing up after my mum cooks hamburgers.*

GRAMMAR

-ing form and infinitive

- Auf einige Verben folgt die *-ing*-Form:
  Ming-Han ***enjoys going*** *to traditional restaurants.*
- Auf andere Verben folgt der Infinitiv:
  The little girl ***wanted to eat*** *a hamburger.*
- Manchmal kann sowohl die *-ing*-Form als auch der Infinitiv folgen:
  We ***love cooking****. / We* ***love to cook****.*

Verb + *-ing*-Form	Verb + Infinitiv	Verb + *-ing*-Form oder Infinitiv
admit, avoid, dislike, don't mind, enjoy, finish, involve, stop, suggest	*agree, choose, decide, expect, hope, learn, manage, prefer, want, would like*	*begin, continue, hate, like, love, start*

c Complete the sentences by putting the verbs in brackets in the correct form.

1 Roslyn likes *running/to run* but I want to *walk*. (run, walk)
2 Keeping fit involves both … right and … . (eat, exercise)
3 I prefer … at home but my wife hates … . (eat, cook)
4 We are looking forward to … a nice Asian meal on Saturday. (have)
5 Would you begin … more foods at home if we agreed … you? (prepare, help)
6 I'm thinking of … the neighbours over for dinner. What do you think? (invite)
7 If we don't start … now, we won't manage … cooking by 8 o'clock. (shop, finish)
8 When you finish … this onion, continue … the others. (chop, chop)

12 **Guess who!**
Interview a person in your class and write sentences about him/her. Each sentence must contain a word or phrase from the grammar box or exercise 12. Everyone gives their papers to the teacher, who reads each one out loud. The class has to guess who it is.

13 Sports vocabulary

Use words in the box to say what is associated with good performance in these sports. There are more words than you need.

football

handball

track and field

tennis

swimming

cheating • doping • drowning • endurance • handling the ball well • injury • jumping very high • scoring points • speed • strategy • strength • teamwork • throwing well

TIP

Bewegen Sie sich!
Vielleicht gehören Sie zu jenen Menschen, die besser lernen, wenn sie sich bewegen. Probieren Sie es aus: Statt im Sitzen Vokabeln zu pauken, gehen Sie dabei durch die Wohnung.

14 Understanding sport reports

3/11

a Listen to the football report and complete the table.

name	team/player	played well/ badly	number of goals scored	won/lost the game	exciting/ boring game
Blackburn	*team*	*well*	*4*	*won*	…
Seamark	…	…	…	…	…
Coppington	…	…	…	…	…
Keepswitch	…	…	…	…	…
Gushing	…	…	…	…	…
Griffin	…	…	…	…	…
Maly	…	…	…	…	…

b The following expressions are used in the report. What do they mean? Use the phrases in brackets to explain the meanings.

1 goal (… try to kick the ball into this object.)
2 score a goal (This is when …)
3 Coppington's chances were nil. (This means …)
4 It was Keepswitch against Gushing. (This means …)
5 semi-finals (This is the phase of the tournament …)
6 the final score (This is the total number of …)

15 Reporting on an event

Bring a photo of a sporting event to class and tell your partner what is happening in the photos. If it's possible in your classroom, project the photos on the wall and tell the whole class. Say where the event took place, who played well, who won, etc.

1 The menu

Read the menu and tell your partner what you would order and why.

This evening's menu

Starter

Hors d'oeuvres buffet plus tomato soup or garden salad

Main course

Pork chops and noodles in wild mushroom sauce, served with green beans

Chicken breast roasted in port wine, served with peas and carrots and boiled potatoes

Fried tofu and wok vegetables in a sweet and spicy sauce, served with rice

Dessert

Assortment of fine cheeses

Apple tart served with vanilla ice cream

TIP

Bestellen sie kein *pig* in einem Restaurant, es sei denn, sie wollen ein neues Haustier! Im Englischen unterscheidet man zwischen den Tieren Rind und Schwein (*cattle and pig*) und ihrem Fleisch (*beef and pork*).

2

3/12

TIP

menu = *Speisekarte* NOT ~~*Menü*~~
chef = *Koch/Köchin*
boss = *Chef*

a Caroline Jones takes her business colleague, John Price, out to dinner after a successful meeting. Listen to the dialogues between the waiter and the guests. What do they order?

b Listen again. All of these phrases are commonly used in a restaurant. Which ones do you hear?

1 What would you like this evening?
2 I'm a vegetarian.
3 I'm allergic to nuts.
4 Do you like spicy foods?
5 I recommend the pork chops.
6 Alright, I'll have that.
7 How was the soup?
8 It was delicious!
9 It was alright.
10 I'm afraid it wasn't so good.
11 This looks delicious!
12 This looks beautiful!
13 Enjoy your meal!
14 May we have the cheque please?
15 Will that be together or separate?
16 It's your treat.
17 I hope to see you again soon.
18 Have a nice evening.

3 Role-play

Complete the following dialogue with a partner.

Waiter	Guest
Begrüßen Sie den Gast und fragen Sie, was er an diesem Abend (essen) möchte.	
	Sie sind entweder Vegetarier(in), allergisch gegen etwas, oder Sie mögen kein scharfes Essen. Bitten Sie um eine Empfehlung.
Empfehlen Sie etwas Angemessenes.	
	Sagen Sie, Sie werden das Empfohlene nehmen.
Servieren Sie dem Gast das Hauptgericht und wünschen Sie ihm einen „guten Appetit!“	
	Sagen Sie, wie das in diesem Moment servierte Hauptgericht aussieht.
Fragen Sie den Gast, wie ihm das Essen geschmeckt hat.	
	Sagen Sie, wie die genannte Vorspeise Ihnen geschmeckt hat. Bitten Sie danach um die Rechnung.
Nennen Sie den zu zahlenden Betrag.	
	Zahlen Sie und vergessen Sie das Trinkgeld nicht.
Bedanken Sie sich und sagen Sie, Sie hoffen, den Gast bald wieder zu sehen.	
	Wünschen Sie dem Kellner/der Kellnerin einen schönen Abend.

Unter WWEU1401 finden Sie Zusatzübungen zum Thema der Unit.

1 Answer the following questions.

1 Why have American teenagers begun to outsource homework? (2 reasons)
2 What does Sawati Patnaik's work usually involve? (4 things)
3 What difficulties are there for the Indian tutors? (2 things)

Outsourcing homework to India

Six days a week in the early hours of the morning, Saswati Patnaik logs into her home computer. Patnaik is a tutor for a Bangalore company called TutorVista and she gets up early to help Western high school students write homework assignments.

Outsourcing started as a way for Western companies to reduce their costs by moving their work to cheaper locations in poorer countries. Hundreds of US businesses regularly outsource work to India.

But now a growing number of individual Americans are outsourcing homework. For $99 a month, they can get unlimited help with English, maths or science from Patnaik or one of her 1,500 fellow tutors at TutorVista.

The economic problems in the USA mean that American families prefer to spend their money on education, rather than goods or holidays. 'More Americans feel that education is the only thing that can help them to stay competitive in this world,' says Krishnan Ganesh, CEO and founder of TutorVista. The service is so popular that TutorVista is adding another 1,500 teachers across India in the next few weeks.

On this particular morning, Patnaik is working with students from Atlanta and New Jersey. She logs into the TutorVista portal, using webchat to greet her student. 'Hello, Brittney,' she says. Her student responds immediately. A polite sentence or two later, the tutor asks, 'How may I help you today?'

The ninth grade student is going to have a test on a famous American novel about the American Civil War, Stephen Crane's *The Red Badge of Courage*. The tutor and student discuss the novel and its characters. Patnaik asks Brittney several questions. She writes the themes in the novel on the digital pad and they discuss them as the words show up on their computers.

Many different types of person work for companies like TutorVista. Among the Indian tutors working for TutorVista are new university graduates who need a job, stay-at-home mothers, retired professionals and those who cannot go out to work because of an illness or disability.

Tutors like Patnaik say some of the students are very good, but many do not work hard enough. 'American kids don't have to deal with the kind of academic pressure that Indian kids have at school and at home,' said Patnaik, who has been tutoring for more than two years.

Older teachers face a culture shock when the kids they are tutoring call them by their first names or criticise them openly. In India, teachers are rarely criticised and always respectfully addressed as 'Ma'am' or 'Sir'.

http://www.watoday.com.au/world/outsourcing-homework-to-india-20100409-ryh3.html#ixzz1UQLjg7Hp (420 words)

Going green

15

1 Warm-up

a Read the newspaper headlines about environmental issues and match them to the most suitable photographs. There are more headlines than you need.

a) New record in CO_2 emissions

b) Arctic environment on thin ice

c) *– Amazon forests protected –*

d) Biofuels create a food crisis

e) EU fishing quotas 'not sustainable'

f) EU exports electronic waste to poor countries

g) World's biggest windfarm goes ahead

h) **Electric car sales rise**

i) *Meltdown at nuclear power plant*

1

2

3

4

5

6

b How do the headlines make you feel? Use the words in the box to discuss your feelings with a partner.

afraid • angry • bored • hopeful • optimistic • pessimistic • uninterested • worried

When I read the headline about the rise in electric car sales, I feel hopeful that we can change things.

3/13

HOME ABOUT ACADEMIC LIFE ADMISSIONS NEWS & EVENTS ATHLETICS GIVING OPPORTUNITIES ALUMNI PARENTS

contact us directories

ACADEMIC LIFE

Everyday heroes: Rudy Sanchez, teen environmental educator

Rudy Sanchez was just your average shy teenager. He was starting 10th grade at his L.A. high school and he was wondering what courses to take. One of those courses changed his life.

Back in those days, Rudy felt negative about 'green' issues: 'When I heard about anything environmental, it was always the negative issues, like: "All these polar bears are dying; the Earth is getting warmer; we have to go buy these expensive solar panels for our roofs." I was never shown a real solution, one that I could apply.'

So Rudy didn't expect much when he took a course called Green Ambassadors. 'I wasn't excited about taking that class to start off. Back then, being 'green' was negative to me, so I didn't want to take a whole class on negativity basically.'

What Rudy learned in that course changed his mind: 'We started off with systems thinking – how are things connected – and we learned it through composting. So Green Ambassadors changed my perspective. Environmentalism went from being a negative movement to being something positive.'

Rudy soon found out that the course wasn't just about the environment: 'They related it to politics and to education and how the community works. It's not just about the environment. It's about living sustainably.'

For Rudy, Green Ambassadors brought him 'out of his shell' and turned him into a teen environmental leader. Before long, Rudy was working locally, nationally and even internationally to turn more teenagers into environmental activists and educators.

At the moment, Rudy is involved with the Plastics Are Forever International Youth Summit. 'I shot a video during the summer on how to give a presentation, so we can empower other students to take action in their community,' says Rudy.

Another project that Rudy is working on is Solar the Sign. The Hollywood sign is a big landmark in Los Angeles and Rudy's group wants to make it eco-friendly: 'Everyone knows the Hollywood sign. What if we use solar panels to power it? What if we make this huge iconic thing a sustainable image, so that people think of a sustainable future when they see it?'

At first, public speaking was difficult for Rudy because of his shyness: 'I wasn't happy at first, but then once I got up there on the stage, I saw that people wanted to hear what I wanted to say.'

Why does Rudy do it? 'I feel that there are so many different solutions out there. Many times you hear a lot of the negative side and I'm trying to offer a "We can do it" approach.'

Anyone can get involved in environmental activism. As Rudy says, 'It doesn't just have to be through public speaking. If you love film, go make a film that promotes something green. If you're into fashion, make your own fashion from recycled material or organic material. We can each be part of the solution and still do what we love to do.'

(495 words)

7 Green Our School!

Students in year 11 of Parkdale High School in Melbourne, Australia are launching a Green Our School campaign. Look at the home page of their website and match the twelve actions (a–l) to the four areas (1–4).

Example: 1c, ...

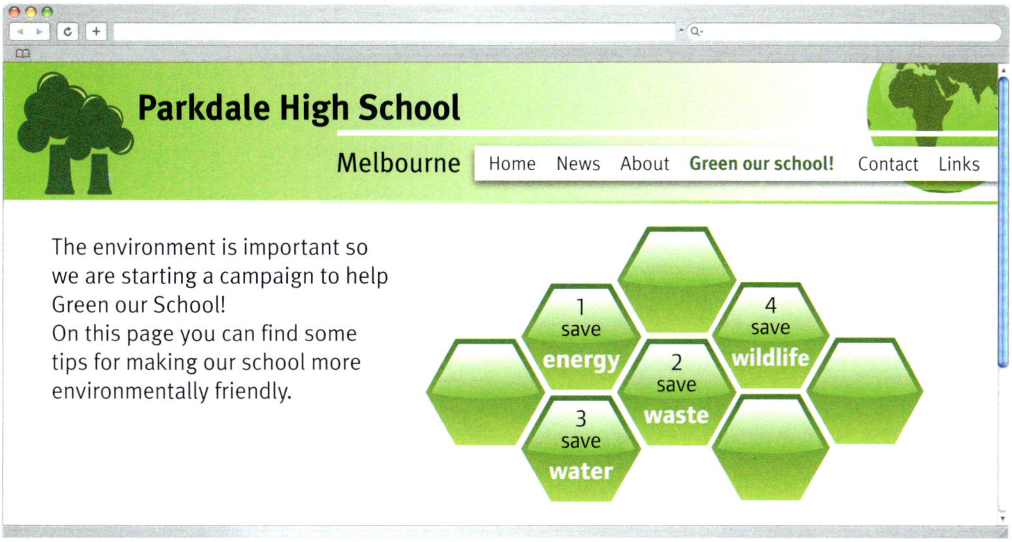

a Build a compost bin for food waste.
b Install rainwater tanks for the toilets, etc.
c Install solar panels and solar hot water.
d Plant more trees in the school grounds.
e Recycle old printer cartridges.
f Replace hard surfaces with grass.
g Bring snacks in reusable containers.
h Switch off the lights when you leave the room.
i Cycle or walk to school, don't drive.
j Re-use paper that is only printed on one side.
k Turn off mobile phones in class.
l Don't buy bottled water or soft drinks.

8 Group project

Work in a group. You're going to plan a Green Our School campaign for your own school.

1 Identify what positive actions your school has already taken. Start with the list from exercise 7, then think of other ideas.
2 Decide what additional actions your school could take. Think of as many ideas as you can.
3 Present your ideas to the class.

We've already installed solar panels, …

We could build a compost bin, …

9 Writing an email

Write an email to your Australian friend about the Green Our School campaign at your school. Describe what you are going to do and how you feel about the campaign. Are you optimistic about its success or pessimistic? Write about 150 words.

GRAMMAR

Revision of tenses

Zeitform	wird gebildet mit …	wird verwendet für …
Simple present	Grundform (+ -s nach *he/she/it*)	gleich bleibende Zustände, regelmäßige Vorgänge
Rudy **lives** in the USA.		
Present progressive	*am/is/are* + *-ing*-Form	vorübergehende Vorgänge
Beispiel: He **is working** on a new project at the moment.		
Simple past	Grundform + *-ed*	abgeschlossene Vorgänge
They **learned** about systems thinking last semester.		
Past progressive	*was/were* + *-ing*-Form	Vorgänge, die in der Vergangenheit andauerten
We realized that we **were wasting** energy.		
Present perfect	*have/has* + Partizip Perfekt (3. Form)	Vorgänge, die irgendwann einmal stattgefunden haben oder bis in die Gegenwart andauern
Our school **has installed** solar panels.		
Past perfect	*had* + Partizip Perfekt (3. Form)	Vorgänge, die bereits abgeschlossen waren, bevor ein 2. Vorgang begann
Once he **had started**, Rudy found public speaking easy.		
***will* future**	*will* + Grundform	Vorhersagen und spontane Entscheidungen, Angebote und Versprechen
Rudy's story **will help** other shy students.		
***going to* future**	*am/is/are* + *going to* + Grundform	feste Pläne und Absichten
We **are going to reduce** our waste.		

10 **Writing about the present**

Complete the text with the simple present or the present progressive of the verbs in brackets.

Experts often *warn* (warn)[1] that the Earth's climate … (change)[2]. CO_2 emissions … (be)[3] the main cause of climate change, they … (say)[4]. Nowadays, most developed countries … (try)[5] to reduce their CO_2 emissions, but most of them … (make)[6] slow progress at the moment. European countries … (spend)[7] billions of euros on wind farms, etc., but at the same time we … (buy)[8] more goods from poorer countries. Industry there produces a lot of CO_2 so some critics … (argue)[9] that we … just … (export)[10] our CO_2 emissions!

11 **Writing about the past**

Choose the correct forms (simple past or present perfect) to complete the text.

Camford United goes green

By our reporter Tim Jones

Camford United Football Club *decide/has decided*[1] to 'go green'. In a meeting last week, the committee *discussed/has discussed*[2] what actions to take.

At the meeting, Club Chairperson Anita Rowan *said/has said*[3]: 'Last year we *installed/have installed*[4] solar panels on the roof of the club house. Since then, many club members *asked/have asked*[5] us to do more to protect the environment. Now we *responded/have responded*[6] to their requests.'

At the meeting, the committee *agreed/has agreed*[7] to install rainwater tanks to save water and *looked/has looked*[8] at ways to reduce waste. Work on 'greening' the club *already began/has already begun*[9]. Since the meeting, maintenance manager Bob Carr *put/has put*[10] recycling bins in the car park. On Monday, students from Camford High School *planted/have planted*[11] 100 trees at the club. Local shop owners *paid/have paid*[12] for the trees.

When we *interviewed/have interviewed*[13] her, Camford Mayor Gina Jenkins *commented/has commented*[14]: 'I'm really pleased that the football club *made/has made*[15] this decision last week.'

12 **Talking about the future**

Complete the dialogue with the *going to* future or *will* future of the verbs in brackets.

Emma	Chloe, are you *going to come* (come)[1] to the disco with me tonight? My dad … (pick)[2] you up, if you like.
Chloe	Sorry, I can't. I … (go)[3] to the Green Ambassadors meeting instead.
Emma	What? You … (sit)[4] in a boring old meeting all evening? Are you crazy? Brad … (probably / be)[5] at the disco, and I know you like him.
Chloe	Umm, actually, Brad … (come)[6] to the meeting with me. So is his friend, Zack.
Emma	Zack … (go)[7] to the Green Ambassadors meeting? He … (be)[8] a Green Ambassador?
Chloe	Yes, that's right. Why?
Emma	Maybe I've changed my mind, Chloe. You're right: green issues are very important. I … (come)[9] to the meeting too. I … (ask)[10] dad to pick you up, if you like.
Chloe	No, thanks. Brad, Zack and I … (ride)[11] our bikes to the meeting. That's better than making an unnecessary car trip.

13 **Past, present and future**

Describe how attitudes to the environment have changed (saving energy, reducing waste, etc.). Write three sentences about:

- how people used to behave
- how they behave now
- how they will behave in the future.

1 First day at school

Discuss with a partner. What do you remember about your first day at vocational school? How did you feel? What did you do?

2 Understanding the text

Read the advice and then match the headings a–j to the most suitable paragraphs.

Tips for surviving your first day at work
by Amanda Evans

Here are just a few tips for getting through the first day at a new job.

1 Have a good night's sleep, get up nice and early and eat a proper breakfast. That's the best preparation to kick-start your first day.
2 There's nothing worse than being 15 minutes late on your first day and blaming it on the traffic is not going to make a very good first impression. This will set a bad precedent for the rest of your time with the company.
3 It's important to find out where you need to go on your first day. If there is an induction course, it may not be in your usual office. Also, make sure you know how to get to work – which train should you catch or which route will you take?
4 You'll need to bring your tax and bank account details so you can get paid for all the hard work you're going to do.
5 It may be difficult to remember everyone's names and roles at the beginning, but try to take note of some of the key people in the office – you may have to call upon them for help later on!
6 Your supervisor or manager may have discussed your duties during the interview, but it is a good idea to make sure what is expected of you on a daily basis.
7 A lot of time may be spent filling out paperwork and familiarising yourself with office procedures and policies – don't expect to do much real work on the first day.
8 It's a good idea to write everything down – there's nothing worse than forgetting where things are or what you're supposed to be doing.
9 Find out whether it's acceptable to have a chat across the office or help yourself to the chocolate biscuits in the kitchen.
10 If you're lazy and take a long lunch break on day one, you'll never get into a constructive work routine.

a Be in the right place
b Bring relevant documentation
c Don't start with bad habits
d Get the day off to a good start
e Keep note
f Know your rights and responsibilities
g Watch your colleagues and follow their example
h Remember names
i Set realistic expectations
j Turn up on time!

3/15 V4

3 Listening: first day blues

Watch or listen to the four speakers. What advice from the text didn't they follow?

Example: *1 – didn't have a good night's sleep, ...*

4 Workplace vocabulary

Match the words to the definitions. All of the words are used in the text.

Example: *1 k – supervisor*

1	This is the person who tells you what work to do.	a	acceptable
2	You should do this before you start a task.	b	bank account
3	This is what others think of you.	c	constructive
4	This is information or training which helps you to do a new job.	d	impression
5	You need one of these to put your salary in.	e	induction
6	It is another word for 'important'.	f	key
7	This is a general word for forms and official documents.	g	paperwork
8	This is the way something is supposed to be done.	h	policy
9	This is a set of rules about how to behave, what to do, etc.	i	preparation
10	Your behaviour at work has to be this, or you will be in trouble!	j	procedure
11	If you want to get work done, you need this kind of attitude.	k	supervisor

5 Words in context

Complete the sentences with words from exercise 3.

1 I'm sorry, Steve, but this work is not *acceptable*. Please do it again.
2 If you don't like ..., you should not have chosen an office job.
3 What is the correct ... for dealing with complaints from customers?
4 Before you start your job, we will give you an ... course to teach you what you need to know.
5 It is a good idea to write down ... information so that you do not forget it.
6 The company has a strict ... about mobile phones in the workplace. Basically, you can't use them.
7 We may have different ideas, but we should discuss them in a ... way. There is no point in being negative.
8 Giving a presentation may seem a difficult task, but it is a lot easier if you do enough ....

6 It's your turn

Write a text advising British students what to do on their first day at vocational school/ college or work experience. Try to think of 8–10 tips to give them.

Listening

3/16 **1** **Today's programme 'Wild World' on the British radio station 'ABC FM' is about how skiing damages the environment. Listen to the programme and complete the summary below. You will listen to the programme twice and can make notes while listening.**

1 Ski lovers are drawn to alpine skiing by the unspoilt nature there: the fresh mountain air, … . Added to this is the healthy exercise.
2 However skiing is … which means a lot of infrastructure.
3 That has a negative impact on …
4 For example, if you compare the numbers of tourists in Austria in winter and in summer …
5 Where the skiing takes place is also important. The alpine environment …
6 Winter tourism uses more energy:
– …
– …
– …
7 However, we don't have to stop skiing completely. We can reduce the negative effects of ski tourism if we …
– …
– …
– …
8 Ski resorts can also become more environmentally-friendly by …
9 That has the advantage that …

3/17 **2** **Your very old neighbour comes from America. Her German is not very good so she likes to use English for important matters. Her German husband has always looked after her official forms and documents but unfortunately he died recently. She is applying for a place in supported accommodation (*eine betreute Wohnung*) and has asked you to help her with the application form. Listen to your neighbour and complete the form for her.**

Name, Vorname:	*Wilkins, Elsie May*
Geburtsdatum:	…
Angehörige (Name, Verwandschaft, Wohnort):	
1 …	
2 …	
Medizinische Probleme:	…
1-Zi. Wohnung ☐	2-Zi. Wohnung ☐
Garten ☐	Garage ☐
Haustiere (bitte auflisten):	…
Wünsche betreffs Wohnung:	…

Writing

3 Choose one of the tasks below. Write at least 150 words.

a Continue the story and give it a title.

It was a nice, sunny day so I went for a walk in the park. A young man on a bike rode past me – he was riding very fast. A 50-euro note fell out of his jeans pocket and landed on the path at my feet. 'Hey! Come back! You've dropped your money!' I called out. But he was already far away and didn't hear me …

b Write an email.

A school in England is starting a project about career perspectives for European teenagers. A 17-year-old student, Matt Price, has written to your school. He would like to know what subjects you are learning, if you have already done a work placement and what you expect from your future workplace.

Grammar

4 Al Gore is an American politician, businessman and environmentalist. Use the information below to write sentences in English about his life.

- 1948 in Washington geboren
- hat vier Kinder
- engagiert sich für die Umwelt seit die 70en
- war von 1993 bis 2001 der Vizepräsident der Vereinigten Staaten
- seit 2004 Vorsitzender der Investmentfirma *Generation Investment Management*
- machte 2006 der Film ‚Eine unbequeme Wahrheit' (*An Inconvenient Truth*)
- bekam 2007 der Friedensnobelpreis (*Nobel Peace Prize*)
- leitet das *Climate Reality Project*, die über 5 Millionen Mitglieder weltweit hat
- möchte in Zukunft sich weiter mit dem Thema Umwelt beschäftigen

5 Compare travelling by bus with travelling by car using the following adjectives: expensive, environmentally friendly, easy. Write four sentences using different comparative forms.

Revision

Modal verbs (▶ S. 82, 202)

1 **Complete these sentences with a suitable modal verb to replace the German verb.**

1 People *könnten* feel pessimistic when they read the newspaper headlines.
2 You *solltest* talk about possible solutions, not just about problems all the time.
3 They *dürfen nicht* cut down those trees unless they plant new ones.
4 Environmentalists say that we *müssen* change our way of life.
5 We *sollen* start a 'Green Our School' campaign.
6 Web users *können nicht* post a comment on the school's website unless they are students at the school.
7 Green Ambassadors *könnte nicht* be the right course for every student.
8 You *müssen nicht* get up on the stage and talk to the audience.
9 Many students *könnten* cycle to school instead of driving.
10 We *sollten nicht* buy bottled water because we *können* drink tap water.

2 **Rewrite the sentences using the phrases in brackets. Change the tense and use substitutes for the modal verbs as necessary.**

1 We can prove the link between CO_2 and climate change. (In the future, …)
2 The school must find ways to reduce waste. (In the last three years, …)
3 We must find ways to live sustainably. (In the future, …)
4 They may (*dürfen*) launch a campaign at their school. (Two years ago, …)
5 This industry need not find ways to save water. (Until now, …)
6 We need not use fossil fuels. (When power is 100 % renewable, …)
7 Perhaps humans can reverse climate change. (… in 100 years' time)
8 They may not (*dürfen nicht*) attend the youth summit. (Last year, …)
9 People cannot understand our attitude to the environment. (Future generations …)
10 Industrialized countries cannot predict the consequences of their actions. (In the 19th century, …)

3 **You are writing tips for a Green Ambassadors website. Suggest actions that young people *can, might, should, must, need not* or *must not* take.**

Example: drive to school – *Students shouldn't drive to school.*

1 get involved in environmental activism
2 drive to school
3 save water and energy
4 buy a wind turbine
5 install solar panels
6 build a compost bin
7 be negative about green issues
8 throw away plastic bags
9 make a film about the environment
10 leave the lights on in an empty classroom

File 1: Unit 1, World of Work, Exercise 3

Partner A

1 You need to find the following items at points A-D on the map below.

vending machine

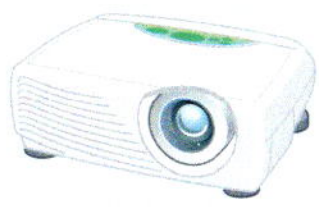
video projector

pot plant

wi-fi modem

Start at the ground floor entrance. Tell your partner how to get to point A. Your partner tells you which object is there. Then, explain how to get from point A to point B, then B to C and finally C to D. At each point, your partner tells you which object you find there.

2 Switch roles with your partner. Start at point D. Follow your partner's directions until he/she finds all the objects on the map below.

Ground floor

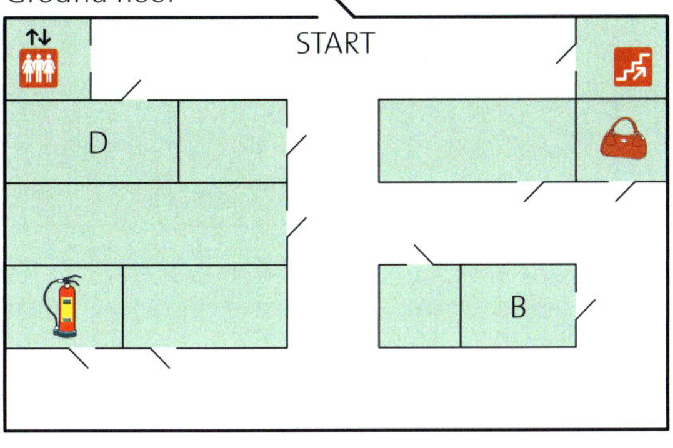

First floor

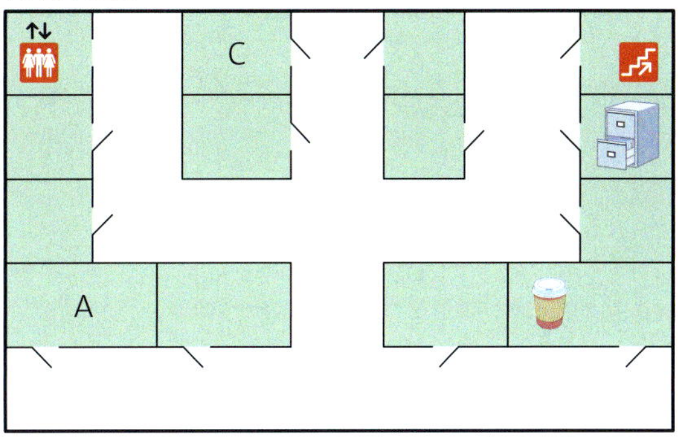

fire extinguisher

lost purse

cup of coffee

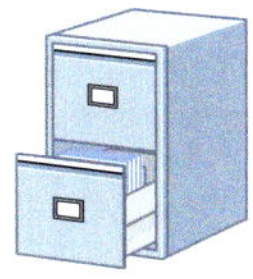
filing cabinet

Explaining the way

Go straight on down the hall.
Go to the end of the hall and turn right/left.
Take the first/second right/left.
It's on your right/left.
It's the first/second/third/last door on your right/left.
It's at the end of the hall.
Take the lift/stairs to the ground/first floor.

File 2: Unit 2, Exercise 1

Partner A

Look at Barack Obama's family tree. It is quite unusual for a US president. Ask your partner questions to get the missing information. The language in the boxes below may help you.

aunt • brother • daughter • father • grandmother • great-grandmother • half-sister • husband • mother • sister • son • stepmother • uncle • wife

What is his mother's/father's/etc. name?
Where is/was … from?
When was … born?

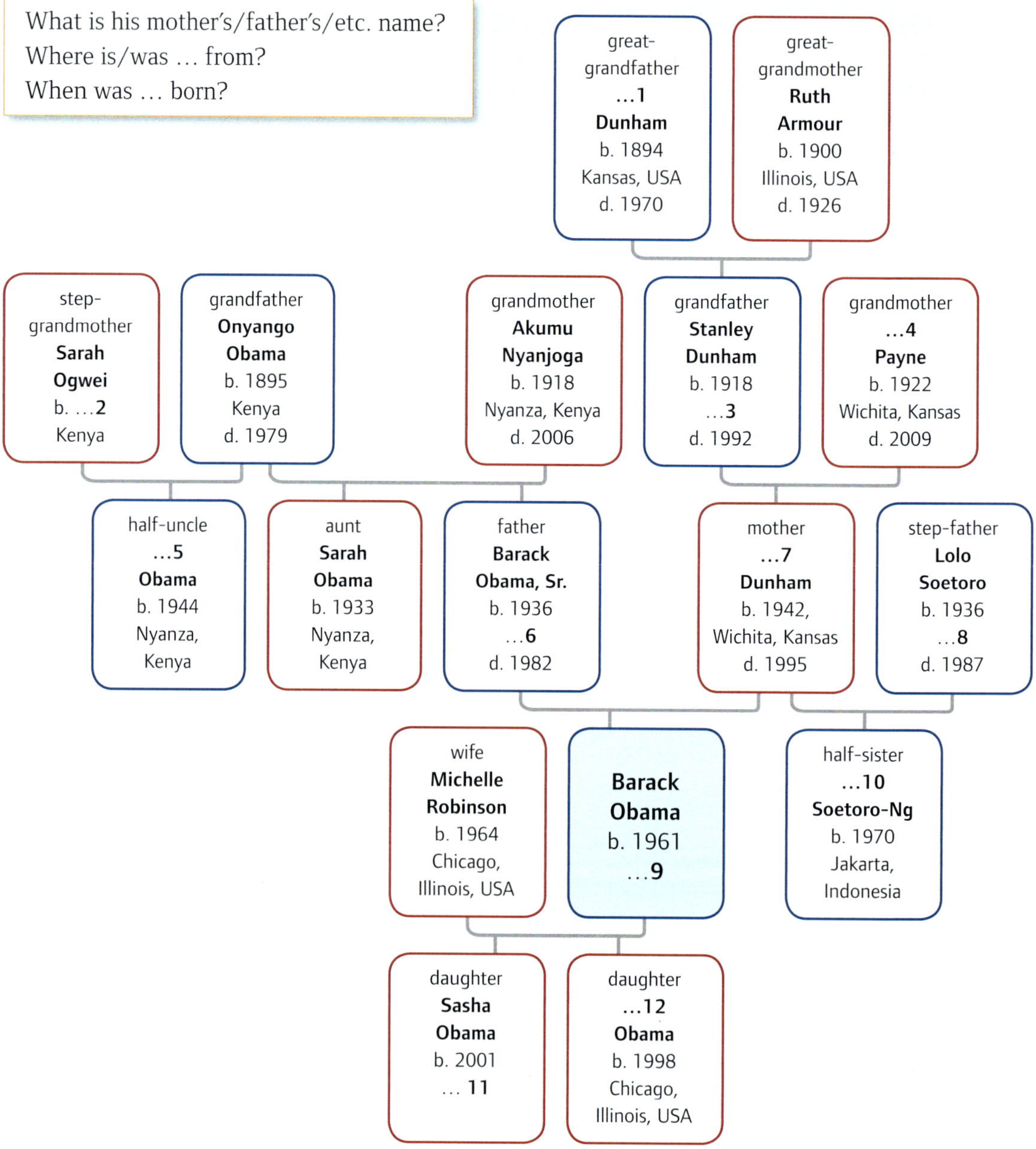

File 3: Unit 7, Exercise 13

Partner A

You are trying to decide what to do in the year after school.

You like …
… working on the computer and making websites.
… films.

You dislike …
… having your work constantly checked by a boss.

You have …
… a rich uncle you can ask for money.

Asking for advice
Do you have any suggestions/ recommendations/advice for me?
What should I do?

Giving advice
Maybe you should (become a police officer) …
I think you should …
Why don't you … ?

File 4: Unit 5, World of Work, Exercise 5 b

Partner A

You are a ticket agent. A customer wants to buy a ticket to Mannheim. Use the details below and the language you have learned on page 55 to act out a dialogue.

- Train leaves at 14.19, arrives at 16.54
- Change trains in Stuttgart
- Costs 45 euros
- Don't need a reservation

File 5: Unit 8, Exercise 3d

Partner A

a **Read the information below and make sure you understand everything. When you are ready, tell Partner B the story. Partner B will take notes. Be prepared to explain if Partner B does not understand something.**

Information: Leena Suominnen is from Finland. She is 25 years old. She was born in Helsinki but lives in Turku now. Leena works in the telecommunications industry. Her hobbies are hiking and watching Formula 1 racing. Her favourite racing star is Mika Häkkinen.

A week before the last race, Leena tried to get tickets online for the Grand Stand at the race track in Nürburgring. She was really disappointed when she got a message saying all the tickets were sold. Then she saw a link on the website which said: "Competition: Your chance to stand in the pits." She entered the competition and won a place in the pits. Leena was really excited because she could meet Mika and the other drivers.

b **Now listen to Partner B's story and make notes. Ask if you don't understand something.**

File 6: Unit 6, How to read effectively

Tim Raue

Cooking is like war

Anyone who knew Tim Raue as a teenager could never have guessed he would become one of the big names in the Berlin restaurant scene. Today, the ghetto kid who hated school and fought in one of the city's toughest gangs, is top of the gourmet league. In his auto-biography, he describes his development from a boy with no future into a man who is doing his dream job.

Early life

Tim Raue was born in 1974 in Kreuzberg, one of the poorest parts of Berlin. His parents divorced when he was three. First, the boy lived with his mother then, at the age of nine, he moved to Stuttgart to live with his father, who beat him. "The people who should have loved and supported me never gave me any love or support," says Raue. At the age of 13, he was so depressed that he tried to commit suicide.

Education

Raue attended 10 schools in 11 years. During his first school years, he was bullied and beaten up; later he became the bully. "I needed a way to let off steam, a way to get rid of all the frustration and humiliation I experienced at home," he explains.

Respect!

During his later years at school, Tim Raue spent most of his time on the streets. He joined "36 Boys", one of the worst gangs in Berlin. He was the only German boy in the gang but the Turkish, Greek and Arab members accepted him because he was a such a vicious fighter. "The gang was my family," he says. "I got a lot of respect and I knew that I could trust the other members of the gang."

A chance

The turning point in Raue's life came when he began to train as a cook. Even though he worked harder and faster than the others in the kitchen, his final mark was 4-. Despite this, he found a job in a Berlin hotel. His girlfriend, Marie-Anne, who he met while training, was the restaurant manager. "She believed in me right from the start and gave me a lot of support," he says. He was promoted quickly and built up his reputation. Together with Marie-Anne, who is now his wife, he opened his own restaurant in 2010.

Cooking is like war

"My past has made me what I am," he says."My childhood taught me self-reliance and my time with the gang helped me develop stamina. Cooking is like war, you have to be able to keep going and focus on what you're doing in order to win," he explains. Tim Raue's past has also made him determined to help others. "Marie-Anne and I employ kids from difficult social backgrounds in service or in the kitchen. We want to give them a chance, too," he says.

461 words, based on material from TV documentary, *Kämpfernaturen – Wenn Krisen stark machen* (VOX, 12.11.2011). Extra information from, Tim Raue: "Ich weiß, Was Hunger ist. Von der Straßengang in die Sterneküche"

File 7: Unit 8, Exercise 3d

Partner B

a Listen to Partner A's story and make notes. Ask if you don't understand something.

b Read the information below and make sure you understand everything. When you are ready, tell Partner A the story. Partner A will take notes. Be prepared to explain if Partner A does not understand something.

Information: Annick Hautefeuille is from France. She is 22 years old. She was born in Lyon but lives in Berlin now. Annick works in the pharmaceutical industry. Her hobbies are swimming and going to rock concerts. Her favourite performer is Rihanna.

A few weeks ago, Annick tried to get tickets for Rihanna's concert in the O2. The tickets were all sold out so she posted a request for a ticket on Rihanna's fan club forum. No-one had a ticket for her, but a guy called Abdi said if Annick met him at Warschauer Brücke, he could give her a backstage pass. Annick didn't want to go alone to meet a stranger so she took her friend Mireille with her. Abdi was really nice and got them both backstage passes.

File 8: Unit 9, World of Work, Exercise 4

Partner A

Use the diary below to arrange an appointment with Mr Barber.

Monday	Tuesday	Wednesday	Thursday	Friday
10 a.m. Appointment with sales team	*3 p.m. Interview for new staff*	*11 a.m. Call Jim in Paris*	*Meeting with Mr Jones all day*	*12 p.m. Lunch meeting with Sarah*

File 9: Unit 7, Exercise 13

Partner C

You are trying to decide what to do in the year after school.

You like …
… machines.
… nature/the outdoors.

You dislike …
… doing the same thing every day.

You have …
… excellent grades in school.

Asking for advice
Do you have any suggestions/recommendations/advice for me?
What should I do?

Giving advice
Maybe you should (become a police officer) …
I think you should …
Why don't you … ?

File 10: Unit 1, World of Work, Exercise 3

Partner B

1 Start at the ground floor entrance on the map below. Follow your partner's directions. Tell your partner what object is in each room he/she directs you to.

2 Now, you need to find the following items at points E-H on the map below.

fire extinguisher lost purse cup of coffee filing cabinet

Start at where your partner finds his/her last object. From there, tell your partner how to get to point E. Your partner tells you which object is there. Then, explain how to get from point E to point F, then F to G and finally G to H. At each point, your partner tells you which object you find there.

vending machine video projector pot plant wi-fi modem

Explaining the way
Go straight on down the hall.
Go to the end of the hall and turn right/left.
Take the first/second right/left.
It's on your right/left.
It's the first/second/third/last door on your right/left.
It's at the end of the hall.
Take the lift/stairs to the ground/first floor.

File 11: Unit 7, Exercise 13

Partner B

You are trying to decide what to do in the year after school.

You like …
… working in teams with other people your age.
… modern music.

You dislike …
… sitting at a desk all day.

You have …
… a mother who works for Lufthansa.
You can fly anywhere in Europe for free.

Asking for advice
Do you have any suggestions/ recommendations/advice for me?
What should I do?

Giving advice
Maybe you should (become a police officer) …
I think you should …
Why don't you … ?

File 12: Unit 5, World of Work, Exercise 5 b

Partner B

You want to buy a ticket to Mannheim and so you ask the ticket agent for help. Use the details below and the language you have learned on page 55 to act out a dialogue.

Ask:
- when the train goes and when it arrives
- if you have to change
- how much it costs
- if you need a reservation

File 13: Unit 9, World of Work, Exercise 4

Partner B

Use the diary below to arrange an appointment with Mr Barber.

Monday	Tuesday	Wednesday	Thursday	Friday
2 p.m. Dentist appointment	*9 a.m. Marketing meeting* *12.30 p.m. Lunch with Olivia*	*10 a.m. Team meeting*	*3 p.m. Training course*	*Holiday*

File 14: Unit 2, Exercise 1

Partner B

Look at Barack Obama's family tree. It is quite unusual for a US president. Ask your partner questions to get the missing information. The language in the boxes below may help you.

aunt • brother • daughter • father • grandmother • great-grandmother • half-sister • husband • mother • sister • son • stepmother • uncle • wife

What is his mother's/father's/etc. name?
Where is/was … from?
When was … born?

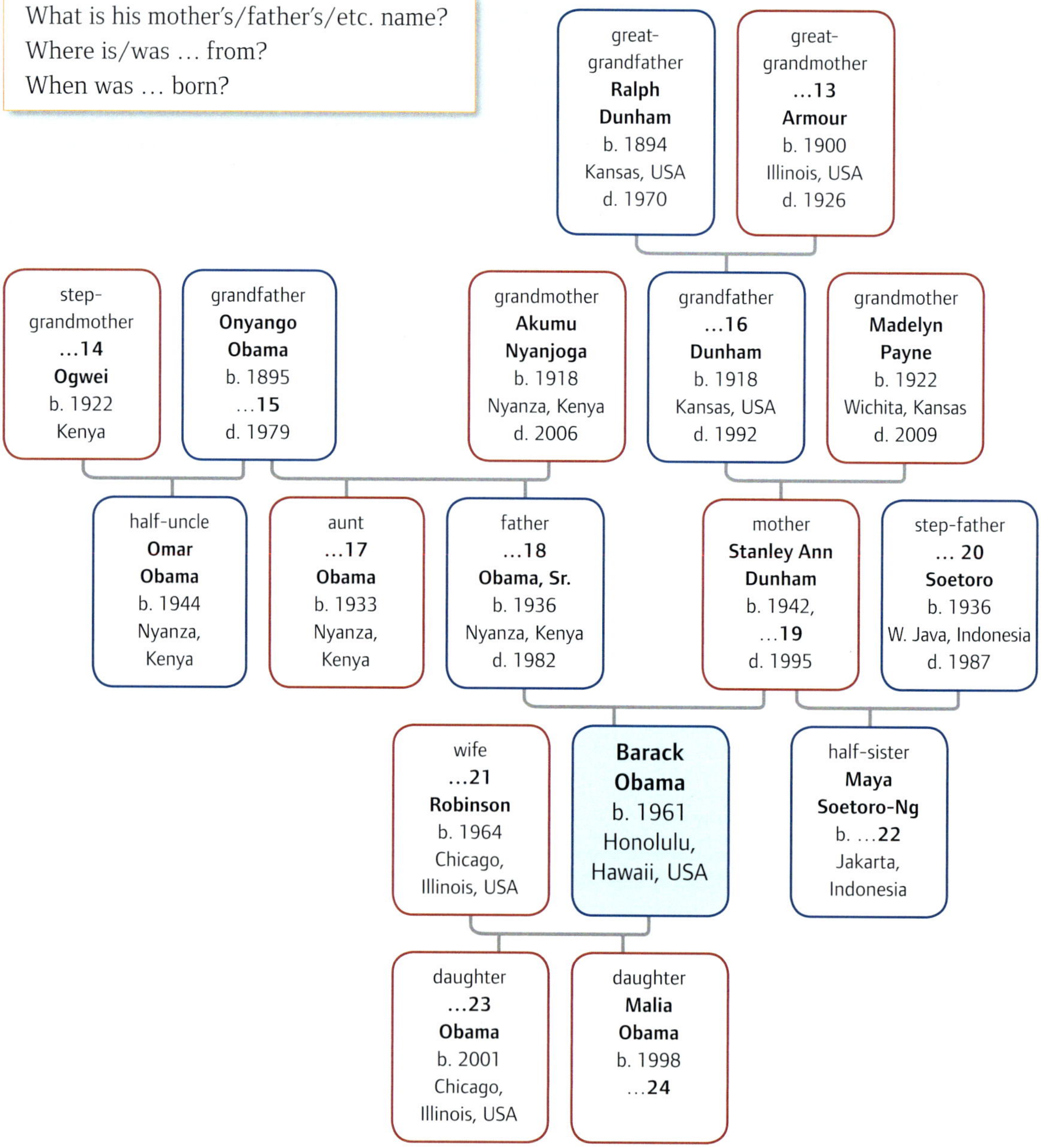

Further reading

Unit 1

English – the global language

A There are over 7 billion people in the world. About 400 million speak English as their native language and, according to surveys, over 1 billion people use English as a second language.

B Talking about native speakers, English is the third most-spoken language in the world after Mandarin Chinese and Spanish. However, when we combine the numbers of native speakers and non-native speakers, English probably moves into first place as the most-spoken global language.

C English is definitely the top language for exchanging information on the internet where it is used more than all the other languages combined.

D Of course, English varies in different parts of the world. Take vocabulary, for example. What the British call *petrol* is called *gas* in the United States and a British *mobile* is a *cell phone* there. The list of UK/USA differences is very long. There are also vocabulary differences in different regions in the same country. When someone in London eats a *bread roll*, people in north-west England eat a *cob*. Most of the English-speaking world writes *colour, humour, flavour, etc.* but the United States spells these words without the *u*.

E Last but not least, as with every language, English pronunciation differs from region to region. It's especially important for learners of English to get used to different pronunciations so try to listen to as much English as possible.

(224 words)

1 Understanding the text

Answer these questions based on the text.

1 How many people speak English as their native language globally? How many non-native speakers are there?
2 When you add native speakers and non-native speakers together, how important is English?
3 How much English is used on the internet?
4 What parts of the language change when you are in different places?
5 Why should learners try to listen to spoken English?

2 Working with words

Find a word or phrase in the text with a similar meaning.

1 mother tongue (Section A)
2 worldwide (Section B)
3 communicating (Section C)
4 areas (Section D)
5 how someone speaks (Section E)

Unit 2

Barack Obama's roots

'What is a family?' This is one of the questions Barack Obama asked himself on his first visit to Kenya.

The 44th president of the United States comes from an African ethnic group. His father was born into a Kenyan tribe called the Luo. When Obama's parents divorced, his father went back to Kenya. Father and son only saw each other a few times after that. Obama Senior died in 1983. Barack Obama decided to visit his father's homeland in 1987.

One of the highlights of the trip was a visit to his paternal grandmother, Akumu. When she welcomed Barack and his half-sister, Auma into her small house, she said in her own language that she had dreamed about this day – the day when she would finally meet the son of her son.

Inside the house, Barack looked at the family photos. One photo showed a young woman with a child on her lap and a young girl standing beside her. 'This is our grandmother,' Auma explained. 'The girl is our aunt Sarah and the baby is our father.'

Barack describes his meeting with his grandmother as a joyful experience. But, when they were alone together, grandmother and grandson realised they could not communicate. Later, Auma told Barack that their grandmother was sad that she could not talk directly to her grandson. Barack explained that he would like to learn Luo, but he was too busy. 'She understands that,' Auma replied, 'but she also says that a man should never be too busy to know his own people.'

During the trip, Barack Obama paid an emotional visit to the graves of his biological father and paternal grandfather. 'For a long time I sat between the two graves and wept,' he said. 'I saw that my life in America was connected with this small plot of earth an ocean away.'

309 words, abridged and adapted from Barack Obama: *Dreams from My Father* (New York, 2004)

1 Understanding the text

Answer these questions on the text.

1 What is the connection between Barack Obama and Kenya?
2 Why was Obama's visit to his grandmother important for her?
3 What piece of good advice does Obama's grandmother give him?
4 How did Barack Obama feel when he visited the graves of his father and grandfather?

2 Working with words

Find words and phrases in the text to match the definitions below.

1 a group made up of parents, children and their relations
2 your father's mother
3 a girl or woman who has either the same father or the same mother as you
4 the sister of your mum or dad
5 someone's real dad

Unit 3

The worst generation ever?

Are young people out of control? Here are some famous quotations:

'Young people no longer respect their parents. They are rude and impatient. They frequently spend time in pubs and have no self-control.'

'What is happening to our young people? They have no respect for older people, they don't obey their parents. They ignore the law.'

'The young people of today think about nothing except themselves. They have no respect for parents or old age.'

Are these criticisms a sign of a problem with young people today? Are today's teenagers really worse than ever before?

Probably not. The first quotation is on the wall of a 6,000-year-old Egyptian tomb; the second comes from the Greek philosopher Plato, 2,300 years ago; the third comes from a religious leader, Peter the Hermit, in AD 1274.

It seems that one thing never changes: adults always think that young people are worse than any previous generation. When today's teenagers are middle-aged, they may say the same about the teenagers of 2050.

If anything is really worse now than in the past, it is the attitude of adults towards teenagers. The media are partly responsible for this: we often read newspaper headlines like 'Out of control British teens the worst behaved in Europe' (Daily Mail) or 'Gangs are getting younger and more violent' (The Telegraph).

As one 16-year-old said in a recent interview: 'People cross the road to avoid me. It's worst when you're wearing a hoodie. The problem is that people read all this bad stuff in newspapers. They focus on the small minority of teenagers who do bad things, they think we're all like that. It's unfair.'

(274 words)

1 Understanding the text

Choose the best summary of the text.

1 Adults think that young people today behave worse than previous generations, but this is probably not true. Newspapers give young people a negative image and adults are afraid of them.
2 Young people behaved much worse in the past, so adults should not complain about them now. Newspapers give young people a negative image and adults are afraid of them.
3 When today's adults were young, they behaved badly. Now they complain about young people and don't want them to have fun. That is unfair and the newspapers should do something about it.

2 Working with words

Find the opposites of these words and expressions in the text.

1 polite
2 rarely
3 pay attention to
4 everything
5 different
6 best
7 meet
8 majority

Unit 4

Illegal music downloads hurt us all

Who do illegal music downloads hurt? Most people would say 'The artist.' Then again, who cares? Pop stars are rich anyway. What does €0.99 mean to them? Not much. Well, that would be true if only one person in the world downloaded files illegally. However, that isn't the case. Millions download free songs every single day.

For instance, let's take a song from the singer Fergie called 'Big Girls Don't Cry.' Let's say 2.5 million people illegally download that song in one week: that adds up to 2.5 million euros. Now multiply that by 52 weeks. That's a lot of money.

The illegal download doesn't just hurt the artist. Who gets a share in that €0.99? Take a look at this list of people: the music recording company; the CD case manufacturer; the CD cover designer; photographers; lawyers for the artist; promotional companies; truck drivers who deliver CDs to stores; the band manager and staff; the CD manufacturer and staff; music stores.

All these people helped the artist to become famous, and without that money, the artist cannot pay these people.

When you think about it, where does most of the money go? That's right: the companies that our families and friends work for. By downloading that song for free, you take away business from the people that need it the most.

In life everything has a consequence; everything you do affects someone in some way. Music companies also have to raise the price of their music to make up for the lost money, which makes it more expensive for you to buy music. So who does it hurt really? Well, in the end it hurts you. Not to mention that it's a crime. Is it worth it?

It is so much smarter and easier to buy the song for €0.99 from the artists themselves or a legal online store. It helps our economy, it keeps you out of trouble and most of all, it keeps the cost down for all of us.

(333 words)

1 Understanding the text

Complete the sentences in your own words.

1 People think that it is OK to download music illegally because pop stars have …
2 Because so many people download music illegally, the amount of money is …

3 As well as the artist, a lot of other people work to …
4 If you download music for free, you hurt people who …
5 When music companies lose a lot of money because of illegal downloads, they …
6 If you want to download music, you should …

2 **Working with words**

Decide which word does not belong in the group. Say why.

1 artist • music • photographer • pop star • singer • truck driver
2 crime • expensive • famous • illegal • legal • rich
3 affect • care • hurt • pay • song • spend

Unit 5

Famous for being famous

What great things has Paris Hilton done? Why is Ashton Kutcher a million dollar star? How can someone become a 'designer' or get a top role on TV when they have no talent? How can a person who has done nothing special in their lives become a celebrity?

Many celebrities are only famous for being famous, for example, the young women who spend huge amounts of money shopping for shoes and going to parties in exclusive night clubs. They are usually girls from rich backgrounds and their only 'achievement' in life is having a dad who has a lot of money.

Another easy way to become a celebrity is to go out with someone who is already famous. Many film stars, sports personalities and politicians like to be seen with someone beautiful, young and sexy. Of course, if the relationship goes wrong, the public often forget about the new celebrity very quickly.

Nevertheless, while they are 'in', tabloid journalism and the paparazzi give these glamorous people a lot of media coverage. Their fabulous lifestyles and the things they do provide many of us with entertainment and perhaps also allow us to share a dream world which we will never live in.

Or might it be possible for you and me to join the rich and famous and become celebrities?

In 1968, the pop art painter Andy Warhol predicted that, in the future, 'Everyone will be world-famous for 15 minutes.'

There are so many ways an individual might become famous today. With reality shows, talent shows, YouTube and other types of popular culture, almost everyone can become famous for a short period of time. Warhol's 15 minutes of fame is achievable. On the other hand, when you see how so many celebrities suffer with the continual attention they get, it might be healthier to stay out of the spotlight.

(308 words)

1 Understanding the text

Choose the most suitable endings for the statements based on the article.

1 Some celebrities are only well known because …
  a they earn huge amounts of money.
  b reports about them appear regularly in the media.
  c they have roles in popular TV programmes.

2 Many famous people have only got where they are because they …
  a have the right connections.
  b go to places which are 'in'.
  c wear designer clothes and shoes.

3 Many people read reports about celebrities to …
  a learn how to become famous.
  b have something to talk about with other people.
  c pass the time and fantasize about fame.

4 New forms of entertainment and communication …
  a cause suffering to many celebrities.
  b have opened up possibilities for all of us.
  c started to develop in the late 1960s.

2 Working with words

Find words and phrases in the text to match the definitions below.

1 a natural ability to do something well
2 a place which not everyone can get into
3 a thing that someone has done successfully
4 a way of reporting news which is not serious
5 the state of being known and talked about

Unit 6

'The fastest man on no legs'

Oscar Pistorius was born on November 22, 1986 in Sandton, Gauteng, South Africa. He was born without bones in his legs, so doctors had to remove both of his legs below the knee when he was just 11 months old.

When Oscar was a baby, his mother wrote a letter for him to read when he was older. In it she wrote: 'A loser is not the one who runs last in the race, but the one who sits and watches and has never tried to run.'

When he was 17 months old, Oscar received his first pair of artificial legs. He did several sports as a child. They included rugby, water polo and tennis. Then in 2004 he started running and has been running ever since. He competes in sprint races from 100 to 400 metres. 'I'm not disabled,' he says, 'I just don't have any legs.'

Oscar has set many world records and won gold medals at both the Paralympic World Cup and also at the Beijing Paralympic Games in 2008. The media often call him 'the fastest man on no legs'. He competes successfully against able-bodied athletes and hopes to run in the Olympic Games. He can run 100 metres in less than 11 seconds and 400 metres in about 45 seconds.

Oscar runs on special J-shaped 'blades' that are made from carbon fibre. Some people claim that these hi-tech 'cheetah legs' give him an unfair advantage. However, Oscar's real advantage is his positive attitude: 'Some people view themselves as disabled because they have one or two disabilities. But what about the millions and millions of abilities they have? So what if you have a leg or two missing? OK, you might not be able to run and jump but there are so many other things you can do.'

(301 words)

1 Understanding the text

Read the sentences below. Decide whether they are true or false. Correct the false ones.

1 Oscar Pistorius lost his legs in a car accident when he was a baby.
2 Oscar does not think that he has a disability.
3 Oscar can run as fast as sprinters who have two legs.
4 Oscar's artificial legs look just like normal legs.

2 Working with words

Match the words to the definitions. There is one definition too many. Find a word in the text which fits it.

1	remove	a	something which makes you able to do something better than others
2	artificial	b	take part in an activity and try to be better than others
3	sprint	c	not natural, made by humans
4	disabled	d	a short, fast race
5	compete	e	something you can do
6	advantage	f	take away, take off
		g	not able to do something that most people can do

Unit 7

Opportunities for girls and boys

We've all heard of 'Girls' Day'. It's the day, once a year, when schoolgirls can find out what it is like to work in jobs which are traditionally seen as 'men's jobs'.

In Germany, 'Girls' Day' was started in 2001. The aim of the event is to encourage girls to train for employment in natural science, skilled trades and the technical professions. The organizers of 'Girls' Day' hoped to make these areas attractive for female pupils. The project is aimed at girls from 5th grade upwards.

At the events, girls can talk to women who are in 'men's jobs' and ask them questions about their work. They can also find out what to do in order to find a job.

In the first ten years of the project, one million teenage girls attended 'Girls' Day' events throughout Germany and about 100,000 girls went on to do practical training or internships in 'men's jobs'.

The first 'Boys' Day' was held in April 2012. One of the organizers of this event said, 'It is equally important to give boys the chance to try out traditionally female jobs. Areas like teaching and the caring professions should be made more attractive to boys. There are very few male role models in these professions,' he said.

Research shows that boys and girls usually decide on 'typical' male or female subjects when they go on to further education. Girls usually study pedagogical subjects, psychology or English while the boys study computer science, manufacturing and engineering. Then they end up in these male/female professions.

Talking about both projects, a spokesperson for the Federal Minister for Family says, 'We hope that what pupils experience at their 'Day' will encourage them to try something different.'

(289 words)

Adapted and abridged from *Zehn Jahre Girls' Day Nach den Mädchen kommen die Jungs*
http://www.faz.net/aktuell/gesellschaft/familie/zehn-jahre-girls-day-nach-den-maedchen-kommen-die-jungs-1970132.html

1 **Understanding the text**

Match the statements (1–6) to people from the text (a–f). Give reasons for your choice.

1 At the start, I had to convince my colleagues that I could do the job.
2 It's great to see how many young people are willing to take a risk.
3 I've just seen a video about electrical engineers. I'm going to apply for training.
4 I would like to work in the wellness sector.
5 There are other opportunities. It doesn't have to be nursing or a cleaning job.
6 Why shouldn't they train to be childminders if they want to?

a a teenage visitor to 'Girls' Day'
b one of the organizers of 'Girls' Day'
c a woman who works as an mechanic
d one of the organizers of 'Boys' Day'
e a teenage visitor to 'Boys' Day'
f a spokesperson from the Federal Ministry for Family

2 **Working with words**

Use the text to find the English for the following German words.

1 Männerberufe
2 Naturwissenschaft
3 Handwerksberufe
4 eine Lehre
5 ein Praktikum
6 Pflegeberufe

Unit 8

Preparing for work in Europe – Europass

So, you'd like to get experience abroad? You're hoping to study or enrol in a training programme? If you're looking for opportunities in Europe, then you should know about Europass.

Europass is a way of making life easier for learners and workers who want to move around Europe. It started in 2004 when the European Parliament realised that trainers and employers have to be able to understand the qualifications and competences of job-seekers from other EU member states.

Europass helps people list their skills, qualifications and experience in a clear way.

It is made up of five documents as follows:

1 Europass Curriculum Vitae (CV)
2 Europass Language Passport
3 Europass Mobility
4 Europass Certificate Supplement
5 Europass Diploma Supplement

You fill in the first two documents yourself to record your qualifications and language abilities. The other three documents are completed for you if you need them.

For example, **Europass Mobility** might be useful if you are doing any of the following: a work placement in a company abroad; a term abroad as part of a higher education programme; or a voluntary placement in a non-governmental organisation (NGO).

Europass Certificate Supplement is for people who have a vocational education and training award.
Europass Diploma Supplement is for graduates of a higher education institution.

All of the documents are available free of charge.

Anyone who would like to use Europass should start by completing the Europass CV. This is a standard CV format which you can use to present details of your skills and qualifications in a way that everybody can understand.

With Europass, you'll be able to move around Europe easily. What are you waiting for? Find out more about Europass on the internet and get to work on your Europass now!

(291 words)

Information from http://www.europass.ie/europass/what.html and http://europass.cedefop.europa.eu/europass/home/hornav/Introduction.csp

1 **Understanding the text**
Answer these FAQs with information from the text.

1 What is Europass?
2 What are the five Europass documents?
3 Which two documents should I complete myself? What information will I give?
4 Does everyone need the other three documents? Who are they aimed at?
5 How much do the Europass documents cost?

2 Working with words

Find words and phrases in the text which you can use to talk about the things below.

1 what you have gained by learning something or working in another country
2 exams you have passed or a course of study you've completed successfully
3 how good you are at talking English or another foreign language
4 part of your course of study where you gained experience of a particular job
5 work you did for free, for example, for an independent organisation

Unit 9

Hip hop without the disrespect

Angelique Nzabanita was born in Rwanda – a poor African nation with a long history of war and violence between its two ethnic groups, the Hutu and the Tutsi. After her parents died, Angelique spent 14 years homeless on the streets of Kigali, Rwanda's capital city. She became a drug addict.

Then football gave Angelique the chance to change her life. At the age of 18, she became a member of Rwanda's team for the 2008 Homeless World Cup in Melbourne, Australia. For her and her team mates, the Homeless World cup gave them something to be proud of. 'I am famous back home and many people recognise me,' she says.

Angelique was able to stay in Australia as a refugee, and now she is one of a small but growing group of African Australians.

While she was homeless in Rwanda, Angelique listened to African-American hip hop. 'Ludacris, Tupac – everyone liked American hip hop,' she says. 'When I was little, I was inspired by them. I love hip hop – it's in me.'

Angelique now calls herself Macc-Too and has a new career – as Melbourne's first female Rwandan-Australian hip hop artist. 'Most African-Australians rap about life, about inspiring people or challenging people. I rap about life – normal life, street life – and to inspire people and sometimes to challenge my haters*.' Her song 'Like a hero' tells us not to judge others by their appearance, because appearance doesn't tell the whole story.

Her fellow rapper, Mxc Wol, left his home country, Sudan, as a child refugee and also came to live in Melbourne. He thinks that American hip hop has changed: 'When hip hop started in America, it was more about story telling … now they just talk about drugs and girls.'

Australian hip hop is different,Mxc Wol says. 'We are just growing. It's not like America, where Africans have been for years. We have more stories to tell.'

Along with Emanuel Jal, who was a child soldier in Sudan but is now a successful musician, Macc-Too and Mxc Wol are part of a new generation of African-Australian hip hop artists who have a positive message for their fans. They have experienced more violence in their lives than any American gangsta rapper, but their message is about peace and respect.

They are a wonderful example of how refugees can give something back to the country which gave them a home, and make a new identity which is both African and Australian.

(407 words)

* hater (Slang) – *Neider/in*

1 Understanding the text

Decide whether the following statements are true, false or not mentioned in the text.

1 When Angelique grew up, Rwanda was a dangerous place to live.
2 Angelique often drank alcohol when she was a teenager.
3 Few people listen to hip hop in Rwanda.
4 Angelique no longer plays football.
5 Mxc Wol left Sudan when he was a young man.
6 Mxc Wol and Emanuel Jal make music which is against violence.
7 Emanuel Jal hopes to be successful one day.
8 Mxc Wol and Emanuel Jal consider themselves Australian, not African.

2 Working with words

Complete the sentences with the most suitable word from the box. There are more words than you need.

appearance • career • hero • homeless • inspire • judge • proud • refugee • violence • wonderful

1 Don't … me by the colour of my skin.
2 That's a great story to … people to do good things.
3 Emanuel Jal is my … – I want to be like him.
4 It's easy to play music as a hobby, but it's very difficult to make a … out of it.
5 I didn't come to this country just to earn more money: I was a … .
6 You should be very … of all the good things that you have done.
7 When she was … , she had to sleep in the street.
8 There is too much … in our towns and cities: people don't feel safe here.

Unit 10

Catch me if you can

For a few years, Frank Abagnale was one of the world's most successful conmen. He was also one of the youngest.

Frank was 14 when his mother left in 1964. He stayed with his father, a wealthy shop owner. Around the same age he became interested in girls and began to use his father's credit card to impress them. Three thousand dollars later, his father sent him to a school for difficult boys. At 16 he left home for good and found that he could get better pay if he lied about his age.

Frank's hair turned grey early, so when he added 10 years to his résumé, it worked. But even with better pay, money was still too tight. Then one day he noticed a group of airline pilots and thought how easy it would be to trick people if he was a pilot. After all, everyone trusts a pilot.

It was a more innocent time, a time when people didn't often ask for your ID. The airline didn't ask many questions when a young man called to say he'd lost his pilot's uniform and needed another one. When a kid called with questions for his high school newspaper story on pilot procedures and documents, the airline was happy to help.

In this way, Frank obtained a pilot's uniform and copied an airline ID badge and pilot's licence. The other airline crew members accepted him as one of them. He took free flights across the country and stayed in hotels where the crews stayed. He wrote false cheques to get money. He made an excuse whenever another pilot offered him a chance to take a turn at the controls.

His intelligence and charm helped him to adopt new identities and make false ID documents. 'What also helped me was being an adolescent and having no fear,' he says now.

He had no permanent home. 'It was a very lonely life,' he says. 'Even though I met all those girls, they all thought I was someone else.' The pilot's uniform made him special, everyone liked and respected him.

After a couple of years of the pilot trick, Frank spent a year as a hospital doctor in Georgia. He didn't plan to do it: he just wanted to rent an apartment and so said he was a doctor to impress the owner. Neighbours introduced him to a hospital manager, who asked him to supervise a ward.

Frank didn't want to admit the lie, so he took the job. Fortunately he never had to make an important medical decision. After that he worked for shorter periods as a college professor and a lawyer – all before he was 21.

Eventually the police caught him, and he spent a few years in French, Swedish and US prisons. When Frank left prison, he became a security consultant – someone who advised companies how to avoid tricks like the ones he had used.

In 1980 he wrote a book about his experiences, and Leonardo DiCaprio played him in the 2002 film 'Catch Me If You Can'.

Now married, the father of three sons and living in Oklahoma, Frank says: 'I hope some day people will judge me on how I've spent the last 25 years of my life and not on a few years as a teenager.'

(552 words)

1 Understanding the text

Put these events in the correct order to make the story of Frank Abagnale's life.

1 He stole money from his father.
2 He went to prison.
3 He became a security consultant.
4 He wrote a book about his life.
5 He left home.
6 He lied about his age on job applications.
7 A film was made about him.
8 He flew all around the USA.
9 He pretended to be a doctor.
10 His mother left him and his father.

2 Working with words

Match the words to the definitions. There are three definitions too many. Find words in the text which fit them.

1	impress	a	to say something which is not true
2	document	b	a piece of paper with information on it, often official
3	trust	c	feeling that you do not have any friends
4	trick	d	to make sure that someone does his/her work properly
5	charm	e	to think that someone is good, honest, etc.
6	supervise	f	having a lot of money
7	lie	g	to make someone think that you are clever, good, etc.
8	advise	h	to make someone believe something which is not true
		i	a trip in an aircraft
		j	to suggest to someone how he/she can do something
		k	a quality that makes people like you

Unit 11

Want to help the Earth? Buy less stuff!

Sometimes it seems that people in our society are in a competition to see who can fill their house with the most stuff. Because our culture trains us to be consumers, we are often unaware of the benefits of having less stuff. Remember, everything that you own 'owns' you.

What I mean by that is: you must maintain, store, repair and clean it. Our stuff quickly becomes a psychological burden. The more things you buy, the more money you need, which increases your time at work – time that you could spend with your family and friends. Finally, making all of our stuff uses up natural resources, so it has a big cost to the environment.

Here are a few tips to help you to buy less stuff:

1 Fix broken things. Our disposable culture encourages us to replace broken items even when they are relatively easy to fix. Just because you can afford a new lawn mower doesn't mean you shouldn't try to fix your old one.

2 Re-use things. You can re-use many so-called disposable items, such as paint brushes, sandwich bags and plastic containers.
3 Borrow from friends. Borrowing saves resources, money and time. It also helps to build a feeling of community. Borrow books, movies and CDs from your local library. Ask your friend if she has an electric drill if you only need it for a day or two.
4 Ask yourself: 'Do I really need it?' Advertising makes us feel that we'll be left out if we don't have the latest gadget or brand of clothing. If we're really honest with ourselves, we don't need much of what we buy.
5 Make a shopping list. Plan ahead before you shop and decide exactly what you want before you go. Otherwise interesting displays, colourful packaging and friendly salespeople might convince you to buy something that you don't need.
6 Avoid impulse buys. Companies actually design their stores to encourage impulse buying. Do you really need any of that junk that surrounds you at the checkout? One powerful technique to avoid expensive impulse buys, such as a new stereo, is to wait two weeks before you buy it. If you still really want it after two weeks, you can get it.

(375 words)

1 Understanding the text

Complete the sentences in your own words.

1 Because we buy so much, our houses …
2 Our stuff becomes a psychological burden because …
3 If we buy less stuff, we can …
4 Instead of replacing an item when it is broken, …
5 Don't throw away things like paint brushes, because …
6 The good thing about libraries is …
7 If your friend has something that you need for a short time, …
8 Because of advertising, we don't …
9 If you write a shopping list, …
10 Because of the way companies design their stores, …

2 Working with words

Complete the sentences with the most suitable word from the box. There are more words than you need.

afford • borrow • convince • encourage • fill • maintain • own • re-use • repair • replace • shop • store

1 I can't … this stereo – it's too expensive.
2 My dad's lawn mower breaks down all the time because he doesn't … it.
3 Don't throw that away – you can easily … it, then you won't have to buy a new one.
4 Can we … this plastic container for something? It might be useful.
5 I left my mobile at home. Can I … yours for a moment, please?

6 Please don't … Mum to buy more stuff. She already buys enough.
7 They … all their furniture every ten years, even though most of it is still OK.
8 How can we … consumers that buying too much stuff is bad for the planet?

Unit 12

Gozo – Malta's mystical island

Gozo is the second largest of the Maltese islands, with a population of approximately 30,000 inhabitants. It is only 5 kilometres away from Malta but it is a very different place from its busy 'sister' island.

Gozo attracts visitors who are looking for a peaceful holiday. The local government has strict controls about building developments so, even though Gozo welcomes tourists, you won't find any huge holiday complexes there. Away from the coast, there are hills and fields as far as the eye can see. Old farmhouses, windmills and quiet villages add to the beauty of the countryside. The coastline has cliffs, steep valleys and beautiful inlets.

The island has many historical sites including one of the group of islands' best-preserved prehistoric temples, Ggantija. The temples are the earliest of a series of temples in Malta. They were built sometime between 3600 and 2500 BC, which makes them one of the world's oldest religious buildings, hundreds of years older than Stonehenge and the Great Pyramids even.

The name, Ggantija, means 'The Giants' Grotto'. According to local folklore, a female giant called Sunsuna built the temples in one day. Because they are round and contained statues of womanly goddesses, archaeologists believe that the temples were made for the Great Earth Mother who was a fertility goddess.

The archaeologists also found evidence that people went to Ggantija to pray for healing. They say that it was a place of pilgrimage for the ancient inhabitants of Malta and for pilgrims from as far away as Sicily and North Africa.

(256 words)

Based on information from www.visitmalta.com

1 **Understanding the text**

The statements below give wrong information. Correct the statements in German. Do not translate word for word.

1 Gozo is bigger than Malta but, apart from that, the islands are very similar.
2 Many areas of Gozo have been turned into holiday camps.
3 The temples on Gozo are copies of Stonehenge and the Pyramids.
4 The Maltese people worshipped a goddess called Sunsuna.
5 In the old days, people went to Ggantija to die.

2 Working with words

Find words in the text which match the definitions below.

1 people who live in a particular place
2 quiet and calm
3 buildings used for the worship of a god or gods
4 the traditions and stories of a country or a community
5 a journey to a holy place

Unit 13

Slumdog millionaire – Jamal, the role model from the slums

Slumdog Millionaire (2008) is a British film which won several awards. It is an adaptation of the novel *Q & A* which was written in 2005 by the Indian author Vikas Swarup.

The film tells the story of Jamal, an 18-year old boy from the slums in Mumbai who is a contestant in the Indian version of *Who wants to be a Millionaire?*. When Jamal answers all the questions correctly, and it looks as if he is going to win the big prize, the game show host thinks he is cheating and hands him over to the police.

To prove his innocence, Jamal tells the story of his life in the slums where he and his brother, Salim, grew up. He describes their adventures together, stealing in order to survive. He talks about the vicious local gangs he knew and about Latika, the girl he loved and lost.

Soon, Jamal convinces the police inspector that his experiences during his short, turbulent life help him work out the answers to the questions on the show. Jamal returns to the show and wins the 20 million rupee prize. He becomes a role model for people all over India and young slum dwellers worship him as their hero.

Many Indian intellectuals criticized the film and said that such a realistic picture of the Indian slums would not help the poor people who live there. Writing on an online film site, one critic said, 'People's negative views about the slums will be reinforced.' Someone else wrote, 'The film supports the views of the people who look down on the slum dwellers.'

On the same website, other Indians praise the film and say that it is about dreams coming true. Many bloggers see Jamal as hopeful and relentless; he is proud of his origins even when people call him a 'slumdog'. One young blogger sums it up: 'Jamal knows that it doesn't matter where you come from, only where you are headed,' he says.

(329 words)

Based on information from http://www.imdb.com/title/tt1010048/; http://en.wikipedia.org/wiki/Slumdog_Millionaire; http://globalvoicesonline.org/2009/01/26/india-reactions-to-slumdog-millionaire/

1 Understanding the text

Match the statements to people from the text. Give reasons for your answers in German.

1 Filmmakers should show India in a more positive way.
2 Jamal inspires us. He gives us hope that we might have a better life.

3 We did some bad things together, but we had to do these things to live.
4 I have told my superiors that I believe Jamal. His explanations are possible.
5 I can't believe that this boy from the slums knows all the answers.
6 Jamal's experience proves that anyone can achieve greatness if they try.
7 The key to the answers is in my life story.
8 I was very surprised when I saw him on TV after all these years.

a some Indian critics
b Jamal
c Jamal's brother
d Latika
e the police inspector
f the quiz master
g a 'slumdog'
h a young, Indian blogger

2 Working with words

Find synonyms in the text.

1 prizes
2 the jackpot
3 to remain alive
4 unsettled
5 idol

Unit 14

The new 'high-fat' Mediterranean diet

A Doctors are continually telling us to follow a Mediterranean diet. They say that eating plenty of vegetables, fruit, fish and olive oil could help us to stay healthy and live longer. According to various studies, it certainly seems that people who eat these types of foods have lower rates of heart disease and cancer compared to people who eat more red meat and dairy products.

B A recent study from the FAO (Food and Agricultural Organization of the United Nations) reports some sad news, however. The report suggests that the people who live around the Mediterranean are eating less of their traditional foods. Instead, they now eat the same kind of meals as people in northern Europe and America.

C One of the researchers involved in the study said, 'People in the area are taking in too many calories. They are eating too much fat, too much salt and too much sugar. As a result, the Mediterranean population is developing the same illnesses as people in the west. There is more diabetes, heart disease and arthritis. The Mediterranean people are getting fatter and these illnesses are the result,' he explained.

D In Greece, three-quarters of the adult population is now overweight or obese. In Italy, Spain and Portugal more than half of the population are overweight. The FAO report suggests that the same developments are likely in the Middle East and North Africa.

E There are many reasons for the change in eating habits. People in the area have more money, and there are more supermarkets and fast food restaurants where they can spend it. Apart from that, more women are going out to work and they no longer have the time or the energy to cook traditional meals.

F The FAO researcher finished by saying, 'Much of the Mediterranean diet doesn't exist in the region any longer. The people who live there prefer to eat unhealthy food.'

(314 words)

based on information from http://www.fao.org/newsroom/en/news/2008/1000871/index.html
and http://lifestyle.t-online.de/fast-food-statt-mozzarella-mittelmeerdiaet-ist-in-suedeuropa-out/id_15751092/index

1 Understanding the text

a Read each paragraph carefully and make notes to complete the sentences below.

1 Experts say that a Mediterranean diet is … (Section A)
2 Recent research indicates that … (Section B)
3 According to a researcher, … (Section C)
4 Many southern European people are … (Section D)
5 The Mediterranean people are eating differently because … (Section E)
6 The researcher believes … (Section F)

b Use your notes to re-write the text in German. Do not translate word for word.

2 Working with words

Find words and phrases in the text to match the definitions below.

1 the food that you eat and drink regularly
2 food and drinks made from milk
3 the kind of meals which people in a certain region have always eaten
4 the units which measure how much energy food produces
5 very fat, in a way that is unhealthy
6 meals that can make people ill

Unit 15

Sea Shepherd – pirates or policemen?

1 Sea Shepherd calls itself a 'conservation society'. That sounds quite harmless, but its activists take direct action of the most aggressive kind. According to its leader, Paul Watson, Sea Shepherd's mission is to protect marine wildlife including seals, dolphins and whales. To do that, they will travel anywhere in the world's seas and oceans and sink or damage ships that endanger marine animals – as long as there is no risk to human life. They see themselves as an international police force, not just a peaceful protest organization like Greenpeace.

2 Sea Shepherd has been very successful. Since Paul Watson started Sea Shepherd in 1979, the organization has sunk 10 ships, but nobody has been killed or seriously injured during any of its actions. Sea Shepherd is extremely well organized and owns three ships and some smaller boats. One of its own boats, a $3 million racer called the *Ady Gil*, was sunk in 2010 during a battle with Japanese whale catchers.

3 The crews of Sea Shepherd's ships come from all over the world and are mostly young people in their 20s and 30s. To become a member of Sea Shepherd crew, you need to have special skills, e.g. as a radio operator, a cook, an engineer or a helicopter pilot. You also need to be extremely brave: Sea Shepherd's campaigns often take place in Arctic and Antarctic waters, where you will only survive for a few minutes if you fall in the water. Activists often use small boats to get in the way of large ships – a very dangerous activity which could easily result in death for the activists.

4 Many well-known people support Sea Shepherd, including actors and rock bands, and it is recognized as a charity in the UK. To many members of the public, Sea Shepherd's activists are heroes and eco-warriors. That positive image is important, because Sea Shepherd needs the public to give money and goods to support its activities. It has filmed a TV series about its campaigns, called *Whale Wars*.

5 On the other hand, its opponents say that Sea Shepherd's activities are illegal. The Japanese government has often asked the USA to treat Sea Shepherd as a terrorist organization. Japan, Norway and Iceland are among the few countries that still kill whales.

6 Even environmentalists are not always sure that Sea Shepherd does more harm than good. Some are worried that the organization gives environmentalists a radical image. It's true that Sea Shepherd's activitists like to look radical: they paint their ships black, wear black uniforms and have a flag which looks very similar to a traditional pirate flag.

7 What do you think? Do ordinary people sometimes have to take direct action to save the planet, or should we rely on our governments to do the right thing? Is it OK to take actions that might put people's lives at risk if the cause is important enough?

1 Understanding the text: reading for gist

Choose a heading for each paragraph of the text. There are more headings than you need.

a Adventure and danger at sea
b Conservation through direct action
c Crisis in the arctic
d Criticism from whalers
e How it all began
f Not the right image?
g Organization is the key
h Putting an end to unsustainable fishing
i Supporting the 'eco-warriors'
j What is your view?

2 Working with words

Complete the sentences with the most suitable word or expression from the box. There are more words than you need.

battle • brave • charity • conservation • direct action • endanger • environmentalist • harm • peaceful • radical • skill • support • survive

1 If we don't spend more on …, we may lose many more species of animal.
2 I don't see the point in passive protest – only … can really change things.

3 Gina and Alex … several different causes, including WWF.
4 He's not really an … , although he is interested in nature.
5 There was a … between a big group of angry protesters and the police.
6 We only use … methods. We are totally against violence.
7 Only … activists use such extreme methods.
8 There is no excuse for actions that … life: we don't want to kill anyone.
9 Sue doesn't eat meat because she is not willing to … animals.
10 That was a very … thing to do: you could have been badly injured.

Simple present (S. 13)

Das *simple present* wird verwendet für gleich bleibende Zustände und regelmäßige, wiederholte Handlungen.

Aussagen	I **play** football. She **eats** a lot of fruit.	*I/we/you/they*: Grundform *he/she/it*: Grundform + *s*
Verneinungen	We **don't like** American films. James **doesn't read** many books.	*I/we/you/they don't* *he/she/it doesn't*
Fragen	**Do** they **listen** to rap music? **Does** it **rain** a lot in England?	*Do I/we/you/they …?* *Does he/she/it …?*

Signalwörter
- always
- never
- often
- sometimes
- usually

Present progressive (S. 22)

Das *present progressive* steht für vorübergehende oder im Moment des Sprechens ablaufende Handlungen und Situationen.

Aussagen	I**'m reading** a book. He**'s taking** a photo. They**'re getting** a new camera.	*am/is/are* + *-ing*-Form des Verbs Verben auf *-e*: das *-e* fällt weg *-m*, *-n* oder *-t* nach kurz gesprochenen Silben verdoppelt
Verneinungen	I**'m not listening** to you. They**'re not coming** with me.	*'m not / isn't / aren't* + *-ing*-Form des Verbs
Fragen	**Are** you **having** fun? **Is** it **raining?**	*am/is/are* wird mit dem Subjekt getauscht

Signalwörter
- at the moment
- now
- just
- still
- today

Simple past (S. 33)

Das *simple past* beschreibt abgeschlossene Ereignisse und Zustände.

Aussagen	I **watched** TV. Jake **bought** a car last week. You **were** young.	regelmäßige Verben: Grundform + *-ed* unregelmäßige Verben: ► S. 262
Verneinungen	I **didn't watch** MTV. Casey **didn't buy** a new phone. I **wasn't** at the party yesterday.	*did not* (*didn't*) + Grundform *to be*: *was* und *were*
Fragen	**Did** you **watch** DVDs? **Did** you **buy** that CD? **Were** you happy?	*did* + Grundform *to be*: *was* und *were*

Signalwörter
- yesterday
- last week/year
- three days ago
- in 2001
- When …?

Present perfect (S. 42)

Man benutzt das *present perfect*, wenn man sagen will, dass etwas in der Vergangenheit begonnen hat und bis in die Gegenwart andauert. Es wird auch für Vorgänge verwendet, die irgendwann einmal – oder noch nie – stattgefunden haben, ohne Angabe des Zeitpunkts.

Aussagen	• I've **(have) posted** a comment already. • He **has been** on Facebook for hours.	regelmäßige Verben: *have/has* + Partizip Perfekt unregelmäßige Verben: ► S. 262
Verneinungen	• He **hasn't read** your email yet. • We **haven't seen** each other since April.	*haven't/hasn't* + Partizip Perfekt
Fragen	• **Have** they **seen** the video yet? • How long **have** you **had** that job?	*have/has* wird mit dem Subjekt getauscht

Signalwörter
already • always • before • ever …? • for three weeks/months/years • How long …? • just • lately • never • recently • since Monday / 2001 • up till now • (not) yet

Past perfect (S. 90)

Mit dem *past perfect* beschreiben wir etwas, das bereits vor einem Zeitpunkt in der Vergangenheit geschah.

Signalwörter
when • as soon as • after

Aussagen	When I **had finished** school, I got a job in a bakery.	*had* + Partizip Perfekt
Verneinungen	I got a bad mark because I **hadn't learned** enough.	*hadn't* + Partizip Perfekt
Fragen	**Had** you **been** to America before you went last year?	*had* wird mit dem Subjekt getauscht

The future (S. 69, 71, 72)

Going to *future*	This is **going to be** a great year! **Are** you **going to move** flat?	für Pläne und Absichten
Will *future*	It **will rain** tomorrow. Hey, what a great offer! **I'll take** it! Don't worry, **I'll do** it tomorrow.	Vorhersage spontane Entscheidung Versprechen/Angebot
Present progressive	Carrie **is going** to Austria in July. When **are** you **going** on holiday?	konkrete Pläne und Absichten (mit Zeitangabe)
Simple present	Our plane **leaves** at six o'clock.	Fahrpläne, Programme usw.

The passive (S. 116)

In einem Passivsatz sagen wir, was mit einer Person oder einer Sache getan wird. Mit *by* können wir sagen, von wem etwas gemacht wird. Meist verwenden wir jedoch das Passiv, wenn es nicht nötig (oder nicht möglich) ist zu sagen, wer etwas tut oder getan hat.

Simple present	Bikes **are stolen** every day in Berlin.	*am/is/are* + Partizip Perfekt
Simple past	My bike **was stolen** yesterday.	*was/were* + Partizip Perfekt
Present perfect	His bike **hasn't been stolen** yet.	*has/have been* + Partizip Perfekt
Will *future*	It **will be stolen** soon though.	*will be* + Partizip Perfekt

Conditonal sentences (S. 105, 126, 127)

Conditional sentences (*if*-Sätze) drücken Bedingungen aus.

Type 1 (S. 105)	für reale Bedingungen	If it **rains**, *if*-Satz: *simple present*	I **will stay** inside today. Hauptsatz: *will future*
Type 2 (S. 126)	für unwahrscheinliche Bedingungen	If I **won** the lottery, *if*-Satz: *simple past*	I **would buy** a fast car. Hauptsatz: *would* + Infinitiv
Type 3 (S. 127)	für Situationen, die in der Vergangenheit geschehen sein könnten, aber nicht geschehen sind	If she **had missed** the bus, *if*-Satz: *past perfect*	she **would have been** late. Hauptsatz: *would have* + Partizip Perfekt

Reported speech (S. 140)

Man verwendet die indirekte Rede um zu berichten, was jemand gesagt hat. Steht das einleitende Verb (*ask, say* usw.) in der Vergangenheit, verschieben sich die Zeiten im Satz.

direkte Rede	***indirekte Rede***
I **play** tennis. **Did** you **play** tennis with Rachel?	She said (that) she **played** tennis. He asked if I **had played** tennis with Rachel.
simple present present progressive simple past present perfect will can past perfect	simple past past progressive past perfect (simple past *auch möglich*) past perfect would could *keine Verschiebung*

Modal verbs (S. 82)

can / be able to *(können)*	• *Can/can't* drücken eine Fähigkeit oder eine Möglichkeit aus. • *Can/can't* werden nur in der Gegenwart benutzt. Das *simple past* lautet *could/couldn't*. • Anderen Zeiten werden mit dem Ersatzverb *to be able to* gebildet.
could / may / might *(könnte/n)*	• *Could, may* und *might* drücken eine Möglichkeit aus.
must / have to *(müssen)*; need not / don't have to *(nicht müssen)*	• *Must* und *have to* drücken eine Verpflichtung oder Notwendigkeit aus. • *Must* wird nur in der Gegenwart benutzt. *Have to* kann in allen Zeiten verwendet werden. • Die Verneinung von *must* ist *need not* oder *not have to* (nicht müssen).
May / be allowed to *(dürfen)*	• *May* und *be allowed to* drücken ein Erlaubnis oder Verbot aus. *May* findet man vor allem im formellen Englisch.
should/shouldn't *(sollen / nicht sollen, sollte/n)*	• *Should/shouldn't* werden benutzt, um Ratschläge zu erteilen bzw. um eine Pflicht hinzuweisen.

Plurals (S. 32)

Die allermeisten Pluralformen werden mit -s gebildet.	*computer* ▸ *computers*
Bei Nomen auf *-y* nach einem Konsonant wird *-y* zu *-ies*.	*family* ▸ *families*
Nomen auf -s und -x bilden die Pluralform mit *-es*.	*bus* ▸ *buses*
Einige häufige Nomen haben unregelmäßige Pluralformen.	*man* ▸ *men, tooth* ▸ *teeth, child* ▸ *children, person* ▸ *people*
Einige Nomen werden immer im Plural verwendet.	*glasses, jeans, trousers, scissors*

Saying how much / how many (S. 32)

Much und *many* stehen in Fragen und verneinten Sätzen. *A lot of* steht in Aussagesätzen. *Few* wird mit zählbaren, *little* mit nicht zählbaren Substantiven verwendet.

how much? *wie viel?*	much / a lot of *viel*	little *wenig*
how many? *wie viele?*	many / a lot of *viele*	few *wenige*

Some/any (S. 43)

Some und *any* bezeichnen eine unbestimmte Menge oder Zahl. *Some* wird vor allem in bejahten Aussagesätzen, Angeboten und Bitten verwendet. *Any* steht meist in verneinten Aussagesätzen und in Fragen.

Aussagen	I downloaded **some** music. **Somebody** sent me a message.
Verneinungen	I didn't download **any** videos. I don't know **anybody** here.
Fragen	Have you received **any** emails today? Has **anybody** seen Emma today?
Bitten/Angebote	Could you send me **some** information? Would you like **something** to drink?

Adverbs of manner (S. 49)

Mit Adverbien beschreibt man, wie etwas geschieht. In der Regel werden Adverbien durch Anhängen von *–ly* an das Adjektiv gebildet.

	Adjektiv	***Adverb***
***Adjektiv* + ly**	quick slow	quickly slowly
***Adjektiv auf* -y ▸ -ily**	happy easy	happily easily
Unregelmäßige Adjektive	good fast hard early late	well fast hard early late

Comparatives and superlatives of adjectives (S. 53)

Adjektive versteigert man mit *-er/-est* oder *more/most*. Vergleiche können mit *–er/more … than* oder *(not) as … as* gebildet werden.

	Adjektiv	***Komparativ***	***Superlativ***
Einsilbige Adjektive	long big	longer bigger	(the) longest (the) biggest
Zweisilbige Adjektive, die auf -y enden	pretty lucky	prettier luckier	prettiest luckiest
Adjektive mit zwei und mehr Silben	famous important	more famous more important	(the) most famous (the) most important
Unregelmäßige Adjektive	good bad	better worse	(the) best (the) worst

Relative clauses (S. 51)

Relativsätze sind Nebensätze, die ein Nomen näher definieren. Sie werden mit Relativpronomen eingeleitet. Das Relativpronomen kann weggelassen werden, wenn der Nebensatz ein anderes Objekt hat.

Personen: *who* oder (seltener) *that*	People **who/that** don't eat meat are vegetarians. That's the girl (**who/that**) I saw at school.
Dinge: *which* oder *that*	He bought the bike **which/that** cost 500 euros. This is the house (**which/that**) I live in.

-*ing* form and infinitive (S. 152)

Auf bestimmte Verben folgt eine -*ing*-Form, während auf andere ein Infinitiv folgt.

Verb + -*ing*-Form	Verb + Infinitiv	Verb + -*ing*-Form oder Infinitiv
I enjoy **dancing** at the disco.	They wanted **to go** on holiday in America.	We love **cooking**. We love **to cook**.
admit, avoid, dislike, don't mind, enjoy, finish, involve, stop, suggest	agree, choose, decide, expect, hope, learn, manage, prefer, want, would like	begin, continue, hate, like, love, start

Chronological word list

Dieses Wörterverzeichnis enthält alle Wörter, die nicht in der Liste des Grundwortschatzes enthalten sind, d.h. die nicht als bekannt vorausgesetzt werden. Wörter aus den Hörverständnisübungen sind gelb hinterlegt und Wörter aus den Partner files sind blau hinterlegt. Die Zahl am linken Rand gibt die Seitenzahl an.
Die neuen Wörtern aus den *Further reading*-Texten sind am Ende des Verzeichnisses. Vorausgesetzt wird jeweils der Wortschatz aus dem Hauptteil des Buches einschließlich der entsprechenden Unit.

AE	= americanisches Englisch	*adv*	= adverb
BE	= britisches Englisch	*inf*	= informal *(informell, Umgangssprache)*
AusE	= australisches Englisch	*phr*	= phrase *(feststehende Wendung)*
n	= noun *(Substantiv)*	*pl*	= plural
v	= verb	*esp*	= especially
adj	= adjective	↔	= opposite *(Gegensatz)*

Unit 1

7	**warm-up**	['wɔːm ʌp]	*v* to warm-up	*Vorbereitung, Aufwärmen*
	phrase	[freɪz]	saying	*Wendung, Formulierung*
	map	[mæp]	atlas	*Landkarte, Karte*
	official language	[əˌfɪʃl 'læŋgwɪdʒ]	national language	*Amtssprache*
	main	[meɪn]	major, central	*Haupt-*
	industry	['ɪndəstri]	*adj* industrial	*Branche, Industriezweig, Industrie*
	capital city	[ˌkæpɪtl 'sɪti]	e.g. The capital city of France is Paris.	*Hauptstadt*
	population	[ˌpɒpju'leɪʃn]	number of people who live in a town or city	*Bevölkerung*
	national holiday	[ˌnæʃnəl 'hɒlədeɪ]	e.g. Christmas Day, New Year's Day	*Nationalfeiertag*
	second-largest	[ˌsekənd 'lɑːdʒɪst]	e.g. The second-largest city in Germany is Hamburg.	*zweitgrößte/r/s*
	square kilometre	[ˌskweə 'kɪləmiːtə]	km²	*Quadratkilometer*
	shipbuilding	['ʃɪpbɪldɪŋ]	making of ships	*Schiffbau*
	manufacturing	[ˌmænju'fæktʃərɪŋ]	*n* manufacturer	*Herstellung, Fertigung*
	automobile	['ɔːtəməbiːl]	car	*Auto, Automobil*
	coal mining	['kəʊlmaɪnɪŋ]	*n* coal miner	*Kohlebergbau*
	chemicals	['kemɪklz]	e.g. chemicals for cleaning	*Chemikalien*
	castle	['kɑːsl]	*esp* where kings and queens live	*Burg, Schloss*
	sausage	['sɒsɪdʒ]	type of meat	*Wurst, Würstchen*
	possible	['pɒsəbl]	↔ impossible	*möglich*
	chancellor	['tʃɑːnsələ]	head of government in some countries	*Kanzler/in*
	to **discuss**	[dɪ'skʌs]	*n* discussion	*besprechen, erörtern, diskutieren*
8	to **match sth**	[mætʃ]	to put two things together	*etw zuordnen*
	to **name**	[neɪm]	e.g. to name a baby	*nennen, benennen*
	G'Day! *(AusE)*	[gə 'deɪ]	*inf* Good afternoon!	*Guten Tag. Hallo.*
	down under	[ˌdaʊn 'ʌndə]	Australia	*Australien*
	national park	[ˌnæʃnəl 'pɑːk]	protected park	*Nationalpark*
	native speaker	[ˌneɪtɪv 'spiːkə]	e.g. British people are native speakers of English.	*Muttersprachler/in*
	billion	['bɪliən]	one thousand million	*Milliarde*
	foreign language	[ˌfɒrən 'læŋgwɪdʒ]	a language you are not a native speaker of	*Fremdsprache*
	religion	[rɪ'lɪdʒən]	*adj* religious	*Religion*
	Rastafarian	[ˌræstə'feəriən]	member of the Rastafarian religion	*Rastafari, Rasta-*
	island	['aɪlənd]	⚠ Aussprache	*Insel*
	except for	[ɪk'sept fə]	↔ including	*außer*
9	**purple**	['pɜːpl]	a colour	*purpur, lila*
	pronunciation	[prəˌnʌnsi'eɪʃn]	how to say a word	*Aussprache*
	either … or	[ˌaɪðə 'ɔː]	↔ neither … nor	*entweder … oder*
	wild	[waɪld]	↔ tame	*wild*
	leopard	['lepəd]	large cat with spots from Africa or Asia	*Leopard*
	lion	['laɪən]	a type of large cat	*Löwe*
	giraffe	[dʒə'rɑːf]	tall, African animal with spots	*Giraffe*
	zebra	['zebrə]	white African horse with black stripes	*Zebra*
	democratic	[ˌdemə'krætɪk]	*n* democracy	*demokratisch*
	election	[ɪ'lekʃn]	*v* to elect	*Wahl*
	independence	[ˌɪndɪ'pendəns]	*adj* independent	*Unabhängigkeit*
	unification	[ˌjuːnɪfɪ'keɪʃn]	*v* to unify	*Vereinigung*
	founding	['faʊndɪŋ]	*v* to found	*Gründung*
	colony	['kɒləni]	*v* to colonise	*Kolonie*
	historic	[hɪ'stɒrɪk]	important	*historisch, geschichtlich*
	event	[ɪ'vent]	sth that is happening	*Ereignis*
	to **celebrate**	['selɪbreɪt]	*n* celebration	*feiern*
	to **land**	[lænd]	*n* landing	*landen*

	to **found**	[faʊnd]	to start	*gründen*
	since	[sɪns]	e.g. Since it happened, I have been...	*seit*
	province	['prɒvɪns]	*adj* provincial	*Provinz*
	to **unify**	['ju:nɪfaɪ]	*n* unity	*vereinigen*
	independent	[ˌɪndɪ'pendənt]	↔ dependent	*unabhängig*
	freedom	['fri:dəm]	*adj* free	*Freiheit*
	to **vote**	[vəʊt]	*n* vote	*abstimmen, wählen*
	to **become**	[bɪ'kʌm]	to later be	*werden*
	grammar	['græmə]	*adj* grammatical	*Grammatik*
	statement	['steɪtmənt]	*v* to state	*Aussage, Behauptung*
	necessary	['nesəsəri]	↔ unnecessary	*nötig, notwendig*
	example	[ɪg'zɑ:mpl]	*adj* exemplary	*Beispiel*
	nowadays	['naʊədeɪz]	↔ back then	*heute, heutzutage*
	not … anymore	[ˌnɒt eni'mɔ:]	no longer	*nicht mehr*
11	**sentence**	['sentəns]	e.g. Please answer using full sentences.	*Satz*
	correct	[kə'rekt]	↔ incorrect	*richtig, korrekt*
	jungle	['dʒʌŋgl]	rainforest	*Dschungel, Urwald*
	less than	['les ðən]	↔ more than	*weniger als*
	to **move**	[mu:v]	e.g. We moved to the US for my father's job.	hier: *übersiedeln*
	home	[həʊm]	*phr* Home sweet home!	hier: *Heimat*
	closed	[kləʊzd]	↔ open	*geschlossen*
	to **mean**	[mi:n]	e.g. What does that mean?	*bedeuten, heißen*
	to **pronounce**	[prə'naʊns]	*n* pronunciation	*aussprechen*
12	to **take part in sth**	[teɪk 'pɑ:t ɪn]	*n* participant	*an etw teilnehmen*
	global	['gləʊbl]	all around the world	*global, weltumspannend*
	conversation	[ˌkɒnvə'seɪʃn]	discussion	*Gespräch, Unterhaltung*
	profile	['prəʊfaɪl]	description	*Profil, Porträt*
	interested in sth	['ɪntrəstɪd ɪn]	*adj* interesting	*an etw interessiert*
	region	['ri:dʒən]	*adj* regional	*Region*
	native language	[ˌneɪtɪv 'læŋgwɪdʒ]	mother tongue	*Muttersprache*
	reason	['ri:zn]	*v* to reason	*Grund*
	to **communicate**	[kə'mju:nɪkeɪt]	*n* communication	*kommunizieren*
	to **do business**	[du 'bɪznəs]	to trade	*Geschäfte machen*
	to **practise**	['præktɪs]	*n* practice	*üben, trainieren*
	globalization	[ˌgləʊbəlaɪ'zeɪʃn]	*adj* globalized	*Globalisierung*
	economy	[ɪ'kɒnəmi]	*adj* economic	*Wirtschaft*
	advantage	[əd'vɑ:ntɪdʒ]	↔ disadvantage	*Vorteil*
	mostly	['məʊstli]	generally, mainly	*hauptsächlich*
	fluent	['flu:ənt]	*adv* fluently	(Sprache:) *fließend*
	national economy	[ˌnæʃnəl ɪ'kɒnəmi]	↔ international economy	*Volkswirtschaft*
13	**mediation**	[ˌmi:di'eɪʃn]	*v* to mediate	*Vermittlung*
	never	['nevə]	↔ always	*nie*
	often	['ɒfn]	e.g. I often swim in the local pool.	*oft*
	usually	['ju:ʒuəli]	↔ seldom, rarely	*gewöhnlich, normalerweise*
	bracket	['brækɪt]	*phr* in brackets	*Klammer*
	comic book	['kɒmɪk bʊk]	*phr* comic book hero	*Comic(heft)*
	voice	[vɔɪs]	e.g. He has a loud voice. He talks loudly.	*Stimme*
	subtitle	['sʌbtaɪtl]	*adj* subtitled	*Untertitel*
	TV series	[ˌti:'vi: sɪəri:z]	e.g. *House*, *Desperate Housewives*, etc.	*Fernsehserie*
	to **chat**	[tʃæt]	*n* chat	*sich unterhalten, chatten*
	accent	['æksent]	way sb from a certain area pronounces words	*Akzent*
14	**receptionist**	[rɪ'sepʃənɪst]	person working at reception	*Empfangsmitarbeiter/in*
	along	[ə'lɒŋ]	e.g. We walked along the river.	*entlang*
	production	[prə'dʌkʃn]	*v* to produce	*Fertigung, Produktion*
	Research & Development (R&D)	[rɪˌsɜ:tʃ ən dɪ'veləpmənt]	department which makes products better or produces new ones	*Forschung(s-) und Entwicklung(sabteilung)*
	Purchasing	['pɜ:tʃəsɪŋ]	*v* to purchase	*Einkauf(sabteilung)*
	logistics	[lə'dʒɪstɪks]	department which organises transport	*Logistik*
	Human Resources (HR)	[ˌhju:mən rɪ'sɔ:sɪz]	department which looks after the people who work in a business	*Personalabteilung*
	advertising	['ædvətaɪzɪŋ]	*n* advertisement	*Werbung, Werbeabteilung*
	Finance	['faɪnæns]	*adj* financial	*Rechnungswesen, Finanzen*
	canteen	[kæn'ti:n]	place where people eat at work	*Kantine*
	Sales	[seɪlz]	*v* to sell	*Vertrieb, Verkauf(sabteilung)*

	customer	['kʌstəmə]	person who buys sth	*Kunde/-in*
	customer service	[ˌkʌstəmə 'sɜːvɪs]	e.g. I wanted to return a dress, so I went to customer service.	*Kundendienst*
	reception	[rɪ'sepʃn]	e.g. Guests go to reception when they arrive.	*Empfang*
	director	[də'rektə]	*v* to direct	*Geschäftsführer/in, Vorstand*
	department	[dɪ'pɑːtmənt]	part of a business	*Abteilung*
	straight on	[ˌstreɪt 'ɒn]	straight ahead	*geradeaus*
	hall	[hɔːl]	corridor	*Flur*
	You're welcome.	[ˌjɔː 'welkəm]	e.g Thank you for your help! You're welcome!	*Bitte (sehr).*
	appointment	[ə'pɔɪntmənt]	an arranged meeting	*Termin*
	job interview	['dʒɒb ɪntəvjuː]	e.g. I had a job interview at the London office.	*Vorstellungsgespräch*
	of course	[əf 'kɔːs]	naturally	*natürlich, selbstverständlich*
	to have lunch	[həv 'lʌntʃ]	to eat lunch	*zu Mittag essen*
	to role-play	['rəʊl pleɪ]	*n* role-play	*mit verteilten Rollen spielen*
	dialogue	['daɪəlɒg]	conversation	*Dialog*
	visitor	['vɪzɪtə]	↔ host/hostess	*Besucher/in*
	to take it in turns	[ˌteɪk ɪt ɪn 'tɜːnz]	e.g. We took it in turns to look after the children.	*sich abwechseln*
	to ask for directions	[ˌɑːsk fə də'rekʃnz]	↔ to give directions	*nach dem Weg fragen*
	area	['eəriə]	part	*Bereich*
	to turn right/left	[ˌtɜːn 'raɪt/'left]	e.g. Turn right at the end of the hall.	*rechts/links abbiegen*
15	**item**	['aɪtəm]	object	*Gegenstand*
	vending machine	['vendɪŋ məʃiːn]	e.g. I bought a drink from the vending machine.	*Automat*
	video projector	['vɪdiəʊ prədʒektə]	⚠ ~~beamer~~	*Beamer*
	pot plant	['pɒt plɑːnt]	e.g. I gave her a pot plant for her new flat.	*Topfpflanze*
	ground floor	[ˌgraʊnd 'flɔː]	floor at the bottom of a building	*Erdgeschoss*
	entrance	['entrəns]	↔ exit	*Eingang*
	object	['ɒbdʒɪkt]	item	*Gegenstand, Objekt*
	finally	['faɪnəli]	at the end	*schließlich*
	to **switch**	[swɪtʃ]	to exchange, to change	*tauschen*
	role	[rəʊl]	*phr* to play a role	*Rolle*
	directions	[də'rekʃnz]	e.g. I gave him directions to the city centre.	*Wegbeschreibung*
	fire extinguisher	['faɪər ɪkstɪŋgwɪʃə]	used to put out fire	*Feuerlöscher*
	rubbish bin *(BE)*	['rʌbɪʃ bɪn]	*AE:* trash can	*Mülleimer*
	purse	[pɜːs]	where you keep your money	*Handtasche (AE), Portemonnaie (BE)*
	filing cabinet	['faɪlɪŋ kæbɪnət]	where you keep files and documents	*Aktenschrank*
	lift *(BE)*	[lɪft]	*AE:* elevator	*Aufzug*
	stairs	[steəz]	e.g. to go up the stairs	*Treppe*
	first floor	[ˌfɜːst 'flɔː]	above the ground floor	*erster Stock*
	to **direct sb somewhere**	[də'rekt]	e.g. Could you please direct me to the manager?	*jdn wohin schicken*
	to call	[kɔːl]	to phone	*jdn anrufen*
	boss	[bɒs]	head of a company/business	*Chef/in*
	business contact	['bɪznəs kɒntækt]	someone you do business with	*Geschäftspartner/in*
	equator	[ɪ'kweɪtə]	line around the middle of the globe	*Äquator*
	behind	[bɪ'haɪnd]	↔ in front of	*nach*
	ahead	[ə'hed]	↔ behind	*vor, voraus*
	to write sth out	[ˌraɪt 'aʊt]	to write down	*etw aufschreiben*
	to calculate	['kælkjuleɪt]	*n* calculation	*rechnen*
	noon	[nuːn]	midday, 12 p.m.	*Mittag*
	midnight	['mɪdnaɪt]	12 a.m.	*Mitternacht*
16	vocabulary book	[və'kæbjələri bʊk]	e.g. Write new words in your vocabulary book.	*Vokabelheft*
	column	['kɒləm]	vertical row or list	*Spalte*
	opposite	['ɒpəzɪt]	↔ synonym	*Gegenteil, Gegensatz*
	synonym	['sɪnənɪm]	↔ opposite	*Synonym*
	sticky notes	['stɪki nəʊts]	e.g. My secretary left a sticky note. It said I should call a customer back.	*Klebezettel*
	to label	['leɪbl]	*n* label	*mit einem Etikett versehen*
	expression	[ɪk'spreʃn]	*v* to express	*Ausdruck*
	unit	['juːnɪt]	chapter	*Lektion*
	translation	[træns'leɪʃn]	*v* to translate	*Übersetzung*
	extra	['ekstrə]	additional	*zusätzlich*
	present	['preznt]	gift	*Geschenk*

Unit 2

17	**family tree**	[ˌfæməli ˈtriː]	chart which describes a family	*Stammbaum*
	wife	[waɪf]	married woman	*Ehefrau*
	husband	[ˈhʌzbənd]	married man	*Ehemann*
	stepmother	[ˈstepmʌðə]	your father's new wife	*Stiefmutter*
	aunt	[ɑːnt]	sister or sister-in-law of a parent	*Tante*
	uncle	[ˈʌŋkl]	brother or brother-in-law of a parent	*Onkel*
	grandmother	[ˈgrænmʌðə]	mother's mother	*Großmutter*
	great-grandmother	[ˈgreɪtgrænmʌðə]	grandmother's mother	*Urgroßmutter*
	half-sister	[ˈhɑːf sɪstə]	sister who has same mum or dad as you	*Halbschwester*
	unusual	[ʌnˈjuːʒuəl]	↔ usual	*ungewöhnlich*
	missing	[ˈmɪsɪŋ]	*v* to miss	*fehlend*
	generation	[ˌdʒenəˈreɪʃn]	people born around the same time	*Generation*
	single parent	[ˌsɪŋgl ˈpeərənt]	parent without a partner	*Alleinerziehende/r*
	same-sex	[ˌseɪm ˈseks]	↔ mixed-sex	*gleichgeschlechtlich*
	adopted	[əˈdɒptɪd]	*v* to adopt	*adoptiert*
	only child	[ˈəʊnlɪ tʃaɪld]	child without brothers or sisters	*Einzelkind*
	siblings	[ˈsɪblɪŋz]	brothers and sisters	*Geschwister*
18	**immigrant**	[ˈɪmɪgrənt]	*v* to immigrate	*Einwanderer/-in*
	ethnic background	[ˌeθnɪk ˈbækgraʊnd]	what race sb / sb's family comes from	*Abstammung*
	grandparents	[ˈgrænpeərənts]	parents of a parent	*Großeltern*
	citizen	[ˈsɪtɪzn]	*n* citizenship	*Staatsbürger*
	passport	[ˈpɑːspɔːt]	document which lets sb travel between countries	*Pass, Reisepass*
	bilingual	[ˌbaɪˈlɪŋgwəl]	able to speak two languages fluently	*zweisprachig*
	relative	[ˈrelətɪv]	family members	*Verwandte/r*
	Kurdish	[ˈkɜːdɪʃ]	of or from Kurdistan	*kurdisch*
	ethnic group	[ˈeθnɪk gruːp]	people with shared cultural or religious traditions	*Volksgruppe*
	traditional	[trəˈdɪʃənl]	*n* tradition	*traditionell*
	middle	[ˈmɪdl]	*phr* in the middle	*Mitte*
	republic	[rɪˈpʌblɪk]	democratic country without a king or queen	*Republik*
	refugee	[ˌrefjuˈdʒiː]	*n* refuge	*Flüchtling*
	war	[wɔː]	e.g. World War II , war in Iraq	*Krieg*
	lots of	[ˈlɒts əv]	↔ few of	*viel(e), eine Menge*
	fighting	[ˈfaɪtɪŋ]	*n* fight	*Kämpfe*
	asylum	[əˈsaɪləm]	*n* asylum seeker	*Asyl*
	connection	[kəˈnekʃn]	*v* to connect	*Verbindung*
	tradition	[trəˈdɪʃn]	*adj* traditional	*Tradition*
	to **telephone**	[ˈtelɪfəʊn]	to call	*telefonieren*
	to **make friends**	[ˌmeɪk ˈfrendz]	*adj* friendly	*Freunde finden/gewinnen*
	dream	[driːm]	↔ nightmare	*Traum*
	education	[ˌedʒuˈkeɪʃn]	*adj* educational	*Schulbildung, Ausbildung*
	member	[ˈmembə]	*phr* to become a member of sth	*Mitglied*
	parliament	[ˈpɑːləmənt]	where government meets	*Parlament*
	background	[ˈbækgraʊnd]	where somebody comes from	*Herkunft*
	complicated	[ˈkɒmplɪkeɪtɪd]	↔ simple	*kompliziert*
	company	[ˈkʌmpəni]	firm, business	*Firma, Unternehmen, Gesellschaft*
	to **give sth up**	[ˌgɪv ˈʌp]	to quit sth	*etw aufgeben*
	future	[ˈfjuːtʃə]	↔ past	*Zukunft*
19	**owner**	[ˈəʊnə]	*v* to own sth	*Inhaber/in*
	to **be at war**	[bi ət ˈwɔː]	⚠ ~~to be in war~~	*im Krieg sein*
	government	[ˈgʌvənmənt]	*v* to govern	*Regierung*
	army	[ˈɑːmi]	soldiers	*Armee*
	rebel	[ˈrebl]	*adj* rebellious	*Rebell*
	rural	[ˈrʊərəl]	in the countryside	*ländlich*
	area	[ˈeəriə]	district, region	*Gebiet*
	urban	[ˈɜːbən]	in the city	*städtisch, Stadt-*
	enormous	[ɪˈnɔːməs]	huge, gigantic	*enorm, gewaltig*
	amount	[əˈmaʊnt]	quantity	*Menge*
	natural	[ˈnætʃrəl]	↔ unnatural	*natürlich*
	resource	[rɪˈsɔːs]	*adj* resourceful	*Ressource, Bodenschatz*
	diamond	[ˈdaɪəmənd]	e.g. a diamond ring	*Diamant*
	conflict	[ˈkɒnflɪkt]	fight, war	*Konflikt, Bürgerkrieg*
	unbelievable	[ˌʌnbɪˈliːvəbl]	*v* to believe	*unglaublich*

	once	[wʌns]	one time	*einmal*
	to imagine sth	[ɪ'mædʒɪn]	*adj* imaginary	*sich etw vorstellen*
	size	[saɪz]	e.g. S, M, L, XL, etc.	*Größe*
	culture	['kʌltʃə]	*adj* cultural	*Kultur*
20	carnival	['kɑ:nɪvl]	a big street party with dancing	*Karneval*
	citizenship	['sɪtɪznʃɪp]	*n* citizen	*Staatsbürgerschaft*
	mixed	[mɪkst]	not all the same	*gemischt*
	to take place	[teɪk 'pleɪs]	to occur, to happen	*stattfinden*
	the Berlin Wall	[ðə ˌbɜ:lɪn 'wɔ:l]	wall around West Berlin from 1961 until 1989	*die Berliner Mauer*
	to criticize	['krɪtɪsaɪz]	*n* critcism	*kritisieren*
	migration	[maɪ'greɪʃn]	*v* to migrate	*Wanderung, Migration*
	organiser	['ɔ:gənaɪzə]	*n* organisation	*Organisator/in*
	celebration	[ˌselɪ'breɪʃn]	*v* to celebrate	*Feier*
	photo(graph)	['fəʊtəʊ, 'fəʊtəgrɑ:f]	*v* to photograph	*Foto(grafie)*
	to dress up	[ˌdres 'ʌp]	e.g. For Hallowe'en I dressed up as a ghost.	*sich verkleiden*
	thousand	['θaʊznd]	1000	*tausend, Tausend*
	to welcome sb	['welkəm]	to say hello	*jdn willkommen heißen*
	bright	[braɪt]	*(hier)* colourful	*(Farbe:) bunt, leuchtend*
	to enjoy doing sth	[ɪn'dʒɔɪ]	*adj* enjoyable	*etw gern tun*
	mirror	['mɪrə]	e.g. I looked in the mirror to check my make-up.	*Spiegel*
	to make yourself up	[ˌmeɪk 'ʌp]	to put on make-up	*sich schminken*
21	at the front of the picture	[ət ðə ˌfrʌnt əv ðə 'pɪktʃə]	↔ at the back of the picture	*vorn im Bild*
	normally	['nɔ:məli]	e.g. I normally eat breakfast before work.	*normalerweise*
	mouse, mice	[maʊs, maɪs]	a small animal	*Maus, Mäuse*
	a day out	[ə ˌdeɪ 'aʊt]	day trip	*ein Ausflug*
	to feed	[fi:d]	*n* food	*füttern*
	duck	[dʌk]	type of bird	*Ente*
	bottom	['bɒtəm]	↔ top	*untere/r/s*
	corner	['kɔ:nə]	e.g. There is a bird in the corner of the photo.	*Ecke*
	face	[feɪs]	part of body at front of the head	*Gesicht*
	chips *(BE)*	[tʃɪps]	*AE:* French fries	*Pommes frites*
	wall	[wɔ:l]	e.g. the Great Wall of China	*Wand*
22	to get ready for sth	[ˌget 'redi fə]	to prepare for sth	*sich auf etw vorbereiten*
	background	['bækgraʊnd]	↔ foreground	*Hintergrund*
	to go for a walk	[ˌgəʊ fər ə 'wɔ:k]	e.g. We went for a walk in the park.	*spazieren gehen*
	to replace	[rɪ'pleɪs]	*n* replacement	*ersetzen, austauschen*
	to rewrite	[ˌri:'raɪt]	to write again	*neu schreiben, neu formulieren*
	relevant	['reləvənt]	↔ irrelevevant	*relevant*
	to add	[æd]	*n* addition	*hinzufügen*
	clause	[klɔ:z]	part of a sentence	*Nebensatz*
	to pick sth	[pɪk]	to choose sth	*etw auswählen, sich etw aussuchen*
	future	['fju:tʃə]	↔ past	*zukünftige/r/s*
	hardly	['hɑ:dli]	almost never	*kaum*
	flat *(BE)*	[flæt]	*AE:* appartment	*Wohnung*
	vegetarian	[ˌvedʒə'teəriən]	someone who doesn't eat meat	*Vegetarier/in*
	to pick sb up	[ˌpɪk 'ʌp]	to collect sb	*jdn abholen*
	task	[tɑ:sk]	*phr* to give sb a task	*Aufgabe*
	based on	['beɪst ɒn]	e.g. She wrote a story based on her life.	*auf Grundlage von*
24	to book	[bʊk]	to order, to reserve	*buchen, reservieren*
	factor	['fæktə]	part	*Faktor*
	location	[ləʊ'keɪʃn]	*v* to locate	*Standort, Lage*
	noisy	['nɔɪzi]	↔ quiet	*laut*
	facilities	[fə'sɪlətiz]	e.g. The school has very good sports facilities.	*Einrichtungen*
	conference room	['kɒnfərəns ru:m]	meeting room	*Konferenzzimmer*
	price	[praɪs]	how much sth costs	*Preis*
	reasonable	['ri:znəbl]	↔ unreasonable	*vernünftig, angemessen*
	past	[pɑ:st]	↔ future	*vergangene/r/s, ehemalige/r/s*
	guest	[gest]	↔ host	*Gast*
	wonderful	['wʌndəfl]	great, super	*wunderbar*
	terrible	['terəbl]	bad, awful	*furchtbar*
	meeting	['mi:tɪŋ]	*v* to meet	*Sitzung, Besprechung*
	to hold a meeting	[ˌhəʊld ə 'mi:tɪŋ]	to have a meeting	*eine Sitzung abhalten*
	presentation	[ˌprezn'teɪʃn]	*v* to present	*Präsentation*

	to **spend**	[spend]	e.g. I spent a year in New York learning English.	*(Zeit) verbringen*
	to **reserve**	[rɪ'zɜːv]	*n* reservation	*reservieren*
	assistant	[ə'sɪstənt]	*v* to assist	*Assistent/in*
	travel arrangements	['trævl əreɪndʒmənts]	*phr* to make travel arrangements	*Reisepläne*
	colleague	['kɒliːg]	sb who works with you	*Kollege/-in*
	to **search for** sth	['sɜːtʃ fə]	to look for sth	*etw suchen*
	private	['praɪvət]	↔ public	*privat, eigene/r/s*
	access	['ækses]	*v* to access	*Zugang, Zugriff*
	free	[friː]	*phr* for free	*kostenlos, gratis*
	I'm afraid	[aɪm ə'freɪd]	unfortunately, sorry	*leider*
	to **share** sth	[ʃeə]	↔ to keep (for oneself)	*(sich) etw teilen*
	to **let** sb **know**	[ˌlet 'nəʊ]	to inform sb of sth	*jdm Bescheid sagen*
	to **make sure**	[ˌmeɪk 'ʃʊə]	to ensure	*sicherstellen, gewährleisten*
	credit card	['kredɪt kɑːd]	e.g. I used my credit card to buy new clothes.	*Kreditkarte*
25	to **receive**	[rɪ'siːv]	*n* receipt	*erhalten, bekommen*
	confirmation	[ˌkɒnfə'meɪʃn]	*v* to confirm	*Bestätigung*
	to **be missing**	[bi 'mɪsɪŋ]	not there	*fehlen*
	surname	['sɜːneɪm]	family name	*Nachname*
	check-in	['tʃekɪn]	e.g. Check-in closes 45 minutes before we fly.	*Ankunft, Anmeldung*
	check-out	['tʃekaʊt]	e.g. Check-out from the hotel is possible until 12.	*Abreise, Abmeldung*
	to **require**	[rɪ'kwaɪə]	*n* requirement	*wünschen, benötigen*
	adult	['ædʌlt]	↔ child	*Erwachsene/r*
	single	['sɪŋgl]	*phr* single bed	*Einzel-*
	double	['dʌbl]	*phr* double room	*Doppel-*
	additional	[ə'dɪʃənl]	extra	*zusätzlich, Zusatz-*
	requirement	[rɪ'kwaɪəmənt]	*v* to require	*Wunsch, Bedürfnis*
	to **confirm**	[kən'fɜːm]	*n* confirmation	*bestätigen*
	to **be able to do** sth	[bi 'eɪbl tə du]	↔ to be unable to do sth	*etw tun können; in der Lage sein, etw zu tun*
	pleasure	['pleʒə]	*adj* pleasurable	*Vergnügen*
	reservation	[ˌrezə'veɪʃn]	*v* to reserve	*Reservierung*
	details	['diːteɪlz]	*phr* contact details	*Angaben, Daten*
	as follows	[əz 'fɒləʊz]	e.g. Your instructions are as follows: ...	*wie folgt*
	to **wish**	[wɪʃ]	*n* wish	*wünschen*
	pleasant	['pleznt]	↔ unpleasant	*angenehm*
	stay	[steɪ]	time sb spends somewhere, e.g. in a hotel	*Aufenthalt*
	Yours faithfully,	[ˌjɔːz 'feɪθfəli]	Yours sincerely,	*(Brief:) Mit freundlichen Grüßen*
	management	['mænɪdʒmənt]	*v* to manage	*Geschäftsleitung*
	mistake	[mɪ'steɪk]	error	*Fehler*
	in advance	[ɪn əd'vɑːns]	before	*im Voraus*
26	**advertisment**	[ædv'ɜːtɪzmənt]	*AE:* commercial	*Werbespot*
	to **be high quality**	[bi ˌhaɪ 'kwɒləti]	↔ to be poor quality	*von hoher Qualität sein*
	located	[ləʊ'keɪtɪd]	*n* location	*gelegen*
	to **take a break from** sth	[ˌteɪk ə 'breɪk frəm]	e.g. She took a break from working to travel the world.	*etw hinter sich lassen, einer Sache entkommen*
	everyday life	[ˌevrideɪ 'laɪf]	what you do everyday	*Alltagsleben*
	outside of	[ˌaʊt'saɪd əv]	↔ inside of	*außerhalb von*
	setting	['setɪŋ]	e.g. It was a beautiful setting.	*Landschaft*
	hiking	['haɪkɪŋ]	*v* to hike	*Wandern*
	sheep, sheep	[ʃiːp, ʃiːp]	type of animal that we get wool from	*Schaf, Schafe*
	goat	[gəʊt]	type of animal	*Ziege*
	chicken	['tʃɪkɪn]	type of bird that we get eggs from	*Huhn*
	star	[stɑː]	e.g. There are a lot of stars in the night sky.	*Stern*
	business person	['bɪznəs pɜːsn]	business man/woman	*Geschäftsmann/-frau*
	nearby	['nɪəbaɪ]	close, near	*in der Nähe*
	several	['sevrəl]	a few, a couple	*mehrere*
	to **work out**	[ˌwɜːk 'aʊt]	to exercise	*trainieren*
	to **offer**	['ɒfə]	*n* offer	*bieten, anbieten*
	cuisine	[kwɪ'ziːn]	a type of cooking	*Küche*
	suitable	['suːtəbl]	↔ unsuitable	*geeignet*
	detail	['diːteɪl]	e.g. contact details	*Detail, Einzelheit*
	detailed	['diːteɪld]	in detail	*detailliert*
	to **mention**	['menʃn]	to name	*erwähnen*

Unit 3

27	granddad	[ˈgrændæd]	*(inf)* grandfather	*Opa*
	fashion	[ˈfæʃn]	*adj* fashionable	*Mode*
	to wear	[weə]	⚠ ~~to carry~~	*(Kleidung:) tragen*
	floral	[ˈflɒrəl]	e.g. She wore a floral dress to the beach.	*Blumen-, mit Blumenmuster*
	shirt	[ʃɜːt]	e.g. I wear a shirt and tie to work every day.	*Hemd*
	decade	[ˈdekeɪd]	10 years	*Jahrzehnt*
	to dye	[daɪ]	*adj* dyed	*färben*
	tight	[taɪt]	↔ loose	*eng, knapp*
	leather	[ˈleðə]	material made from animal skin	*Leder*
	jacket	[ˈdʒækɪt]	light coat	*Jacke*
	suit	[suːt]	formal clothing usually worn with a tie	*Anzug*
	bald	[bɔːld]	with no hair	*glatzköpfig*
	cardigan	[ˈkɑːdɪgən]	a type of clothing	*Strickjacke*
	sunglasses	[ˈsʌnglɑːsɪz]	glasses to protect eyes from sun	*Sonnenbrille*
	chain	[tʃeɪn]	necklace	*Kette*
	tracksuit	[ˈtræksuːt]	clothes you wear to do exercise	*Trainingsanzug*
28	Second World War	[ˌsekənd ˌwɜːld ˈwɔː]	world war between 1939 and 1945	*der Zweite Weltkrieg*
	moon	[muːn]	e.g. There's a full moon tonight.	*Mond*
	landing	[ˈlændɪŋ]	*v* to land	*Landung*
	TV set	[ˌtiːˈviː set]	television	*Fernsehgerät, -apparat*
	mobile phone *(BE)*	[ˌməʊbaɪl ˈfəʊn]	*AE:* cell phone	*Handy, Mobiltelefon*
	to save sth	[seɪv]	*n* saving	*etw sparen*
	comfortable	[ˈkʌmftəbl]	↔ uncomfortable	*gemütlich, bequem*
	to settle down	[ˌsetl ˈdaʊn]	e.g. After getting married, they settled down and started a family.	*sesshaft werden, zur Ruhe kommen, es sich bequem machen*
	to drop out	[ˌdrɒp ˈaʊt]	to leave	*aussteigen*
	instead	[ɪnˈsted]	e.g. We didn't go out. We stayed at home instead.	*stattdessen*
	optimism	[ˈɒptɪmɪzəm]	↔ pessimism	*Optimismus*
	flower	[ˈflaʊə]	*n* to flower	*Blume*
	power	[ˈpaʊə]	strength	*Kraft, Energie*
	to worry about sth	[ˈwʌri əbaʊt]	*n* worry	*sich um etw Sorgen machen*
	nuclear	[ˈnjuːkliə]	*phr* nuclear energy	*Atom-*
	to ban	[bæn]	*n* ban	*verbieten, abschaffen*
	bomb	[bɒm]	explosive substance	*Bombe*
	hard-working	[ˌhɑːd ˈwɜːkɪŋ]	↔ lazy	*fleißig, hart arbeitend*
	record	[ˈrekɔːd]	larger, old-fashioned CD	*Schallplatte*
	record player	[ˈrekɔːd pleɪə]	machine for playing records	*Schallplattenspieler*
	to stick sth	[stɪk]	to put	*etw stecken, stechen*
	pin	[pɪn]	needle	*Stecknadel, Anstecknadel*
	ear	[ɪə]	part of the body on side of the head	*Ohr*
	lip	[lɪp]	part of the mouth	*Lippe*
	to come down	[ˌkʌm ˈdaʊn]	↔ to go up, to rise	*einstürzen, fallen*
	smart	[smɑːt]	clever, intelligent	*clever, schick*
	Communist	[ˈkɒmjənɪst]	*phr* the Communist Party	*kommunistisch, Kommunist/in*
	to own	[əʊn]	*n* owner	*besitzen*
	collection	[kəˈlekʃn]	*v* to collect	*Sammlung*
	to include	[ɪnˈkluːdɪŋ]	e.g. The price of the room includes breakfast.	*einschließen, beinhalten*
	endless	[ˈendləs]	without an end	*endlos*
	to earn sb sth	[ɜːn]	to give sb sth	*jdm etw einbringen*
	nickname	[ˈnɪkneɪm]	name your friends and family call you	*Spitzname*
	however	[haʊˈevə]	but, on the other hand	*dagegen, allerdings, jedoch*
	to grow up	[ˌgrəʊ ˈʌp]	to become an adult	*erwachsen werden*
	the Gulf War	[ðə ˈgʌlf wɔː]	war against Iraq in 1991	*der Golfkrieg*
	shock	[ʃɒk]	*phr* to be in shock	*Schock*
	climate	[ˈklaɪmət]	weather	*Klima*
	climate change	[ˈklaɪmət tʃeɪndʒ]	e.g. Scientists met to discuss climate change.	*Klimawandel*
	optimist	[ˈɒptɪmɪst]	↔ pessimist	*Optimist/in*
29	technology	[tekˈnɒlədʒi]	*adj* technological	*Technologie, Technik*
	characteristic	[ˌkærəktəˈrɪstɪk]	feature	*Merkmal, Eigenschaft*
	attitude	[ˈætɪtjuːd]	belief	*Einstellung, Haltung*
	to seem	[siːm]	to appear	*scheinen*
	to brainstorm	[ˈbreɪnstɔːm]	to collect ideas	*Ideen sammeln*

	research	[rɪ'sɜːtʃ]	*v* to research	*Nachforschungen, Recherche*
	to find out	[ˌfaɪnd 'aʊt]	to discover	*herausfinden*
30	lyrics	['lɪrɪks]	songtext	*Liedtext*
	to put sb down	[ˌpʊt 'daʊn]	to criticise	*jdn demütigen, jdn herabsetzen*
	to get around	[ˌget ə'raʊnd]	to mix with people	*herumkommen*
	awful	['ɔːfl]	terrible	*furchtbar*
	to fade away	[ˌfeɪd ə'weɪ]	to disappear	*verschwinden*
	to dig	[dɪg]	to understand or like sth	*(ugs.) verstehen*
	to cause	[kɔːz]	*n* cause	*verursachen*
	sensation	[sen'seɪʃn]	*adj* sensational	*Sensation*
	verse	[vɜːs]	part of a song that you sing more than once	*Strophe*
	meaning	['miːnɪŋ]	*v* to mean	*Bedeutung*
	to drop	[drɒp]	to let sth fall	*fallen lassen*
	unimportant	[ˌʌnɪm'pɔːtənt]	↔ important	*unwichtig, unbedeutend*
	to kill	[kɪl]	e.g. The fire killed 10 people.	*töten*
	circle	['sɜːkl]	*phr* circle of friends	*Kreis*
	to mix with sb	['mɪks wɪð]	to talk or be friends with sb	*mit jdm verkehren*
	to avoid	[ə'vɔɪd]	to try not to do sth	*vermeiden, meiden*
	hole	[həʊl]	e.g. Be careful of the hole in the ground!	*Loch*
	ground	[graʊnd]	floor, earth	*Erde*
31	to support	[sə'pɔːt]	*n* support	*unterstützen, untermauern*
	to earn	[ɜːn]	*n* earnings	*verdienen*
	specific	[spə'sɪfɪk]	particular	*speziell*
	original	[ə'rɪdʒənl]	*adv* originally	*ursprünglich*
	to be alive	[bi ə'laɪv]	↔ to be dead	*am Leben sein*
	to appear	[ə'pɪə]	*n* appearance	*vorkommen, erscheinen*
	to prepare	[prɪ'peə]	*n* preparation	*(sich) vorbereiten*
	actor	['æktə]	*v* to act	*Schauspieler*
	producer	[prə'djuːsə]	*v* to produce	*Produzent/in*
	heart attack	['hɑːt ətæk]	*phr* to have a heart attack	*Herzinfarkt*
	because of	[bɪ'kɒz əv]	due to, thanks to	*aufgrund*
	cocaine	[kəʊ'keɪn]	*phr* to take cocaine	*Kokain*
	overdose	['əʊvədəʊs]	*v* to overdose	*Überdosis*
	Guess what?	[ˌges 'wɒt]	e.g. Guess what? I got the job!	*Stellen Sie sich/Stell dir vor!*
	pill	[pɪl]	tablet	*Pille, Tablette*
	at least	[ət 'liːst]	↔ at most	*mindestens*
	music lessons	['mjuːzɪk lesnz]	*phr* to take music lessons	*Musikunterricht*
	active	['æktɪv]	↔ inactive, passive	*aktiv*
	career	[kə'rɪə]	*phr* to start a career	*Karriere*
	discussion	[dɪ'skʌʃn]	*v* to discuss	*Diskussion, Erörterung*
	to look sth up	[ˌlʊk 'ʌp]	to look in a dictionary	*etw (in einem Wörterbuch) nachschlagen*
	to represent	[ˌreprɪ'zent]	*n* representation	*vertreten, repräsentieren*
32	tooth	[tuːθ, tiːθ]	*pl* teeth	*Zahn, Zähne*
	while	[waɪl]	at the same time as sth else	*während*
	to look after sb/sth	[ˌlʊk 'ɑːftə]	e.g. The babysitter looked after the children.	*sich um jdn/etw kümmern*
	to behave	[bɪ'heɪv]	*n* behaviour	*sich verhalten, sich benehmen*
	housewife	['haʊswaɪf]	e.g. She stayed at home and became a housewife.	*Hausfrau*
	spiky	['spaɪki]	e.g. Bart Simpson has spiky hair.	*stachelig*
	coloured	['kʌləd]	colourful, full of colour	*farbig, bunt*
	result	[rɪ'zʌlt]	consequence	*Ergebnis, Folge*
	pressure	['preʃə]	*phr* to put sb under pressure	*Druck*
33	to happen	['hæpən]	to occur	*geschehen, passieren*
	dear	[dɪə]	e.g. Look after yourself, dear.	*meine Liebe/mein Lieber, Schatz*
	step	[step]	*phr* step by step	*Schritt*
	giant	['dʒaɪənt]	huge, enormous	*riesig*
	leap	[liːp]	large jump	*Sprung*
	mankind	[mæn'kaɪnd]	all humans	*Menschheit*
	at all	[ət 'ɔːl]	e.g. That was no fun at all!	*überhaupt*
	disappointed	[ˌdɪsə'pɔɪntɪd]	*n* disappointment	*enttäuscht*
	march	[mɑːtʃ]	*v* to march	*Marsch*
	to smoke	[sməʊk]	*n* smoker	*rauchen*
	marijuana	[ˌmærə'wɑːnə]	cannabis	*Marihuana*
	certain	['sɜːtn]	↔ uncertain	*gewiss, bestimmt*

	silly	['sɪli]	funny, stupid	*albern, dumm*
	documentary	[ˌdɒkju'mentri]	TV programme about things that really happened	*Dokumentation, Dokumentarfilm*
	to be fun	[bi 'fʌn]	↔ to be boring	*Spaß machen, unterhaltsam sein*
	miniskirt	['mɪniskɜːt]	short skirt	*Minirock*
	serious	['sɪəriəs]	sensible	*ernst, ernsthaft*
34	sales assistant	['seɪlz əsɪstənt]	e.g. I worked as a sale assistant in a supermarket.	*Verkäufer/in*
	seaside	['siːsaɪd]	next to the sea	*am Meer, Küsten-*
	to introduce sb to sb	[ˌɪntrə'djuːs tə]	e.g. Let me introduce you to my father.	*jdm jdn vorstellen*
	to fit	[fɪt]	to be right	*passen*
	so far	[ˌsəʊ 'fɑː]	until now	*bis jetzt, so weit*
	forest	['fɒrɪst]	wood	*Wald*
	by the way	[ˌbaɪ ðə 'weɪ]	e.g. By the way, have you heard about Paul?	*übrigens*
	to improve	[ɪm'pruːv]	↔ to get worse	*verbessern, (sich) bessern*
	to get the hang of it	[ˌget ðə 'hæŋ əv ɪt]	to get used to sth	*etw hinbekommen*
	work experience	['wɜːk ɪkspɪəriəns]	*phr* to do work experience	*Praktikum*
	definitely	['defɪnətli]	↔ possibly	*bestimmt, absolut*
	manager	['mænɪdʒə]	*v* to manage	*Geschäftsführer/in*
35	interest	['ɪntrəst]	*v* to interest sb	*Interesse*
	to sound	[saʊnd]	e.g. That sounds like a great plan!	*klingen*
	unfriendly	[ʌn'frendli]	↔ friendly	*unfreundlich*
	politics	['pɒlətɪks]	*n* poltician	*Politik*
36	unknown	[ˌʌn'nəʊn]	↔ known	*unbekannt*
	to panic	['pænɪk]	↔ to relax	*in Panik geraten*
	to work sth out	[ˌwɜːk 'aʊt]	to solve	*etw herausbekommen*
	in bold	[ɪn 'bəʊld]	e.g. This word is in **bold**.	*fettgedruckt*
	Englishman	['ɪŋglɪʃmən]	man from England	*Engländer*
	relaxing	[rɪ'læksɪŋ]	*v* to relax	*erholsam*
	excitement	[ɪk'saɪtmənt]	*adj* exciting	*Aufregung, Spannung*
	dear	[dɪə]	expensive	*lieb, teuer*
	cheap	[tʃiːp]	inexpensive	*billig*
	close to	['kləʊs tə]	↔ far from	*nahe bei*
	to taste	[teɪst]	*n* taste	*schmecken*
	to throw sth away	[ˌθrəʊ ə'weɪ]	to put in the rubbish	*etw wegwerfen*

Unit 4

37	social	['səʊʃl]	↔ antisocial	*sozial, gesellschaftlich*
	media	['miːdiə]	TV, radio, internet, newspaper, etc.	*Medien*
	multi-player	[ˌmʌlti 'pleɪə]	*phr* multi-player game	*mit mehreren Spielern*
	network	['netwɜːk]	*phr* social network	*Netzwerk*
	to reply	[rɪ'plaɪ]	*n* reply	*antworten*
	stranger	['streɪndʒə]	sb you don't know	*Fremde/r*
	to exchange	[ɪks'tʃeɪndʒ]	*n* exchange	*austauschen*
	user	['juːzə]	*v* to use	*Benutzer/in*
	kind	[kaɪnd]	type, sort	*Art*
	diary	['daɪəri]	journal (*esp AE*)	*Tagebuch*
	to upload	[ˌʌp'ləʊd]	↔ to download	*hochladen*
	to interest	['ɪntrəst]	*adj* interesting	*interessieren*
	personal	['pɜːsənl]	↔ public, shared	*persönlich, eigene/r/s*
	to link	[lɪŋk]	*n* link	*verlinken*
	permission	[pə'mɪʃn]	*v* to permit	*Erlaubnis, Genehmigung*
	rarely	['reəli]	*adj* rare	*selten, kaum*
	all the time	[ˌɔːl ðə 'taɪm]	↔ never	*ständig, andauernd*
	vocabulary	[və'kæbjələri]	*phr* to expand one's vocabulary	*Wortschatz*
	concept	['kɒnsept]	idea, term	*Begriff*
	update	['ʌpdeɪt]	*v* to update	*Aktualisierung*
	privacy	['prɪvəsi]	*adj* private	*Privatsphäre*
	setting	['setɪŋ]	*phr* security settings	*Einstellung*
	to point to sth	['pɔɪnt tə]	to show	*auf etw (ver)weisen*
	to control	[kən'trəʊl]	*n* control	*steuern*
	space	[speɪs]	area	*Raum, Platz*
	to post sth	[pəʊst]	e.g. I posted new photos on my Facebook profile.	*etw* (am Schwarzen Brett) *anschlagen, aushängen*
	to allow	[ə'laʊ]	to let sb do sth	*erlauben, gestatten*
38	tragedy	['trædʒədi]	*adj* tragic	*Tragödie*

	to **keep in touch**	[ˌkiːp ɪn ˈtʌtʃ]	to stay in contact	*in Verbindung bleiben*
	to **contact sb**	[ˈkɒntækt]	to get in touch with	*Kontakt zu jdm aufnehmen*
	to **accept**	[əkˈsept]	*n* acceptance	*akzeptieren, annehmen*
	guitar	[gɪˈtɑː]	*n* guitarist	*Gitarre*
	drums	[drʌmz]	*n* drummer	*Schlagzeug*
	since then	[sɪns ˈðen]	e.g. I liked it and since then I have been often.	*seitdem*
	boat	[bəʊt]	small ship	*Boot*
	fishing	[ˈfɪʃɪŋ]	catching fish	*Angeln, Fischen*
	difficulty	[ˈdɪfɪkəlti]	*adj* difficult	*Schwierigkeit*
	overweight	[ˌəʊvəˈweɪt]	↔ underweight	*übergewichtig*
	depressed	[dɪˈprest]	↔ happy	*niedergeschlagen, deprimiert*
	to **rush**	[rʌʃ]	to do sth quickly	*eilen*
	puzzled	[ˈpʌzld]	confused	*verwirrt*
	nasty	[ˈnɑːsti]	cruel, bad	*gemein, böse*
	to **cry**	[kraɪ]	e.g. Don't cry, it will be alright!	*schreien, weinen*
	to **trust**	[trʌst]	↔ to distrust	*vertrauen*
	rude	[ruːd]	↔ polite	*unhöflich, unverschämt*
	shocked	[ʃɒkt]	surprised	*schockiert*
	to **turn sth off**	[ˌtɜːn ˈɒf]	↔ to turn sth on	*etw ausschalten*
	to **shout at sb**	[ˈʃaʊt ət]	to say sth very loudly	*jdn anschreien*
	to **be supposed to do sth**	[bi səˈpəʊzd tə du]	e.g. I am sorry, but don't understand what I am supposed to do.	*(eigentlich) etw tun sollen*
	obviously	[ˈɒbviəsli]	clearly	*offensichtlich*
	upset	[ˌʌpˈset]	*v* to upset sb	*bestürzt, aufgeregt*
	suddenly	[ˈsʌdnli]	↔ gradually	*plötzlich*
	horrible	[ˈhɒrəbl]	awful	*schrecklich*
	feeling	[ˈfiːlɪŋ]	*phr* to have a feeling that...	*Gefühl, Eindruck*
	upstairs	[ˌʌpˈsteəz]	↔ downstairs	*oben, nach oben*
	closet (AE)	[ˈklɒzɪt]	*BE:* wardrobe	*begehbarer Kleiderschrank*
	belt	[belt]	e.g. I am wearing jeans with a leather belt.	*Gürtel*
	neck	[nek]	part of the body between the head and shoulders	*Hals*
	account	[əˈkaʊnt]	e.g. Facebook account or profile	*Konto*
	final	[ˈfaɪnl]	last	*letzte/r/s*
39	**whether**	[ˈweðə]	if	*ob*
	true	[truː]	*n* truth	*wahr*
	false	[fɔːls]	↔ true	*falsch*
	opposite	[ˈɒpəzɪt]	on the other side	*gegenüber*
	to **feel sorry**	[ˌfiːl ˈsɒri]	to be sorry	*Leid tun*
	afterwards	[ˈɑːftəwədz]	↔ before	*hinterher*
	joke	[dʒəʊk]	e.g. He tells funny jokes.	*Witz, Streich*
	lie	[laɪ]	↔ truth	*Lüge*
	feeling	[ˈfiːlɪŋ]	view, opinion	*Ansicht, Meinung*
	to **be afraid of sth**	[bi əˈfreɪd əv]	to be scared of sth	*vor etw Angst haben*
40	**gist**	[dʒɪst]	the most important points	*das Wesentliche*
	thread	[θred]	e.g. forum thread (in internet)	*Faden*
	What is the point of …	[ˌwɒt ɪz ðə ˈpɔɪnt əv]	e.g. I am sorry, but what is the point of this meeting?	*Welchen Sinn hat es, …*
	to **call**	[kɔːl]	e.g. Don't call me bad names!	*nennen*
	insecure	[ˌɪnsɪˈkjʊə]	↔ secure, safe	*unsicher*
	popular	[ˈpɒpjələ]	↔ unpopular	*beliebt*
	might	[maɪt]	e.g. I might come but I don't know yet.	*können*
	site	[saɪt]	website	*Website*
	to **delete**	[dɪˈliːt]	*n* deletion	*löschen*
	face-to-face	[ˌfeɪs tə ˈfeɪs]	in person	*persönlich*
	weird	[wɪəd]	↔ normal	*seltsam, verrückt*
	to **agree with sb**	[əˈgriː wɪð]	↔ to disagree with sb	*jdm zustimmen, jdm Recht geben*
	lonely	[ˈləʊnli]	alone	*einsam*
	personality	[ˌpɜːsəˈnæləti]	a person's character	*Persönlichkeit*
41	**bullying**	[ˈbʊliɪŋ]	*n* bully	*Mobbing*
	cyberbullying	[ˈsaɪbəbʊliɪŋ]	bullying on the internet	*Mobbing im Internet*
	youth	[juːθ]	*adj* young	*Jugend*
	programme	[ˈprəʊgræm]	e.g. My favourite TV programme is *Wetten das?*	*(Radio-/TV-)Sendung*
	choice	[tʃɔɪs]	*v* to choose	*Wahl, Entscheidung*
	bully	[ˈbʊli]	*v* to bully sb	*Mobber/in, Tyrann*

	comment	[ˈkɒment]	*v* to comment	*Kommentar, Bemerkung*
	mouth	[maʊθ]	*phr* word of mouth	*Mund*
	to **complain**	[kəmˈpleɪn]	*n* complaint	*sich beschweren*
	to **steal**	[stiːl]	to take away	*stehlen, hier: ausspannen*
	to **get even with sb**	[ˌget ˈiːvn wɪð]	to get revenge	*es jdm heimzahlen*
	exact	[ɪgˈzækt]	↔ inexact	*genau*
	embarrassing	[ɪmˈbærəsɪŋ]	*v* to embarrass sb	*peinlich*
	text message	[ˈtekst mesɪdʒ]	short message sent on a mobile phone	*SMS*
	fair	[feə]	↔ unfair	*gerecht, fair*
	to **disagree with sb**	[ˌdɪsəˈgriː wɪð]	*n* disagreement	*jdm widersprechen, anderer Meinung als jd sein*
	stupid	[ˈstjuːpɪd]	↔ clever, intelligent	*dumm, doof*
	mean	[miːn]	↔ kind	*gemein*
	to **threaten**	[ˈθretn]	*n* threat	*drohen*
	to **lose**	[luːz]	↔ to win	*verlieren*
	to **annoy sb**	[əˈnɔɪ]	*adj* annoying	*jdn belästigen, nerven*
	to **upset sb**	[ˌʌpˈset]	*adj* upsetting	*jdn ärgern, aufregen*
	to **scare sb**	[skeə]	to frighten sb	*jdm Angst einjagen, jdn verängstigen*
	threat	[θret]	*adj* threatening	*Drohung*
	insult	[ˈɪnsʌlt]	*adj* insulting	*Beleidigung*
	victim	[ˈvɪktɪm]	*phr* victim of bullying	*Opfer*
	to **hurt sb**	[hɜːt]	to injure sb	*jdn verletzen*
	excuse	[ɪkˈskjuːs]	reason	*Entschuldigung, Ausrede*
	to **report**	[rɪˈpɔːt]	*n* report	*berichten, Bericht erstatten*
42	**lately**	[ˈleɪtli]	in recent times	*in letzter Zeit*
	recently	[ˈriːsntli]	lately	*neulich*
	up till now	[ˌʌp tɪl ˈnaʊ]	↔ from now on	*bis jetzt*
	yet	[jet]	already	*schon, bereits*
44	**reputation**	[ˌrepjuˈteɪʃn]	what people think of sb	*Ruf, Ansehen*
	title	[ˈtaɪtl]	name	*Titel*
	to **connect (to sb)**	[kəˈnekt]	*n* connection	*(sich mit jdm) verbinden*
	client	[ˈklaɪənt]	business customer	*Kunde/-in*
	potential	[pəˈtenʃl]	possible	*potentiell*
	employer	[ɪmˈplɔɪə]	↔ employee	*Arbeitgeber/in*
	to **check**	[tʃek]	to make sure	*überprüfen*
	applicant	[ˈæplɪkənt]	*n* application	*Bewerber/in*
	unsuitable	[ʌnˈsuːtəbl]	↔ suitable, appropriate	*ungeeignet, unpassend*
	dressed up	[ˌdrest ˈʌp]	↔ dressed down	*schick angezogen*
	to **create**	[kriˈeɪt]	*n* creation	*schaffen, erzeugen*
	impression	[ɪmˈpreʃn]	*v* to impress	*Eindruck*
	professional	[prəˈfeʃənl]	*n* profession	*professionell*
	current	[ˈkʌrənt]	↔ out-of-date, old	*aktuell*
	wise	[waɪz]	*n* wisdom	*klug*
	public	[ˈpʌblɪk]	↔ private	*öffentlich*
	innocent	[ˈɪnəsnt]	*n* innocence	*unschuldig, harmlos*
	to **impress**	[ɪmˈpres]	*adj* impressive	*beeindrucken*
	to **match sth**	[mætʃ]	to go well together	*zu etw passen*
	CV *(BE)*	[ˌsiː ˈviː]	*AE:* résumé	*Lebenslauf*
	charity work	[ˈtʃærəti wɜːk]	work that sb does for no money	*ehrenamtliche Tätigkeit*
	captain	[ˈkæptɪn]	head of a team	*Kapitän*
	interview	[ˈɪntəvjuː]	e.g. job interview	*Vorstellungsgespräch*
	unprofessional	[ˌʌnprəˈfeʃənl]	↔ professional	*unprofessionell*
	thank God	[ˌθæŋk ˈgɒd]	e.g. Thank God that's over! It was awful!	*Gott sei Dank*
	bored	[bɔːd]	↔ interested	*gelangweilt*
	security	[sɪˈkjʊərəti]	*adj* secure	*Sicherheit*
	fully	[ˈfʊli]	completely	*vollständig, völlig*
	to **make sure**	[ˌmeɪk ˈʃʊə]	to ensure	*sich vergewissern*
	although	[ɔːlˈðəʊ]	even though, though	*obwohl*
	to **remove**	[rɪˈmuːv]	*n* removal	*entfernen*
	advice	[ədˈvaɪs]	*v* to advise	*Rat, Ratschlag*
	to **lock**	[lɒk]	↔ to unlock	*sperren*
	use	[juːs]	*n* user	*Gebrauch, Benutzung*
45	to **distribute**	[dɪˈstrɪbjuːt]	*n* distribution	*vertreiben*
	cartoon	[kɑːˈtuːn]	a funny drawing	*Karikatur*

	…-**based**	[beɪst]	*v* to be based in	*in … lebend/ansässig*
	to **reproduce**	[ˌriːprəˈdjuːs]	*n* reproduction	*abdrucken, reproduzieren*
	message	[ˈmesɪdʒ]	*n* messenger	*Botschaft*
	view	[vjuː]	*phr* point of view	*Ansicht, Meinung*
	to **make a point**	[ˌmeɪk ə ˈpɔɪnt]	to show	*auf etw hinweisen*
	cartoonist	[kɑːˈtuːnɪst]	person who draws cartoons	*Karikaturist/in*
	clear	[klɪə]	↔ unclear	*klar, deutlich*
46	**tool**	[tuːl]	*phr* toolbox	*Werkzeug*
	to **recognise**	[ˈrekəgnaɪz]	e.g. He had changed so I didn't recognise him.	*erkennen, wiedererkennen*
	feature	[ˈfiːtʃə]	characteristic	*Eigenschaft, Merkmal*
	to **suggest**	[səˈdʒest]	*n* suggestion	*vorschlagen*
	to **type**	[taɪp]	e.g. to type in the box	*tippen, eingeben*
	search	[sɜːtʃ]	*phr* search engine	*Suche*
	article	[ˈɑːtɪkl]	*esp* text in a newspaper	*Artikel*
	signed	[saɪnd]	with a name written on it	*unterzeichnet*

Unit 5

47	**celebrity**	[səˈlebrəti]	famous person	*Prominente/r, Promi*
	circus	[ˈsɜːkəs]	e.g. circus tent	*Zirkus*
	headline	[ˈhedlaɪn]	title of an article	*Überschrift*
	violent	[ˈvaɪələnt]	*n* violence	*brutal, gewalttätig*
	attack	[əˈtæk]	*n* attacker	*Angriff, Übergriff*
	to **adopt**	[əˈdɒpt]	*n* adoption	*adoptieren*
	rehab	[ˈriːhæb]	rehabiliation centre	*Entzug*
	drug	[drʌg]	*phr* drug abuse	*Droge, Drogen-*
	scandal	[ˈskændl]	*adj* scandalous	*Skandal*
	bold	[bəʊld]	brave, not afraid	*kühn, provokant*
	arrest	[əˈrest]	*v* to arrest	*Verhaftung*
	secretly	[ˈsiːkrətli]	*n* secret	*heimlich*
	awards show	[əˈwɔːdz ʃəʊ]	e.g. The biggest film awards show is the Oscars.	*Preisverleihung*
	to **catch**	[kætʃ]	to find	*fangen, erwischen, verwickeln*
	to **make sth up**	[ˌmeɪk ˈʌp]	to invent, to create	*sich etw ausdenken, etw erfinden*
48	**fame**	[feɪm]	*adj* famous	*Ruhm*
	plastic surgery	[ˌplæstɪk ˈsɜːdʒəri]	e.g. Many famous people have plastic surgery in order to look younger.	*kosmetische Chirurgie, Schönheitsoperation(en)*
	to **take off your clothes**	[teɪk ˌɒf jɔː ˈkləʊðz]	↔ to put on your clothes	*sich ausziehen*
	dangerous	[ˈdeɪndʒərəs]	*n* danger	*gefährlich*
	fabulous	[ˈfæbjələs]	wonderful, incredible	*fabelhaft*
	attention	[əˈtenʃn]	*adj* attentive	*Aufmerksamkeit*
	glamorous	[ˈglæmərəs]	*n* glamour	*glamourös*
	countless	[ˈkaʊntləs]	a lot, many	*unzählig, zahllos*
	to **appear**	[əˈpɪə]	*n* appearance	*scheinen, erscheinen*
	tragic	[ˈtrædʒɪk]	*n* tragedy	*tragisch*
	ultimate	[ˈʌltɪmət]	big, ideal	*größte/r/s, endgültig*
	miserable	[ˈmɪzrəbl]	*n* misery	*unglücklich, elend*
	to **be addicted to sth**	[bi əˈdɪktɪd tə]	*n* addiction	*nach etw süchtig sein, von etw abhängig sein*
	unfortunately	[ʌnˈfɔːtʃənətli]	↔ fortunately	*leider, unglücklicherweise*
	happiness	[ˈhæpinəs]	↔ unhappiness, misery	*Zufriedenheit, Glück*
	shocking	[ˈʃɒkɪŋ]	e.g. The effects of the earthquake were shocking.	*schockierend*
	obscene	[əbˈsiːn]	*n* obscenity	*unverschämt, obszön*
	to **insult sb**	[ɪnˈsʌlt]	*n* insult	*jdn beleidigen*
	in public	[ɪn ˈpʌblɪk]	↔ in private	*öffentlich*
	to **tell lies**	[ˌtel ˈlaɪz]	to not tell the truth	*Lügen verbreiten*
	to **hide**	[haɪd]	to keep secret	*verbergen, verheimlichen*
	sexuality	[ˌsekʃuˈæləti]	*adj* sexual	*Sexualität*
	to **undress**	[ˌʌnˈdres]	↔ to dress	*sich ausziehen*
	to **appear on television**	[əˌpɪər ɒn ˈtelɪvɪʒn]	*n* television appearance	*ins Fernsehen kommen*
	to **put pressure on sb**	[ˌpʊt ˈpreʃə ɒn]	to pressurise sb	*auf jdn Druck ausüben*
	to **destroy**	[dɪˈstrɔɪ]	*n* destruction	*zerstören*
	to **dislike**	[dɪsˈlaɪk]	↔ to like	*nicht mögen*
	desperate	[ˈdespərət]	*n* desperation	*verzweifelt*

	impossible	[ɪm'pɒsəbl]	↔ possible	*unmöglich*
	talent agent	['tælənt eɪdʒənt]	sb who finds and looks after celebrities	*(Schauspiel-)Agent/in, (Künstler-) Vermittler/in*
	to **agree with sth**	[ə'gri: wɪð]	*n* agreement	*einer Sache zustimmen*
	aspect	['æspekt]	side	*Aspekt, Seite*
49	**author**	['ɔ:θə]	writer	*Autor/in*
	manner	['mænə]	way	*Art (und Weise)*
	to **get married**	[ˌget 'mærid]	e.g. They were together for five years before they got married.	*heiraten*
	marriage	['mærɪdʒ]	↔ divorce	*Ehe*
	director	[də'rektə]	*v* to direct	*Regisseur/in*
	kick	[kɪk]	*phr* kick-off	*Tritt, Schuss*
	to **kick**	[kɪk]	e.g. The footballer kicked the ball.	*treten, schießen*
	to **dress**	[dres]	to put on clothes	*sich kleiden, sich anziehen*
	runner	['rʌnə]	*v* to run	*Läufer/in*
	heavy	['hevi]	↔ light	*schwer*
	drinker	['drɪŋkə]	*v* to drink	*Trinker/in*
	scientist	['saɪəntɪst]	*n* science	*(Natur-)Wissenschaftler/in*
50	**keyboard**	['ki:bɔ:d]	sth you type on	*Tastatur*
	shelf, shelves	[ʃelf, ʃelvz]	*n* bookshelf	*Regal, Regale*
	pin board	['pɪn bɔ:d]	somewhere you can stick notices	*Pinnwand*
	printer	['prɪntə]	*n* to print	*Drucker*
	wastebasket	['weɪstbɑ:skɪt]	somewhere to put rubbish	*Papierkorb*
	next to	['nekst tə]	beside	*neben*
	stationery	['steɪʃənri]	pens, paper, etc.	*Schreibwaren, Briefpapier*
	file	[faɪl]	records	*Ordner, Akte*
51	**voicemail**	['vɔɪsmeɪl]	answerphone	*Anrufbeantworter*
	skill	[skɪl]	*adj* skilled	*Fähigkeit, Fertigkeit*
	messenger	['mesɪndʒə]	*n* message	*Bote, Kurier*
	blonde	[blɒnd]	e.g. Monroe was famous for her blonde hair.	*blond*
	guy	[gaɪ]	man	*Typ, Kerl*
	on top of	[ɒn 'tɒp əv]	↔ at the bottom of	*auf*
	to **record**	['rekɔ:d]	*n* recording	*aufnehmen*
	furniture	['fɜ:nɪtʃə]	e.g. chairs, tables, desks, etc.	*Möbel*
	piece of furniture	[ˌpi:s əf 'fɜ:nɪtʃə]	e.g. sofa, wardrobe, table, etc.	*Möbelstück*
	to **hold sth**	[həʊld]	*(hier)* to store	*etw fassen, für etw Platz haben*
	generally	['dʒenrəli]	↔ specifically	*im Allgemeinen*
	pay	[peɪ]	money you earn for doing a job	*Lohn, Gage*
	wrestling	['reslɪŋ]	*phr* wrestling ring	*Ringen*
	wrestler	['reslə]	*v* to wrestle	*Ringer/in*
	huge	[hju:dʒ]	↔ tiny	*riesig, gewaltig*
	smart	[smɑ:t]	clever, intelligent	*intelligent, clever*
	successful	[sək'sesfl]	↔ unsuccessful	*erfolgreich*
52	to **have sth in common**	[həv ɪn 'kɒmən]	to like the same things as sb	*etw gemeinsam haben*
	drag	[dræg]	when a man wears women's clothes	*Frauenkleider (von Männern getragen)*
	feminine	['femənɪn]	↔ masculine	*weiblich*
	to **host**	[həʊst]	*n* host	*moderieren*
	to **compete**	[kəm'pi:t]	*n* competition	*konkurrieren, (in einem Wettbewerb) antreten*
	challenge	['tʃælɪndʒ]	*v* to challenge	*Herausforderung*
	to **involve**	[ɪn'vɒlv]	*n* involvement	*beinhalten, einbeziehen*
	spectacular	[spek'tækjələ]	really good, amazing	*spektakulär*
	performer	[pə'fɔ:mə]	*v* to perform	*Mitwirkende/r*
	loser	['lu:zə]	*v* to lose	*Verlierer/in*
	trainee	[treɪ'ni:]	*n* traineeship	*Auszubildende/r*
	religious	[rɪ'lɪdʒəs]	*n* religion	*Religions-*
	to **counsel sb**	['kaʊnsl]	*n* counsellor *(BE)*, counselor *(AE)*	*jdn beraten*
	married couple	[ˌmærɪd 'kʌpl]	husband and wife	*Ehepaar*
	mosque	[mɒsk]	Islamic place of worship	*Moschee*
	Grand Mufti	[ˌgrænd 'mʌfti]	highest official of Islamic law in a country	*Großmufti*
	to **judge**	[dʒʌdʒ]	*n* judgement	*beurteilen*
	performance	[pə'fɔ:məns]	*n* performer	*Leistung, Darbietung, Aufführung*

	to eliminate sb	[ɪ'lɪmɪneɪt]	to send sb home	*jdn ausschließen*
	contestant	[kən'testənt]	participant, player	*Kandidat/in*
	winner	['wɪnə]	*v* to win	*Gewinner/in*
	trip	[trɪp]	*phr* to go on a trip	*Reise*
	scholarship	['skɒləʃɪp]	*phr* to apply for a scholarship	*Stipendium*
	to act	[ækt]	*n* actor	*handeln, sich verhalten*
	aggressive	[ə'gresɪv]	violent	*aggressiv*
	problematic	[ˌprɒblə'mætɪk]	↔ straightforward	*problematisch, Problem-*
	old-fashioned	[ˌəʊld 'fæʃənd]	↔ modern	*altmodisch*
	finishing school	['fɪnɪʃɪŋ sku:l]	old-fashioned place where girls learned how to behave properly	*Mädchenpensionat*
	conservative	[kən'sɜ:vətɪv]	↔ liberal	*konservativ*
	etiquette	['etɪket]	good behaviour, way to behave	*Etikette, richtiges Benehmen*
	aristocrat	['ærɪstəkræt]	*adj* aristocratic	*Aristokrat/in*
	prize	[praɪz]	e.g. I won a prize for my photograph.	*Preis, Gewinn*
53	comparison	[kəm'pærɪsn]	*v* to compare	*Vergleich*
	to create	[kri'eɪt]	to think up, to invent	*hier: sich ausdenken*
	concept	['kɒnsept]	e.g. We met to discuss the concept of the advert.	*Konzept*
	to present	[prɪ'zent]	*n* presentation	*vorstellen, präsentieren*
	to perform	[pə'fɔ:m]	*n* performance	*ausführen, aufführen*
54	itinerary	[aɪ'tɪnərəri]	schedule	*Reiseroute*
	business associate	['bɪznəs əsəʊʃiət]	business partner	*Geschäftspartner/in*
	to fill sth in	[ˌfɪl 'ɪn]	to complete	*etw ausfüllen*
	length	[leŋθ]	*adj* long	*Länge*
	departure	[dɪ'pɑ:tʃə]	↔ arrival	*Abfahrt, Abreise*
	to change trains	[ˌtʃeɪndʒ 'treɪnz]	e.g. I had to change trains twice to get here.	*umsteigen*
	convenient	[kən'vi:niənt]	↔ inconvenient	*praktisch, bequem*
	journey	['dʒɜ:ni]	trip	*Fahrt, Reise*
	Oh my goodness!	[ˌəʊ maɪ 'gʊdnəs]	you say this when you are surprised/shocked	*Du meine Güte!*
	to mind	[maɪnd]	to be okay	*etw dagegen haben*
	platform	['plætfɔ:m]	where you stand and wait for a train	*Bahnsteig, Gleis*
	restaurant car	['restrɒnt kɑ:]	place on a train where you can buy food	*Speisewagen*
	ticket machine	['tɪkɪt məʃi:n]	machine where you can buy tickets	*Fahrkartenautomat*
	track	[træk]	what the train travels on	*Gleis*
	conductor	[kən'dʌktə]	person who works on the train	*Schaffner/in, Zugbegleiter/in*
	bench	[bentʃ]	place to sit	*Bank*
	car	[kɑ:]	wagon on a train	*(Eisenbahn-)Wagen*
55	to depart	[dɪ'pɑ:t]	*n* departure	*abfahren, abreisen*
	seat	[si:t]	*phr* to take a seat	*Platz, Sitz*
	safely	['seɪfli]	*adj* safe	*sicher*
	agent	['eɪdʒənt]	e.g. ticket agent	*Verkäufer/in*
	alright	[ɔ:l'raɪt]	okay	*gut, in Ordnung*
56	grammatical	[grə'mætɪkl]	*n* grammar	*grammatikalisch*
	mark	[mɑ:k]	grade	*Note*
	stylistical	[staɪ'lɪstɪkl]	*n* style	*stilistisch*
	to think about sth	['θɪŋk əbaʊt]	to consider sth	*sich über etw Gedanken machen*
	not … yet	[ˌnɒt 'jet]	↔ already	*noch nicht*
	mind	[maɪnd]	head	*Geist, Hirn, Kopf*
	TV show	[ˌti: 'vi: ʃəʊ]	TV programme	*Fernsehsendung, -serie*
	to reform	[rɪ'fɔ:m]	to change	*reformieren, (grundsätzlich) ändern*
	channel	['tʃænl]	e.g. TV channel	*Kanal*
	to exercise	['eksəsaɪz]	to work out, to do sport	*sich körperlich betätigen*
	obese	[əʊ'bi:s]	↔ thin	*fettleibig*
	in addition	[ɪn ə'dɪʃn]	also	*darüber hinaus*
	unhealthy	[ˌʌn'helθi]	*adv* unhealthily	*ungesund*
	criminal	['krɪmɪnl]	*n* crime	*verbrecherisch, kriminell*
	to conclude	[kən'klu:d]	*n* conclusion	*abschließend*
	arrow	['ærəʊ]	line which points to sth	*Pfeil*

Unit 6

57	lifetime	['laɪftaɪm]	*phr* the opportunity of a lifetime	*Leben, Lebenszeit*
	goal	[gəʊl]	aim, target	*Ziel*
	to fit sb/sth	[fɪt]	to match	*zu jdm/etw passen*
	parent	['peərənt]	mother or father	*Vater/Mutter, Elternteil*

	to **protect**	[prə'tekt]	*n* protection	*schützen, beschützen*
	to **push**	[pʊʃ]	↔ to pull	*schieben, drücken*
	limit	['lɪmɪt]	*v* to limit	*Grenze*
	to **save**	[seɪv]	e.g. He saved my life after the car accident.	*retten*
	to **entertain sb**	[ˌentə'teɪn]	*n* entertainment	*jdn unterhalten*
	to **solve**	[sɒlv]	*n* solution	*lösen*
	technical	['teknɪkl]	*n* technician	*technisch*
	creative	[kri'eɪtɪv]	*v* to create	*kreativ*
58	**success**	[sək'ses]	*v* to succeed	*Erfolg*
	against the odds	[əˌgenst ði 'ɒdz]	unexpectedly	*wider Erwarten, wider alle Wahrscheinlichkeit*
	wealthy	['welθi]	↔ poor	*wohlhabend, reich*
	dyslexia	[dɪs'leksiə]	*adj* dyslexic	*Legasthenie*
	to **start a company**	[ˌstɑːt ə 'kʌmpəni]	to create a new business	*ein Unternehmen gründen*
	to **build**	[bɪld]	to construct	*bauen, aufbauen, erbauen*
	recording studio	[rɪ'kɔːdɪŋ stjuːdiəʊ]	where you record music	*Tonstudio*
	to **sign sb**	[saɪn]	to give sb a contract	*jdn unter Vertrag nehmen*
	to **continue to do sth**	[kən'tɪnjuː]	*adj* continuous	*etw weiterhin tun*
	risk	[rɪsk]	*adj* risky	*Risiko*
	to **take a risk**	[ˌteɪk ə 'rɪsk]	to risk	*ein Risiko eingehen*
	airline	['eəlaɪn]	company which sells flights	*Fluglinie*
	railway	['reɪlweɪ]	to do with trains	*Eisenbahn*
	brand	[brænd]	sort	*Marke*
	space	[speɪs]	e.g. space shuttle	*Weltraum*
	tourism	['tʊərɪzəm]	*n* tourist	*Tourismus*
	adventurer	[əd'ventʃərə]	*n* adventure	*Abenteurer/in*
	to **break**	[breɪk]	↔ to repair	*brechen*
	world record	[ˌwɜːld 'rekɔːd]	e.g. world record holder	*Weltrekord*
	hot air balloon	[ˌhɒt 'eə bəluːn]		*Heißluftballon*
	to **cross**	[krɒs]	*n* crossing	*überqueren*
	to **set**	[set]	e.g. to set a challenge	*setzen*
	to **rise above sth**	['raɪz əbʌv]	to go further	*über etw hinausgehen, etw überwinden*
	to **afford sth**	[ə'fɔːd]	*adj* affordable	*sich etw leisten (können)*
	fee	[fiː]	price you pay for sth	*Gebühr*
	to **return**	[rɪ'tɜːn]	to come back	*zurückkehren*
	limited	['lɪmɪtɪd]	↔ unlimited	*begrenzt, beschränkt*
	electricity	[ɪˌlek'trɪsəti]	*adj* electrical	*Strom, Elektrizität*
	running water	[ˌrʌnɪŋ 'wɔːtə]	water that comes from a tap	*fließendes Wasser, Trinkwasser*
	village	['vɪlɪdʒ]	↔ city, town	*Dorf*
	local	['ləʊkl]	↔ foreign	*örtlich, lokal*
	library	['laɪbrəri]	place where you can take books for a short time	*Bibliothek*
	to **pick sth up**	[ˌpɪk 'ʌp]	to take	*etw nehmen, etw aufheben*
	windmill	['wɪndmɪl]	structure that takes power from the wind	*Windmühle*
	to pump	[pʌmp]	*n* pump	*pumpen*
	turbine	['tɜːbaɪn]	e.g. turbine engine	*Turbine*
	tractor	['træktə]	machine found on a farm	*Traktor*
	pipe	[paɪp]	tube	*Rohr, Röhre*
	to **generate**	['dʒenəreɪt]	to make	*erzeugen*
	power	['paʊə]	energy	*Strom*
	light	[laɪt]	↔ dark	*Licht*
	to **separate**	['sepəreɪt]	*n* separation	*sich trennen*
	pregnant	['pregnənt]	*n* pregnancy	*schwanger*
	despite	[dɪ'spaɪt]	e.g. Despite problems, the project was a success!	*trotz*
	to **express**	[ɪk'spres]	*n* expression	*ausdrücken*
	worth	[wɜːθ]	*adj* worthy	*wert*
	to **set sth up**	[ˌset 'ʌp]	to found	*etw aufbauen, gründen*
	to **give away**	[ˌgɪv ə'weɪ]	*n* giveaway	*schenken, verschenken, spenden*
	ability	[ə'bɪləti]	↔ inability	*Fähigkeit, Möglichkeit*
	to **make a difference**	[ˌmeɪk ə 'dɪfrəns]	e.g. Thank you for help, it made a difference.	*etw bewirken*
59	**trouble**	['trʌbl]	*adj* troublesome	*Ärger, Schwierigkeiten, Probleme*
	sailing boat	['seɪlɪŋ bəʊt]	e.g. When he retired, he bought a sailing boat.	*Segelboot*
	bit	[bɪt]	*phr* bit by bit	*Stück, Teil*
	preparation	[ˌprepə'reɪʃn]	*v* to prepare	*Vorbereitung*

	achievement	[ə'tʃi:vmənt]	*v* to achieve	*Errungenschaft, Erfolg*
	interviewee	[ˌɪntəvju:'i:]	↔ interviewer	*Person, die interviewt wird*
60	to **record**	[rɪ'kɔ:d]	*n* record	*aufzeichnen, aufnehmen*
	autobiography	[ˌɔ:təbaɪ'ɒgrəfi]	*adj* autobiographical	*Autobiografie*
	founder	['faʊndə]	*v* to found	*Gründer/in*
	apparently	[ə'pærəntli]	*adj* apparent	*anscheinend*
	flight	[flaɪt]	*v* to fly	*Flug*
61	**biographical**	[ˌbaɪə'græfɪkl]	*n* biography	*biografisch*
	remarkable	[rɪ'mɑ:kəbl]	incredible	*bemerkenswert, erstaunlich*
	athlete	['æθli:t]	*adj* athletic	*Sportler/in*
62	**twice**	[twaɪs]	two times	*zweimal*
	doctor	['dɒktə]	sb who you go to if you are not well	*Arzt/Ärztin*
	lawyer	['lɔ:jə]	sb who works with the law	*Anwalt/Anwältin*
	president	['prezɪdənt]	head of government	*Präsident/in*
	policeman	[pə'li:smən]	police officer	*Polizist*
	firefighter *(AE)*	['faɪəfaɪtə]	*BE:* fireman	*Feuerwehrmann*
	dreamer	['dri:mə]	*n* dream	*Träumer*
	to **last**	[lɑ:st]	*adj* lasting	*dauern*
	forever	[fə'revə]	↔ temporary	*ewig*
	to **hold on to sth**	[ˌhəʊld 'ɒn tə]	↔ to let go of sth	*an etw festhalten*
	to **reach**	[ri:tʃ]	e.g. to reach a decision	*erreichen*
	top	[tɒp]	↔ bottom	*Spitze, Gipfel*
	to **matter**	['mætə]	to mean a lot, to be important	*wichtig sein*
	caught up	[ˌkɔ:t 'ʌp]	*v* to catch	*gefangen*
	stream	[stri:m]	river	*Strom*
	to **focus**	['fəʊkəs]	to concentrate	*(sich) konzentrieren*
	luxury	['lʌkʃəri]	*adj* luxurious	*Luxus*
	to **inspire**	[ɪn'spaɪə]	*adj* inspirational	*anregen, inspirieren*
	naive	[naɪ'i:v]	↔ wise	*naiv*
	idealistic	[ˌaɪdiə'lɪstɪk]	*n* ideal	*idealistisch*
	catchy	['kætʃi]	e.g. catchy song	*eingängig*
63	**order**	['ɔ:də]	sequence	*Reihenfolge*
	to **come true**	[ˌkʌm 'tru:]	to become real	*wahr werden, sich verwirklichen*
	chorus	['kɔ:rəs]	part of a song that is repeated	*Refrain*
	realistic	[ˌri:ə'lɪstɪk]	↔ unrealistic	*realistisch*
	to **consider**	[kən'sɪdə]	*adj* considerate	*berücksichtigen, in Betracht ziehen*
	essay	['eseɪ]	text about a particular subject	*Aufsatz*
	to **consider**	[kən'sɪdə]	*n* consideration	*betrachten*
	on the one hand	[ɒn ðə 'wʌn hænd]	e.g. On the one hand, I like her, but...	*einerseits*
	on the other hand	[ɒn ði 'ʌðə hænd]	e.g. ...on the other hand, my family hate her.	*andererseits*
	to **state**	[steɪt]	*n* statement	*sagen, erklären, angeben*
	to **summarize**	['sʌməraɪz]	*n* summary	*zusammenfassen*
	to **close**	[kləʊz]	↔ to open	*schließen, zum Ende kommen*
	to **sum up**	[ˌsʌm 'ʌp]	to conclude	*zusammenfassen*
	to **waste**	[weɪst]	e.g. waste of time/money	*verschwenden, vergeuden*
	energy	['enədʒi]	*adj* energetic	*Energie*
	effort	['efət]	e.g. to make an effort	*Mühe, Anstrengung*
	satisfied	['sætɪsfaɪd]	*n* satisfactory	*zufrieden*
	to **hold sb back**	[ˌhəʊld 'bæk]	to stop sb doing sth	*jdn zurückhalten*
	to **achieve sth**	[ə'tʃi:v]	*n* achievement	*etw erreichen*
	to **aim**	[eɪm]	to have as a goal	*zielen*
	to **aim high**	[ˌeɪm 'haɪ]	to be ambitious	*hoch hinaus wollen*
	possibility	[ˌpɒsə'bɪləti]	*adj* possible	*Möglichkeit*
64	**résumé** *(AE)*	['rezjumeɪ]	*BE:* curriculum vitae (CV)	*Lebenslauf*
	to **apply for sth**	[ə'plaɪ fə]	*n* application	*sich um etw bewerben*
	voluntary	['vɒləntri]	without getting paid	*freiwillig, ehrenamtlich*
	birth	[bɜ:θ]	↔ death	*Geburt*
	date of birth	[ˌdeɪt əv 'bɜ:θ]	when sb was born	*Geburtsdatum*
	primary school *(BE)*	['praɪməri sku:l]	*AE:* elementary school	*Grundschule*
	secondary school *(BE)*	['sekəndri sku:l]	*AE:* high school	*Hauptschule/Realschule*
	vocational college	[vəʊˌkeɪʃənl 'kɒlɪdʒ]	school which prepares sb for a job	*Berufsfachschule*
	work experience	['wɜ:k ɪkspɪəriəns]	e.g. to get work experience	*Berufserfahrung*
	work placement	['wɜ:k pleɪsmənt]	e.g. to be on work placement	*Praktikum*
	salesperson	['seɪlzpɜ:sn]	sales assistant	*Verkäufer/in*

	Easter	['iːstə]	e.g. Easter egg	*Ostern*
	conservation	[ˌkɒnsə'veɪʃn]	protection of animals and plants	*Naturschutz*
	veterinary clinic	[ˌvetnri 'klɪnɪk]	place you take sick animals	*Tierklinik*
	basic	['beɪsɪk]	↔ advanced	*elementar,* hier: *Grundkenntnisse*
	first aid	[ˌfɜːst 'eɪd]	help you give sb who has had an accident	*Erste Hilfe*
	certificate	[sə'tɪfɪkət]	document which shows you have a qualification	*Urkunde, Zeugnis*
	health	[helθ]	*adj* healthy	*Gesundheit*
	reference	['refərəns]	e.g. job reference	*Referenz*
	available	[ə'veɪləbl]	↔ unavailable	*erhältlich, verfügbar*
	request	[rɪ'kwest]	e.g. to make a request	*Bitte, Wunsch*
	experience	[ɪk'spɪəriəns]	*v* to experience	*Erfahrung*
	outdoors	[ˌaʊt'dɔːz]	↔ indoors	*draußen, im Freien*
	study	['stʌdi]	*v* to study	*Studium*
65	**equivalent**	[ɪ'kwɪvələnt]	the same as	*Entsprechung*
	disadvantage	[ˌdɪsəd'vɑːntɪdʒ]	↔ advantage	*Nachteil*
	wide	[waɪd]	↔ narrow	*breit, weit*
	to **get out of touch with sb**	[get ˌaʊt əv 'tʌtʃ wɪð]	to lose contact with sb	*den Kontakt zu jdm verlieren*
	It's your turn.	[ˌɪts 'jɔː tɜːn]	e.g. I paid last time - it's your turn now!	*Du bist dran.*
	model	['mɒdl]	example	*Muster, Modell*
66	**effective**	[ɪ'fektɪv]	e.g. The medicine was effective against my headache.	*effektiv, wirksam*
	prediction	[prɪ'dɪkʃn]	*v* to predict	*Voraussage, Vorhersage*
	to **skim**	[skɪm]	to read something quickly	*(Text) überfliegen*
	to **scan**	[skæn]	*n* scanner	*absuchen, (Text) überfliegen*
	significance	[sɪg'nɪfɪkəns]	*adj* significant	*Bedeutung*
	incorrect	[ˌɪnkə'rekt]	↔ correct, right	*falsch, nicht korrekt*
	to **fight**	[faɪt]	*n* fighter	*kämpfen*
	tough	[tʌf]	difficult	*hart*
	gourmet	['gʊəmeɪ]	sb who likes high-quality food	*Feinschmecker*
	league	[liːg]	e.g. football league	*Liga*
	development	[dɪ'veləpmənt]	*v* to develop	*Entwicklung*
	to **divorce**	[dɪ'vɔːs]	↔ to get married	*sich scheiden lassen*
	anger	['æŋgə]	*adj* angry	*Wut, Hass*
	to **take sth out on sb**	[ˌteɪk 'aʊt ɒn]	e.g. It wasn't me so don't take your anger out on me!	*etw an jdm auslassen*
	to **beat sb**	[biːt]	to hit sb	*jdn schlagen*
	support	[sə'pɔːt]	*v* to support sb/sth	*Unterstützung*
	suicide	['suːɪsaɪd]	to kill oneself	*Selbstmord*
	to **commit sth**	[kə'mɪt]	*phr* to commit a crime	*etw (Tat etc.) begehen*
	to **attend sth**	[ə'tend]	*n* attendance	*etw besuchen, an etw teilnehmen*
	to **bully**	['bʊli]	*n* bully	*mobben, tyrannisieren*
	to **beat sb up**	[ˌbiːt 'ʌp]	to violently attack sb	*jdn verprügeln*
	to **let off steam**	[let ˌɒf 'stiːm]	to let out anger	*Dampf ablassen*
	to **get rid of sth**	[ˌget 'rɪd əv]	to dispose of sth	*etw loswerden*
	humiliation	[hjuːˌmɪli'eɪʃn]	*v* to humiliate sb	*Erniedrigung*
	to **experience**	[ɪk'spɪəriəns]	*n* experience	*erleben, erfahren*
	to **join**	[dʒɔɪn]	to become part of	*sich anschließen, beitreten*
	vicious	['vɪʃəs]	aggressive	*brutal, bissig*
	fighter	['faɪtə]	*v* fight	*Kämpfer/in*
	turning point	['tɜːnɪŋ pɔɪnt]	changing point	*Wendepunkt*
	to **train as**	['treɪn əz]	to learn to become	*eine Ausbildung zum/zur … machen*
	even though	['iːvn ðəʊ]	although	*obwohl*
	training	['treɪnɪŋ]	*v* to train	*Ausbildung*
	to **promote sb**	[prə'məʊt]	*n* promotion	*jdn befördern*
	past	[pɑːst]	↔ future	*Vergangenheit*
	childhood	['tʃaɪldhʊd]	↔ adulthood	*Kindheit*
	self-reliance	[ˌself rɪ'laɪəns]	↔ dependence	*Selbstständigkeit*
	to **develop**	[dɪ'veləp]	*n* development	*entwickeln*
	stamina	['stæmɪnə]	e.g. to have/possess stamina	*Durchhaltevermögen, Ausdauer*
	determined	[dɪ'tɜːmɪnd]	*n* determination	*entschlossen*
	to **employ sb**	[ɪm'plɔɪ]	*n* employee	*jdn beschäftigen*

Unit 7

67	**questionnaire**	[ˌkwestʃəˈneə]	list of questions	*Fragebogen*
	to **be prepared to do sth**	[bi prɪˈpeəd tə]	*n* preparation	*bereit/willens sein, etw zu tun*
	to **manage sth**	[ˈmænɪdʒ]	*n* management	*etw verwalten*
	to **prepare**	[prɪˈpeə]	to make sth ready	*zubereiten*
	to **deal with sb/sth**	[ˈdiːl wɪð]	to handle, to behave towards	*mit jdm/etw zu tun haben, zurechtkommen, umgehen*
	to **look forward to sth**	[ˌlʊk ˈfɔːwəd tə]	to be excited about sth in the future	*sich auf etw freuen*
	responsibility	[rɪˌspɒnsəˈbɪləti]	*adj* responsible	*Verantwortung, Verantwortlichkeit*
	to **move ahead**	[ˌmuːv əˈhed]	to go forward	*vorankommen, Fortschritte machen*
	married	[ˈmærid]	*v* to marry	*verheiratet*
	pet	[pet]	animal you keep at home	*Haustier*
	to **rank**	[ræŋk]	to put in order	*einstufen, (an-, ein)ordnen*
	poll	[pəʊl]	*v* to poll	*Umfrage, Abstimmung*
68	**childminding**	[ˈtʃaɪldmaɪndɪŋ]	babysitting	*Kinderbetreuung*
	empathy	[ˈempəθi]	understanding people's feelings	*Einfühlungsvermögen*
	artistic	[ɑːˈtɪstɪk]	creative	*künstlerisch*
	construction	[kənˈstrʌkʃn]	*v* to construct	*Bau, Hausbau*
	further education	[ˌfɜːðər edʒuˈkeɪʃn]	e.g. college, university, etc.	*Weiterbildung*
	original	[əˈrɪdʒənl]	new, different	*originell*
	to **volunteer**	[ˌvɒlənˈtɪə]	to do sth without getting paid	*ehrenamtlich/unentgeltlich arbeiten*
	religious	[rɪˈlɪdʒəs]	*n* religion	*religiös*
	orphanage	[ˈɔːfənɪdʒ]	place where children with no mother or father live	*Waisenhaus*
	attention	[əˈtenʃn]	*phr* to have sb's attention	*Zuwendung*
	to **announce**	[əˈnaʊns]	to tell	*ankündigen*
	to **join sb/sth**	[dʒɔɪn]	to put together	*bei jdm/etw mitmachen*
	bus driver	[ˈbʌs draɪvə]	*v* to drive	*Busfahrer/in*
	financial	[faɪˈnænʃl]	*n* finance	*finanziell, Finanz-*
	investment	[ɪnˈvestmənt]	*v* to invest	*Investition*
	school-leaver	[ˌskuːlˈliːvə]	sb who has finished school	*Schulabgänger/in*
	common	[ˈkɒmən]	popular	*verbreitet, häufig*
	graphic artist	[ˌgræfɪk ˈɑːtɪst]	sb who creates graphics	*Grafiker/in*
	automobile	[ˈɔːtəməbiːl]	to do with cars	*Auto-*
	innovative	[ˈɪnəveɪtɪv]	new and original	*innovativ*
	internship	[ˈɪntɜːnʃɪp]	traineeship in a company	*Praktikum*
	lorry	[ˈlɒri]	truck	*Lastwagen*
	motorcycle	[ˈməʊtəsaɪkl]	motorbike	*Motorrad*
	dealership	[ˈdiːləʃɪp]	place that sells cars	*Händler*
	to **be in need**	[bi ˌɪn ˈniːd]	to require	*bedürftig sein*
	mechanic	[mɪˈkænɪk]	sb who repairs cars, etc.	*(Kfz-)Mechaniker/in*
	to **look ahead**	[ˌlʊk əˈhed]	to look forward	*nach vorn schauen*
69	**arrogant**	[ˈærəgənt]	too confident	*überheblich, arrogant*
	to **come of age**	[ˌkʌm əv ˈeɪdʒ]	to become an adult	*erwachsen werden*
	to **control**	[kənˈtrəʊl]	to monitor, to watch closely	*kontrollieren, überwachen*
	historical	[hɪˈstɒrɪkl]	*n* history	*historisch, Historien-*
	isolated	[ˈaɪsəleɪtɪd]	*n* isolation	*abgesondert, abgelegen, isoliert*
	community	[kəˈmjuːnəti]	people who live together in an area	*Gemeinschaft, Gemeinde*
	strict	[strɪkt]	firm	*streng*
	rule	[ruːl]	regulation	*Regel, Vorschrift*
	dress	[dres]	clothes sb wears	*Kleidung*
	period	[ˈpɪəriəd]	length of time	*Zeitabschnitt*
	the movies	[ðə ˈmuːviz]	cinema	*Kino*
	alcohol	[ˈælkəhɒl]	e.g. beer, wine, vodka, etc.	*Alkohol*
70	**careers counsellor**	[kəˈrɪəz kaʊnsələ]	sb who helps you decide what job you want to do	*Berufsberater/in*
	unsure	[ˌʌnˈʃʊə]	not certain	*unsicher*
	to **stress sb out**	[ˌstres ˈaʊt]	to make sb stressed	*jdn stressen, jdn fertig machen*
	set	[set]	group	*Reihe, Menge, Gruppe*
	to **have no idea**	[həv ˌnəʊ aɪˈdɪə]	to not know	*keine Ahnung haben*
	activity	[ækˈtɪvəti]	*adj* active	*Tätigkeit, Aktivität*
	case	[keɪs]	example	*Fall*
	hopeless	[ˈhəʊpləs]	↔ hopeful	*hoffnungslos*
	to **analyse**	[ˈænəlaɪz]	*n* analysis	*analysieren*
	to **jump out at sb**	[ˌdʒʌmp ˈaʊt]	to be prominent	*jdm ins Auge springen*

	skyscraper	['skaɪskreɪpə]	very tall building	*Wolkenkratzer, Hochhaus*
	architect	['ɑ:kɪtekt]	sb who designs buildings	*Architekt/in*
	thought	[θɔ:t]	*v* to think	*Gedanke*
	at first	[ət 'fɜ:st]	firstly	*zunächst*
	to **wander**	['wɒndə]	to move aimlessly	*wandern, schlendern*
	wish	[wɪʃ]	desire	*Wunsch*
	suggestion	[sə'dʒestʃən]	*v* to suggest	*Vorschlag*
	messenger	['mesɪndʒə]	sb who brings letters and parcels	*Bote/Botin*
	shape	[ʃeɪp]	form of sth	*Form*
	driver	['draɪvə]	*v* to drive	*Fahrer/in*
	tour guide	['tʊə gaɪd]	sb who shows tourists around a place	*Reiseführer/in, Reiseleiter/in*
	to **deliver**	[dɪ'lɪvə]	*n* delivery	*liefern, ausliefern*
	to **research sth**	[rɪ'sɜ:tʃ]	to look for information about sth	*recherchieren, Nachforschungen anstellen*
	employment	[ɪm'plɔɪmənt]	*v* to employ	*Beschäftigung, Anstellung*
	employment office	[ɪm'plɔɪmənt ɒfɪs]	job centre	*Arbeitsamt*
	job advertisment	['dʒɒb ədvɜ:tɪsmənt]	text a firm writes when they want new employees	*Stellenanzeige*
	right away	[ˌraɪt ə'weɪ]	immediately	*sofort*
	to **do research**	[ˌdu: rɪ'sɜ:tʃ]	to find information	*recherchieren*
	nightmare	['naɪtmeə]	bad dream	*Albtraum*
	to **paraphrase**	['pærəfreɪz]	to write/say in a different way	*umschreiben, anders ausdrücken*
	crowd	[kraʊd]	a large group of people	*Menschenmenge*
	highway	['haɪweɪ]	motorway	*Autobahn*
71	**offer**	['ɒfə]	when sb says they will do sth	*Angebot*
	spontaneous	[spɒn'teɪniəs]	without thinking	*spontan*
	promise	['prɒmɪs]	when sb says they will definitely do sth	*Versprechen*
	graduation	[ˌgrædʒu'eɪʃn]	*v* to graduate	*Abschluss*
	boredom	['bɔ:dəm]	*adj* bored	*Langeweile*
	exciting	[ɪk'saɪtɪŋ]	*n* excitement	*aufregend, spannend*
	to **take care of sb/sth**	[ˌteɪk 'keər əv]	to look after	*sich um jdn/etw kümmern*
	flatmate	['flætmeɪt]	sb you live with	*Mitbewohner/in*
	rather	['rɑ:ðə]	quite	*ziemlich, ganz schön*
72	**recommendation**	[ˌrekəmen'deɪʃn]	*v* to recommend	*Empfehlung*
	constantly	['kɒnstəntli]	always, continuously	*ständig, andauernd*
	the outdoors	[ði ˌaʊt'dɔ:z]	↔ inside	*die freie Natur*
	excellent	['eksələnt]	very good	*ausgezeichnet, hervorragend*
	calendar	['kælɪndə]	diary	*Kalender*
	organic	[ɔ:'gænɪk]	made/grown without chemicals	*Bio-, Öko-*
	grocer's shop	['grəʊsəz ʃɒp]	store where you buy food	*Lebensmittelhandlung*
	bakery	['beɪkəri]	place where you buy bread	*Bäckerei*
	to **specialise in sth**	['speʃəlaɪz ɪn]	*adj* special	*sich auf etw spezialisieren*
73	**Ladies and gentlemen**	[ˌleɪdiz ən 'dʒentlmən]	e.g. Ladies and gentlemen, please take a seat.	*Meine Damen und Herren*
	to **shoot**	[ʃu:t]	to film / take a photo	*(Film-, Foto-)Aufnahmen machen*
	costume	['kɒstju:m]	clothes an actor wears in a play/film	*Kostüm*
	to **pick sb up**	[ˌpɪk 'ʌp]	to lift sb	*jdn hochheben*
	ice-cold	[ˌaɪs 'kəʊld]	very, very cold	*eiskalt*
	setting	['setɪŋ]	surroundings	*Umgebung, Rahmen, Umfeld*
	industrial	[ɪn'dʌstriəl]	*n* industry	*Industrie-, industriell*
	casual(ly)	['kæʒuə]	↔ formal	(Kleidung:) *leger*
	emotional	[ɪ'məʊʃənl]	*n* emotion	*emotional*
	reward	[rɪ'wɔ:d]	sth you get when you do sth well	*Lohn*
	company car	['kʌmpəni kɑ:]	car that an employee gets for work	*Firmenwagen*
	supplier	[sə'plaɪə]	*v* to supply	*Zulieferer, Lieferant/in*
	satisfaction	[ˌsætɪs'fækʃn]	*v* to satisfy	*Genugtuung*
	to **be passionate about sth**	[bi 'pæʃənət əbaʊt]	to really like or care about sth	*sich für etw leidenschaftlich begeistern*
	term	[tɜ:m]	word for sth	*Begriff*
	gap	[gæp]	hole	*Lücke*
	gap year	['gæp jɪə]	year a student takes between school and university/work	*Jahr zwischen Schule und Studium bzw. Berufsanfang*
74	**covering letter**	[ˌkʌvərɪŋ 'letə]	letter you send with a job application	*Anschreiben, Begleitschreiben*
	similar	['sɪmələ]	nearly the same	*ähnlich*
	to **stand out**	[ˌstænd 'aʊt]	to be individual/different	*hervorstechen, herausragen*

	photographer	[fəˈtɒɡrəfə]	sb who takes photos	*Fotograf/in*
	duty	[ˈdjuːti]	sth you have to do	*Aufgabe, Pflicht*
	to **carry sth out**	[ˌkæri ˈaʊt]	to conduct, to do sth	*etw ausführen, durchführen*
	display	[dɪˈspleɪ]	where you show sth to sb	*Ausstellung*
	to **set up**	[ˌset ˈʌp]	to start, to build	*aufbauen, aufstellen*
	exhibit	[ɪɡˈzɪbɪt]	*n* exhibition	*Ausstellungsstück*
	art	[ɑːt]	e.g. paintings, sculptures, etc.	*Kunst*
	art gallery	[ˈɑːt ɡæləri]	place which displays art	*Kunst-, Gemäldegalerie*
	artwork	[ˈɑːtwɜːk]	piece of art	*Kunstwerke, -gegenstände*
	artist	[ˈɑːtɪst]	sb who draws/paints/etc.	*Künstler/in*
	organized	[ˈɔːɡənaɪzd]	*v* to organize	*(gut) organisiert*
	to **care about sth**	[ˈkeər əbaʊt]	to feel passionate about	*am Herzen liegen*
	human rights	[ˌhjuːmən ˈraɪts]	when you think all people are equal and should be treated well	*Menschenrechte*
	justice	[ˈdʒʌstɪs]	making sure things are right	*Gerechtigkeit*
	to **seek**	[siːk]	to look for	*suchen*
	personnel	[ˌpɜːsəˈnel]	staff, employees	*Mitarbeiter, Personal*
	campaign	[kæmˈpeɪn]	movement, action	*Kampagne, Aktion*
	intensive	[ɪnˈtensɪv]	*adj* intense	*intensiv*
	donor	[ˈdəʊnə]	*v* to donate	*Spender/in*
	furniture store	[ˈfɜːnɪtʃə stɔː]	place that sells beds, chairs, etc.	*Möbelhaus*
	to **run (a business)**	[rʌn]	to manage	*(ein Geschäft) leiten, führen*
	programmer	[ˈprəʊɡræmə]	*v* to programme	*Programmierer/in*
	caregiver	[ˈkeəɡɪvə]	carer, care assistant	*Pfleger/in*
	injured	[ˈɪndʒəd]	hurt	*verletzt*
	orphaned	[ˈɔːfnd]	without parents	*verwaist*
	to **respect**	[rɪˈspekt]	to think a lot of	*respektieren*
	wildlife	[ˈwaɪldlaɪf]	animals, etc.	*Tierwelt, Tier-*
	biology	[baɪˈɒlədʒi]	study of animals, plants, etc.	*Biologie*
	medication	[ˌmedɪˈkeɪʃn]	medicine, e.g. tablets	*Medikamente*
75	**communicative**	[kəˈmjuːnɪkətɪv]	*n* communication	*kommunikativ*
	analytical	[ˌænəˈlɪtɪkl]	*v* to analyse	*analytisch*
	technically minded	[ˈteknɪkli maɪndɪd]	liking technology	*technikinteressiert*
	outgoing	[ˈaʊtɡəʊɪŋ]	sociable	*kontaktfreudig*
	responsible	[rɪˈspɒnsəbl]	*n* responsibility	*verantwortungsbewusst*
	reliable	[rɪˈlaɪəbl]	*v* to rely on	*zuverlässig*
	a good cause	[ə ˌɡʊd ˈkɔːz]	sth worthwhile	*ein guter Zweck, eine gute Sache*
	course work	[ˈkɔːs wɜːk]	work you have to do as part of your studies	*Unterrichtsaufgaben, Klausuren*
	to **coordinate**	[kəʊˈɔːdɪneɪt]	to organise	*koordinieren*
	computer science	[kəmˈpjuːtə saɪəns]	information technology	*Informatik*
	groceries	[ˈɡrəʊsəriːz]	food	*Lebensmittel*
	medical assistant	[ˌmedɪkl əˈsɪstənt]	doctor's assistant	*Medizinische/r Fachangestellte/r*
	Yours sincerely	[ˌjɔːz sɪnˈsɪəli]	what you write at the end of a letter	*Mit freundlichen Grüßen*
76	to **take sb/sth seriously**	[ˌteɪk ˈsɪəriəsli]	to think sb/sth is important	*jdn/etw ernst nehmen*
	unprepared	[ˌʌnprɪˈpeəd]	not ready	*unvorbereitet*
	disorganised	[dɪsˈɔːɡənaɪzd]	not well organised	*unorganisiert*
	balance	[ˈbæləns]	amount of money you have in your bank	*Kontostand*
	relationship	[rɪˈleɪʃnʃɪp]	connection you have with sb	*Beziehungen*
	to **work out**	[ˌwɜːk ˈaʊt]	to go well	*klappen, funktionieren*
	profession	[prəˈfeʃn]	job	*Beruf*
	outline	[ˈaʊtlaɪn]	summary, framework	*Übersicht, Stichpunkte*
	recipe	[ˈresəpi]	instructions how to make a type of food	*(Koch-)Rezept*
	fascinated	[ˈfæsɪneɪtɪd]	*v* to fascinate	*fasziniert*
	Too bad.	[ˌtuː ˈbæd]	Bad luck!	*Pech gehabt!*
	impressive	[ɪmˈpresɪv]	*v* to impress	*beeindruckend, eindrucksvoll*
	statistic	[stəˈtɪstɪk]	number or fact	*Statistik*
	listener	[ˈlɪsnə]	audience member	*Zuhörer/in*
	to **break a leg**	[ˌbreɪk ə ˈleɡ]	e.g. She had an accident and broke her leg.	*sich ein Bein brechen*
	ever since	[ˌevə ˈsɪns]	since then	*seitdem*
	romantic relationship	[rəʊˌmæntɪk rɪˈleɪʃnʃɪp]	e.g. He's in a romantic relationship with Sue. She's his girlfriend.	*Liebesbeziehung*
	destination	[ˌdestɪˈneɪʃn]	place where you are going	*Ziel*
	to **beat**	[biːt]	to pump	*schlagen*

	beat	[biːt]	e.g. heartbeat	*Schlag*
	healthy	['helθi]	↔ ill, sick	*gesund*
	to **structure**	['strʌktʃə]	to put in a good order	*strukturieren*
	to **introduce**	[ˌɪntrə'djuːs]	to begin	*einführen, vorstellen*
	argument	['ɑːgjumənt]	point	*Argument*

Unit 8

77	**geographical**	[ˌdʒiːə'græfɪkl]	*n* geography	*geographisch*
	unified	['juːnɪfaɪd]	joined together	*vereint, vereinigt*
	diversity	[daɪ'vɜːsəti]	*adj* diverse	*Vielfalt*
	to **conquer**	['kɒŋkə]	to beat	*erobern*
	to **abolish**	[ə'bɒlɪʃ]	to stop, to remove	*abschaffen*
	monarchy	['mɒnəki]	kings and queens	*Monarchie*
78	**opportunity**	[ˌɒpə'tjuːnəti]	chance	*Möglichkeit, Gelegenheit, Chance*
	to **set up**	[ˌset 'ʌp]	to start	*sich niederlassen*
	to **expand**	[ɪk'spænd]	to make bigger	*expandieren*
	border	['bɔːdə]	where one country finishes and another begins	*Grenze*
	chef	[ʃef]	cook	*Koch/Köchin, Chefkoch/-köchin*
	cruise	[kruːz]	holiday where you travel around on a ship	*Kreuzfahrt*
	stressful	['stresfl]	hard, difficult	*anstrengend, stressig*
	office management assistant	[ˌɒfɪs 'mænɪdʒmənt əsɪstənt]	sb who works in an office	*Bürokaufmann/-frau*
	based in …	['beɪst ɪn]	situated in …	*mit Sitz in …, ansässig in …*
	abroad	[ə'brɔːd]	in another country	*im/ins Ausland*
	temporary	['temprəri]	↔ permanent	*(Stelle:)* *befristet*
	position	[pə'zɪʃn]	place, job	*Stelle, Stellung, Position*
	subsidiary	[səb'sɪdiəri]	smaller office that is not the main one	*Niederlassung*
	apprenticeship	[ə'prentɪʃɪp]	traineeship	*Lehre, Ausbildung*
	accommodation	[əˌkɒmə'deɪʃn]	place to stay	*Unterkunft*
	to **hold**	[həʊld]	e.g. You never know what the future holds!	*bereithalten*
	in the meantime	[ɪn ðə 'miːntaɪm]	until then	*in der Zwischenzeit*
79	**host country**	['həʊst kʌntri]	country where sb has gone to visit	*Gastgeberland*
	enthusiastic about sth	[ɪnˌθjuːzi'æstɪk əbaʊt]	*n* enthusiasm	*von etw begeistert*
	heading	['hedɪŋ]	title	*Überschrift*
	to **overcome sth**	[ˌəʊvə'kʌm]	to get better at sth	*etw überwinden*
	unfamiliar	[ˌʌnfə'mɪliə]	strange, unknown	*unbekannt*
	instruction	[ɪn'strʌkʃn]	what sb has to do	*Anweisung*
	to **get sth across**	[ˌget ə'krɒs]	to make sb understand sth	*etw verständlich machen, etw vermitteln*
	majority	[mə'dʒɒrəti]	↔ minority	*Mehrheit*
	to **act**	[ækt]	e.g. Brad Pitt acted in the film *Troy*.	*spielen, darstellen*
	to **mime**	[maɪm]	to act without speaking	*pantomimisch darstellen*
	to **point to sth**	['pɔɪnt tə]	to show	*auf etw zeigen*
	to **draw**	[drɔː]	e.g. to draw a picture/graph	*zeichnen*
	telecommunications industry	[ˌtelikəˌmjuːnɪ'keɪʃnz ɪndəstri]	e.g. phone companies, internet firms, etc.	*Telekommunikationsbranche*
	Formula 1	[ˌfɔːmjələ 'wʌn]	car racing	*Formel 1*
	racing	['reɪsɪŋ]	*v* to race	*Rennsport, Rennen*
	race	[reɪs]	when everyone tries to be first	*Rennen*
	grand stand	['grænd stænd]	place where you can sit	*Haupttribüne*
	race track	['reɪs træk]	where race takes place	*Rennstrecke*
	competition	[ˌkɒmpə'tɪʃn]	*v* to compete	*Wettbewerb*
	pit	[pɪt]	place where you can sit	*Box*
	to **enter a competition**	[ˌentər ə kɒmpə'tɪʃn]	to take part in a competition	*an einem Wettbewerb teilnehmen*
	excited	[ɪk'saɪtɪd]	enthusiastic	*aufgeregt, begeistert*
	clarification	[ˌklærɪfɪ'keɪʃn]	*v* to clarify	*Erläuterung, Klärung*
	pharmaceutical	[ˌfɑːmə'suːtɪkl]	to do with medicine	*Pharma-*
	performer	[pə'fɔːmə]	singer, artist	*Sänger/in, Künstler/in*
	pass	[pɑːs]	e.g. a backstage pass	*Ausweis, Pass*
80	**polling firm**	['pəʊlɪŋ fɜːm]	company that collects information by asking people questions	*Meinungsforschungsinstitut*
	permanent(ly)	['pɜːmənənt]	↔ temporarily	*dauerhaft*
	opinion poll	[ə'pɪniən pəʊl]	when you ask many people what they think about sth	*Meinungsumfrage*

	survey	['sɜːveɪ]	opinion poll	*Umfrage, Gutachten*
	inquiry	[ɪn'kwaɪəri]	when sb tries to find sth out	*Untersuchung*
	selection	[sɪ'lekʃn]	choice	*Auswahl*
	by chance	[baɪ 'tʃɑːns]	by accident	*per Zufall, zufällig*
	to **fall in love with sb**	[ˌfɔːl ɪn 'lʌv wɪð]	when you start to love sb	*sich in jdn verlieben*
	flexible	['fleksəbl]	happy to change	*flexibel*
	willing	['wɪlɪŋ]	happy to do sth	*bereit, willens*
	to **survey sb**	['sɜːveɪ]	to ask sb questions	*jdn befragen*
	specifically	[spə'sɪfɪkli]	particularly	*speziell*
	participant	[pɑː'tɪsɪpənt]	sb who is taking part in sth	*Teilnehmer/in*
	interestingly	['ɪntrəstɪŋli]	*adj* interesting	*interessanterweise*
	mainly	['meɪnli]	mostly	*hauptsächlich*
	to **relocate**	[ˌriːləʊ'keɪt]	to move somewhere new	*umsiedeln, umziehen*
	to **number**	['nʌmbə]	to add up to	*aufzählen*
	to **be made up of**	[bi ˌmeɪd 'ʌp əv]	to consist of	*bestehen aus*
	aged …	[eɪdʒd]	at the age of …	*im Alter von … Jahren*
	age span	['eɪdʒ spæn]	from age … to age …	*Altersspanne*
	postgraduate degree	[pəʊstˌgrædʒuət dɪ'griː]	a second degree	*weiterführender Studienabschluss (z. B. Promotion)*
	to **look closely at sth**	[ˌlʊk 'kləʊsli ət]	to examine	*sich etw genau ansehen*
	educated	['edʒukeɪtɪd]	*n* education	*ausgebildet, gebildet*
	to **get established**	[ˌget ɪ'stæblɪʃt]	to start	*sich etablieren*
	vocational training	[vəʊˌkeɪʃənl 'treɪnɪŋ]	job training	*Berufsausbildung*
	to **attract**	[ə'trækt]	*n* attraction	*anziehen, anlocken*
	knowledge	['nɒlɪdʒ]	what sb knows	*Wissen, Kenntnis(se)*
	job satisfaction	['dʒɒb sætɪsfækʃn]	happiness at work	*Arbeitszufriedenheit*
	dissatisfied	[dɪs'sætɪsfaɪd]	not happy	*unzufrieden*
	pay	[peɪ]	how much money you get paid at work	*Bezahlung, Lohn*
	workmate	['wɜːkmeɪt]	sb you work with	*Arbeitskollege/-in*
	working hours	[ˌwɜːkɪŋ 'aʊəz]	how long you work	*Arbeitszeiten*
	sick leave	['sɪk liːv]	time you get off work because you are not well	*Krankheitsurlaub, Krankschreibung*
	to **poll sb**	[pəʊl]	to ask sb questions	*jdn befragen*
	slightly	['slaɪtli]	a little bit	*ein bisschen, etwas*
	to **predict**	[prɪ'dɪkt]	to guess what will happen	*vorhersagen*
	benefits	['benɪfɪts]	extra rewards	*Zulagen, Sozialleistungen*
	to **adapt to sth**	[ə'dæpt tə]	to change to fit sth	*sich an etw anpassen*
	work environment	['wɜːk ɪnvaɪrənmənt]	what the atmosphere is like at work	*Arbeitsumfeld*
	paid sick leave	[ˌpeɪd 'sɪk liːv]	when you have time off work because you are ill but still get paid	*Lohnfortzahlung im Krankheitsfall*
81	**complaint**	[kəm'pleɪnt]	*v* to complain	*Klage, Beschwerde*
	to **rise**	[raɪz]	to go up	*steigen, ansteigen*
	meanwhile	['miːnwaɪl]	during that time	*währenddessen*
	wages	['weɪdʒɪz]	money you get paid at work	*Lohn, Gehalt*
	to **regret**	[rɪ'gret]	to wish you hadn't done sth	*bereuen*
	common	['kɒmən]	*phr* to have sth in common	*gemeinsam*
	graph	[grɑːf]	diagram showing figures	*Diagram, Grafik*
	bar chart	['bɑː tʃɑːt]	type of graph with columns	*Säulendiagramm*
	dissatisfaction	[ˌdɪsˌsætɪs'fækʃn]	↔ satisfaction	*Unzufriedenheit*
	percentage	[pə'sentɪdʒ]	number out of 100	*Anteil, Prozentsatz*
	co-worker	['kəʊwɜːkə]	sb you work with	*Arbeitskollege/-in*
	waste of time	[ˌweɪst əf 'taɪm]	when sth wasn't worth doing	*Zeitverschwendung*
82	**substitute**	['sʌbstɪtjuːt]	replacement	*Ersatz, Ersetzung*
	to **be allowed to do sth**	[bi ə'laʊd tə duː]	to be permitted to do sth	*etw tun dürfen*
	alarm clock	[ə'lɑːm klɒk]	clock that wakes you up in the morning	*Wecker*
	examination	[ɪgˌzæmɪ'neɪʃn]	test, exam	*Prüfung*
83	to **be brought up**	[bi ˌbrɔːt 'ʌp]	e.g. My parents brought me up well.	*aufwachsen*
	to **work overtime**	[ˌwɜːk 'əʊvətaɪm]	to work longer than normal	*Überstunden machen*
	presenter	[prɪ'zentə]	e.g. TV presenter	*Moderator/in, Präsentator/in*
	application	[ˌæplɪ'keɪʃn]	*v* to apply	*Bewerbung*
	to **operate**	['ɒpəreɪt]	to make sth work	*bedienen*
	to **have a day off**	[həv ə ˌdeɪ 'ɒf]	to not have to work on that day	*einen Tag frei bekommen*
	rent	[rent]	money you pay for your house/flat	*Miete*
	sign	[saɪn]	e.g. a stop sign	*Schild*

	to **handle sth**	[ˈhændl]	*phr* to handle with care	*mit etw hantieren, mit etw umgehen*
	spillage	[ˈspɪlɪdʒ]	*v* to spill	*Verschütten*
	machinery	[məˈʃiːnəri]	different machines	*Maschinen, Geräte*
	danger of fire	[ˌdeɪndʒər əv ˈfaɪə]	possible that there could be a fire	*Brandgefahr*
	to **pass sth**	[pɑːs]	to give sth to sb else	*etw weitergeben, weiterreichen*
84	**dos and don'ts**	[ˌduːz ən ˈdəʊnts]	what you should and shouldn't to	*Dinge, die man tun und lassen sollte*
	to **study**	[ˈstʌdi]	to learn about sth	*studieren*
	to **allow sth**	[əˈlaʊ]	*(hier)* to calculate	*etw einkalkulieren*
	relaxed	[rɪˈlækst]	↔ stressed	*entspannt*
	to **dress up**	[ˌdres ˈʌp]	to put on good, smart clothes	*sich elegant anziehen*
	electronics	[ˌɪlekˈtrɒnɪks]	*n* electricity	*Elektronik*
85	**strength**	[streŋθ]	*adj* strong	*Stärke*
	weakness	[ˈwiːknəs]	*adj* weak	*Schwäche*
	lack of sth	[ˈlæk əv]	not enough	*Mangel an etw*
	eye contact	[ˈaɪ kɒntækt]	when you look sb in the eye	*Blickkontakt*
	to **advertise a job**	[ˌædvətaɪz ə ˈdʒɒb]	*n* job advert	*eine Stelle ausschreiben*
	purchasing assistant	[ˈpɜːtʃəsɪŋ əsɪstənt]	sb whose job it is to help buy things	*Assistent/in im Einkauf*
	drawing	[ˈdrɔːɪŋ]	diagram	*(technische) Zeichnung*
	contract	[ˈkɒntrækt]	e.g. work contract	*Vertrag*
	support	[səˈpɔːt]	help	*Unterstützung, Hilfe*
	administrative	[ədˈmɪnɪstrətɪv]	*n* administration	*Verwaltungs-*
	school leaving certificate	[ˌskuːl liːvɪŋ səˈtɪfɪkət]	qualification you get at the end of school	*Schulabgangszeugnis*
	level	[ˈlevl]	grade, rank	*Niveau*
	flexibility	[ˌfleksəˈbɪləti]	*adj* flexible	*Flexibilität*
	carer	[ˈkeərə]	sb whose job it is to look after people	*Pfleger/in*
	care	[keə]	*n* carer	*Pflege*
	facility	[fəˈsɪləti]	building/place that provides a certain service	*Einrichtung*
	elderly	[ˈeldəli]	old	*älter, alt*
	desire	[dɪˈzaɪə]	wish	*Wunsch*
	habit	[ˈhæbɪt]	sth you do often	*Gewohnheit*
	process	[ˈprəʊses]	series of actions, procedure	*Verfahren*
86	**underground (train)**	[ˈʌndəgraʊnd]	train that travels underground	*U-Bahn*
	the Tube	[ðə ˈtjuːb]	the underground in London	*die Londoner U-Bahn*
	past sth	[pɑːst]	e.g. We went past the church on the way to school.	*an etw vorbei*
	traffic lights	[ˈtræfɪk laɪts]	lights which tell cars when to stop and go	*Ampel*
	post office	[ˈpəʊst ɒfɪs]	where you post letters	*Postamt*

Unit 9

87	to **judge**	[dʒʌdʒ]	to think sth about sb	*hier:* *verurteilen*
	to **be suspicious of sb/sth**	[bi səˈspɪʃəs əv]	*n* suspicion	*gegenüber jdm/etw misstrauisch/ argwöhnisch sein*
	to **be intolerant of sb/ sth**	[bi ɪnˈtɒlərənt əv]	↔ to be tolerant of sb/sth	*gegenüber jdm/etw intolerant sein*
	to **feel uncomfortable**	[ˌfiːl ʌnˈkʌmftəbl]	to not feel right	*sich unwohl fühlen*
	race	[reɪs]	e.g. Hispanic, Asian, etc.	*Rasse*
	lifestyle	[ˈlaɪfstaɪl]	way you live your life	*Lebensweise*
	belief	[bɪˈliːf]	*v* to believe	*Glaube*
	disability	[ˌdɪsəˈbɪləti]	*adj* disabled	*Behinderung*
88	**charity**	[ˈtʃærəti]	*adj* charitable	*Wohltätigkeitsorganisation*
	unity	[ˈjuːnəti]	*v* to unify	*Einheit*
	shooting	[ˈʃuːtɪŋ]	*v* to shoot	*Schießerei*
	goose	[guːs]	type of bird	*Gans*
	fair	[feə]	a small carnival	*Jahrmarkt, Rummel, Kirmes*
	gun	[gʌn]	type of weapon	*Pistole, Gewehr*
	to **point sth at sb**	[ˈpɔɪnt ət]	e.g. Don't point that gun at me!	*etw auf jdn richten*
	to **fire**	[ˈfaɪə]	to shoot a gun	*schießen, abfeuern*
	bullet	[ˈbʊlɪt]	*phr* hit by a bullet	*(Gewehr-)Kugel*
	to **hit**	[hɪt]	*phr* hit by a bullet	*treffen*
	stomach	[ˈstʌmək]	part of the body	*Bauch*
	crime	[kraɪm]	*adj* criminal	*Verbrechen*
	district	[ˈdɪstrɪkt]	area, region	*Bezirk*
	nearby	[ˈnɪəbaɪ]	close	*nahe gelegen*
	to **be unlucky**	[bi ʌnˈlʌki]	to have bad luck	*kein Glück haben*

	murder	['mɜːdə]	when sb kills sb	*Mord*
	tipping point	['tɪpɪŋ pɔɪnt]	the point when sth has to change	*der Tropfen, der das Fass zum Überlaufen bringt*
	crime	[kraɪm]	*adj* criminal	*Kriminalität*
	table tennis	['teɪbl tenɪs]	type of tennis played on a table	*Tischtennis*
	to **come up with sth**	[ˌkʌm 'ʌp wɪð]	*phr* to come up with a good idea	*sich etw einfallen lassen, sich etw ausdenken*
	rival	['raɪvl]	↔ friend	*rivalisierend, Rivale*
	to **recruit**	[rɪ'kruːt]	to bring people into a group	*anwerben*
	to **persuade**	[pə'sweɪd]	to talk sb into doing sth	*überzeugen, überreden*
	tie	[taɪ]	*phr* to wear a suit and tie	*Krawatte*
	to **sign up**	[ˌsaɪn 'ʌp]	to join	*sich anmelden, sich einschreiben*
	to **throw sb out**	[ˌθrəʊ 'aʊt]	to make sb leave	*jdn hinauswerfen*
	head teacher	[ˌhed 'tiːtʃə]	the top person in a school	*Schulleiter/in*
	dressing room	['dresɪŋ ruːm]	where you change your clothes	*Umkleidekabine*
	enemy	['enəmi]	↔ friend	*Feind*
	brilliant	['brɪliənt]	really good	*toll, super*
	rivalry	['raɪvlri]	*n* rival	*Rivalität*
	disabled	[dɪs'eɪbld]	*n* disability	*behindert*
	gym instructor	['dʒɪm ɪnstrʌktə]	sb who works in a gym	*Fitnesstrainer/in*
	to **run sth**	[rʌn]	to manage	*etw anbieten, durchführen*
	aim	[eɪm]	target	*Ziel*
	qualification	[ˌkwɒlɪfɪ'keɪʃn]	sth you get at the end of a course of study	*Abschluss, Qualifikation*
	compulsory	[kəm'pʌlsəri]	sth you must do	*Pflicht-, obligatorisch, verpflichtend*
	session	['seʃn]	course, lesson	*Sitzung, Stunde*
	maintenance	['meɪntənəns]	*v* to maintain	*Wartung, Instandhaltung, Pflege*
	to **prevent**	[prɪ'vent]	*n* prevention	*verhindern, vorbeugen*
	involved with sth	[ɪn'vɒlvd wɪð]	*n* involvement	*an etw beteiligt*
	to **offend**	[ə'fend]	*n* offence	*straffällig werden*
	murderer	['mɜːdərə]	killer	*Mörder/in*
89	**violence**	['vaɪələns]	*adj* violent	*Gewalt*
	cause	[kɔːz]	reason	*Ursache, Grund*
	nation	['neɪʃn]	country	*Nation, Volk*
	illegal	[ɪ'liːgl]	↔ legal	*illegal*
	authority	[ɔː'θɒrəti]	e.g. teachers, parents, police, etc.	*Autorität*
	to **score**	[skɔː]	*phr* to score a goal	(Tore, Punkte etc.) *erzielen, schießen*
90	to **reduce**	[rɪ'djuːs]	to make sth smaller	*reduzieren, senken*
	desperately	['despərətli]	*adj* desperate	*verzweifelt, händeringend*
	to **put**	[pʊt]	to say	*formulieren, sagen*
	fairy godmother	[ˌfeəri 'gɒdmʌðə]	sb who really helps sb	*gute Fee*
	to **doubt**	[daʊt]	to not be sure about sth	*bezweifeln*
	to **say sth to sb's face**	[ˌseɪ tə sʌmbədiz 'feɪs]	to tell sb in person, not on the phone	*jdm etw ins Gesicht sagen*
	agreement	[ə'griːmənt]	*v* to agree	*Zustimmung*
	disagreement	[ˌdɪsə'griːmənt]	*v* to disagree	*Ablehnung, Meinungsverschiedenheit*
	to **be in agreement**	[bi ˌɪn ə'griːmənt]	to agree	*einer Meinung sein*
91	to **shoot sb**	[ʃuːt]	e.g. to shoot sb with a gun	*auf jdn schießen, jdn erschießen*
	boot	[buːt]	type of shoe	*Stiefel*
	to **get in trouble**	[get ˌɪn 'trʌbl]	e.g. to get in trouble with the police	*Ärger/Schwierigkeiten bekommen*
	tired	['taɪəd]	↔ lively	*müde*
	timeline	['taɪmlaɪn]	the order that things happened in	*Zeitachse, Zeitstrahl*
	to **get involved in sth**	[ˌget ɪn'vɒlvd ɪn]	to do sth with sb/sth	*mit etw zu tun haben, in etw hineingeraten*
92	to **equal**	['iːkwəl]	to be the same	*gleich(wertig) sein*
	skin	[skɪn]		*Haut*
	vision	['vɪʒn]	ideal	*Vision*
	bond	[bɒnd]	connection	*Bindung*
	to **tear**	[teə]	to rip	*zerreißen*
	evil	['iːvl]	↔ good	*(das) Böse*
	to **make a stand**	[ˌmeɪk ə 'stænd]	to do sth about sth	*für etw eintreten*
	racism	['reɪsɪzəm]	*adj* racist	*Rassismus*
	within	[wɪ'ðɪn]	inside	*innen*
	harmony	['hɑːməni]	*adj* harmonic	*Harmonie*

	wheelchair	['wiːltʃeə]	what a person who can't walk sits in	*Rollstuhl*
	to **embrace sth**	[ɪm'breɪs]	to adopt, to take on	*etw annehmen, einsehen*
	ignorance	['ɪgnərəns]	*adj* ignorant	*Ignoranz, Unwissen*
93	**image**	['ɪmɪdʒ]	picture	*Bild*
	to **justify**	['dʒʌstɪfaɪ]	to give reasons	*begründen, rechtfertigen*
	to **illustrate**	['ɪləstreɪt]	*n* illustration	*illustrieren*
	advertising agency	['ædvətaɪzɪŋ eɪdʒənsi]	company that makes adverts	*Werbeagentur*
	underlined	[ˌʌndə'laɪnd]	*v* to underline	*unterstrichen*
	individual	[ˌɪndɪ'vɪdʒuəl]	one person	*Einzelperson*
	weak	[wiːk]	↔ strong	*schwach*
	fairy tale	['feəri teɪl]	e.g. Snow White, Goldilocks, etc.	*Märchen*
	goodness	['gʊdnəs]	↔ evil	*das Gute, Gut, Güte*
	billionaire	[ˌbɪljə'neə]	sb who has over a billion euros	*Milliardär/in*
	solution	[sə'luːʃn]	answer	*Lösung*
94	**Red Cross**	[ˌred 'krɒs]	a charity	*Rotes Kreuz*
	to **have in mind**	[həv ɪn 'maɪnd]	to think about	*beabsichtigen, daran denken*
	to **realise**	['rɪəlaɪz]	*n* realisation	*klar werden, bewusst werden*
	apology	[ə'pɒlədʒi]	*v* to apologise	*Entschuldigung*
	to **arrange**	[ə'reɪndʒ]	to make (an appointment)	*(Termin)* ***ausmachen***
	memo	['meməʊ]	a short note	*Notiz, Mitteilung*
95	**staff**	[stɑːf]	people who work in a company	*Mitarbeiter*
	dentist	['dentɪst]	sb who looks after your teeth	*Zahnarzt/-ärztin*
	to **swap**	[swɒp]	to change with sb	*tauschen*
	to **agree sth**	[ə'griː]	to decide with sb	*sich auf etw einigen*
	to **suit**	[suːt]	to fit well	*passen*
	tied up	[ˌtaɪd 'ʌp]	busy	*beschäftigt, verhindert*
	to **cancel**	['kænsl]	to say sth won't happen anymore	*absagen, stornieren*
	Never mind.	[ˌnevə 'maɪnd]	Oh well.	*Das macht nichts.*
	to **apologize**	[ə'pɒlədʒaɪz]	*n* apology	*sich entschuldigen*
	inconvenience	[ˌɪnkən'viːniəns]	problems	*Unannehmlichkeiten*
97	**pocket**	['pɒkɪt]	e.g. coat pocket	*(Hemd-, Jacken-, Hosen-)Tasche*
	to **mean**	[miːn]	to want to do sth	hier: ***beabsichtigen, wollen***
	kind	[kaɪnd]	nice, friendly	*nett, freundlich*

Unit 10

99	**risky**	['rɪski]	*n* risk	*riskant*
	behaviour	[bɪ'heɪvjə]	*v* to behave	*Verhalten*
	risk-taker	['rɪsk teɪkə]	sb who takes risks	*risikobereite Person*
	to **exist**	[ɪg'zɪst]	to be	*existieren*
	funfair	['fʌnfeə]	carnival with amusement rides	*Jahrmarkt, Rummel, Kirmes*
	ride	[raɪd]	e.g. rollercoaster, big wheel, carousel, etc.	*Fahrgeschäft, Karussel*
	in case	[ɪn 'keɪs]	*phr* just in case	*für den Fall, dass*
	action	['ækʃn]	sth sb does	*Handlung, Aktion*
	optimistic	[ˌɒptɪ'mɪstɪk]	*n* optimism	*optimistisch*
	to **hand in**	[ˌhænd 'ɪn]	to give sb sth	*einreichen, abgeben*
	safety gear	['seɪfti gɪə]	clothes and equipment you use to keep you safe	*Sicherheitskleidung, -ausrüstung*
	to **ride (a bike)**	[raɪd]	to cycle	*(Fahrrad) fahren*
	speed	[spiːd]	how fast sth is	*Geschwindigkeit*
	entrepreneur	[ˌɒntrəprə'nɜː]	e.g. business entrepreneur	*Unternehmer/in*
	physical	['fɪzɪkl]	↔ mental	*körperlich*
	police officer	[pə'liːs ɒfɪsə]	sb who works in the police	*Polizist/in*
	security guard	[sɪ'kjʊərəti gɑːd]	sb who keeps a building safe	*Wachmann/-frau*
	to **play it safe**	[ˌpleɪ ɪt 'seɪf]	↔ to take risks	*auf Nummer sicher gehen*
	to **require**	[rɪ'kwaɪə]	to need	*erfordern*
	health care	['helθ keə]	care you get to keep you healthy and not sick	*Gesundheitswesen*
	potential	[pə'tenʃl]	possible	*Potenzial*
	foolish	['fuːlɪʃ]	↔ clever	*dumm, leichtsinnig*
	too good to be true	[tuː ˌgʊd tə bi 'truː]	unbelievable	*zu schön, um wahr zu sein*
	to **blind**	[blaɪnd]	*adj* blind	*blenden*
	enthusiasm	[ɪn'θjuːziæzəm]	*adj* enthusiastic	*Begeisterung*
	to **resist**	[rɪ'zɪst]	to say no	*widerstehen*
	peers	[pɪəz]	people the same age as you	*Gleichaltrige, Umgebung*
	to **visualize sth**	['vɪʒuəlaɪz]	to see sth in pictures	*sich etw bildlich vorstellen*

	to **worry**	['wʌri]	to be unsure/anxious	*beunruhigen*
100	**universe**	['ju:nɪvɜ:s]	world	*Universum*
	quote	[kwəʊt]	sth that sb said	*Zitat*
	rider	['raɪdə]	cyclist	*(Motorrad-)Fahrer/in*
	bridge	[brɪdʒ]	e.g. the Millenium Bridge in London	*Brücke*
	rail tunnel	['reɪl tʌnl]	place a train goes through	*Eisenbahntunnel*
	to **run sb over**	[ˌrʌn 'əʊvə]	e.g. He died when he was run over by a car.	*jdn überfahren*
	to **be addictive**	[bi ə'dɪktɪv]	*n* addiction	*süchtig machen*
	to **injure**	['ɪndʒə]	*n* injury	*verletzen*
	white water	[ˌwaɪt 'wɔ:tə]	*phr* white water kayaking	*Wildwasser*
	kayaking	['kaɪækɪŋ]	similar to canoeing	*Kayakfahren*
	thrill	[θrɪl]	*adj* thrilling	*Nervenkitzel*
	adrenaline	[ə'drenəlɪn]	e.g. an adrenaline high	*Adrenalin*
	high	[haɪ]	e.g. Taking risks give me a high.	*Rausch*
	to **increase**	[ɪn'kri:s]	to go up	*steigen*
	to **provide**	[prə'vaɪd]	to give	*liefern, bieten*
	to **push**	[pʊʃ]	*phr* to push to the limit	*treiben*
	beyond	[bɪ'jɒnd]	over	*darüber hinaus*
	advanced	[əd'vɑ:nst]	difficult, challenging	*fortgeschritten*
	slope	[sləʊp]	e.g. skiing slope	*Piste*
	off piste	[ˌɒf 'pi:st]	when you don't ski on the slopes	*abseits der Piste*
	accident	['æksɪdənt]	*adv* accidentally	*Unfall*
	paraplegic	[ˌpærə'pli:dʒɪk]	a disabled person who can't move	*Querschnittgelähmte/r*
	to **ruin**	['ru:ɪn]	to destroy	*zugrunde richten, ruinieren*
	to **endanger**	[ɪn'deɪndʒə]	to put at risk	*gefährden*
	youth	[ju:θ]	young people	*Jugendliche/r*
	fight	[faɪt]	*n* fighter	*Kampf*
	shoplifting	['ʃɒplɪftɪŋ]	stealing from a shop	*Ladendiebstahl*
	proud	[praʊd]	*n* pride	*stolz*
101	to **go ahead**	[ˌgəʊ ə'hed]	to start	*anfangen, loslegen*
	law	[lɔ:]	*adj* legal	*Gesetz(e), Recht*
102	**human being**	[ˌhju:mən 'bi:ɪŋ]	person	*Mensch*
	hang glider	['hæŋ glaɪdə]	*v* to go hang gliding	*Drachen, Deltasegler*
	after all	[ˌɑ:ftər 'ɔ:l]	in the end	*schließlich, letzten Endes*
	pointless	['pɔɪntləs]	without any purpose	*sinnlos*
	racing driver	['reɪsɪŋ draɪvə]	sb who takes part in races	*Rennfahrer/in*
	(steering) wheel	['stɪərɪŋ wi:l]	wheel you use to move a car in the right direction	*Lenkrad, Steuer*
	to **affect sth**	[ə'fekt]	to influence	*etw beeinflussen, sich auf etw auswirken*
	hooliganism	['hu:lɪgənɪzm]	e.g. football hooliganism	*Rowdytum*
	binge drink	['bɪndʒ drɪŋk]	drinking too much alcohol in a short time period	*Sauftour, Kampftrinken*
	to **vandalize**	['vændəlaɪz]	to destroy things	*verwüsten, mutwillig beschädigen*
	property	['prɒpəti]	sth sb owns	*Eigentum, Immobilie*
103	**consequence**	['kɒnsɪkwəns]	result	*Konsequenz*
	social(ly)	['səʊʃl]	*n* society	*sozial, gesellschaftlich*
	to **embarrass sb**	[ɪm'bærəs]	e.g. He embarrassed me in front of all those people!	*jdn in Verlegenheit bringen, jdn bloßstellen*
	criminal record	['krɪmɪnl rekɔ:d]	sth which shows what crimes you have done	*Vorstrafenregister*
	unprotected	[ˌʌnprə'tektɪd]	*v* to protect	*ungeschützt*
	part-time	[ˌpɑ:t'taɪm]	↔ full-time	*Teilzeit-*
104	**Listen up.**	[ˌlɪsn 'ʌp]	Pay attention.	*Hört mal her!*
	to **take off**	[ˌteɪk 'ɒf]	to move into the air	*abheben, starten*
	to **depend on sth**	[dɪ'pend ɒn]	to rely on sth	*von etw abhängen*
	wing	[wɪŋ]	e.g. the wing of a plane	*Flügel, Tragfläche*
	to **steer**	[stɪə]	to control direction	*steuern*
	to **shift**	[ʃɪft]	to move	*verlagern*
	weight	[weɪt]	*v* to weigh	*Gewicht*
	to **drop down**	[ˌdrɒp 'daʊn]	to move downwards	*sich senken*
	to **speed up**	[ˌspi:d 'ʌp]	to go faster	*beschleunigen*
	to **lift**	[lɪft]	to move upwards	*hochgehen*
	to **slow down**	[ˌsləʊ 'daʊn]	to go slower	*bremsen, langsamer werden*
	to **push**	[pʊʃ]	↔ to pull	*stoßen, drücken*
	ground	[graʊnd]	earth	*Boden*
	handbook	['hændbʊk]	book of instructions	*Handbuch*

	to **sail**	[seɪl]	to travel on the sea	*segeln*
105	**skier**	['ski:ə]	sb who skis	*Skifahrer/in*
	reaction	[ri'ækʃn]	*v* to react	*Reaktion*
	to **lie (to sb)**	[laɪ]	to not tell the truth	*lügen, jdn belügen*
	to **ring**	[rɪŋ]	e.g. Your phone is ringing.	*läuten, schellen*
	to **ground sb**	[graʊnd]	to not let sb leave the house	*jdn unter Hausarrest stellen*
	lottery	['lɒtəri]	competition where you can win a lot of money	*Lotto, Lotterie*
	to **win the lottery**	[ˌwɪn ðə 'lɒtəri]	e.g. I won the lottery! I'm rich!	*im Lotto gewinnen*
106	**pain**	[peɪn]	*phr* to be in pain	*Schmerz(en)*
	shoulder	['ʃəʊldə]	part of the body at top of arm	*Schulter*
	prescription	[prɪ'skrɪpʃn]	sth the doctor gives you to get medicine	*(ärztliches) Rezept*
	pharmacy	['fɑ:məsi]	chemist's	*Apotheke*
	receipt	[rɪ'si:t]	piece of paper you get when you buy sth	*Quittung*
	tablet	['tæblɪt]	pill	*Tablette*
	change	[tʃeɪndʒ]	money you get back when you pay for sth	*Wechselgeld*
	painkiller	['peɪnkɪlə]	tablet which stops pain	*Schmerzmittel*
	to **lie down**	[ˌlaɪ 'daʊn]	e.g. to lie down in bed	*sich hinlegen*
	dizzy	['dɪzi]	when you feel like everything is spinning	*schwindlig*
	side-effect	['saɪdɪfekt]	sth that happens to you when you take medicine	*Nebenwirkung*
	dizziness	['dɪzinəs]	*adj* dizzy	*Schwindel*
	the day after tomorrow	[ðə ˌdeɪ ɑ:ftə tə'mɒrəʊ]	e.g. I'll come the day after tomorrow.	*übermorgen*
	vitamin	['vɪtəmɪn]	*phr* vitamin pill	*Vitamin*
	to **respond (to sb/sth)**	[rɪ'spɒnd]	to reply	*(jdm) antworten, (auf etw) reagieren*
107	to **interpret**	[ɪn'tɜ:prɪt]	to mediate	*übersetzen*
	pack	[pæk]	packet	*Packung*
108	to **delay**	[dɪ'leɪ]	to make sth late	*sich verzögern, sich verspäten*
	overnight	[ˌəʊvə'naɪt]	from one day to the next	*über Nacht*
	hopefully	['həʊpfli]	*n* hope	*hoffentlich*
	fridge	[frɪdʒ]	cold place where you keep milk, cheese, etc.	*Kühlschrank*
	kipper	['kɪpə]	type of fish	*Räucherhering*
	obvious	['ɒbviəs]	clear	*klar erkennbar, offensichtlich*
	parental	[pə'rentl]	to do with your mother and father	*elterlich*
	researcher	[rɪ'sɜ:tʃə]	*v* to research	*Forscher/in*
	range	[reɪndʒ]	variety	*Reihe, Auswahl*
	income	['ɪnkʌm]	money you get from work	*Einkommen*
	unemployment	[ˌʌnɪm'plɔɪmənt]	not having a job	*Arbeitslosigkeit*
	to **remain**	[rɪ'meɪn]	to stay	*bleiben*
	to **do well**	[ˌdu: 'wel]	to be successful	*(es) gut gehen*
	recent	['ri:snt]	current, modern	*jüngst*
	recession	[rɪ'seʃn]	time when the economy is bad	*Rezession*
	loan	[ləʊn]	money which you have to give back to sb later	*Darlehen, Kredit*
	to **owe**	[əʊ]	to have to give sb sth back	*schulden*
	eventually	[ɪ'ventʃuəli]	in the end	*schließlich, endlich*
	considering	[kən'sɪdərɪŋ]	if you think about	*angesichts der Umstände*
	health and safety	[ˌhelθ ənd 'seɪfti]	e.g. You have to wear a hat for health and safety.	*Arbeitsschutz, Arbeitssicherheit*
	incident	['ɪnsɪdənt]	event	*Zwischenfall, Vorfall*
	site	[saɪt]	e.g. building site	*Baustelle*
	to **cut wood**	[ˌkʌt 'wʊd]	to make pieces of wood smaller	*Holz hacken/sägen*
	to **fall off**	[ˌfɔ:l 'ɒf]	e.g. He fell off the chair.	*herunterfallen*
	obviously	['ɒbviəsli]	clearly	*versteht sich*
	medical	['medɪkl]	*n* medicine	*ärztlich, medizinisch*
	treatment	['tri:tmənt]	*v* to treat	*Behandlung*
	proper	['prɒpə]	real	*richtig, ordentlich*
	check-up	['tʃekʌp]	medical check	*Untersuchung*
109	to **get off**	[ˌget 'ɒf]	e.g. to get off the train/bus	(Zug etc.:) *aussteigen*
	stop	[stɒp]	e.g. bus stop	*Haltestelle*
	to **go for a walk**	[ˌgəʊ fər ə 'wɔ:k]	e.g. He went for a walk with his dog.	*spazieren gehen*
	path	[pɑ:θ]	walkway	*Weg*
	to **pack**	[pæk]	to put in a bag or suitcase	*einpacken*
	jumper	['dʒʌmpə]	pullover	*Pullover*
110	to **take sth up**	[ˌteɪk 'ʌp]	to start	*mit etw anfangen, etw annehmen*
	sailor	['seɪlə]	*v* to sail	*Segler/in*

	round-the-world sailor	[raʊnd ðə ˌwɜːld ˈseɪlə]	*v* to sail around the world	*Weltumsegler/in*
	yacht	[jɒt]	type of sailing boat	*Yacht*
	lionheart	[ˈlaɪənhɑːt]	used to describe sb brave	*Löwenherz*
	adventure	[ədˈventʃə]	*adj* adventurous	*Abenteuer*
	modest	[ˈmɒdɪst]	↔ arrogant	*bescheiden*
	to **prove**	[pruːv]	*n* proof	*beweisen*
	to **be critical of sb**	[bi ˈkrɪtɪkl əv]	*n* criticism	*jdm kritisch gegenüberstehen*
	irresponsible	[ˌɪrɪˈspɒnsəbl]	↔ responsible	*verantwortungslos*
	to **attempt sth**	[əˈtemt]	to try sth	*etw versuchen*
	criticism	[ˈkrɪtɪsɪzəm]	*v* to criticise	*Kritik*
	to **direct sth at sb**	[dəˈrekt ət]	*n* direction	*etw an jdn richten*
	terrifying	[ˈterɪfaɪɪŋ]	scary	*schrecklich, furchterregend*
	fortunately	[ˈfɔːtʃənətli]	thankfully	*glücklicherweise, zum Glück*

Unit 11

111	**consumer**	[kənˈsjuːmə]	*v* to consume	*Verbraucher/in, Konsument/in*
	heaven	[ˈhevn]	*(hier)* really good place	*Himmel*
	advertisment	[ədˈvɜːtɪsmənt]	*inf* ad, advert	*Anzeige, Werbung*
	ordinary	[ˈɔːdnri]	normal	*gewöhnlich, normal, mittelmäßig*
	artificial	[ˌɑːtɪˈfɪʃl]	↔ natural	*künstlich*
	advertiser	[ˈædvətaɪzə]	sb who makes adverts	*Werbetreibende/r, Anzeigenkunde/-in*
	nostalgia	[nɒˈstældʒə]	*adj* nostalgic	*Nostalgie*
	power	[ˈpaʊə]	*adj* powerful	*Macht*
	findings	[ˈfaɪndɪŋz]	results	*Ergebnisse*
	clothing	[ˈkləʊðɪŋ]	what people wear	*Kleidung, Bekleidung, Kleider*
	to **number**	[ˈnʌmbə]	to add up to	*nummerieren*
	ethical	[ˈeθɪkl]	*n* ethics	*ethisch, moralisch*
	to **harm sb**	[hɑːm]	↔ to protect sb	*jdm schaden*
	environment	[ɪnˈvaɪrənmənt]	the atmosphere and things around us	*Umwelt*
112	**retail**	[ˈriːteɪl]	to do with selling	*Einzelhandel*
	retail outlet	[ˈriːteɪl aʊtlet]	shop	*(Einzelhandels-)Geschäft*
	cotton	[ˈkɒtn]	a type of material	*Baumwolle*
	inside out	[ˌɪnsaɪd ˈaʊt]	e.g You have to wash the shirt inside out.	(Wäsche:) *links, auf links gewendet*
	separately	[ˈseprətli]	not together	*getrennt*
	label	[ˈleɪbl]	tag	*Etikett*
	van	[væn]	e.g. delivery van	*Lieferwagen*
	warehouse	[ˈweəhaʊs]	where products are stored	*Lager, Lagerhalle*
	sewing machine	[ˈsəʊɪŋ məʃiːn]	e.g. She makes clothes on her sewing machine.	*Nähmaschine*
	zip	[zɪp]	e.g. She broke the zip on her skirt so couldn't wear it.	*Reißverschluss*
	robot	[ˈrəʊbɒt]	machine	*Roboter*
	bonus	[ˈbəʊnəs]	extra	*Zulage*
	safety guard	[ˈseɪfti gɑːd]	sth to protect your safety	*Schutzblende, Sicherheitsabdeckung*
	to **concentrate**	[ˈkɒnsntreɪt]	*n* concentration	*sich konzentrieren*
	sharp	[ʃɑːp]	e.g. a sharp knife	*scharf, spitz*
	needle	[ˈniːdl]	you use this to sew	*Nadel*
	machinist	[məˈʃiːnɪst]	sb who uses a machine	*Maschinist/in*
	sense	[sens]	e.g. touch, taste, smell, etc.	*Sinn*
	component	[kəmˈpəʊnənt]	part, piece	*Teil, Komponente*
	roll	[rəʊl]	e.g. a roll of cloth	*Ballen, Rolle*
	cloth	[klɒθ]	material	*Stoff, Tuch*
	to **weave**	[wiːv]	*adj* woven	*weben*
	to **colour**	[ˈkʌlə]	to dye	*färben*
	synthetic	[sɪnˈθetɪk]	artificial	*synthetisch, künstlich hergestellt*
	dye	[daɪ]	sth used to colour material	*Färbemittel, Farbstoff*
	to **cut**	[kʌt]	to make smaller	(Stoff) *zuschneiden*
	to **sew**	[səʊ]	to join material together	*nähen*
	volcanic stone	[vɒlˌkænɪk ˈstəʊn]	rock from volcano	*Vulkangestein, Vulkansteine*
	soft	[sɒft]	↔ hard	*weich*
	comfortable	[ˈkʌmftəbl]	*n* comfort	*angenehm, bequem*
	profit	[ˈprɒfɪt]	money you earn when you sell sth	*Gewinn*
	tonne	[tʌn]	1000 kg	*Tonne*
	to **stitch sth together**	[ˌstɪtʃ təˈgeðə]	to sew sth together	*zusammennähen*

	to combine	[kəm'baɪn]	to put or mix together	*kombinieren, zusammenfügen*
	button	['bʌtn]	e.g. a button on a shirt	*Knopf*
	zinc	[zɪŋk]	a type of metal	*Zink*
	copper	['kɒpə]	a type of metal	*Kupfer*
	pile	[paɪl]	heap	*Stapel*
113	**sheet (of paper)**	[ˌʃi:t əv 'peɪpə]	piece (of paper)	*Blatt (Papier)*
	manufacture	[ˌmænju'fæktʃə]	making of sth	*Herstellung, Fertigung*
	range	[reɪndʒ]	variety	*Sortiment, Palette*
	to feed sb	[fi:d]	to give sb food	*jdn ernähren*
	wage	[weɪdʒ]	money sb earns at work	*Lohn*
	drum	[drʌm]	a musical instrument you hit	*Fass, Trommel*
114	**various**	['veəriəs]	different types of	*verschiedene/r/s*
	reply	[rɪ'plaɪ]	answer	*Antwort*
	to grow	[grəʊ]	to plant	*(Feldfrucht) anbauen*
	baby changing room	[ˌbeɪbi 'tʃeɪndʒɪŋ ru:m]	place where you can change babies' nappies	*Wickelraum*
	car park	['kɑ: pɑ:k]	place where you leave cars	*Parkplatz, Parkhaus, Tiefgarage*
	escalator	['eskəleɪtə]	moving stairs	*Rolltreppe*
	medical centre	['medɪkl sentə]	where you can see the doctor	*Ärztehaus, medizinisches Zentrum*
	meeting point	['mi:tɪŋ pɔɪnt]	place to meet people	*Treffpunkt*
	playground	['pleɪgraʊnd]	where children can play	*Spielplatz*
	bin	[bɪn]	where you put rubbish	*Mülleimer, Mülltonne*
	to enter	['entə]	to go into	*(Gebäude etc.) betreten*
115	**adequate**	['ædɪkwət]	enough, sufficient	*ausreichend, angemessen*
	store	[stɔ:]	shop	*Laden, Geschäft*
	rubbish	['rʌbɪʃ]	things you throw away	*Abfall, Müll*
	ramp	[ræmp]	e.g. a ramp for a wheelchair	*Rampe*
	ideally	[aɪ'di:əli]	at best	*im Idealfall*
	to gather	['gæðə]	to collect	*sammeln, zusammentragen*
	shopper	['ʃɒpə]	sb who is buying things	*Käufer/in*
	to shut sb out	[ˌʃʌt 'aʊt]	to not let sb in	*jdn aussperren*
	focus group	['fəʊkəs gru:p]	a group you ask questions to to get information	*Fokusgruppe, Diskussionsgruppe*
	drop-in centre	[ˌdrɒp 'ɪn sentə]	e.g. youth drop-in centre	*Anlaufstelle*
116	**fashions**	['fæʃnz]	what people like at a certain time	*modische Kleidung(sstücke)*
	works	[wɜ:ks]	factory	*Werk*
	loom	[lu:m]	sth you use to weave clothes	*Webmaschine, Webstuhl*
117	**sale**	[seɪl]	when things are sold cheaply	*Schlussverkauf*
	clothes rail	['kləʊðz reɪl]	where clothes can be hung	*Kleiderstange*
	litter	['lɪtə]	rubbish	*Abfall, Müll*
	sweater	['swetə]	jumper, pullover	*Pullover*
	to mix sth up	[ˌmɪks 'ʌp]	*n* mixture	*etw durcheinander bringen/werfen*
	scene	[si:n]	what sth looks like	*Szene, Vorfall, Anblick*
	to hit	[hɪt]	e.g. I was angry so I hit him.	*schlagen*
118	**to put sb through**	[ˌpʊt 'θru:]	to pass sb to sb else on the phone	*(Telefon:) jdn durchstellen*
	to hold (the line)	[ˌhəʊld ðə 'laɪn]	to wait a moment	*(Telefon:) am Apparat bleiben*
	to take a message	[ˌteɪk ə 'mesɪdʒ]	↔ to leave a message	*(Telefon:) jdm etw ausrichten*
120	**sand blasting**	['sænd blɑ:stɪŋ]	using sand to make material look old	*Sandstrahlen*
	distressed	[dɪ'strest]	made to look old	*auf alt gemacht, Used-Look-*
	import	['ɪmpɔ:t]	sth brought into a country from abroad	*Einfuhr*
	to blast with sand	[ˌblɑ:st wɪð 'sænd]	to use sand to make material look old	*sandstrahlen*
	to breathe	[bri:ð]	e.g. to breathe heavily	*atmen*
	dust	[dʌst]	fine particles in the air	*Staub*
	anonymously	[ə'nɒnɪməsli]	when you do sth without giving your name	*anonym*
	effect	[ɪ'fekt]	result	*Auswirkung, Folge*
	hose	[həʊz]	e.g. a water hose	*Schlauch*
	air compressor	['eə kəmpresə]	*v* to compress	*Druckluftkompressor*
	to blow	[bləʊ]		*blasen*
	worn	[wɔ:n]	*v* to wear	*abgenutzt, abgetragen*
	to soften	['sɒfn]	↔ to harden	*weicher machen*
	silicosis	[ˌsɪlɪ'kəʊsɪs]	a type of illness	*Silikose, Staublunge*
	to cough	[kɒf]	e.g. He coughed a lot because of the dust.	*husten*
	weight loss	['weɪt lɒs]	when sb weighs less than they did before	*Gewichtsverlust*
	exporter	[ɪk'spɔ:tə]	sb who sells things to people abroad	*Exporteur*
	military service	[ˌmɪlətri 'sɜ:vɪs]	time in the army	*Militärdienst, Wehrdienst*

	to argue	['ɑːgjuː]	to state	*argumentieren*
	to take responsibility	[ˌteɪk rɪˌspɒnsə'bɪləti]	*adj* responsible	*Verantwortung übernehmen*
	to suffer sth	['sʌfə]	e.g. to suffer from an illness	*etw erleiden*
121	emergency	[ɪ'mɜːdʒənsi]	e.g. I need help quickly – it's an emergency!	*Notfall*
	Accident & Emergency	[ˌæksɪdənt ənd ɪ'mɜːdʒənsi]	part of hospital where people go in an emergency	*Notaufnahme*
	injury	['ɪndʒəri]	*v* to injure	*Verletzung*
	illness	['ɪlnəs]	sickness	*Krankheit*
	unit	['juːnɪt]	*v* to unify	*Einheit*
	equivalent	[ɪ'kwɪvələnt]	*v* to equal	*Entsprechung, Gegenwert*
	say	[seɪ]	for example	*zum Beispiel*
	study	['stʌdi]	*v* to study	*Untersuchung, Studie*
	frequently	['friːkwəntli]	often	*oft, häufig*
	quantity	['kwɒntəti]	amount	*Menge*
	to affect	[ə'fekt]	to influence	*beeinträchtigen*
	fall	[fɔːl]	*v* to fall	*Sturz*
	balance	['bæləns]	*v* to balance	*Gleichgewicht(ssinn)*
	co-ordination	[kəʊˌɔːdɪ'neɪʃn]	*v* to co-ordinate	*Koordination*
	facial	['feɪʃl]	*n* face	*Gesichts-*
	mood	[muːd]	how sb feels	*Stimmung, Laune*
	mental	['mentl]	↔ physical	*geistig*
122	games arcade	['geɪmz ɑːkeɪd]	games hall	*Spielhalle*
	sales manager	['seɪlz mænɪdʒə]	*v* to manage	*Verkaufsleiter/in, Vertriebsleiter/in*

Unit 12

123	sight	[saɪt]	*v* to see	*Sehenswürdigkeit*
	cave	[keɪv]	e.g. It was dark in the cave.	*Höhle*
	grotto	['grɒtəʊ]	e.g. Santa's grotto	*Grotte*
	palace	['pæləs]	where kings and queens live	*Palast*
	ruin	['ruːɪn]	very old building	*Ruine*
	walls	[wɔːlz]	e.g. the city walls	*Stadtmauer*
	Grand Master	[ˌgrænd 'mɑːstə]		*Großmeister*
	knight	[naɪt]	e.g. The queen made Sir David Beckham a knight.	*Ritter*
	cathedral	[kə'θiːdrəl]	a big church	*Dom, Kathedrale*
	lizard	['lɪzəd]	a type of animal	*Eidechse*
	pie	[paɪ]	a type of food	*Kuchen, Torte*
124	package holiday	['pækɪdʒ hɒlədeɪ]	holiday which includes flight and accomodation	*Pauschalreise*
	leisure	['leʒə]	freetime	*Freizeit*
	chamber	['tʃeɪmbə]	room	*Kammer*
	ancient	['eɪnʃənt]	very old	*alt*
	bus pass	['bʌs pɑːs]	a ticket for the bus for a longer period of time	*Zeitkarte für den Bus*
	pass	[pɑːs]	ticket	*Eintrittskarte*
	the Middle Ages	[ðə ˌmɪdl 'eɪdʒɪz]	period in history from around the fifth to the fifteenth century	*Mittelalter*
	discount	['dɪskaʊnt]	when you have to pay less for an item	*Rabatt, Nachlass*
	horseback riding	[ˌhɔːsbæk 'raɪdɪŋ]	*v* to ride on a horse	*Reiten (auf dem Pferd)*
	in the countryside	[ɪn ðə 'kʌntrisaɪd]	↔ in the city	*auf dem Land*
	scuba diving	['skuːbə daɪvɪŋ]	*v* to dive	*Gerätetauchen*
	introduction	[ˌɪntrə'dʌkʃn]	*v* to introduce	*Einführung*
125	traveller	['trævələ]	*v* to travel	*Reisende/r*
	entry	['entri]	*v* to enter	*Eintrag*
	site	[saɪt]	e.g. a tourist site	*Stätte, Platz, Schauplatz*
	sunburn	['sʌnbɜːn]	*adj* sunburnt	*Sonnenbrand*
126	wet	[wet]	↔ dry	*feucht, nass*
	century	['sentʃəri]	100 years	*Jahrhundert*
	embassy	['embəsi]	e.g. the German Embassy in the UK	*Botschaft*
127	swimsuit	['swɪmsjuːt]	what you wear to go swimming	*Badehose, -anzug, Bikini*
128	terrace	['terəs]	patio	*Terrasse*
	balcony	['bælkəni]	e.g. a hotel room with a balcony	*Balkon*
129	plate	[pleɪt]	what you put your food on	*Teller*
	greeting	['griːtɪŋ]	*v* to greet	*Gruß*
130	counter	['kaʊntə]	e.g. ticket counter	*Schalter*
	to check in	[ˌtʃek 'ɪn]	to register (e.g. for a flight)	*einchecken, (Gepäck) aufgeben*
	luggage	['lʌgɪdʒ]	bags and suitcases	*Gepäck*

	limit	['lɪmɪt]	sth you are not allowed to have more than	*Höchstgrenze*
	extra charge	[ˌekstrə 'tʃɑːdʒ]	extra money you have to pay for sth	*Aufschlag, Gebühr*
	aisle	[aɪl]	↔ window (seat)	*Gang*
	boarding pass	['bɔːdɪŋ pɑːs]	document you need to get on a plane	*Bordkarte*
	gate	[geɪt]	where you go to get on a plane	*Flugsteig*
	to **board**	[bɔːd]	to get on a plane	*an Bord gehen*
	security	[sɪ'kjʊərəti]	where sb checks your bags at the airport	*Sicherheitskontrollen, Sicherheitspersonal*
	agent	['eɪdʒənt]	e.g. travel agent, check-in agent	*hier: Schaltermitarbeiter/in*
	to **improvise**	['ɪmprəvaɪz]	to make up	*improvisieren*
	via	['vaɪə]	place where you go through on a journey	*über*
	scale	[skeɪl]	what you use to weigh things	*Waage*
131	to **confiscate**	['kɒnfɪskeɪt]	to take away	*konfiszieren, sicherstellen*
	announcement	[ə'naʊnsmənt]	*v* to announce	*Durchsage*
	due to	['djuː tə]	because of	*aufgrund*
	to **regret**	[rɪ'gret]	to be sorry	*bedauern*
	to **proceed**	[prə'siːd]	to go on	*gehen, sich begeben*
	to **inform**	[ɪn'fɔːm]	to let sb know	*informieren*
	platinum	['plætɪnəm]	a type of metal	*Platin*
	beverage	['bevərɪdʒ]	drink	*Getränk*
133	**luckily**	['lʌkɪli]	↔ unluckily, unfortunately	*glücklicherweise*
134	**mountainous**	['maʊntənəs]	*n* mountain	*bergig*
	hill	[hɪl]	small mountain	*Hügel, Berg*
	to **retire**	[rɪ'taɪə]	to stop working	*sich zur Ruhe setzen*

Unit 13

135	**role model**	['rəʊl mɒdl]	sb you want to be like	*Vorbild*
	talented	['tæləntɪd]	*n* talent	*talentiert*
	courageous	[kə'reɪdʒəs]	*n* courage	*mutig*
	gifted	['gɪftɪd]	talented	*begabt*
	influential	[ˌɪnflu'enʃl]	*n* influence	*einflussreich*
	generous	['dʒenərəs]	*n* generosity	*großzügig*
	polite	[pə'laɪt]	*n* politeness	*höflich*
	to **look up at sb**	[ˌlʊk 'ʌp ət]	to admire	*jdn bewundern*
	to **be good at sth**	[bi 'gʊd ət]	to be talented	*etw gut können, gut in etw sein*
	to **try one's hand at sth**	[ˌtraɪ wʌnz 'hænd ət]	to try out	*sich in etw versuchen*
136	**rickshaw**	['rɪkʃɔː]	small vehicle with three wheels	*Rikscha*
	tiny	['taɪni]	very small	*winzig*
	three-wheeled	['θriː wiːld]	with three wheels	*dreirädrig*
	transportation	[ˌtrænspɔː'teɪʃn]	*v* to transport	*Beförderung*
	to **charge sb sth**	[tʃɑːdʒ]	to ask sb to pay for sth	*etw* (Gebühren, Geld etc.) *von jdm verlangen*
	to **fund**	[fʌnd]	to give money for sth	*finanzieren*
	donation	[dəʊ'neɪʃn]	*v* to donate	*Spende*
	board	[bɔːd]	e.g. The teacher wrote the answer on the board.	*Tafel*
	electrical	[ɪ'lektrɪkl]	*n* electricity	*elektrisch, Elektro-*
	device	[dɪ'vaɪs]	machine, gadget	*Gerät*
	monsoon	[ˌmɒn'suːn]	very heavy rain	*Monsun*
	monsoon season	[ˌmɒn'suːn siːzn]	time when it rains a lot	*Regenzeit*
	to **abridge**	[ə'brɪdʒ]	to shorten (a text)	(Text) *kürzen*
	to **adapt**	[ə'dæpt]	to change	(Text) *bearbeiten*
137	to **be literate**	[bi 'lɪtərət]	to be able to read and write	*lesen und schreiben können*
	to **educate**	['edʒukeɪt]	to teach	*unterrichten*
	to **be fortunate**	[bi 'fɔːtʃənət]	to be lucky	*Glück haben, sich glücklich schätzen können*
	fortune	['fɔːtʃuːn]	luck	*Glück*
	to **be entitled to sth**	[bi ɪn'taɪtld tə]	*n* entitlement	*auf etw Anspruch haben*
	computer-assisted	[kəm'pjuːtər əsɪstɪd]	with the help of a computer	*computergestützt*
	education	[ˌedʒu'keɪʃn]	schooling	*Schulwesen, Bildungswesen*
	caste	[keɪst]	group of society in India	*Kaste*
	dozen	['dʌzn]	12	*Dutzend*
	profession	[prə'feʃn]	job, career	*Beruf, Berufsgruppe*
	gender	['dʒendə]	male or female	*Geschlecht*

	discrimination	[dɪˌskrɪmɪ'neɪʃn]	*v* to discriminate	*Diskriminierung*
	official	[ə'fɪʃl]	*adv* officially	*offiziell*
138	**beneath**	[bɪ'ni:θ]	under	*unter*
	shadow	['ʃædəʊ]		*Schatten*
	sunlight	['sʌnlaɪt]	e.g. That sunlight is very bright.	*Sonnenlicht*
	content	[kən'tent]	satisfied, happy	*zufrieden*
	to **shine**	[ʃaɪn]	e.g. The sun is shining brightly today.	*scheinen, glänzen*
	glory	['glɔ:ri]	*adj* glorious	*Ruhm*
	hero	['hɪərəʊ]	e.g. He's my hero. I really admire him.	*Held*
	eagle	['i:gl]	a type of bird	*Adler*
	to **go unnoticed**	[gəʊ ˌʌn'nəʊtɪst]	to not notice sth	*nicht beachtet werden*
	truth	[tru:θ]	*adj* true	*Wahrheit*
	to **touch**	[tʌtʃ]	*n* touch	*berühren*
139	**call-in programme**	[ˌkɔ:l 'ɪn prəʊgræm]	radio/TV programme when people phone in to say their opinions	*Sendung mit Zuschauer-/ Zuhörerbeteiligung per Telefon*
	to **imitate**	['ɪmɪteɪt]	*n* imitation	*nachahmen, imitieren*
	to **confront**	[kən'frʌnt]	*n* confrontation	*konfrontieren*
	idol	['aɪdl]	idol, role model	*Idol*
	youth worker	['ju:θ wɜ:kə]	sb who helps young people with their problems	*Sozialpädagoge/-in, Erzieher/in, Jugendarbeiter/in*
	adolescence	[ˌædə'lesns]	*n* adolescent	*Jugend, Pubertät*
	to **gain**	[geɪn]	to get	*erwerben, erlangen*
	outlook	['aʊtlʊk]	perspective, way sb sees things	*Einstellung, Perspektive*
	to **succeed**	[sək'si:d]	*n* success	*Erfolg haben, erfolgreich sein*
	honest	['ɒnɪst]	*n* honesty	*ehrlich*
	taste	[teɪst]	what sb likes and dislikes	*Geschmack*
	sensible	['sensəbl]	↔ silly	*vernünftig*
	to **influence**	['ɪnfluəns]	*n* influence	*beeinflussen*
	eating disorder	[ˌi:tɪŋ dɪs'ɔ:də]	e.g. anorexia, bulimia, etc.	*Essstörung*
	starved	[stɑ:vd]	*v* to starve	*ausgehungert*
	to **look on the bright side**	[ˌlʊk ɒn ðə 'braɪt saɪd]	to think positively	*das Positive sehen, es positiv sehen*
	to **sort sth out**	[ˌsɔ:t 'aʊt]	to arrange sth	*etw in Ordnung bringen*
	character trait	['kærəktə treɪ]	way sb is	*Charakterzug*
	selfishness	['selfɪʃnəs]	*adj* selfish	*Egoismus, Selbstsucht*
	to **trash sth**	[træʃ]	to destroy sth	*etw kaputtschlagen*
	abusive	[ə'bju:sɪv]	*n* abuse	*ausfallend, gewalttätig*
	to **praise**	[preɪz]	to tell sb when they have done sth good	*loben*
	to **get away with sth**	[ˌget ə'weɪ wɪð]	↔ to be punished	*mit etw davonkommen*
	to **come across**	[ˌkʌm ə'krɒs]	to be given	*ankommen, vermittelt werden*
	disregard	[ˌdɪsrɪ'gɑ:d]	↔ regard	*Missachtung*
	to **glorify**	['glɔ:rɪfaɪ]	*n* glory	*verherrlichen*
	judgement	['dʒʌdʒmənt]	*v* to judge	*Urteil*
	to **be sb's fault**	[bi ˌsʌmbədiz 'fɔ:lt]	e.g. It was his fault. He caused the problem.	*jds Schuld sein, an etw Schuld sein*
	to **get around to sth**	[ˌget ə'raʊnd tə]	to find time for sth	*zu etw kommen*
	anyway	['eniweɪ]	e.g. He's ill but he's going to the party anyway.	*sowieso, ohnehin*
	turbulent	['tɜ:bjələnt]	↔ peaceful	*turbulent*
	value	['vælju:]	how much sth is worth	*Wert, Wertvorstellung*
140	to **admit**	[əd'mɪt]	e.g. He admitted the truth. He had lied.	*zugeben, eingestehen*
141	**unemployment benefit**	[ˌʌnɪm'plɔɪmənt benɪfɪt]	money you get from the government when you don't have a job	*Arbeitslosengeld*
	to **tolerate**	['tɒləreɪt]	*n* tolerance	*tolerieren*
	to **cope with sth**	['kəʊp wɪð]	to deal with sth	*mit etw zurechtkommen, mit etw fertigwerden*
	to **react**	[ri'ækt]	*n* reaction	*reagieren*
142	**purpose**	['pɜ:pəs]	reason	*Zweck*
	versus (vs.)	['vɜ:səs]	contrasted with	*gegenüber, im Gegensatz zu*
	to **pass an exam**	[ˌpɑ:s ən ɪg'zæm]	↔ to fail an exam	*eine Prüfung bestehen*
	abbreviation	[əˌbri:vi'eɪʃn]	short form	*Abkürzung*
	concept	['kɒnsept]	term	*Begriff, Konzept*
	reference information	['refərəns ɪnfəmeɪʃn]	e.g. Could you give me the relevant reference information, please?	etwa: *relevante Angaben, Zusatzinformationen*
	to **call a meeting**	[ˌkɔ:l ə 'mi:tɪŋ]	e.g. He called a meeting to discuss some new ideas.	*eine Sitzung einberufen*
	event	[ɪ'vent]	happening	*Veranstaltung*

	product launch	['prɒdʌkt lɔ:ntʃ]	when you start to sell a new product	*Produkteinführung*
	directive	[də'rektɪv]	instruction	*Anweisung, Direktive*
	display	[dɪ'spleɪ]	*v* to display	*Display, Auslage, Ausstellung*
	pyrotechnics	[,paɪrə'teknɪks]	fireworks	*Feuerwerk*
	scheduling	['ʃedju:lɪŋ]	*v* to schedule	*Zeitplan, Zeitplanung*
143	chief executive officer (CEO)	[,tʃi:f ɪg'zekjətɪv ɒfɪsə]	head of a company	*Vorstandsvorsitzende/r, Geschäftsführer/in*
	technician	[tek'nɪʃn]	*adj* technical	*Techniker/in*
	attendee	[ə,ten'di:]	*v* to attend	*Teilnehmer/in*
	to launch (a product)	[lɔ:ntʃ]	to bring a product onto the market	*(ein Produkt) auf den Markt bringen, einführen*
	final	['faɪnl]	last	*fertig, endgültig*
	to display	[dɪ'spleɪ]	*n* display	*ausstellen, zeigen*
	pyramid	['pɪrəmɪd]	e.g. the ancient pyramids in Egypt	*Pyramide*
	Oh my gosh!	[,əʊ maɪ 'gɒʃ]	e.g. Oh my gosh! I can't believe that!	*Ach du liebe Zeit!*
	to force	[fɔ:s]	to make sb do sth	*zwingen*
	to review	[rɪ'vju:]	to check, to think about sth	*überprüfen, überdenken, Revue passieren lassen*
	venue	['venju:]	place where events are held	*Veranstaltungsort*
	installation	[,ɪnstə'leɪʃn]	*v* to install	*Aufbau, Installation*
	to install	[ɪn'stɔ:l]	to set up	*aufbauen, installieren*
	intern	['ɪntɜ:n]	trainee	*Praktikant/in*
	to assume	[ə'sju:m]	*n* assumption	*annehmen, vermuten*
	stage	[steɪdʒ]	e.g. The stage is big in this theatre.	*Bühne*
	screen	[skri:n]	e.g. It was only a small screen in the cinema.	*Leinwand*
	finale	[fɪ'nɑ:li:]	big end of a show	*Finale*
144	importance	[ɪm'pɔ:tns]	*adj* important	*Bedeutung, Wichtigkeit*
	character	['kærəktə]	e.g. Who's your favourite character in the film?	*(Roman, Film etc.:) Figur, Person*
	magic	['mædʒɪk]	*adj* magical	*Zauberei*
	to do magic	[du 'mædʒɪk]	*n* magician	*zaubern*
	learning difficulty	['lɜ:nɪŋ dɪfɪkəlti]	when sb has a problem learning	*Lernschwäche, Lernbehinderung*
	to get sb down	[,get 'daʊn]	to depress sb	*jdn deprimieren*
	to suppose	[sə'pəʊz]	to think	*annehmen, glauben*
	slim	[slɪm]	↔ fat	*schlank*
	cattle	['kætl]	e.g. cows, bulls, etc.	*Vieh*
	remote	[rɪ'məʊt]	very far away and isolated	*entlegen, abgelegen*
	rough	[rʌf]	↔ easy	*rau, holprig, einfach*
	dirt road	['dɜ:t rəʊd]	e.g. It was only a dirt road, not a real street.	*unbefestigte Straße, Sandpiste*
	supplies	[sə'plaɪz]	e.g. Have you got supplies for the camping trip?	*Vorräte*
	boarding school	['bɔ:dɪŋ sku:l]	school where students live	*Internat*
	distant	['dɪstənt]	↔ near	*fern*
	to be considered sth	[bi kən'sɪdəd]	to be thought of as	*als etw gelten*
	radio	['reɪdiəʊ]	e.g. I used the radio to call for help.	*Funkgerät, Funk*
	means of communication	[,mi:nz əf kəmju:nɪ'keɪʃn]	way to communicate	*Kommunikationsmittel*
	worksheet	['wɜ:kʃi:t]	e.g. We have to fill in this worksheet for homework.	*Arbeitsblatt*
	pedal radio	[,pedl 'reɪdiəʊ]	old style of radio	*Pedalfunk, Pedalfunkgerät*
	satellite	['sætəlaɪt]	e.g. We have satellite TV.	*Satellit*
	broadband	['brɔ:dbænd]	e.g. broadband internet connection	*Breitband-*
145	housekeeper	['haʊski:pə]	e.g The housekeeper looks after the house.	*(Hotel:) Zimmermädchen, Zimmerservice*
	glasses	['glɑ:sɪz]	e.g. She can't see without her glasses.	*Brille*
	initials	[ɪ'nɪʃlz]	Her initials are KS.	*Initialien*
	case	[keɪs]	e.g. glasses case	*Etui*
	entertainment	[,entə'teɪnmənt]	*v* to entertain	*Unterhaltung*
146	inspiring	[ɪn'spaɪrɪŋ]	*n* inspiration	*inspirierend, anregend*
	unless	[ən'les]	e.g. She can't come unless I pick her up in the car.	*außer wenn, es sei denn*
	principal	['prɪnsəpl]	headteacher	*Schuldirektor/in*
	to discriminate against sb	[dɪ'skrɪmɪneɪt əgenst]	*n* discrimination	*jdn diskriminieren*
	uncountable	[,ʌn'kaʊntəbl]	↔ countable	*unzählbar*

Unit 14

147	**dairy**	['deəri]	products made of milk	*Milchprodukte*
	exercise	['eksəsaɪz]	*v* to exercise	*Bewegung*
	poultry	['pəʊltri]	e.g. chicken, turkey, etc.	*Geflügel*
	nutritional supplements	[nju,trɪʃənl 'sʌplɪmənt]	*n* nutrition	*Nahrungsergänzungsmittel*
	plant oil	['plɑ:nt ɔɪl]	e.g. sunflower oil	*Pflanzenöl*
	starchy	['stɑ:tʃi]	*n* starch	*stärkehaltig*
	whole grain	[,həʊl 'greɪn]	e.g. whole grain bread	*Vollkorn*
	berry	['beri]	e.g. strawberry, blueberry, etc.	*Beere*
	fizzy drink	['fɪzi drɪŋk]	e.g. cola, lemonade, etc.	*Erfrischungsgetränk* (mit Kohlensäure)
	multi-vitamin pill	[mʌlti ,vɪtəmɪn 'pɪl]	pill which gives you extra vitamins	*Multivitamintablette*
	salmon	['sæmən]	type of fish	*Lachs*
	scale	[skeɪl]	e.g. Remove scales from the fish before you cook it.	*(Fisch-)Schuppe*
	sunflower	['sʌnflaʊə]	a big, yellow flower	*Sonnenblume*
	mat	[mæt]	e.g. yoga mat	*Matte*
	dose	[dəʊs]	portion	*Portion, Menge, Dosis*
148	**nutrition**	[nju'trɪʃn]	*adj* nutritious	*Nahrung, Ernährung*
	myth	[mɪθ]	legend	*Gerücht, Mythos*
	protein	['prəʊti:n]	e.g. You get a lot of protein from meat.	*Eiweiß, Protein(e)*
	to **catch**	[kætʃ]	to get	(Krankheit) *bekommen*
	flu	[flu:]	a type of illness like a bad cold	*Grippe*
	source	[sɔ:s]	where sth comes from	*Quelle*
	fibre	['faɪbə]	e.g. There is a lot of fibre in whole grain bread.	*Ballaststoffe*
	gas	[gæs]		*Blähungen*
	nutrient	['nju:triənt]	e.g. vitamins, etc.	*Nährstoff*
	gram	[græm]	e.g. A thousand grams is one kilogram.	*Gramm*
	to **soak sth**	[səʊk]	to leave sth in water	*etw einweichen (lassen)*
	supplement	['sʌplɪmənt]	extra	*Zusatz*
	to **contain**	[kən'teɪn]	to hold, to include	*enthalten*
	disease	[dɪ'zi:z]	illness	*Erkrankung, Krankheit*
	breast	[brest]	part of the body	*Brust*
	cancer	['kænsə]	e.g. Cancer is an awful illness.	*Krebs*
	influenza	[,ɪnflu'enzə]	*inf* flu	*Grippe*
	virus	['vaɪrəs]	type of illness	*Virus*
	to **strengthen**	['streŋθn]	to make stronger	*stärken*
	immune system	[ɪ'mju:n sɪstəm]	what fights against illness in your body	*Immunsystem*
	diet	['daɪət]	what you eat normally	*Kost, Ernährung*
	saturated	['sætʃəreɪtɪd]	*v* to saturate	*gesättigt*
	bone	[bəʊn]	e.g. I don't like eating meat with bones.	*Knochen*
	leafy vegetables	[,li:fi 'vedʒtəblz]	e.g. spinach, cabbage, etc.	*Blattgemüse*
	spinach	['spɪnɪtʃ]	a type of vegetable	*Spinat*
	baked beans	[,beɪkt 'bi:nz]	e.g. The British eat baked beans with their breakfast.	*weiße Bohnen in Tomatensoße* (brit. Nationalgericht)
	to **deep fry**	[,di:p 'fraɪ]	to fry in a lot of oil	*fritieren*
	unsaturated	[,ʌn'sætʃəreɪtɪd]	e.g. unsaturated fats	*ungesättigt*
	olive	['ɒlɪv]		*Olive*
	fatty	['fæti]	with a lot of fat	*fettreich*
149	**pork**	[pɔ:k]	a type of meat	*Schweinefleisch*
	health spa	['helθ spɑ:]	wellness centre	*Kurort, Heilbad*
	balanced	['bælənst]	*v* to balance	*ausgewogen*
150	**dish**	[dɪʃ]	meal	*Gericht*
	side dish	['saɪd dɪʃ]	sth you eat with the main part of your meal	*Beilage*
	ingredient	[ɪn'gri:diənt]	what you need to make a meal	*Zutat*
	roasted	['rəʊstɪd]	e.g. roasted potatoes	*geröstet, gebraten*
	shrimp	[ʃrɪmp]	a type of fish	*Garnele*
	paste	[peɪst]	a mixture you use for cooking	*Paste*
	fresh	[freʃ]	e.g. Fresh vegetables are better than frozen ones.	*frisch*
	curcuma	[kɜ:'kju:mɑ:]		*Gelbwurz*
	ginger	['dʒɪndʒə]		*Ingwer*
	preparation	[,prepə'reɪʃn]	*v* to prepare	*Zubereitung*
	to **chop**	[tʃɒp]	to cut into small pieces	*hacken, kleinschneiden*
	to **boil**	[bɔɪl]	to cook in water	*kochen*

	rest	[rest]	break	*Erholung, Pause, Ruhe*
	relaxation	[ˌriːlæk'seɪʃn]	*v* to relax	*Entspannung*
	crowded	['kraʊdɪd]	full, busy	*überfüllt, voll(gestopft)*
	to wait in line	[ˌweɪt ɪn 'laɪn]	to queue	*sich in einer Warteschlange anstellen*
	to feed sb sth	[fiːd]	to give sb sth to eat	*jdm etw zu essen geben*
	relatively	['relətɪvli]	quite	*verhältnismäßig, relativ*
	to hit	[hɪt]	to reach	*erreichen, betreffen*
	resident	['rezɪdənt]	inhabitant	*Bewohner, Einwohner*
	menu	['menjuː]	e.g. The restaurant has a big menu.	*Speisekarte*
	cosmetic	[kɒz'metɪk]	to do with how sth looks	*kosmetisch*
	to top	[tɒp]	to put on top	(eine Speise mit Soße) *überziehen, übergießen*
	fried	[fraɪd]	*v* to fry	*gebraten*
	patty	['pæti]		*Pastete, Bratling*
	filet	['fɪlɪt]	e.g. filet of fish	*Filet*
152	to exercise	['eksəsaɪz]	to move, to do exercise	*sich bewegen*
	to manage	['mænɪdʒ]	e.g. After a lot of trying, he finally managed it.	*es schaffen*
153	to associate	[ə'səʊʃieɪt]	*n* association	*in Verbindung bringen, assoziieren*
	performance	[pə'fɔːməns]	*v* to perform	*Leistung*
	track and field	[ˌtræk ənd 'fiːld]	type of athletics	*Leichtathletik*
	to cheat	[tʃiːt]	e.g. He cheated! He broke the rules!	*betrügen*
	to drown	[draʊn]	to die in the water	*ertrinken*
	endurance	[ɪn'djʊərəns]	*v* to endure	*Ausdauer*
	strategy	['strætədʒi]	*adj* strategic	*Strategie*
	report	[rɪ'pɔːt]	e.g. a sports report	*Reportage*
	goal	[gəʊl]	e.g. He scored three goals in the football match.	(Fußball etc.:) *Tor*
	nil	[nɪl]	zero	*null, gleich null*
	exceptionally	[ɪk'sepʃənəli]	*n* exception	*außergewöhnlich*
	finals	['faɪnlz]	last game of a competition	*Finale*
	semi-finals	[ˌsemi'faɪnlz]	game before the final	*Halbfinale*
	remarkably	[rɪ'mɑːkəbli]	*adj* remarkable	*erstaunlich*
	goalkeeper	['gəʊlkiːpə]	e.g. The goalkeeper was good. No goals were scored.	*Torwart, Torfrau*
	to pass sb by	[ˌpɑːs 'baɪ]	to go past sb	*an jdm vorbeigehen*
	to sweat	[swet]	e.g. It was so hot that I sweated a lot!	*schwitzen*
	stadium	['steɪdiəm]	e.g. football stadium	*Stadion*
	final score	[ˌfaɪnl 'skɔː]	end result	*Endstand, Endergebnis*
	tournament	['tʊənəmənt]	sports competition	*Turnier*
154	starter	['stɑːtə]	what you eat before your main meal	*Vorspeise*
	hors d'oeuvre	[ˌɔː 'dɜːv]	starter	*Vorspeise*
	buffet	['bʊfeɪ]	food from a selection of dishes	*Büfett*
	main course	[ˌmeɪn 'kɔːs]	what you eat after your starter	*Hauptgang*
	chop	[tʃɒp]	e.g. a pork chop	*Kotelett*
	noodle	['nuːdl]	a type of pasta	*Nudel*
	sauce	[sɔːs]	e.g. chips with tomato sauce	*Soße*
	to roast	[rəʊst]	to cook in the oven	*braten*
	port wine	[ˌpɔːt 'waɪn]		*Portwein*
	spicy	['spaɪsi]	*n* spice	*würzig, scharf*
	dessert	[dɪ'zɜːt]	sweet food you eat at the end of a meal	*Nachtisch, Dessert*
	assortment	[ə'sɔːtmənt]	variety	*Auswahl*
	apple tart	['æpl tɑːt]	type of apple cake	*Apfelkuchen*
	vanilla	[və'nɪlə]		*Vanille*
	invitation	[ˌɪnvɪ'teɪʃn]	*v* to invite	*Einladung*
	allergic to	[ə'lɜːdʒɪk tə]	*n* allergy	*allergisch gegen*
	cream	[kriːm]	e.g. strawberries and cream	*Sahne*
	stomach	['stʌmək]	part of the body where your food goes	*Magen*
	delicious	[dɪ'lɪʃəs]	e.g. This cake is delicious! I really like it!	*köstlich*
	Enjoy your meal.	[ɪnˌdʒɔɪ jə 'miːl]	what a waiter says when he brings you your meal	*Guten Appetit!*
	bill	[bɪl]	what the waiter brings at the end of the meal which says how much the food cost	*Rechnung*
	cheque (AE)	[tʃek]	BE: bill	*Rechnung*
	separate	['seprət]	↔ together	*getrennt*
	It's my treat.	[ɪts 'maɪ triːt]	I'll pay.	*Das geht auf mich. Du bist eingeladen.*
156	to outsource	['aʊtsɔːs]	e.g. We outsourced the call centre to India.	(Arbeit) *auslagern*

	tutor	['tju:tə]	teacher	*(Betreuungs-)Lehrer/in*
	assignment	[ə'saınmənt]	task	*Aufgabe*
	unlimited	[ʌn'lımıtıd]	*v* to limit	*unbegrenzt*
	fellow	['feləʊ]	e.g. a fellow classmate	*Kollege/-in, Mit-*
	economic	[,i:kə'nɒmık]	*n* economy	*wirtschaftlich, Wirtschafts-*
	competitive	[kəm'petətıv]	*n* competition	*wettbewerbsfähig*
	across (India)	[ə'krɒs]	all over	*in ganz (Indien)*
	particular	[pə'tıkjələ]	certain	*spezielle/r/s*
	grade	[greıd]	class at school	*Klasse(nstufe)*
	novel	['nɒvl]	e.g. *Oliver Twist* is a novel by Charles Dickens.	*Roman*
	civil war	[,sıvl 'wɔ:]	war where people from the same country fight each other	*Bürgerkrieg*
	badge	[bædʒ]		*Abzeichen, Orden*
	courage	['kʌrıdʒ]	*adj* courageous	*Mut*
	to **show up**	[,ʃəʊ 'ʌp]	to appear	*auftauchen, sichtbar werden*
	graduate	['grædʒuət]	sb who has finished school/university	*Absolvent/in*
	retired	[rı'taıəd]	no longer working	*im Ruhestand, pensioniert*
	to **tutor**	['tju:tə]	to teach after school	*unterrichten*
	to **face sth**	[feıs]	e.g. to face a problem	*vor etw stehen, mit etw zu kämpfen haben*
	rarely	['reəli]	↔ often	*(nur) selten*
	respectful	[rı'spektfl]	*n* respect	*respektvoll*
	to **address sb**	[ə'dres]	to call sb	*jdn anreden*
157	**virtual**	['vɜ:tʃuəl]	↔ real	*virtuell*
	sale	[seıl]	when things are sold cheaply	*Verkauf*
	aid	[eıd]	help	*Hilfe*
	item	['aıtəm]	article, thing	*Artikel, Gegenstand*
	to **estimate**	['estımət]	to guess	*schätzen*
	game money	['geım mʌni]	e.g. He lost all his game money.	*Spielgeld*
	to **encourage**	[ın'kʌrıdʒ]	*n* encouragement	*fördern*
	to **aid**	[eıd]	to help	*helfen, unterstützen*
	lineage	['laınıdʒ]	background	*Abstammung, Herkunft*
	warcraft	['wɔ:krɑ:ft]	to do with war	*Kriegshandwerk*
	to **revolve around sth**	[rı'vɒlv əraʊnd]	to turn around	*sich um etw drehen*
	to **equip**	[ı'kwıp]	*n* equipment	*ausrüsten*
	equipment	[ı'kwıpmənt]	the things you need to do sth	*Ausrüstung*
	powerful	['paʊəfl]	strong	*stark, mächtig*
	to **suggest sth**	[sə'dʒest]	*n* suggestion	*auf etw hindeuten*
	supplier	[sə'plaıə]	*v* to supply	*Anbieter*
	annual	['ænjuəl]	yearly	*jährlich, Jahres-*
	trade	[treıd]	business	*Handel, Branche*
	to **spoil**	[spɔıl]	to ruin	*verderben*
	processing fee	['prəʊsesıŋ fi:]	money you have to pay when sth is processed	*Bearbeitungsgebühr*
	to **split**	[splıt]	to break up	*teilen, aufteilen*
	retailer	['ri:teılə]	e.g. a jeans retailer	*Einzelhändler*
	to **contrast sth with sth**	[kən'trɑ:st wıð]	to compare	*etw einer Sache gegenüberstellen*
	to **farm**	[fɑ:m]	e.g. to farm the fields	(Feldfrucht) *anbauen*
	significant	[sıg'nıfıkənt]	important	*erheblich, bedeutend*
	impact	['ımpækt]	influence	*Einfluss, Auswirkung(en)*
158	**Look out!**	[,lʊk 'aʊt]	Watch out!	*Achtung! Vorsicht!*
	cookery course	['kʊkəri kɔ:s]	where you learn how to cook	*Kochkurs*
	aboard	[ə'bɔ:d]	e.g. aboard a ship	*an Bord*
	bacon	['beıkən]		*Speck*
	sliced	[slaıst]	cut into slices	*in Scheiben*
	tasty	['teısti]	delicious	*schmackhaft, lecker*

Unit 15

159	**environmental**	[ın,vaırən'mentl]	to do with the environment	*Umwelt-*
	issue	['ıʃu:]	question, problem	*Frage, Streitpunkt, Problem*
	biofuel	[,baıəʊ'fju:əl]	fuel made from organic material	*Biokraftstoff*
	crisis	['kraısıs]	big problem	*Krise*
	fishing quota	['fıʃıŋ kwəʊtə]	how much fish you are allowed to catch somewhere	*Fangquote(n)*
	sustainable	[sə'steınə'bl]	*v* to sustain	*nachhaltig*

	electronic waste	[ɪlekˌtrɒnɪk 'weɪst]	electronic rubbish	Elektronikschrott
	sales	[seɪlz]	how much of sth is sold	Absatz
	meltdown	['meltdaʊn]	e.g. a nuclear meltdown	Kernschmelze
	nuclear power plant	[ˌnju:kliə 'paʊə plɑ:nt]	where electricity is produced using nuclear energy	Atomkraftwerk
	hopeful	['həʊpfl]	optimistic	zuversichtlich, optimistisch
160	everyday	['evrideɪ]	normal	Alltags-
	educator	['edʒukeɪtə]	v to educate	Pädagoge/-in
	average	['ævərɪdʒ]	normal	Durchschnitt(s-), durchschnittlich
	shy	[ʃaɪ]	quiet, nervous with people you don't know	schüchtern
	polar bear	['pəʊlə beə]	e.g. There are lots of polar bears in the North Pole.	Eisbär
	solar panel	[ˌsəʊlə 'pænl]	e.g. We get our electricity from solar panels.	Solarzelle
	roof	[ru:f]	top of a building	Dach
	to apply sth	[ə'plaɪ]	to use sth	etw anwenden
	ambassador	[æm'bæsədə]	e.g. UN ambassador	Botschafter/in
	negativity	[ˌnegə'tɪvəti]	↔ positivity	negative Einstellung
	to change sb's mind	[ˌtʃeɪndʒ sʌmbədiz 'maɪnd]	to make sb have a different opinion	seine Meinung ändern
	systems thinking	['sɪstəmz θɪŋkɪŋ]		Systemdenken
	to compost	['kɒmpɒst]	phr compost heap	kompostieren
	perspective	[pə'spektɪv]	viewpoint	Blickwinkel, Perspektive
	environmentalism	[ɪnˌvaɪrən'mentlɪzm]	adj environmental	Umweltschutz(bewegung)
	movement	['mu:vmənt]	v to move	Bewegung
	to relate sth to sth	[rɪ'leɪt tə]	n relation	etw zu etw in Beziehung setzen
	shell	[ʃel]	phr to come out of his shell	Schneckenhaus
	summit	['sʌmɪt]	conference	Gipfel
	to shoot	[ʃu:t]	e.g. to shoot a video	(Foto, Video etc.) aufnehmen
	to empower sb	[ɪm'paʊə]	n power	jdn befähigen
	to take action	[ˌteɪk 'ækʃn]	to do sth	tätig werden, Maßnahmen ergreifen
	landmark	['lændmɑ:k]	e.g. a landmark building	Wahrzeichen
	to power sth	['paʊə]	to give sth electricity	etw mit Strom versorgen
	iconic	[aɪ'kɒnɪk]	n icon	symbolträchtig, Symbol-
	shyness	['ʃaɪnəs]	adj shy	Schüchternheit
	approach	[ə'prəʊtʃ]	way of doing sth	Herangehensweise, Ansatz
	to promote sth	[prə'məʊt]	n promotion	für etw werben, etw fördern
161	to launch sth	[lɔ:ntʃ]	n launch	etw starten
	to benefit from sth	['benɪfɪt frəm]	n benefit	von etw profitieren
162	water conservation	['wɔ:tə kɒnsəveɪʃn]	v to conserve water	Wassersparen, Wasserreinhaltung
	to advertise sth	['ædvətaɪz]	n advertisement	für etw werben/Werbung machen
	to highlight	['haɪlaɪt]	to draw attention to	hervorheben, verdeutlichen
	to raise funds	[ˌreɪz 'fʌndz]	to collect money	Spenden sammeln
	reusable	[ˌri:'ju:zəbl]	able to be used again	wiederverwendbar
	station	['steɪʃn]	e.g. TV/radio station	(Radio-, Fernseh-)Sender
	press release	['pres rɪli:s]	e.g. The press release told the media all about it.	Pressemitteilung
	to melt	[melt]	e.g. The ice is melting in Antarctica.	schmelzen
	convinced	[kən'vɪnst]	v to convince	überzeugt
163	environmentally friendly	[ɪnvaɪrənˌmentəli 'frendli]	not damaging the environment	umweltfreundlich
	compost bin	['kɒmpɒst bɪn]	e.g. Put the remaining food in the compost bin.	Komposttonne, Kompostierfass
	waste	[weɪst]	rubbish	Abfall
	to plant	[plɑ:nt]	e.g. to plant trees	pflanzen
	cartridge	['kɑ:trɪdʒ]	e.g. printer cartridge	Kartusche
	surface	['sɜ:fɪs]	e.g. on the surface	Oberfläche
	container	[kən'teɪnə]	e.g. Put it in this container.	Behälter, Behältnis
	to switch off	[ˌswɪtʃ 'ɒf]	to turn off	ausschalten, ausmachen
	to cycle	['saɪkl]	to go by bicycle	(mit dem) Fahrrad fahren
	to re-use	[ˌri:'ju:z]	to use again	wiederverwenden
	bottled	['bɒtld]	put in bottles	in Flaschen abgefüllt
	to identify	[aɪ'dentɪfaɪ]	n identification	herausfinden, feststellen
164	to warn	[wɔ:n]	e.g. I warned you it would be a problem.	(davor) warnen
	emission	[ɪ'mɪʃn]	v to emit	Emission
	progress	['prəʊgres]	v to progress	Fortschritt(e)
	critic	['krɪtɪk]	e.g. He's my biggest critic. He always disagrees with me.	Kritiker/in
165	chairperson	['tʃeəpɜ:sn]	the head person (in a committee for example)	Vorsitzende/r
	to comment	['kɒment]	to say sth	sagen, bemerken

	unnecessary	[ʌnˈnesəsəri]	↔ necessary	*unnötig*
166	**vocational school**	[vəʊˌkeɪʃənl ˈskuːl]	school which prepares sb for work life	*Berufsschule*
	paragraph	[ˈpærəgrɑːf]	e.g. Write a paragraph about the environment.	(Text:) *Absatz*
	to **survive**	[səˈvaɪv]	to live through	*überleben*
	to **blame sb/sth**	[bleɪm]	to say that sth is sb's fault	*jdm/einer Sache die Schuld geben*
	precedent	[ˈpresɪdent]	previous example	*Beispiel, Präzedenzfall*
	induction	[ɪnˈdʌkʃn]	introduction	*Einführung*
	route	[ruːt]	way to get somewhere	*Weg, Route*
	tax	[tæks]	e.g. I have to pay car tax.	*Steuer*
	key	[kiː]	main, important	*wichtigste/r/s, Haupt-*
	supervisor	[ˈsuːpəvaɪzə]	*v* to supervise	*Vorgesetzte/r*
	paperwork	[ˈpeɪpəwɜːk]	forms	*Unterlagen*
	to **familiarise oneself with sth**	[fəˈmɪliəraɪz wɪð]	to get to know sth	*sich mit etw vertraut machen*
	procedure	[prəˈsiːdʒə]	way sth should happen	*Ablauf, Verfahren*
	policy	[ˈpɒləsi]	way a certain person does sth	*Vorgehensweise, Linie, Politik*
	acceptable	[əkˈseptəbl]	*v* to accept	*akzeptabel, in Ordnung*
	chat	[tʃæt]	discussion	*Unterhaltung, Schwätzchen*
	to **help oneself to sth**	[ˈhelp wʌnself tə]	to take sth	*sich etw (zu essen) nehmen*
	lazy	[ˈleɪzi]	↔ hard-working	*faul*
	documentation	[ˌdɒkjumenˈteɪʃn]	*v* to document	*Unterlagen*
	expectation	[ˌekspekˈteɪʃn]	*v* to expect	*Erwartung*
	to **turn up**	[ˌtɜːn ˈʌp]	to show up	*kommen, auftauchen*
167	**the blues** (*pl.*)	[ðə ˈbluːz]	depression	*Niedergeschlagenheit, Depressionen*
	disaster	[dɪˈzɑːstə]	*adj* disastrous	*Katastrophe*
	timetable	[ˈtaɪmteɪbl]	e.g. bus timetable	*Fahrplan*
	trial run	[ˈtraɪəl rʌn]	when you practise sth before you really do it	*Probelauf*
	disappointment	[ˌdɪsəˈpɔɪntmənt]	*v* to disappoint	*Enttäuschung*
	chatty	[ˈtʃæti]	talkative	*gesprächig*
	to **have a laugh**	[ˌhəv ə ˈlɑːf]	to have fun	*lachen, Witze machen*
	salary	[ˈsæləri]	how much you get paid at work	*Lohn, Gehalt*
168	**environmental impact**	[ɪnvaɪrənˌmentl ˈɪmpækt]	how sth affects the environment	*Umweltbelastung, Umweltfolgen*
	to **draw**	[drɔː]	to take	*ziehen*
	crisp	[krɪsp]	e.g. crisp, fresh snow	*frisch*
	unspoilt	[ʌnˈspɔɪlt]	*v* to spoil	*unverdorben, unverbaut*
	scenery	[ˈsiːnəri]	e.g. beautiful mountain scenery	*Landschaft, Kulisse*
	to **uncover**	[ʌnˈkʌvə]	to discover	*aufdecken*
	infrastructure	[ˈɪnfrəstrʌktʃə]	the structure of a system	*Infrastruktur*
	resort	[rɪˈzɔːt]	e.g. holiday resort	*Ferienort*
	to **recover**	[rɪˈkʌvə]	to relax	*sich erholen*
	hiker	[ˈhaɪkə]	*v* to hike	*Wanderer*
	lodge	[rɪˈzɔːt lɒdʒ]	e.g. a holiday lodge	*Hütte*
	heating	[ˈhiːtɪŋ]	*v* to heat	*Heizung*
	to **disturb**	[dɪˈstɜːb]	to interrupt	*stören*
	to **operate**	[ˈɒpəreɪt]	to work	*betreiben*
	application form	[ˌæplɪˈkeɪʃn fɔːm]	*v* to apply	*Antragsformular*
	relation	[rɪˈleɪʃn]	relative	*Angehörige/r*
	blind	[blaɪnd]	unable to see	*blind*
	garage	[ˈgærɑːʒ]	e.g. The car is in the garage.	*Garage*
169	**workplace**	[ˈwɜːkpleɪs]	where you work	*Arbeitsplatz*
	politician	[ˌpɒləˈtɪʃn]	*n* politics	*Politiker/in*
170	to **cut down**	[ˌkʌt ˈdaʊn]	e.g. to cut down trees	(Baum) *fällen*
	tap water	[ˈtæp wɔːtə]	↔ bottled water	*Leitungswasser*
	fossil fuels	[ˈfɒsl fjuːəlz]	e.g. coal, oil, gas	*fossile Brennstoffe*
	to **reverse**	[rɪˈvɜːs]	to change back	*rückgängig machen, umkehren*

Further Reading 1

179	**survey**	['sɜ:veɪ]	*Umfrage, Untersuchung*
	to **combine**	[kəm'baɪn]	*zusammenzählen*
	definitely	['defɪnətli]	*sicher(lich), bestimmt*
	to exchange	[ɪks'tʃeɪndʒ]	*austauschen*
	to **vary**	['veəri]	*variieren*
	vocabulary	[və'kæbjələri]	*Wortschatz*
	petrol	['petrəl]	*Benzin* (BE)
	gas	[gæs]	*Benzin* (AE)
	mobile	['məʊbaɪl]	*Handy* (BE)
	cell phone	['sel fəʊn]	*Handy* (AE)
	bread roll	[ˌbred 'rəʊl]	*Brötchen*
	humour	['hju:mə]	*Humor, Stimmung*
	flavour	['fleɪvə]	*Aroma, Geschmack*
	to **differ**	['dɪfə]	*sich unterscheiden, unterschiedlich sein*
	especially	[ɪ'speʃəli]	*besonders*
	based on	['beɪst ɒn]	*auf Grundlage der/s*
	to **add**	[æd]	*zusammenzählen, addieren*
	feature	['fi:tʃə]	*Eigenschaft, Merkmal*
	mother tongue	['mʌðə tʌŋ]	*Muttersprache*

Further Reading 2

180	**root**	[ru:t]	*Wurzel*
	president	['prezɪdənt]	*Präsident/in*
	tribe	[traɪb]	*Stamm*
	to **divorce**	[dɪ'vɔ:s]	*sich scheiden lassen*
	homeland	['həʊmlænd]	*Heimat, Heimatland*
	highlight	['haɪlaɪt]	*Höhepunkt*
	trip	[trɪp]	*Reise*
	paternal	[pə'tɜ:nl]	*väterlicherseits*
	finally	['faɪnəli]	*endlich*
	to **study**	['stʌdi]	*studieren, sich etw genau ansehen*
	lap	[læp]	*Schoß*
	beside	[bɪ'saɪd]	*neben*
	meeting	['mi:tɪŋ]	*Begegnung, Treffen*
	joyful	['dʒɔɪfl]	*freudig, froh*
	experience	[ɪk'spɪəriəns]	*Erlebnis, Erfahrung*
	to **realise**	['rɪəlaɪz]	*klar werden, bewusst werden*
	to **reply**	[rɪ'plaɪ]	*antworten*
	to **pay a visit to sth**	[ˌpeɪ ə 'vɪzɪt tə]	*etw besuchen*
	emotional	[ɪ'məʊʃənl]	*emotional*
	grave	[greɪv]	*Grab*
	biological	[ˌbaɪə'lɒdʒɪkl]	*biologisch*
	to **weep**	[wi:p]	*weinen*
	to **connect**	[kə'nekt]	*verbinden*
	plot of earth	[ˌplɒt əv 'ɜ:θ]	*Stück Land*
	ocean	['əʊʃn]	*Ozean*
	to **abridge**	[ə'brɪdʒ]	(Text) *kürzen*
	to **adapt**	[ə'dæpt]	(Text) *bearbeiten*
	(piece of) advice	[əd'vaɪs]	*Rat, Ratschlag*
	relation	[rɪ'leɪʃn]	*Angehörige/r*

Further Reading 3

181	**out of control**	[ˌaʊt əv kən'trəʊl]	*außer Kontrolle*
	quotation	[kwəʊ'teɪʃn]	*Zitat*
	to **respect**	[rɪ'spekt]	*respektieren*
	rude	[ru:d]	*unhöflich, unverschämt*
	impatient	[ɪm'peɪʃnt]	*ungeduldig, unduldsam*
	frequently	['fri:kwəntli]	*oft, häufig*
	self-control	[ˌself kən'trəʊl]	*Selbstbeherrschung*
	respect	[rɪ'spekt]	*Respekt*
	to **obey**	[ə'beɪ]	*gehorchen*
	to **ignore**	[ɪg'nɔ:]	*missachten*
	law	[lɔ:]	*Gesetz(e)*
	criticism	['krɪtɪsɪzəm]	*Kritik*
	sign	[saɪn]	*Zeichen, Anzeichen*
	tomb	[tu:m]	*Grabkammer*
	philosopher	[fə'lɒsəfə]	*Philosoph/in*
	religious leader	[rɪˌlɪdʒəs 'li:də]	*Religionsführer/in*
	hermit	['hɜ:mɪt]	*Einsiedler/in*
	previous	['pri:viəs]	*vorherig, vorig*
	middle-aged	[ˌmɪdl'eɪdʒd]	*mittleren Alters*
	partly	['pɑ:tli]	*teilweise, zum Teil*
	headline	['hedlaɪn]	*Überschrift*
	violent	['vaɪələnt]	*brutal, gewalttätig*
	recent	['ri:snt]	*aktuell, jüngst*
	to **cross**	[krɒs]	*überqueren*
	to **avoid sb**	[ə'vɔɪd]	*jdm aus dem Weg gehen*
	stuff	[stʌf]	*Zeug(s)*
	to **focus on sb/sth**	['fəʊkəs ɒn]	*sich auf jdn/etw konzentrieren*
	minority	[maɪ'nɒrəti]	*Minderheit*
	to **be afraid of sb/sth**	[bi ə'freɪd əv]	*vor jdm/etw Angst haben*
182	**polite**	[pə'laɪt]	*höflich*
	rarely	['reəli]	*selten, kaum*
	to **pay attention to sb**	[ˌpeɪ ə'tenʃn tə]	*auf etw achten, etw beachten*
	majority	[mə'dʒɒrəti]	*Mehrheit*

Further Reading 4

	illegal	[ɪ'li:gl]	*illegal*
	artist	['ɑ:tɪst]	*Künstler/in*
	Who cares?	[ˌhu: 'keəz]	*Was soll's? Wen juckt's?*
	anyway	['eniweɪ]	*sowieso, ohnehin*
	case	[keɪs]	*Fall*
	for instance	[fə'r ɪnstəns]	*zum Beispiel*
	to **add up to sth**	[ˌæd 'ʌp tə]	*etw ergeben*
	to **multiply sth by sth**	['mʌltɪplaɪ baɪ]	*etw mit etw multiplizieren*
	share	[ʃeə]	*Anteil, Teil*
	music recording company	['mju:zɪk rɪkɔ:dɪŋ kʌmpəni]	*Plattenfirma*
	case	[keɪs]	*Etui, Hülle*
	photographer	[fə'tɒgrəfə]	*Fotograf/in*
	lawyer	['lɔ:jə]	*Anwalt/Anwältin*
	promotional company	[prəˌməʊʃənl 'kʌmpəni]	*Werbefirma*
	truck driver	['trʌk draɪvə]	*LKW-Fahrer/in*
	to **deliver**	[dɪ'lɪvə]	*liefern, ausliefern*
	staff	[stɑ:f]	*Mitarbeiter, Personal*
	consequence	['kɒnsɪkwəns]	*Konsequenz*
	to affect sb/sth	[ə'fekt]	*sich auf jdn/etw auswirken*
	to **raise**	[reɪz]	*erhöhen*

to make up for sth	[ˌmeɪk ˈʌp fə]	*etw ausgleichen, etw wieder gutmachen*
in the end	[ɪn ði ˈend]	*letzten Endes*
crime	[kraɪm]	*Straftat, Verbrechen*
worth	[wɜːθ]	*wert*
legal	[ˈliːgl]	*legal*
to keep sb out of trouble	[kiːp ˌaʊt əf ˈtrʌbl]	*jdm Ärger ersparen*
183 as well as	[əz ˈwel əz]	*ebenso wie*

Further Reading 5

achievement	[əˈtʃiːvmənt]	*Leistung, Errungenschaft, Erfolg*
politician	[ˌpɒləˈtɪʃn]	*Politiker/in*
relationship	[rɪˈleɪʃnʃɪp]	*Beziehung*
nevertheless	[ˌnevəðəˈles]	*nichtsdestotrotz, trotzdem*
tabloid journalism	[ˌtæblɔɪd ˈdʒɜːnəlɪzəm]	*Boulevardpresse*
coverage	[ˈkʌvərɪdʒ]	*Berichterstattung*
fabulous	[ˈfæbjələs]	*fabelhaft, sagenhaft*
to provide	[prəˈvaɪd]	*liefern, bieten*
entertainment	[ˌentəˈteɪnmənt]	*Unterhaltung*
to join sb	[dʒɔɪn]	*sich jdm anschließen*
painter	[ˈpeɪntə]	*Maler/in*
to predict	[prɪˈdɪkt]	*vorhersagen*
individual	[ˌɪndɪˈvɪdʒuəl]	*Einzelperson*
popular culture	[ˌpɒpjələ ˈkʌltʃə]	*Popularkultur*
period	[ˈpɪəriəd]	*Zeitabschnitt*
fame	[feɪm]	*Ruhm*
achievable	[əˈtʃiːvəbl]	*erreichbar, machbar*
on the other hand	[ɒn ði ˈʌðə hænd]	*andererseits*
to suffer	[ˈsʌfə]	*leiden*
continual	[kənˈtɪnjuəl]	*ständig, dauernd*
healthy	[ˈhelθi]	*gesund*
spotlight	[ˈspɒtlaɪt]	*Rampenlicht*
184 to fantasize	[ˈfæntəsaɪz]	*träumen*
suffering	[ˈsʌfərɪŋ]	*Leid, Leiden*
possibility	[ˌpɒsəˈbɪləti]	*Möglichkeit*
ability	[əˈbɪləti]	*Fähigkeit, Möglichkeit*
artificial	[ˌɑːtɪˈfɪʃl]	*künstlich*
state	[steɪt]	*Zustand*

Further Reading 6

bone	[bəʊn]	*Knochen*
race	[reɪs]	*Rennen*
water polo	[ˈwɔːtə pəʊləʊ]	*Wasserball*
to compete	[kəmˈpiːt]	*antreten, an Wettbewerben teilnehmen*
disabled	[dɪsˈeɪbld]	*behindert*
medal	[ˈmedl]	*Medaille*
able-bodied	[ˌeɪblˈbɒdid]	*nicht behindert*
athlete	[ˈæθliːt]	*Sportler/in, Athlet/in*
185 J-shaped	[ˈdʒeɪ ʃeɪpt]	*J-förmig*
blade	[bleɪd]	*Blatt, Klinge, Schaufel*
carbon fibre	[ˈkɑːbən faɪbə]	*Kohlefaser*
to claim	[kleɪm]	*behaupten*
cheetah	[ˈtʃiːtə]	*Gepard*
to view	[vjuː]	*betrachten, sehen*
disability	[ˌdɪsəˈbɪləti]	*Behinderung*
accident	[ˈæksɪdənt]	*Unfall*
human	[ˈhjuːmən]	*Mensch*

Further Reading 7

opportunity	[ˌɒpəˈtjuːnəti]	*Möglichkeit, Gelegenheit, Chance*
aim	[eɪm]	*Ziel*
event	[ɪˈvent]	*Veranstaltung*
to train	[treɪn]	*eine Ausbildung machen*
employment	[ɪmˈplɔɪmənt]	*Beschäftigung, Anstellung*
skilled trade	[ˌskɪld ˈtreɪd]	*Handwerksberuf*
attractive	[əˈtræktɪv]	*attraktiv*
to be aimed at sb	[bi ˈeɪmd ət]	*sich an jdn richten*
upwards	[ˈʌpwədz]	*aufwärts*
186 equally	[ˈiːkwəli]	*genauso, gleichermaßen*
caring professions	[ˈkeərɪŋ prəfeʃnz]	*Pflege-/Betreuungsberufe*
role model	[ˈrəʊl mɒdl]	*Vorbild*
pedagogical	[ˌpedəˈgɒdʒɪkl]	*pädagogisch*
psychology	[saɪˈkɒlədʒi]	*Psychologie*
engineering	[ˌendʒɪˈnɪərɪŋ]	*Ingenieurwesen, Maschinenbau*
to end up	[ˌend ˈʌp]	*landen*
spokesperson	[ˈspəʊkspɜːsn]	*Sprecher/in*
federal	[ˈfedərəl]	*Bundes-*
to encourage	[ɪnˈkʌrɪdʒ]	*ermutigen, ermuntern*
to convince	[kənˈvɪns]	*überzeugen*
willing	[ˈwɪlɪŋ]	*bereit, willens*
nursing	[ˈnɜːsɪŋ]	*Krankenpflege*
childminder	[ˈtʃaɪldmaɪndə]	*Tagesmutter/-vater*

Further Reading 8

to enrol	[ɪnˈrəʊl]	*sich anmelden, sich einschreiben*
187 parliament	[ˈpɑːləmənt]	*Parlament*
qualification	[ˌkwɒlɪfɪˈkeɪʃn]	*Abschluss, Qualifikation*
job-seeker	[ˈdʒɒbsiːkə]	*Arbeitssuchende/r*
member state	[ˈmembə steɪt]	*Mitgliedsstaat*
supplement	[ˈsʌplmənt]	*Zusatz, Ergänzung*
term	[tɜːm]	*Trimester, Semester*
non-governmental organisation	[ˌnɒn gʌvənˌmentl ɔːgənaɪˈzeɪʃn]	*Nichtregierungsorganisation*
graduate	[ˈgrædʒuət]	*Absolvent/in*
free of charge	[ˌfriː əv ˈtʃɑːdʒ]	*gebührenfrei, kostenlos*
to gain	[geɪn]	*erwerben, erlangen*
188 to pass an exam	[ˌpɑːs ən ɪgˈzæm]	*eine Prüfung bestehen*
course of study	[ˌkɔːs əf ˈstʌdi]	*Studiengang*

Further Reading 9

disrespect	[ˌdɪsrɪˈspekt]	*Mangel an Respekt, Missachtung*
homeless	[ˈhəʊmləs]	*obdachlos*
drug addict	[ˈdrʌg ædɪkt]	*Drogensüchtige/r*
team mate	[ˈtiːm meɪt]	*Mannschaftskamerad/in*
proud	[praʊd]	*stolz*
challenging	[ˈtʃælɪndʒɪŋ]	*fordernd*
to challenge sb	[ˈtʃælɪndʒ]	*jdn herausfordern*
hater	[ˈheɪtə]	*Neider/in*
hero	[ˈhɪərəʊ]	*Held*
to judge	[dʒʌdʒ]	*verurteilen, beurteilen*
appearance	[əˈpɪərəns]	*Erscheinung(sbild)*
fellow	[ˈfeləʊ]	*Kollege/-in, Mit-*
along with	[əˈlɒŋ wɪð]	*(gemeinsam) mit*

	soldier	['səʊldʒə]	*Soldat/in*
	musician	[mju:'zɪʃn]	*Musiker/in*
	peace	[pi:s]	*Frieden*
189	identity	[aɪ'dentəti]	*Identität*
	to split	[splɪt]	*teilen, spalten*

Further Reading 10

	to catch sb	[kætʃ]	*jdn fangen, erwischen, kriegen*
	conman	['kɒnmæn]	*Trickbetrüger*
	wealthy	['welθi]	*wohlhabend*
	for good	[fə 'gʊd]	*endgültig*
190	tight	[taɪt]	*knapp*
	to trust sb	[trʌst]	*jdm vertrauen*
	innocent	['ɪnəsnt]	*unschuldig*
	ID	[ˌaɪ 'di:]	*Ausweis*
	procedure	[prə'si:dʒə]	*Verfahren, Ablauf*
	to obtain	[əb'teɪn]	*erhalten, bekommen*
	to copy	['kɒpi]	*nachmachen*
	badge	[bædʒ]	*Abzeichen, Anstecker, (Namens-)Schild*
	crew	[kru:]	*Besatzung*
	to write a cheque	[ˌraɪt ə 'tʃek]	*einen Scheck ausstellen*
	to take a turn at the controls	[teɪk ə ˌtɜ:n ət ðə kən'trəʊlz]	*das Steuer übernehmen*
	intelligence	[ɪn'telɪdʒəns]	*Intelligenz*
	charm	[tʃɑ:m]	*Charme*
	to adopt sth	[ə'dɒpt]	*etw annehmen*
	adolescent	[ˌædə'lesnt]	*Heranwachsende/r*
	fear	[fɪə]	*Angst*
	to rent	[rent]	*mieten*
	apartment	[ə'pɑ:tmənt]	*Wohnung (AE)*
	owner	['əʊnə]	*Besitzer/in, Eigentümer/in*
	to supervise	['su:pəvaɪz]	*leiten, führen, beaufsichtigen*
	ward	[wɔ:d]	*Station, Abteilung (im Krankenhaus)*
	to admit	[əd'mɪt]	*zugeben, eingestehen*
	prison	['prɪzn]	*Gefängnis*
	consultant	[kən'sʌltənt]	*Berater/in*
191	to advise sb	[əd'vaɪz]	*jdn beraten*
	to pretend	[prɪ'tend]	*vorgeben, sich ausgeben als*
	honest	['ɒnɪst]	*ehrlich*
	aircraft	['eəkrɑ:ft]	*Flugzeug*

Further Reading 11

	society	[sə'saɪəti]	*Gesellschaft*
	to be unaware of sth	[bi ˌʌnə'weə əv]	*sich einer Sache nicht bewusst sein*
	benefit	['benɪfɪt]	*Vorteil*
	to maintain sth	[meɪn'teɪn]	*etw warten, unterhalten, instandhalten*
	to store	[stɔ:]	*lagern*
	psychological	[ˌsaɪkə'lɒdʒɪkl]	*psychologisch*
	burden	['bɜ:dn]	*Last, Belastung*
	to increase	['ɪŋkri:s]	*erhöhen*
	to use sth up	[ju:z 'ʌp]	*etw aufbrauchen, etw verbrauchen*
	to fix	[fɪks]	*reparieren*
	broken	['brəʊkən]	*kaputt*
192	disposable	[dɪ'spəʊzəbl]	*Wegwerf-*
	lawn mower	['lɔ:n məʊə]	*Rasenmäher*
	paint brush	['peɪnt brʌʃ]	*Farbpinsel*
	container	[kən'teɪnə]	*Behälter*
	to borrow	['bɒrəʊ]	*(sich etw) leihen*
	electric drill	[ɪ'lektrɪk drɪl]	*Bohrmaschine*
	advertising	['ædvətaɪzɪŋ]	*Werbung*
	to be left out	[bi ˌleft 'aʊt]	*übergangen werden, alleine dastehen*
	gadget	['gædʒɪt]	*Gerät, Spielerei*
	ahead	[ə'hed]	*voraus*
	display	[dɪ'spleɪ]	*Auslage*
	colourful	['kʌləfl]	*farbenfroh, bunt*
	packaging	['pækɪdʒɪŋ]	*Verpackung*
	impulse buy	['ɪmpʌls baɪ]	*Impulskauf*
	junk	[dʒʌŋk]	*Schrott*
	to surround	[sə'raʊnd]	*umgeben, umzingeln*
	checkout	['tʃekaʊt]	*Kasse*
	technique	[tek'ni:k]	*Methode, Technik*
	stereo	['steriəʊ]	*Stereoanlage*
	to break down	[ˌbreɪk 'daʊn]	*kaputtgehen*

Further Reading 12

193	mystical	['mɪstɪkl]	*geheimnisvoll*
	approximately	[ə'prɒksɪmətli]	*ungefähr, zirka*
	inhabitant	[ɪn'hæbɪtənt]	*Einwohner/in*
	peaceful	['pi:sfl]	*ruhig*
	building development	['bɪldɪŋ dɪveləpmənt]	*Bauvorhaben, Neubauten*
	farmhouse	['fɑ:mhaʊs]	*Bauernhaus*
	windmill	['wɪndmɪl]	*Windmühle*
	to add to sth	['æd tə]	*zu etw beitragen*
	beauty	['bju:ti]	*Schönheit*
	coastline	['kəʊstlaɪn]	*Küste*
	cliff	[klɪf]	*Klippe, Fels*
	valley	['væli]	*Tal*
	steep	[sti:p]	*steil, (Tal:) eng*
	inlet	['ɪnlet]	*Bucht*
	preserved	[prɪ'zɜ:vd]	*erhalten*
	prehistoric	[ˌpri:hɪ'stɒrɪk]	*prähistorisch, vorgeschichtlich*
	temple	['templ]	*Tempel*
	series	['sɪəri:z]	*Reihe*
	BC (= before Christ)	[ˌbi: 'si: / bɪˌfɔ: 'kraɪst]	*v. Chr. (= vor Christus)*
	pyramid	['pɪrəmɪd]	*Pyramide*
	giant	['dʒaɪənt]	*Riese*
	folklore	['fəʊklɔ:]	*volkstümliche Überlieferung*
	to contain	[kən'teɪn]	*enthalten*
	statue	['stætʃu:]	*Statue*
	womanly	['wʊmənli]	*weiblich, fraulich*
	goddess	['gɒdes]	*Göttin*
	fertility	[fə'tɪləti]	*Fruchtbarkeit*
	archaeologist	[ˌɑ:ki'ɒlədʒɪst]	*Archäologe/-in*
	evidence	['evɪdəns]	*Beweise, Hinweise*
	to pray	[preɪ]	*beten*
	healing	['hi:lɪŋ]	*Heilung*
	place of pilgrimage	[ˌpleɪs əf 'pɪlgrɪmɪdʒ]	*Wallfahrtsort*
	pilgrim	['pɪlgrɪm]	*Pilger*
	apart from	[ə'pɑ:t frəm]	*außer, abgesehen von*
	to worship	['wɜ:ʃɪp]	*anbeten, verehren*
194	calm	[kɑ:m]	*ruhig, still*
	holy	['həʊli]	*heilig*

Further Reading 13

	award	[ə'wɔ:d]	*Preis, Auszeichnung*
	adaptation	[,ædæp'teɪʃn]	*Verfilmung*
	novel	['nɒvl]	*Roman*
	contestant	[kən'testənt]	*Teilnehmer/in (eines Wettbewerbs)*
	millionaire	[,mɪljə'neə]	*Millionär/in*
	prize	[praɪz]	*Gewinn, Preis*
	host	[həʊst]	*Moderator/in*
	to **cheat**	[tʃi:t]	*schummeln, betrügen*
	to **hand sb/sth over**	[,hænd 'əʊvə]	*jdn/etw übergeben*
	innocence	['ɪnəsns]	*Unschuld*
	to **survive**	[sə'vaɪv]	*überleben*
	rupee	[ru:'pi:]	*Rupie*
	dweller	['dwelə]	*Bewohner/in*
	intellectual	[,ɪntə'lektʃʊəl]	*Intellektuelle/r*
	to **reinforce**	[,ri:ɪn'fɔ:s]	*verstärken, bestärken*
	relentless	[rɪ'lentləs]	*unbarmherzig, schonungslos*
	origins	['ɒrɪdʒɪnz]	*Herkunft*
	to **be headed somewhere/ for sth**	[bi 'hedɪd]	*wohin unterwegs sein, auf etw zugehen*
196	**superior**	[su:'pɪəriə]	*Vorgesetzte/r*
	greatness	['greɪtnəs]	*Großes, Größe*
	critic	['krɪtɪk]	*Kritiker/in*
	unsettled	[ʌn'setld]	*turbulent, stürmisch*

Further Reading 14

	rate	[reɪt]	*Quote*
	heart disease	['hɑ:t dɪzi:z]	*Herzkrankheit*
	agricultural	[,ægrɪ'kʌltʃərəl]	*landwirtschaftlich, Landwirtschafts-*
	calorie	['kæləri]	*Kalorie*
	diabetes	[,daɪə'bi:ti:z]	*Diabetes*
	arthritis	[ɑ:'θraɪtɪs]	*Arthritis*
196	to **indicate**	['ɪndɪkeɪt]	*darauf hindeuten*
	to **measure**	['meʒə]	*messen*

Further Reading 15

	shepherd	['ʃepəd]	*Schäfer*
	pirate	['paɪrət]	*Pirat*
	harmless	['hɑ:mləs]	*harmlos*
	marine	[mə'ri:n]	*Meeres-*
	seal	[si:l]	*Robbe*
	dolphin	['dɒlfɪn]	*Delphin*
	whale	[weɪl]	*Wal*
	to **sink sth**	[sɪŋk]	*etw versenken*
	police force	[pə'li:s fɔ:s]	*Polizeitruppe*
	peaceful	['pi:sfl]	*friedlich*
	racer	['reɪsə]	*Schnellboot*
	whale catcher	['weɪl kætʃə]	*Walfänger*
197	**radio operator**	[,reɪdiəʊ 'ɒpəreɪtə]	*Funker/in*
	brave	[breɪv]	*mutig*
	eco-	['i:kəʊ]	*Öko-*
	warrior	['wɒriə]	*Krieger/in*
	harm	[hɑ:m]	*Schaden*
	to **do harm**	[du 'hɑ:m]	*Schaden anrichten*
	to **paint sth**	[peɪnt]	*etw anmalen, etw streichen*
	flag	[flæg]	*Flagge*
	to **rely on sb**	[rɪ'laɪ ɒn]	*sich auf jdn verlassen*
	to **put an end to sth**	[,pʊt ən 'end tə]	*unter etw einen Schlussstrich ziehen*
	unsustainable	[,ʌnsə'steɪnəbl]	*nicht nachhaltig*
	cause	[kɔ:z]	*Anliegen, Sache*
	species	['spi:ʃi:z]	*Art*
	passive	['pæsɪv]	*passiv*

Alphabetical word list

ABC

A

abbreviation 142 Abkürzung
ability 58, 184 Fähigkeit, Möglichkeit
able, to **be ~ to do sth** 25 etw tun können; in der Lage sein, etw zu tun
able-bodied 184 nicht behindert
aboard 158 an Bord
to **abolish** 77 abschaffen
to **abridge** 136, 180 *(Text)* kürzen
abroad 78 im/ins Ausland
abusive 139t ausfallend, gewalttätig
accent 13 Akzent
to **accept** 38 akzeptieren, annehmen
acceptable 166 akzeptabel, in Ordnung
access 24 Zugang, Zugriff
accident 100 Unfall
Accident & Emergency 121 Notaufnahme
accommodation 78 Unterkunft
account 38 Konto
to **achieve sth** 63 etw erreichen
achievable 183 erreichbar, machbar
achievement 59, 183 Errungenschaft, Erfolg
across (India) 156 in ganz (Indien)
to **act** 52 handeln, sich verhalten; 79 spielen, darstellen
action 99 Handlung, Aktion
action, to **take ~** 160 tätig werden, Maßnahmen ergreifen
active 31t aktiv
activity 70t Tätigkeit, Aktivität
actor 31t Schauspieler
to **adapt** 136, 180 *(Text)* bearbeiten
to **adapt to sth** 80 sich an etw anpassen
adaptation 194 Verfilmung
to **add** 22 hinzufügen; 179 zusammenzählen, addieren
to **add to sth** 193 zu etw beitragen
to **add up to sth** 182 etw ergeben
addicted, to **be ~ to sth** 48 nach etw süchtig sein, von etw abhängig sein
addictive, to **be ~** 100 süchtig machen
addition, **in ~** 56 darüber hinaus
additional 25 zusätzlich, Zusatz-
to **address sb** 156 jdn anreden
adequate 115t ausreichend, angemessen
administrative 85 Verwaltungs-
to **admit** 140, 190 zugeben, eingestehen
adolescence 139t Jugend, Pubertät
adolescent 190 Heranwachsende/r
to **adopt** 47 adoptieren
to **adopt sth** 190 etw annehmen
adopted 17 adoptiert
adrenaline 100 Adrenalin
adult 25 Erwachsene/r
advance, **in ~** 25 im Voraus
advanced 100 fortgeschritten
advantage 12 Vorteil
adventurer 58 Abenteurer/in
to **advertise sth** 162t für etw werben / Werbung machen
to **advertise a job** 85 eine Stelle ausschreiben
advertiser 111 Werbetreibende/r, Anzeigenkunde/-in
advertising 14 Werbung, Werbeabteilung
advertising agency 93 Werbeagentur
advertisment 26 Werbespot; 111 Anzeige, Werbung
advice 44 Rat, Ratschlag
to **advise sb** 190 jdn beraten
to **affect** 121 beeinträchtigen
to **affect sth** 102t, 182 etw beeinflussen, sich auf etw auswirken
to **afford sth** 58 sich etw leisten (können)
afraid, to **be ~ of sb/sth** 39, 181 vor jdm/etw Angst haben
afraid, I'm ~ 24 leider
after all 102t schließlich, letzten Endes
afterwards 39 hinterher
against the odds 58 wider Erwarten, wider alle Wahrscheinlichkeit
age, to **come of ~** 69 erwachsen werden
age span 80t Altersspanne
aged … 80t im Alter von … Jahren
agent 55 Verkäufer/in; 130 Schaltermitarbeiter/in
aggressive 52 aggressiv
to **agree with sb** 40 jdm zustimmen, jdm Recht geben
to **agree with sth** 48 einer Sache zustimmen
to **agree sth** 95 sich auf etw einigen
agreement 90 Zustimmung
agreement, to **be in ~** 90 einer Meinung sein
agricultural 195 landwirtschaftlich, Landwirtschafts-
ahead 15 vor, voraus
to **aid** 157 helfen, unterstützen
aid 157 Hilfe
aid, first ~ 64 Erste Hilfe
to **aim** 63 zielen
to **aim high** 63 hoch hinaus wollen
aim 88, 185 Ziel
aimed, to **be ~ at sb** 185 sich an jdn richten
air compressor 120 Druckluftkompressor
aircraft 191 Flugzeug
airline 58 Fluglinie
aisle 130t Gang
alarm clock 82 Wecker
alcohol 69 Alkohol
alive, to **be ~** 31 am Leben sein
all the time 37 ständig, andauernd
allergic to 154t allergisch gegen
to **allow** 37 erlauben, gestatten
to **allow sth** 84 etw einkalkulieren
allowed, to **be ~ to do sth** 82 etw tun dürfen
along 14 entlang
along with 188 (gemeinsam) mit
alright 55 gut, in Ordnung
although 44 obwohl
ambassador 160 Botschafter/in
amount 19 Menge
to **analyse** 70t analysieren
analytical 75 analytisch
ancient 124 alt
anger 66p Wut, Hass
to **announce** 68 ankündigen
announcement 131 Durchsage
to **annoy sb** 41 jdn belästigen, nerven
annual 157 jährlich, Jahres-
anonymously 120 anonym
anyway 139t, 182 sowieso, ohnehin
apart from 193 außer, abgesehen von
apartment 190 Wohnung *(AE)*
to **apologize** 95 sich entschuldigen
apology 94t Entschuldigung
apparently 60 anscheinend
to **appear** 31 vorkommen, erscheinen; 48 scheinen
to **appear on television** 48 ins Fernsehen kommen
appearance 188 Erscheinung(sbild)
apple tart 154 Apfelkuchen
applicant 44 Bewerber/in
application 83 Bewerbung
application form 168 Antragsformular
to **apply for sth** 64 sich um etw bewerben
to **apply sth** 160 etw anwenden
appointment 14t Termin
apprenticeship 78 Lehre, Ausbildung
approach 160 Herangehensweise, Ansatz
approximately 193 ungefähr, zirka
archaeologist 193 Archäologe/-in
architect 70t Architekt/in
area 14 Bereich; 19 Gebiet
to **argue** 120 argumentieren
argument 76 Argument
aristocrat 52 Aristokrat/in
army 19 Armee
to **arrange** 94t *(Termin)* ausmachen
arrest 47 Verhaftung
arrogant 69 überheblich, arrogant
arrow 56 Pfeil
art 74 Kunst
art gallery 74 Kunst-, Gemäldegalerie
arthritis 195 Arthritis
article 46 Artikel
artificial 111, 184 künstlich
artist 74, 182 Künstler/in
artistic 68 künstlerisch
artwork 74 Kunstwerke, -gegenstände
as follows 25 wie folgt
as well as 183 ebenso wie
to **ask for directions** 14 nach dem Weg fragen
aspect 48 Aspekt, Seite
assignment 156 Aufgabe
assistant 24 Assistent/in
to **associate** 153 in Verbindung bringen, assoziieren
assortment 154 Auswahl
to **assume** 143t annehmen, vermuten
asylum 18 Asyl
at all 33 überhaupt
at first 70t zunächst
at least 31t mindestens
athlete 61, 184 Sportler/in, Athlet/in
to **attack** 88 angreifen
attack 47 Angriff, Übergriff
to **attempt sth** 110 etw versuchen
to **attend sth** 66p etw besuchen, an etw teilnehmen
attendee 143 Teilnehmer/in
attention 48 Aufmerksamkeit; 68 Zuwendung
attention, to **pay ~ to sb** 182 auf etw achten, etw beachten
attitude 29 Einstellung, Haltung
to **attract** 80 anziehen, anlocken
attractive 185 attraktiv
aunt 17 Tante
author 49 Autor/in
authority 89 Autorität
autobiography 60 Autobiografie
automobile 7 Auto(-), Automobil(-)
available 64 erhältlich, verfügbar
average 160 Durchschnitt(s-), durchschnittlich
to **avoid** 30 vermeiden, meiden
to **avoid sb** 181 jdm aus dem Weg gehen
award 194 Preis, Auszeichnung
awards show 47 Preisverleihung
awful 30 furchtbar

B

baby changing room 114 Wickelraum
background 18 Herkunft; 22 Hintergrund
background, ethnic ~ 18 Abstammung
bacon 158 Speck
badge 156, 190 Abzeichen, Orden, Anstecker, (Namens-)Schild
baked beans 148 weiße Bohnen in Tomatensoße *(brit. Nationalgericht)*
bakery 72t Bäckerei
balance 76t Kontostand; 121 Gleichgewicht(ssinn)
balanced 149 ausgewogen
balcony 128 Balkon
bald 27 glatzköpfig
to **ban** 28 verbieten, abschaffen
bar chart 81 Säulendiagramm
…-based 45 in … lebend/ansässig
based in … 78 mit Sitz in …, ansässig in …
based on 23, 179 auf Grundlage von/der/s
basic 64 elementar, *hier:* Grundkenntnisse
BC (= before Christ) 193 v. Chr. (= vor Christus)
beach 123 Strand
beat 76t Schlag
to **beat** 76t schlagen
to **beat sb** 66p jdn schlagen
to **beat sb up** 66p jdn verprügeln
beauty 193 Schönheit
because of 31t aufgrund
to **become** 10 werden

to **behave** 32 sich verhalten, sich benehmen
behaviour 99 Verhalten
behind 15 nach
belief 87 Glaube
belt 38 Gürtel
bench 54 Bank
beneath 138 unter
to **benefit from sth** 161 von etw profitieren
benefit 191 Vorteil
benefits 80 Zulagen, Sozialleistungen
the Berlin Wall 20 die Berliner Mauer
berry 147 Beere
beside 180 neben
beverage 131t Getränk
beyond 100 darüber hinaus
bilingual 18 zweisprachig
bill 154t Rechnung
billion 8 Milliarde
billionaire 93 Milliardär/in
bin 114 Mülleimer, Mülltonne
to **binge drink** 102 eine Sauftour machen, kampftrinken
biofuel 159 Biokraftstoff
biographical 60 biografisch
biological 180 biologisch
biology 74 Biologie
birth 64 Geburt
bit 59 Stück, Teil
blade 185 Blatt, Klinge, Schaufel
to **blame sb/sth** 166 jdm/einer Sache die Schuld geben
to **blast with sand** 120 sandstrahlen
the blues (pl.) 167 Niedergeschlagenheit, Depressionen
blind 168t blind
to **blind** 99 blenden
blonde 51t blond
to **blow** 120 blasen
board 136 Tafel
to **board** 130t an Bord gehen
boarding pass 130t Bordkarte
boarding school 144t Internat
boat 38 Boot
to **boil** 150 kochen
bold 47 kühn, provokant
bold, in ~ 36 fettgedruckt
bomb 28 Bombe
bond 92 Bindung
bone 148, 184 Knochen
bonus 112 Zulage
to **book** 24 buchen, reservieren
boot 91 Stiefel
border 78 Grenze
bored 44 gelangweilt
boredom 71 Langeweile
to **borrow** 192 (sich etw) leihen
boss 15 Chef/in
bottled 163 in Flaschen abgefüllt
bottom 21t untere/r/s
bracket 13 Klammer
to **brainstorm** 29 Ideen sammeln
brand 58 Marke
brave 197 mutig
bread roll 179 Brötchen
break, to **take a ~ from sth** 26t etw hinter sich lassen, einer Sache entkommen
to **break** 58 brechen
to **break a leg** 76t sich ein Bein brechen
to **break down** 192 kaputtgehen
breast 148 Brust
to **breathe** 120 atmen
bridge 100 Brücke
bright 20 *(Farbe:)* bunt, leuchtend
bright side, to **look on the ~** 139t das Positive sehen, es positiv sehen
brilliant 88 toll, super
broadband 144t Breitband-
broken 191 kaputt
brought up, to **be ~** 83 aufwachsen
buffet 154 Büfett
to **build** 58 bauen, aufbauen, erbauen
building development 193 Bauvorhaben, Neubauten
bullet 88 (Gewehr-)Kugel
to **bully** 66p mobben, tyrannisieren
bully 41 Mobber/in, Tyrann
bullying 41 Mobbing
burden 191 Last, Belastung
bus driver 68 Busfahrer/in
bus pass 124 Zeitkarte für den Bus
business, to **do ~** 12 Geschäfte machen
business associate 54 Geschäftspartner/in
business contact 15 Geschäftspartner/in
business person 26t Geschäftsmann/-frau
button 112 Knopf
by chance 80 per Zufall, zufällig
by the way 34 übrigens

C

to **calculate** 15 rechnen
calendar 72 Kalender
to **call** 15 jdn anrufen; 40 nennen
to **call a meeting** 142 eine Sitzung einberufen
call-in programme 139 *Sendung mit Zuschauer-/ Zuhörerbeteiligung per Telefon*
calm 194 ruhig, still
calorie 195 Kalorie
campaign 74 Kampagne, Aktion
to **cancel** 95 absagen, stornieren
cancer 148 Krebs
canteen 14 Kantine
capital city 7 Hauptstadt
captain 44 Kapitän
car 54 (Eisenbahn-)Wagen
car park 114 Parkplatz, Parkhaus, Tiefgarage
carbon fibre 185 Kohlefaser
cardigan 27 Strickjacke
care 85 Pflege
care, to **take ~ of sb/sth** 71 sich um jdn/etw kümmern
to **care about sth** 74 am Herzen liegen
care, Who ~s? 182 Was soll's? Wen juckt's?
career 31t Karriere
careers counsellor 70 Berufsberater/in
caregiver 74 Pfleger/in
carer 85 Pfleger/in
caring professions 186 Pflege-/ Betreuungsberufe
carnival 20 Karneval
to **carry sth out** 74 etw ausführen, durchführen
cartoon 45 Karikatur
cartoonist 45 Karikaturist/in
cartridge 163 Kartusche
case 70t, 182 Fall; 145t, 182 Etui, Hülle
case, in ~ 99 für den Fall, dass
caste 137 Kaste
castle 7 Burg, Schloss
casual(ly) 73 *(Kleidung:)* leger
to **catch** 47, 189 fangen, erwischen, verwickeln; 148 *(Krankheit)* bekommen
catchy 62 eingängig
cathedral 123 Dom, Kathedrale
cattle 144t Vieh
caught up 62 gefangen
to **cause** 30 verursachen
cause 89 Ursache, Grund; 197 Anliegen, Sache
cause, a good ~ 75 ein guter Zweck, eine gute Sache
cave 123 Höhle
to **celebrate** 10t feiern
celebration 20 Feier
celebrity 47 Prominente/r, Promi
cell phone 179 Handy *(AE)*
century 126 Jahrhundert
certain 33 gewiss, bestimmt
certificate 64 Urkunde, Zeugnis
chain 27 Kette
chairperson 165 Vorsitzende/r
challenge 52 Herausforderung, (schwierige) Aufgabe
to **challenge sb** 188 jdn herausfordern
challenging 188 fordernd
chamber 124 Kammer
chance, by ~ 80 per Zufall, zufällig
chancellor 7 Kanzler/in
change 106 Wechselgeld
to **change sb's mind** 160 seine Meinung ändern
to **change trains** 54 umsteigen
channel 56 Kanal
character 144t *(Roman, Film etc.:)* Figur, Person, Rolle
character trait 139t Charakterzug
characteristic 29 Merkmal, Eigenschaft
to **charge sb sth** 136 etw *(Gebühren, Geld etc.)* von jdm verlangen
charge, extra ~ 130t Aufschlag, Gebühr
charge, free of ~ 188 gebührenfrei, kostenlos
charity 88 Wohltätigkeitsorganisation
charity work 44 ehrenamtliche Tätigkeit
charm 190 Charme
chart, bar ~ 81 Säulendiagramm
chat 166 Unterhaltung, Schwätzchen
to **chat** 13 sich unterhalten, chatten
chatty 167t gesprächig
cheap 36 billig
to **cheat** 153, 194 betrügen, schummeln
to **check** 44 überprüfen
to **check in** 130 einchecken, *(Gepäck)* aufgeben
check-in 25 Ankunft, Anmeldung
check-out 25 Abreise, Abmeldung
check-up 108t Untersuchung
checkout 192 Kasse
cheetah 185 Gepard
chef 78 Koch/Köchin, Chefkoch/-köchin
chemicals 7 Chemikalien
cheque 154 Rechnung
cheque, to **write a ~** 190 einen Scheck ausstellen
chicken 26t Huhn
chief executive officer (CEO) 143 Vorstandsvorsitzende/r, Geschäftsführer/in
childhood 66p Kindheit
childminder 186 Tagesmutter/-vater
childminding 68 Kinderbetreuung
chips (BE) 21 Pommes frites
choice 41 Wahl, Entscheidung
chop 154 Kotelett
to **chop** 150 hacken, kleinschneiden
chorus 63 Refrain
church 123 Kirche
circle 30 Kreis
circus 47 Zirkus
citizen 18 Staatsbürger
citizenship 20 Staatsbürgerschaft
civil war 156 Bürgerkrieg
to **claim** 185 behaupten
clarification 79p Erläuterung, Klärung
clause 22 Nebensatz
clear 45 klar, deutlich
client 44 Kunde/-in
cliff 193 Klippe, Fels
climate 28 Klima
climate change 28 Klimawandel
to **close** 63 schließen, zum Ende kommen
close to 36 nahe bei
closed 11 geschlossen
closet (AE) 38 begehbarer Kleiderschrank
cloth 112 Stoff, Tuch
clothes rail 117 Kleiderstange
clothing 111 Kleidung, Bekleidung, Kleider
coal mining 7 Kohlebergbau
coastline 193 Küste
cocaine 31t Kokain
colleague 24 Kollege/-in
collection 28 Sammlung
colony 10 Kolonie
to **colour** 112 färben
coloured 32 farbig, bunt
colourful 192 farbenfroh, bunt
column 16 Spalte
to **combine** 112 kombinieren, zusammenfügen; 179 zusammenzählen
to **come across** 139t ankommen, vermittelt werden

to **come down** 28 einstürzen, fallen
to **come of age** 69 erwachsen werden
to **come true** 63 wahr werden, sich verwirklichen
to **come up with sth** 88 sich etw einfallen lassen, sich etw ausdenken
comfortable 28 gemütlich, bequem; 112 angenehm
comic book 13 Comic(heft)
comment 41 Kommentar, Bemerkung
to **comment** 165 sagen, bemerken
to **commit sth** 66p etw *(Tat etc.)* begehen
common 68 verbreitet, häufig; 81 gemeinsam
common, to **have sth in ~** 52 etw gemeinsam haben
to **communicate** 12 kommunizieren
communicative 75 kommunikativ
Communist 28 kommunistisch, Kommunist/in
community 69 Gemeinschaft, Gemeinde
company 18 Firma, Unternehmen, Gesellschaft
company, to **start a ~** 58 ein Unternehmen gründen
company car 73t Firmenwagen
comparison 52 Vergleich
to **compete** 52, 184 konkurrieren, (in einem Wettbewerb) antreten, antreten
competition 79p Wettbewerb
competition, to **enter a ~** 79p an einem Wettbewerb teilnehmen
competitive 156 wettbewerbsfähig
to **complain** 41t sich beschweren
complaint 81 Klage, Beschwerde
complicated 18 kompliziert
component 112 Teil, Komponente
to **compost** 160 kompostieren
compost bin 163 Komposttonne, Kompostierfass
compulsory 88 Pflicht-, obligatorisch, verpflichtend
computer science 75 Informatik
computer-assisted 137 computergestützt
to **concentrate** 112 sich konzentrieren
concept 37, 142 Begriff; 53 Konzept
conclude, to **~** 56 abschließend
conductor 54 Schaffner/in, Zugbegleiter/in
conference room 24 Konferenzzimmer
to **confirm** 25 bestätigen
confirmation 25 Bestätigung
to **confiscate** 131 konfiszieren, sicherstellen
conflict 19 Konflikt, Bürgerkrieg
to **confront** 139 konfrontieren
conman 189 Trickbetrüger
to **connect (to sb)** 44, 180 (sich mit jdm) verbinden
connection 18 Verbindung
to **conquer** 77 erobern
consequence 103, 182 Konsequenz
conservation 64 Naturschutz
conservative 52 konservativ
to **consider** 63 berücksichtigen, in Betracht ziehen; 63 betrachten
considered, to **be ~ sth** 144t als etw gelten
considering 108t angesichts der Umstände
constantly 72p ständig, andauernd
construction 68 Bau, Hausbau
consultant 190 Berater/in
consumer 111 Verbraucher/in, Konsument/in
to **contact sb** 38 Kontakt zu jdm aufnehmen
to **contain** 148, 193 enthalten
container 163, 192 Behälter, Behältnis
content 138 zufrieden
contestant 52 Kandidat/in; 194 Teilnehmer/in (eines Wettbewerbs)
continual 183 ständig, dauernd
to **continue to do sth** 58 etw weiterhin tun
contract 85 Vertrag
to **contrast sth with sth** 157 etw einer Sache gegenüberstellen
to **control** 37 steuern; 69 kontrollieren, überwachen
control, out of ~ 181 außer Kontrolle
convenient 54 praktisch, bequem
conversation 12 Gespräch, Unterhaltung
to **convince** 186 überzeugen
convinced 162 überzeugt
cookery course 158 Kochkurs
to **coordinate** 75 koordinieren
co-ordination 121 Koordination
to **cope with sth** 141 mit etw zurechtkommen, mit etw fertigwerden
copper 112 Kupfer
to **copy** 190 nachmachen
corner 21t Ecke
correct 11 richtig, korrekt
cosmetic 150 kosmetisch
costume 73 Kostüm
cotton 112 Baumwolle
to **cough** 120 husten
to **counsel sb** 52 jdn beraten
counter 130 Schalter
countless 48 unzählig, zahllos
countryside, in the ~ 124 auf dem Land
courage 156 Mut
courageous 135 mutig
course, main ~ 154 Hauptgang
course, of ~ 14t natürlich, selbstverständlich
course of study 188 Studiengang
course work 75 Unterrichtsaufgaben, Klausuren
coverage 183 Berichterstattung
covering letter 74 Anschreiben, Begleitschreiben
co-worker 81 Arbeitskollege/-in
cream 154t Sahne
to **create** 44 schaffen, erzeugen; 53 sich ausdenken
creative 57 kreativ
credit card 24 Kreditkarte
crew 190 Besatzung
crime 88 Verbrechen; 88 Kriminalität; 182 Straftat
criminal 56 verbrecherisch, kriminell
criminal record 103 Vorstrafenregister
crisis 159 Krise
crisp 168t frisch
critic 164, 195 Kritiker/in
critical, to **be ~ of sb** 110 jdm kritisch gegenüber stehen
criticism 110, 181 Kritik
to **criticize** 20 kritisieren
to **cross** 58, 181 überqueren
crowd 70 Menschenmenge
crowded 150 überfüllt, voll(gestopft)
cruise 78 Kreuzfahrt
to **cry** 38 schreien, weinen
cuisine 26t Küche
culture 19 Kultur
curcuma 150 Gelbwurz
current 44 aktuell
customer 14 Kunde/-in
customer service 14 Kundendienst
to **cut** 112 *(Stoff)* zuschneiden
to **cut down** 170 *(Baum)* fällen
to **cut wood** 108t Holz hacken/sägen
CV (BE) 44 Lebenslauf
cyberbullying 41 Mobbing im Internet
to **cycle** 163 (mit dem) Fahrrad fahren

D

dairy 147 Milchprodukte
danger of fire 83 Brandgefahr
dangerous 48 gefährlich
date of birth 64 Geburtsdatum
day, to **have a ~ off** 83 einen Tag frei bekommen
the day after tomorrow 106t übermorgen
a day out 21t ein Ausflug
to **deal with sb/sth** 67 mit jdm/etw zu tun haben, zurechtkommen, umgehen
dealership 68 Händler
dear 33 meine Liebe/mein Lieber, Schatz; 36 lieb, teuer
decade 27 Jahrzehnt
to **deep fry** 148 fritieren
definitely 34, 179 bestimmt, absolut
to **delay** 108t sich verzögern, sich verspäten, aufhalten
to **delete** 40 löschen
delicious 154t köstlich
to **deliver** 70t, 182 liefern, ausliefern
democratic 10 demokratisch
dentist 95p Zahnarzt/-ärztin
to **depart** 54 abfahren, abreisen
department 14t Abteilung
departure 54 Abfahrt, Abreise
to **depend on sth** 104t von etw abhängen, auf etw ankommen
depressed 38 niedergeschlagen, deprimiert
desire 85 Wunsch
desperate 48 verzweifelt
desperately 90 verzweifelt, händeringend
despite 58 trotz
dessert 154 Nachtisch, Dessert
destination 76t Ziel
to **destroy** 48 zerstören
detail 26 Detail, Einzelheit
detailed 26 detailliert
details 25 Angaben, Daten
determined 66p entschlossen
to **develop** 66p entwickeln
development 66p Entwicklung
device 136 Gerät
diabetes 195 Diabetes
dialogue 14 Dialog
diamond 19 Diamant
diary 37 Tagebuch
diet 148 Kost, Ernährung
to **differ** 179 sich unterscheiden, unterschiedlich sein
difference, to **make a ~** 58 etw bewirken
difficulty 38 Schwierigkeit
difficulty, learning ~ 144t Lernschwäche, Lernbehinderung
to **dig** 30 *(ugs.)* verstehen
to **direct sth at sb** 110 etw an jdn richten
to **direct sb somewhere** 15p jdn wohin schicken
directions 15p Wegbeschreibung
directions, to **ask for ~** 14 nach dem Weg fragen
directive 142 Anweisung, Direktive
director 14 Geschäftsführer/in, Vorstand; 49 Regisseur/in
dirt road 144t unbefestigte Straße, Sandpiste
disability 87, 185 Behinderung
disabled 88, 184 behindert
disadvantage 65 Nachteil
to **disagree with sb** 41t jdm widersprechen, anderer Meinung als jd sein
disagreement 90 Ablehnung, Meinungsverschiedenheit
disappointed 33 enttäuscht
disappointment 167t Enttäuschung
disaster 167t Katastrophe
discount 124 Rabatt, Nachlass
to **discriminate against sb** 146 jdn diskriminieren
discrimination 137 Diskriminierung
to **discuss** 7 besprechen, erörtern, diskutieren
discussion 31 Diskussion, Erörterung
disease 148 Erkrankung, Krankheit
dish 150 Gericht
dish, side ~ 150 Beilage
to **dislike** 48 nicht mögen
disorganised 76 unorganisiert
display 74 Ausstellung; 142, 192 Display, Auslage, Ausstellung
to **display** 143t ausstellen, zeigen
disposable 192 Wegwerf-
disregard 139t Missachtung

disrespect 188 Mangel an Respekt, Missachtung
dissatisfaction 81 Unzufriedenheit
dissatisfied 80 unzufrieden
distant 144t fern
distressed 120 auf alt gemacht, Used-Look-
to **distribute** 45 vertreiben
district 88 Bezirk
to **disturb** 168t stören
diversity 77 Vielfalt
to **divorce** 66p, 180 sich scheiden lassen
dizziness 106 Schwindel
dizzy 106 schwindlig
to **do business** 12 Geschäfte machen
to **do harm** 198 Schaden anrichten
to **do magic** 144t zaubern
to **do research** 70t recherchieren, Nachforschungen anstellen
to **do well** 108t (es) gut gehen
doctor 62 Arzt/Ärztin
documentary 33 Dokumentation, Dokumentarfilm
documentation 166 Unterlagen
dolphin 196 Delphin
donation 136 Spende
donor 74 Spender/in
dos and don'ts 84 Dinge, die man tun und lassen sollte
dose 147 Portion, Menge, Dosis
double 25 Doppel-
to **doubt** 90 bezweifeln
down under 8t Australien
dozen 137 Dutzend
drag 52 Frauenkleider *(von Männern getragen)*
to **draw** 79 zeichnen; 168t ziehen
drawing 85 (technische) Zeichnung
dream 18 Traum
dreamer 62 Träumer
dress 69 Kleidung
to **dress** 49 sich kleiden, sich anziehen
to **dress up** 20 sich verkleiden; 84 sich elegant anziehen
dressed up 44 schick angezogen
dressing room 88 Umkleidekabine
drill, electric ~ 192 Bohrmaschine
drinker 49 Trinker/in
driver 70t Fahrer/in
to **drop** 30 fallen lassen
to **drop down** 104t sich senken
to **drop out** 28 aussteigen
drop-in centre 115 Anlaufstelle
to **drown** 153 ertrinken
drug 47 Droge, Drogen-
drug addict 188 Drogensüchtige/r
drum 113 Fass, Trommel
drums 38 Schlagzeug
duck 21t Ente
due to 131t aufgrund
dust 120 Staub
duty 74 Aufgabe, Pflicht
dweller 194 Bewohner/in
dye 112 Färbemittel, Farbstoff
to **dye** 27 färben
dyslexia 58 Legasthenie

E

eagle 138 Adler
ear 28 Ohr
to **earn** 31 verdienen
to **earn sb sth** 28 jdm etw einbringen
Easter 64 Ostern
eating disorder 139t Essstörung
eco- 197 Öko-
economic 156 wirtschaftlich, Wirtschafts-
economy 12 Wirtschaft
to **educate** 137 unterrichten
educated 80t ausgebildet, gebildet
education 18 Schulbildung, Ausbildung; 137 Schulwesen, Bildungswesen
education, further ~ 68 Weiterbildung
educator 160 Pädagoge/-in
effect 120 Auswirkung, Folge
effective 65 effektiv, wirksam
effort 63 Mühe, Anstrengung
either ... or 9 entweder ... oder
elderly 85 älter, alt
election 10 Wahl
electric drill 192 Bohrmaschine
electrical 136 elektrisch, Elektro-
electricity 58 Strom, Elektrizität
electronic waste 159 Elektronikschrott
electronics 84 Elektronik
to **eliminate sb** 52 jdn ausschließen
to **embarrass sb** 103 jdn in Verlegenheit bringen, jdn bloßstellen
embarrassing 41t peinlich
embassy 126 Botschaft
to **embrace sth** 92 etw annehmen, einsehen
emergency 121 Notfall
Emergency, Accident & ~ 121 Notaufnahme
emission 164 Emission
emotional 73, 180 emotional
empathy 68 Einfühlungsvermögen
to **employ sb** 66p jdn beschäftigen
employer 44 Arbeitgeber/in
employment 70t, 185 Beschäftigung, Anstellung
employment office 70t Arbeitsamt
to **empower sb** 160 jdn befähigen
to **encourage** 157 fördern; 186 ermutigen, ermuntern
to **end up** 186 landen
end, in the ~ 182 letzten Endes
end, to put an ~ to sth 198 unter etw einen Schlussstrich ziehen
to **endanger** 100 gefährden
endless 28 endlos
endurance 153 Ausdauer
enemy 88 Feind
energy 63 Energie
engineering 186 Ingenieurwesen, Maschinenbau
Englishman 36 Engländer
to **enjoy doing sth** 20 etw gern tun
Enjoy your meal. 154t Guten Appetit!
enormous 19 enorm, gewaltig
to **enrol** 186 sich anmelden, sich einschreiben
to **enter** 114 *(Gebäude etc.)* betreten
to **enter a competition** 79p an einem Wettbewerb teilnehmen
to **entertain sb** 57 jdn unterhalten
entertainment 145, 183 Unterhaltung
enthusiasm 99 Begeisterung
enthusiastic about sth 79 von etw begeistert
entitled, to **be ~ to sth** 137 auf etw Anspruch haben
entrance 15p Eingang
entrepreneur 99 Unternehmer/in
entry 125 Eintrag
environment 111 Umwelt
environmental 159 Umwelt-
environmental impact 168 Umweltbelastung, Umweltfolgen
environmentalism 160 Umweltschutz(bewegung)
environmentally friendly 163 umweltfreundlich
to **equal** 92 gleich(wertig) sein
equally 186 genauso, gleichermaßen
equator 15 Äquator
to **equip** 157 ausrüsten
equipment 157 Ausrüstung
equivalent 64 Entsprechung; 121 Gegenwert
escalator 114 Rolltreppe
especially 179 besonders
essay 63 Aufsatz
established, to **get ~** 80t sich etablieren
to **estimate** 157 schätzen
ethical 111 ethisch, moralisch
ethnic background 18 Abstammung
ethnic group 18 Volksgruppe
etiquette 52 Etikette, richtiges Benehmen
even, to **get ~ with sb** 41t es jdm heimzahlen
even though 66p obwohl
event 10 Ereignis; 142, 185 Veranstaltung
eventually 108t schließlich, endlich
ever since 76t seitdem
everyday 160 Alltags-
everyday life 26t Alltagsleben
evidence 193 Beweise, Hinweise
evil 92 (das) Böse
exact 41t genau
examination 82 Prüfung
example 10 Beispiel
excellent 72p ausgezeichnet, hervorragend
except for 8 außer
exceptionally 153t außergewöhnlich
to **exchange** 37, 179 austauschen
excited 79p aufgeregt, begeistert
excitement 36 Aufregung, Spannung
exciting 71 aufregend, spannend
excuse 41 Entschuldigung, Ausrede
exercise 147 Bewegung
to **exercise** 56 sich körperlich betätigen; 152 sich bewegen
exhibit 74 Ausstellungsstück
to **exist** 99 existieren
to **expand** 78 expandieren
expectation 166 Erwartung
experience 64, 180 Erfahrung, Erlebnis
to **experience** 66p erleben, erfahren
exporter 120 Exporteur
to **express** 58 ausdrücken
expression 16 Ausdruck
extra 16 zusätzlich
extra charge 130t Aufschlag, Gebühr
eye contact 85 Blickkontakt

F

fabulous 48, 183 fabelhaft, sagenhaft
to **face sth** 156 vor etw stehen, mit etw zu kämpfen haben
face 21 Gesicht
face, to **say sth to sb's ~** 90 jdm etw ins Gesicht sagen
face-to-face 40 persönlich
facial 121 Gesichts-
facilities 24 Einrichtungen
facility 85 Einrichtung
factor 24 Faktor
to **fade away** 30 verschwinden
fair 41t gerecht, fair; 88 Jahrmarkt, Rummel, Kirmes
fairy godmother 90 gute Fee
fairy tale 93 Märchen
fall 121 Sturz
to **fall in love with sb** 80t sich in jdn verlieben
to **fall off** 108t herunterfallen
false 39 falsch
fame 48, 183 Ruhm
to **familiarise oneself with sth** 166 sich mit etw vertraut machen
family tree 17 Stammbaum
to **fantasize** 184 träumen
to **farm** 157 *(Feldfrucht)* anbauen
farmhouse 193 Bauernhaus
fascinated 76t fasziniert
fashion 27 Mode
fashions 116 modische Kleidung(sstücke)
fatty 148 fettreich
fault, to **be sb's ~** 139t jds Schuld sein, an etw Schuld sein
fear 190 Angst
feature 46, 179 Eigenschaft, Merkmal
federal 186 Bundes-
fee 58 Gebühr
to **feed** 21t füttern
to **feed sb** 113 jdn ernähren
to **feed sb sth** 150 jdm etw zu essen geben
to **feel sorry** 39 Leid tun
feeling 38 Gefühl, Eindruck; 39 Ansicht, Meinung
fellow 156, 188 Kollege/-in, Mit-
feminine 52 weiblich
fertility 193 Fruchtbarkeit
fibre 148 Ballaststoffe
to **fight** 66 kämpfen
fight 100 Kampf

fighter 66p Kämpfer/in
fighting 18 Kämpfe
file 50 Ordner, Akte
filet 150 Filet
filing cabinet 15p Aktenschrank
to **fill sth in** 54 etw ausfüllen
final 38 letzte/r/s; 143t fertig, endgültig
final score 153t Endstand, Endergebnis
finale 143t Finale
finally 15p schließlich
finally 180 endlich
finals 153t Finale
Finance 14 Rechnungswesen, Finanzen
financial 68 finanziell, Finanz-
to **find out** 29 herausfinden
findings 111 Ergebnisse
finishing school 52 Mädchenpensionat
to **fire** 88 schießen, abfeuern
fire, danger of ~ 83 Brandgefahr
fire extinguisher 15p Feuerlöscher
firefighter (AE) 62 Feuerwehrmann
first, at ~ 70t zunächst
first aid 64 Erste Hilfe
first floor 15p erster Stock
fishing 38 Angeln, Fischen
fishing quota 159 Fangquote(n)
to **fit** 34 passen
to **fit sb/sth** 57 zu jdm/etw passen
to **fix** 191 reparieren
fizzy drink 147 Erfrischungsgetränk *(mit Kohlensäure)*
flag 197 Flagge
flat (BE) 23 Wohnung
flatmate 71 Mitbewohner/in
flavour 179 Aroma, Geschmack
flexibility 85 Flexibilität
flexible 80t flexibel
flight 60 Flug
floor, first ~ 15p erster Stock
floor, ground ~ 15p Erdgeschoss
floral 27 Blumen-, mit Blumenmuster
flower 28 Blume
flu 148 Grippe
fluent 12 *(Sprache:)* fließend
to **focus (on sb/sth)** 62, 181 sich (auf jdn/etw) konzentrieren
focus group 115 Fokusgruppe, Diskussionsgruppe
folklore 193 volkstümliche Überlieferung
follow, as ~s 25 wie folgt
foolish 99 dumm, leichtsinnig
for good 189 endgültig
for instance 182 zum Beispiel
to **force** 143 zwingen
foreign language 8 Fremdsprache
forest 34 Wald
forever 62 ewig
Formula 1 79p Formel 1
fortunate, to **be ~** 137 Glück haben, sich glücklich schätzen können
fortunately 110 glücklicherweise
fortune 137 Glück
fossil fuels 170 fossile Brennstoffe
to **found** 10t gründen
founder 60 Gründer/in
founding 10 Gründung
free 24 kostenlos, gratis
free of charge 187 gebührenfrei, kostenlos
freedom 10t Freiheit
frequently 121, 181 oft, häufig
fresh 150 frisch
fridge 108t Kühlschrank
fried 150 gebraten
friend, to **make ~s** 18 Freunde finden/gewinnen
front, at the ~ of the picture 21 vorn im Bild
fuel, fossil ~s 170 fossile Brennstoffe
fully 44 vollständig, völlig
fun, to **be ~** 33 Spaß machen, unterhaltsam sein
to **fund** 136 finanzieren
funds, to **raise ~** 162t Spenden sammeln
funfair 99 Jahrmarkt, Rummel, Kirmes
furniture 51 Möbel
furniture, piece of ~ 51 Möbelstück
furniture store 74 Möbelhaus
further education 68 Weiterbildung
future 18 Zukunft; 23 zukünftige/r/s

G

G'Day! (AusE) 8t Guten Tag. Hallo.
gadget 192 Gerät, Spielerei
to **gain** 139t, 187 erwerben, erlangen
game money 157 Spielgeld
games arcade 122 Spielhalle
gap 73 Lücke
gap year 73 *Jahr zwischen Schule und Studium bzw. Berufsanfang*
garage 168t Garage
gas 148 Blähungen; 179 Benzin *(AE)*
gate 130t Flugsteig
to **gather** 115t sammeln, zusammentragen
gender 137 Geschlecht
generally 51 im Allgemeinen
to **generate** 58 erzeugen
generation 17 Generation
generous 135 großzügig
geographical 77 geographisch
to **get around** 30 herumkommen
to **get around to sth** 139t zu etw kommen
to **get away with sth** 139t mit etw davonkommen
to **get established** 80t sich etablieren
to **get even with sb** 41t es jdm heimzahlen
to **get in trouble** 91 Ärger/ Schwierigkeiten bekommen
to **get involved in sth** 91 mit etw zu tun haben, in etw hineingeraten
to **get married** 49 heiraten
to **get off** 109 *(Zug etc.:)* aussteigen
to **get out of touch with sb** 65 den Kontakt zu jdm verlieren
to **get ready for sth** 22 sich auf etw vorbereiten, sich für etw fertig machen
to **get rid of sth** 66p etw loswerden
to **get rid of sth** 139t etw loswerden
to **get sb down** 144t jdn deprimieren
to **get sth across** 79 etw verständlich machen, etw vermiteln
to **get the hang of it** 34 etw hinbekommen
giant 33 riesig; 193 Riese
gifted 135 begabt
ginger 150 Ingwer
giraffe 9 Giraffe
gist 40 das Wesentliche
to **give away** 58 schenken, verschenken, spenden
to **give sth up** 18 etw aufgeben
glamorous 48 glamourös
glasses 145t Brille
global 12 global, weltumspannend
globalization 12 Globalisierung
to **glorify** 139t verherrlichen
glory 138 Ruhm
to **go ahead** 101 anfangen, loslegen
to **go for a walk** 22, 109 spazieren gehen
to **go unnoticed** 138 nicht beachtet werden
goal 57 Ziel; 153 *(Fußball etc.:)* Tor
goalkeeper 153t Torwart, Torfrau
goat 26t Ziege
goddess 193 Göttin
godmother, fairy ~ 90 gute Fee
good, for ~ 190 endgültig
good, too ~ to be true 99 zu schön, um wahr zu sein
good, to **be ~ at sth** 135 etw gut können, gut in etw sein
goodness 93 das Gute, Gut, Güte
goodness, Oh my ~! 54t Du meine Güte!
goose 88 Gans
gosh, Oh my ~! 143t Ach du liebe Zeit!
gourmet 66p Feinschmecker
government 19 Regierung
governmental, non-~ organisation 187 Nichtregierungsorganisation
grade 156 Klasse(nstufe)
graduate 156, 187 Absolvent/in
graduation 71 Abschluss
grain, whole ~ 147 Vollkorn
gram 148 Gramm
grammar 10 Grammatik
grammatical 55 grammatikalisch
Grand Master 123 Großmeister
Grand Mufti 52 Großmufti
granddad 27 Opa
grandmother 17 Großmutter
grandparents 18 Großeltern
grand stand 79p Haupttribüne
graph 81 Diagram, Grafik
graphic artist 68 Grafiker/in
grave 180 Grab
great-grandmother 17 Urgroßmutter
greatness 195 Großes, Größe
greeting 129 Gruß
grocer's shop 72t Lebensmittelhandlung
groceries 75 Lebensmittel
grotto 123 Grotte
to **ground sb** 105 jdn unter Hausarrest stellen
ground 30 Erde; 104t Boden
ground floor 15p Erdgeschoss
to **grow** 114 *(Feldfrucht)* anbauen
to **grow up** 28 erwachsen werden
Guess what? 31t Stellen Sie sich / Stell dir vor!
guest 24 Gast
guitar 38 Gitarre
the Gulf War 28 der Golfkrieg
gun 88 Pistole, Gewehr
guy 51t Typ, Kerl
gym instructor 88 Fitnesstrainer/in

H

habit 85 Gewohnheit
half-sister 17 Halbschwester
hall 14t Flur
hand, on the one ~ 63 einerseits
hand, on the other ~ 63, 183 andererseits
hand, to **try one's ~ at sth** 135 sich in etw versuchen
to **hand in** 99 einreichen, abgeben
to **hand sb/sth over** 194 jdn/etw übergeben
handbook 104 Handbuch
to **handle sth** 83 mit etw hantieren, mit etw umgehen
hang, to **get the ~ of it** 34 etw hinbekommen
hang glider 102t Drachen, Deltasegler
to **happen** 33 geschehen, passieren
happiness 48 Zufriedenheit, Glück
hard-working 28 fleißig, hart arbeitend
hardly 23 kaum
harm 197 Schaden
harm, to **do ~** 197 Schaden anrichten
to **harm sb** 111 jdm schaden
harmless 196 harmlos
harmony 92 Harmonie
hat 127 Hut
hater 188 Neider/in
to **have a day off** 83 einen Tag frei bekommen
to **have a laugh** 167t lachen, Witze machen
to **have in mind** 94 beabsichtigen, daran denken
to **have lunch** 14 zu Mittag essen
to **have no idea** 70t keine Ahnung haben
to **have sth in common** 52 etw gemeinsam haben
head teacher 88 Schulleiter/in

headed, to be ~ somewhere/for sth 194 wohin unterwegs sein, auf etw zugehen
heading 79 Überschrift
headline 47, 181 Überschrift
healing 193 Heilung
health 64 Gesundheit
health and safety 108t Arbeitsschutz, Arbeitssicherheit
health care 99 Gesundheitswesen
health spa 149 Kurort, Heilbad
healthy 76t, 183 gesund
heart attack 31t Herzinfarkt
heart disease 195 Herzkrankheit
heating 168t Heizung
heaven 111 Himmel
heavy 49 schwer
to **help oneself to sth** 166 sich etw (zu essen) nehmen
hermit 181 Einsiedler/in
hero 138, 188 Held
to **hide** 48 verbergen, verheimlichen
high 100 Rausch
highlight 180 Höhepunkt
to **highlight** 162t hervorheben, verdeutlichen
highway 70 Autobahn
hiker 168t Wanderer
hiking 26t Wandern
hill 134 Hügel, Berg
historic 10 historisch, geschichtlich
historical 69 historisch, Historien-
to **hit** 88 treffen; 117 schlagen; 150 erreichen, betreffen
to **hold** 78 bereithalten
to **hold sth** 51 etw fassen, für etw Platz haben
to **hold on to sth** 62 an etw festhalten
to **hold sb back** 63 jdn zurückhalten
to **hold (the line)** 118 *(Telefon:)* am Apparat bleiben
to **hold a meeting** 24 eine Sitzung abhalten
hole 30 Loch
holy 194 heilig
home 11 *hier:* Heimat
homeland 180 Heimat, Heimatland
homeless 188 obdachlos
honest 139t, 191 ehrlich
hooliganism 102 Rowdytum
hopeful 159 zuversichtlich, optimistisch
hopefully 108t hoffentlich
hopeless 70t hoffnungslos
horrible 38 schrecklich
hors d'oeuvre 154 Vorspeise
horseback riding 124 Reiten (auf dem Pferd)
hose 120 Schlauch
to **host** 52 moderieren
host 194 Moderator/in
host country 79 Gastgeberland
hot air balloon 58 Heißluftballon
housekeeper 145t *(Hotel:)* Hausdame, Zimmermädchen
housewife 32 Hausfrau
however 28 dagegen, allerdings, jedoch
huge 51 riesig, gewaltig
human 185 Mensch
human being 102t Mensch
Human Resources (HR) 14 Personalabteilung
human rights 74 Menschenrechte
humiliation 66p Erniedrigung
humour 179 Humor, Stimmung
to **hurt sb** 41 jdn verletzen
husband 17 Ehemann

I

ice-cold 73 eiskalt
iconic 160 symbolträchtig, Symbol-
ID 190 Ausweis
idea, to have no ~ 70t keine Ahnung haben
idealistic 62 idealistisch
ideally 115t im Idealfall
to **identify** 163 herausfinden, feststellen
identity 189 Identität
idol 139 Idol
ignorance 92 Ignoranz, Unwissen
to **ignore** 181 missachten
illegal 89, 182 illegal
illness 121 Krankheit
to **illustrate** 93 illustrieren
image 93 Bild
to **imagine sth** 19 sich etw vorstellen
to **imitate** 139 nachahmen, imitieren
immigrant 18 Einwanderer/-in
immune system 148 Immunsystem
impact 157 Einfluss, Auswirkung(en)
impatient 181 ungeduldig, unduldsam
import 120 Einfuhr
importance 144 Bedeutung, Wichtigkeit
impossible 48 unmöglich
to **impress** 44 beeindrucken
impression 44 Eindruck
impressive 76 beeindruckend, eindrucksvoll
to **improve** 34 verbessern, (sich) bessern
to **improvise** 130 improvisieren
impulse buy 192 Impulskauf
incident 108t Zwischenfall, Vorfall
to **include** 28 einschließen, beinhalten
income 108t Einkommen
inconvenience 95 Unannehmlichkeiten
incorrect 66 falsch, nicht korrekt
to **increase** 100 steigen; 191 erhöhen
independence 10 Unabhängigkeit
independent 10t unabhängig
to **indicate** 196 darauf hindeuten
individual 93, 183 Einzelperson
induction 166 Einführung
industrial 73 Industrie-, industriell
industry 7 Branche, Industriezweig, Industrie
to **influence** 139t beeinflussen
influential 135 einflussreich
influenza 148 Grippe
to **inform** 131t informieren
infrastructure 168t Infrastruktur
ingredient 150 Zutat
inhabitant 193 Einwohner/in
initials 145t Initialien
to **injure** 100 verletzen
injured 74 verletzt
injury 121 Verletzung
inlet 193 Bucht
innocence 194 Unschuld
innocent 44, 190 unschuldig, harmlos
innovative 68 innovativ
inquiry 80 Untersuchung
insecure 40 unsicher
inside out 112 *(Wäsche:)* links, auf links gewendet
to **inspire** 62 anregen, inspirieren
inspiring 146 inspirierend, anregend
to **install** 143 aufbauen, installieren
installation 143 Aufbau, Installation
instance, for ~ 182 zum Beispiel
instead 28 stattdessen
instruction 79 Anweisung
insult 41 Beleidigung
to **insult sb** 48 jdn beleidigen
intellectual 194 Intellektuelle/r
intelligence 190 Intelligenz
intensive 74 intensiv
interest 35 Interesse
to **interest** 37 interessieren
interested in sth 12 an etw interessiert
interestingly 80t interessanterweise
intern 143t Praktikant/in
to **interpret** 107 übersetzen
internship 68 Praktikum
interview 44 Vorstellungsgespräch
interviewee 59 *Person, die interviewt wird*
intolerant, to be ~ of sb/sth 87 gegenüber jdm/etw intolerant sein
to **introduce (sb to sb)** 34 jdm jdn vorstellen; 76 einführen
introduction 124 Einführung
investment 68 Investition
invitation 154t Einladung
to **involve** 52 beinhalten, einbeziehen, mit sich bringen
involved with sth 88 an etw beteiligt
involved, to get ~ in sth 91 mit etw zu tun haben, in etw hineingeraten
irresponsible 110 verantwortungslos
island 8 Insel
isolated 69 abgesondert, abgelegen, isoliert
issue 159 Frage, Streitpunkt, Problem
item 15p Gegenstand; 157 Artikel
itinerary 53 Reiseroute

J

J-shaped 185 J-förmig
jacket 27 Jacke
job advertisment 70t Stellenanzeige
job interview 14t Vorstellungsgespräch
job satisfaction 80 Arbeitszufriedenheit
job-seeker 187 Arbeitssuchende/r
to **join** 66p, 183 sich anschließen, beitreten
to **join sb/sth** 68 bei jdm/etw mitmachen
joke 39 Witz, Streich
journey 54 Fahrt, Reise
joyful 180 freudig, froh
to **judge** 52, 188 verurteilen, beurteilen
judgement 139t Urteil
to **jump out at sb** 70t jdm ins Auge springen
jumper 109 Pullover
jungle 11 Dschungel, Urwald
junk 192 Schrott
justice 74 Gerechtigkeit
to **justify** 93 begründen, rechtfertigen

K

kayaking 100 Kayakfahren
to **keep in touch** 38 in Verbindung bleiben
to **keep sb out of trouble** 182 jdm Ärger ersparen
key 166 wichtigste/r/s, Haupt-
keyboard 50 Tastatur
kick 49 Tritt, Schuss
to **kick** 49 treten, schießen
to **kill** 30 töten
kind 37 Art; 97 nett, freundlich
kipper 108t Räucherhering
knight 123 Ritter
knowledge 80 Wissen, Kenntnis(se)
Kurdish 18 kurdisch

L

label 112 Etikett
to **label** 16 etikettieren, mit einem Etikett versehen
lack of sth 85 Mangel an etw
Ladies and gentlemen 73 Meine Damen und Herren
to **land** 10t landen
landing 28 Landung
landmark 160 Wahrzeichen
lap 180 Schoß
to **last** 62 dauern
lately 42 in letzter Zeit
laugh, to have a ~ 167t lachen, Witze machen
to **launch (a product)** 143t (ein Produkt) auf den Markt bringen, einführen
to **launch sth** 161 etw starten
law 101, 181 Gesetz(e), Recht
lawn mower 192 Rasenmäher
lawyer 62, 182 Anwalt/Anwältin
lazy 166 faul
leafy vegetables 148 Blattgemüse
league 66p Liga
leap 33 Sprung
learning difficulty 144t Lernschwäche, Lernbehinderung
least, at ~ 31t mindestens
leather 27 Leder

left out, to **be ~** 192 übergangen werden, alleine dastehen
legal 182 legal
leisure 124 Freizeit
length 54 Länge
leopard 9 Leopard
less than 11 weniger als
to **let off steam** 66p Dampf ablassen
to **let sb know** 24 jdm Bescheid sagen
level 85 Niveau
library 58 Bibliothek
lie 39 Lüge
lie, to **tell ~s** 48 Lügen verbreiten
to **lie (to sb)** 105 lügen, jdn belügen
to **lie down** 106 sich hinlegen
lifestyle 87 Lebensweise
lifetime 56 Leben, Lebenszeit
lift (BE) 15p Aufzug
to **lift** 104t hochgehen
light 58 Licht
limit 57 Grenze; 130t Höchstgrenze
limited 58 begrenzt, beschränkt, eingeschränkt
line, to **wait in ~** 150 sich in einer Warteschlange anstellen
lineage 157 Abstammung, Herkunft
to **link** 37 verlinken
lion 9 Löwe
lionheart 110 Löwenherz
lip 28 Lippe
Listen up. 104t Hört mal her!
listener 76 Zuhörer/in
literate, to **be ~** 137 lesen und schreiben können
litter 117 Abfall, Müll
lizard 123 Eidechse
loan 108t Darlehen, Kredit
local 58 örtlich, lokal
located 26 gelegen
location 24 Standort, Lage
to **lock** 44 sperren
lodge 168t Hütte
logistics 14 Logistik
lonely 40 einsam
to **look after sb/sth** 32 sich um jdn/etw kümmern
to **look ahead** 68 nach vorn schauen
to **look closely at sth** 80t sich etw genau ansehen
to **look forward to sth** 67 sich auf etw freuen
to **look sth up** 31 etw *(in einem Wörterbuch)* nachschlagen
to **look up at sb** 135 jdn bewundern
to **look on the bright side** 139t das Positive sehen, es positiv sehen
Look out! 158 Achtung! Vorsicht!
loom 116 Webmaschine, Webstuhl
lorry 68 Lastwagen
to **lose** 41t verlieren
loser 52 Verlierer/in
lots of 18 viel(e), eine Menge
lottery 105 Lotto, Lotterie
lottery, to **win the ~** 105 im Lotto gewinnen
love, to **fall in ~ with sb** 80t sich in jdn verlieben
luckily 133 glücklicherweise
luggage 130t Gepäck
lunch, to **have ~** 14 zu Mittag essen
luxury 62 Luxus
lyrics 30 Liedtext

M

machinery 83 Maschinen, Geräte
machinist 112 Maschinist/in
made up, to **be ~ of** 80t bestehen aus
magic 144t Zauberei
magic, to **do ~** 144t zaubern
main 7 Haupt-
main course 154 Hauptgang
mainly 80t hauptsächlich
to **maintain sth** 191 etw warten, unterhalten, instandhalten
maintenance 88 Wartung, Instandhaltung, Pflege
majority 79, 182 Mehrheit
to **make sure** 24 sicherstellen, gewährleisten; 44 sich vergewissern
to **make sth up** 47 sich etw ausdenken, etw erfinden
to **make yourself/sb up** 20 sich schminken
to **make up for sth** 182 etw ausgleichen, etw wieder gutmachen
to **make a difference** 58 etw bewirken
to **make a point** 45 auf etw hinweisen
to **make a stand** 92 für etw eintreten
to **make friends** 18 Freunde finden/gewinnen
to **manage** 152 es schaffen; 67 etw verwalten
management 25 Geschäftsleitung
manager 34 Geschäftsführer/in
mankind 33 Menschheit
manner 49 Art (und Weise)
manufacture 113 Herstellung, Fertigung
manufacturing 7 Herstellung, Fertigung
map 7 Landkarte, Karte
march 33 Marsch
marijuana 33 Marihuana
marine 196 Meeres-
mark 56 Note
marriage 49 Ehe
married 67 verheiratet
married, to **get ~** 49 heiraten
married couple 52 Ehepaar
mat 147 Matte
to **match sth** 8 etw zuordnen; 44 zu etw passen
to **matter** 62 wichtig sein
mean 41t gemein
to **mean** 11 bedeuten, heißen; 97 beabsichtigen, wollen
meaning 30 Bedeutung
means of communication 144t Kommunikationsmittel
meantime, in the ~ 78 in der Zwischenzeit
meanwhile 81 währenddessen
to **measure** 196 messen
mechanic 68 (Kfz-)Mechaniker/in
medal 184 Medaille
media 37 Medien
mediation 13 Vermittlung
medical 108t ärztlich, medizinisch
medical assistant 75 Medizinische/r Fachangestellte/r
medical centre 114 Ärztehaus, medizinisches Zentrum
medication 74 Medikamente
meeting 24 Sitzung, Besprechung; 180 Begegnung, Treffen
meeting, to **hold a ~** 24 eine Sitzung abhalten
meeting point 114 Treffpunkt
to **melt** 162 schmelzen
meltdown 159 Kernschmelze
member 18 Mitglied
member state 187 Mitgliedsstaat
memo 94 Notiz, Mitteilung
mental 121 geistig
to **mention** 26 erwähnen
menu 150 Speisekarte
message 45 Botschaft
message, to **take a ~** 118 *(Telefon:)* jdm etw ausrichten
messenger 51t Bote/Botin, Kurier
middle 18 Mitte
middle-aged 181 mittleren Alters
the Middle Ages 124 Mittelalter
midnight 15 Mitternacht
might 40 können
migration 20 Wanderung, Migration
military service 120 Militärdienst, Wehrdienst
millionaire 194 Millionär/in
to **mime** 79 pantomimisch darstellen
mind 56 Geist, Hirn, Kopf
mind, to **change sb's ~** 160 seine Meinung ändern
mind, to **have in ~** 94 beabsichtigen, daran denken
to **mind** 54 etw dagegen haben
mind, Never ~. 95 Das macht nichts.
miniskirt 33 Minirock
minority 181 Minderheit
mirror 20 Spiegel
miserable 48 unglücklich, elend
missing 17p fehlend
missing, to **be ~** 25 fehlen
mistake 25 Fehler
to **mix sth up** 117 etw durcheinander bringen/werfen
to **mix with sb** 30 mit jdm verkehren
mixed 20 gemischt
mobile 179 Handy *(BE)*
mobile phone (BE) 28 Handy, Mobiltelefon
model 65 Muster, Modell
modest 110 bescheiden
monarchy 77 Monarchie
monsoon 136 Monsun
monsoon season 136 Regenzeit
mood 121 Stimmung, Laune
moon 28 Mond
mosque 52 Moschee
mostly 12 hauptsächlich
mother tongue 179 Muttersprache
motorcycle 68 Motorrad
mountainous 134 bergig
mouse, mice 21t Maus, Mäuse
mouth 41t Mund
to **move** 11 übersiedeln
to **move ahead** 67 vorankommen, Fortschritte machen
movement 160 Bewegung
the movies 69 Kino
multi-player 37 mit mehreren Spielern
to **multiply sth by sth** 182 etw mit etw multiplizieren
multi-vitamin pill 147 Multivitamintablette
murder 88 Mord
murderer 88 Mörder/in
music lessons 31t Musikunterricht
music recording company 182 Plattenfirma
musician 188 Musiker/in
mystical 193 geheimnisvoll
myth 148 Gerücht, Mythos

N

naive 62 naiv
to **name** 8 nennen, benennen
nasty 38 gemein, böse
nation 89 Nation, Volk
national economy 12 Volkswirtschaft
national holiday 7 Nationalfeiertag
national park 8t Nationalpark
native language 12 Muttersprache
native speaker 8t Muttersprachler/in
natural 19 natürlich
nearby 26t in der Nähe
nearby 88 nahe gelegen
necessary 10 nötig, notwendig
neck 38 Hals
need, to **be in ~** 68 bedürftig sein
needle 112 Nadel
negativity 160 negative Einstellung
network 37 Netzwerk
never 13 nie
Never mind. 95 Das macht nichts.
nevertheless 183 nichtsdestotrotz, trotzdem
next to 50 neben
nickname 28 Spitzname
nightmare 70t Albtraum
nil 153t null, gleich null
noisy 24 laut
non-governmental organisation 187 Nichtregierungsorganisation
noodle 154 Nudel
noon 15 Mittag
normally 21 normalerweise
nostalgia 111 Nostalgie
not … anymore 10 nicht mehr
not … yet 56 noch nicht
novel 156, 194 Roman
nowadays 10 heute, heutzutage
nuclear 28 Atom-
nuclear power plant 159 Atomkraftwerk
to **number** 80t aufzählen; 111 nummerieren
nursing 186 Krankenpflege

nutrient 148 Nährstoff
nutrition 148 Nahrung, Ernährung
nutritional supplements 147 Nahrungsergänzungsmittel

O

obese 56 fettleibig
to **obey** 181 gehorchen
object 15p Gegenstand, Objekt
obscene 48 unverschämt, obszön
to **obtain** 190 erhalten, bekommen
obvious 108t klar erkennbar, offensichtlich
obviously 38 offensichtlich; 108t versteht sich
ocean 180 Ozean
odds, against the ~ 58 wider Erwarten, wider alle Wahrscheinlichkeit
of course 14t natürlich, selbstverständlich
off, to **have a day ~** 83 einen Tag frei bekommen
off piste 100 abseits der Piste
to **offend** 88 straffällig werden
offer 71 Angebot
to **offer** 26t bieten, anbieten
office management assistant 78 Bürokaufmann/-frau
official 137 offiziell
official language 7 Amtssprache
often 13 oft
old-fashioned 52 altmodisch
olive 148 Olive
on the one hand 63 einerseits
on the other hand 63, 183 andererseits
on top of 51t auf
once 19 einmal
only child 17 Einzelkind
to **operate** 83 bedienen; 168t betreiben
opinion poll 80 Meinungsumfrage
opportunity 78, 185 Möglichkeit, Gelegenheit, Chance
opposite 16 Gegenteil, Gegensatz; 39 gegenüber
optimism 28 Optimismus
optimist 28 Optimist/in
optimistic 99 optimistisch
order 62 Reihenfolge
ordinary 111 gewöhnlich, normal, mittelmäßig
organic 72 Bio-, Öko-
organiser 20 Organisator/in
organized 74 (gut) organisiert
original 31 ursprünglich; 68 originell
origins 194 Herkunft
orphanage 68 Waisenhaus
orphaned 74 verwaist
out of control 181 außer Kontrolle
outdoors 64 draußen, im Freien
the outdoors 72p die freie Natur
outgoing 75 kontaktfreudig
outline 76t Übersicht, Stichpunkte
outlook 139t Einstellung, Perspektive
outside of 26t außerhalb von
to **outsource** 156 *(Arbeit)* auslagern
to **overcome sth** 79 etw überwinden
overdose 31t Überdosis
overnight 108t über Nacht
overtime, to **work ~** 83 Überstunden machen
overweight 38 übergewichtig
to **owe** 108t schulden
owner 19 Inhaber/in; 190 Besitzer/in, Eigentümer/in
to **own** 28 besitzen

P

pack 107 Packung
to **pack** 109 einpacken
package holiday 124 Pauschalreise
packaging 192 Verpackung
paid sick leave 80 Lohnfortzahlung im Krankheitsfall
pain 106 Schmerz(en)
painkiller 106 Schmerzmittel
to **paint sth** 197 etw anmalen, etw streichen
paint brush 192 Farbpinsel
painter 183 Maler/in
palace 123 Palast
to **panic** 36 in Panik geraten
paperwork 166 Unterlagen
paragraph 166 *(Text:)* Absatz
to **paraphrase** 70 umschreiben, anders ausdrücken
paraplegic 100 Querschnittgelähmte/r
parent 57 Vater/Mutter, Elternteil
parental 108t elterlich
parliament 18, 187 Parlament
part-time 103 Teilzeit-
participant 80t Teilnehmer/in
particular 156 spezielle/r/s
partly 181 teilweise, zum Teil
pass 79p Ausweis, Pass; 124 Eintrittskarte
to **pass sth** 83 etw weitergeben, weiterreichen
to **pass sb by** 153t an jdm vorbeigehen
to **pass an exam** 142, 188 eine Prüfung bestehen
passionate, to **be ~ about sth** 73t sich für etw (leidenschaftlich) begeistern
passive 197 passiv
passport 18 Pass, Reisepass
past 24 vergangene/r/s, ehemalige/r/s; 66p Vergangenheit
past sth 86 an etw vorbei
paste 150 Paste
paternal 180 väterlicherseits
path 109 Weg
patty 150 Pastete, Bratling
pay 51 Lohn, Gage; 80 Bezahlung
to **pay a visit to sth** 180 etw besuchen
to **pay attention to sb** 182 auf etw achten, etw beachten
peace 188 Frieden
peaceful 193 ruhig; 196 friedlich
pedagogical 186 pädagogisch
pedal radio 144t Pedalfunk, Pedalfunkgerät
peers 99 Gleichaltrige, Umgebung
percentage 81 Anteil, Prozentsatz
to **perform** 53 ausführen, aufführen
performance 52 Leistung, Darbietung, Aufführung
performer 52 Mitwirkende/r; 79p Sänger/in, Künstler/in
period 69, 183 Zeitabschnitt
permanent(ly) 80 dauerhaft
permission 37 Erlaubnis, Genehmigung
personal 37 persönlich, eigene/r/s
personality 40 Persönlichkeit
personnel 74 Mitarbeiter, Personal
perspective 160 Blickwinkel, Perspektive
to **persuade** 88 überzeugen, überreden
pet 67 Haustier
petrol 179 Benzin *(BE)*
pharmaceutical 79p Pharma-
pharmacy 106 Apotheke
philosopher 181 Philosoph/in
photo(graph) 20 Foto(grafie)
photographer 74, 182 Fotograf/in
phrase 7 Wendung, Formulierung
physical 99 körperlich
to **pick sth** 22 etw auswählen, sich etw aussuchen
to **pick sth up** 58 etw nehmen, etw aufheben
to **pick sb up** 23 jdn abholen; 73 jdn hochheben
pie 123 Kuchen, Torte
piece of furniture 51 Möbelstück
pile 112 Stapel
pilgrim 193 Pilger
pilgrimage, place of ~ 193 Wallfahrtsort
pill 31t Pille, Tablette
pin 28 Stecknadel, Anstecknadel
pin board 50 Pinnwand
pipe 58 Rohr, Röhre
pirate 196 Pirat
piste, off ~ 100 abseits der Piste
pit 79p Box
place of pilgrimage 193 Wallfahrtsort
to **plant** 163 pflanzen
plant oil 147 Pflanzenoil
plastic surgery 48 kosmetische Chirurgie, Schönheitsoperation(en)
plate 129 Teller
platform 54 Bahnsteig, Gleis
platinum 131t Platin
to **play it safe** 99 auf Nummer sicher gehen
playground 114 Spielplatz
pleasant 25 angenehm
pleasure 25 Vergnügen
plot of earth 180 Stück Land
pocket 97 (Hemd-, Jacken-, Hosen-)Tasche
to **point sth at sb** 88 etw auf jdn richten
to **point to sth** 37 auf etw (ver)weisen; 79 auf etw zeigen
point, to **make a ~** 45 auf etw hinweisen
point, What is the ~ of … 40 Welchen Sinn hat es, …
pointless 102t sinnlos
polar bear 160 Eisbär
police force 196 Polizeitruppe
police officer 99 Polizist/in
policeman 62 Polizist
policy 166 Vorgehensweise, Linie, Politik
polite 135, 182 höflich
politician 169, 183 Politiker/in
politics 35 Politik
poll 67 Umfrage, Abstimmung
to **poll sb** 80 jdn befragen
polling firm 80 Meinungsforschungsinstitut
popular 40 beliebt
popular culture 183 Popularkultur
population 7 Bevölkerung
pork 149 Schweinefleisch
port wine 154 Portwein
position 78 Stelle, Stellung, Position
possibility 63, 184 Möglichkeit
possible 7 möglich
to **post sth** 37 etw *(am Schwarzen Brett)* anschlagen, aushängen
post office 86 Postamt
postgraduate degree 80t weiterführender Studienabschluss *(z. B. Promotion)*
pot plant 15p Topfpflanze
potential 44 potentiell; 99 Potenzial
poultry 147 Geflügel
power 28 Kraft, Energie; 58 Strom; 111 Macht
to **power sth** 160 etw mit Strom versorgen
powerful 157 stark, mächtig
to **practise** 12 üben, trainieren
to **praise** 139t loben
to **pray** 193 beten
precedent 166 Beispiel, Präzedenzfall
to **predict** 80, 183 vorhersagen
prediction 66 Voraussage, Vorhersage
pregnant 58 schwanger
prehistoric 193 prähistorisch, vorgeschichtlich
preparation 59 Vorbereitung; 150 Zubereitung
to **prepare** 31 (sich) vorbereiten; 67 zubereiten
prepared, to **be ~ to do sth** 67 bereit/willens sein, etw zu tun
prescription 106 (ärztliches) Rezept
present 16 Geschenk
to **present** 53 vorstellen, präsentieren
presentation 24 Präsentation
presenter 83 Moderator/in, Präsentator/in
preserved 193 erhalten
president 62, 180 Präsident/in
press release 162t Pressemitteilung
pressure 32 Druck
pressure, to **put ~ on sb** 48 auf jdn Druck ausüben
to **pretend** 191 vorgeben, sich ausgeben als
to **prevent** 88 verhindern, vorbeugen
previous 181 vorherig, vorig
price 24 Preis

primary school (BE) 64 Grundschule
principal 146 Schuldirektor/in
printer 50 Drucker
prison 190 Gefängnis
privacy 37 Privatsphäre
private 24 privat, eigene/r/s
prize 52, 194 Preis, Gewinn
problematic 52 problematisch, Problem-
to **proceed** 131t gehen, sich begeben
procedure 166, 190 Ablauf, Verfahren
process 85 Verfahren
processing fee 157 Bearbeitungsgebühr
producer 31t Produzent/in
product launch 142 Produkteinführung
production 14 Fertigung, Produktion
profession 76t Beruf
professional 44 professionell
profile 12 Profil, Porträt
profit 112 Gewinn
programme 41 (Radio-/TV-) Sendung
programmer 74 Programmierer/in
progress 164 Fortschritt(e)
promise 71 Versprechen
to **promote sb** 66p jdn befördern
to **promote sth** 160 für etw werben, etw fördern
promotional company 182 Werbefirma
to **pronounce** 11 aussprechen
pronunciation 9 Aussprache
proper 108t richtig, ordentlich
property 102 Eigentum, Immobilie
to **protect** 57 schützen, beschützen
protein 148 Eiweiß, Protein(e)
proud 100, 188 stolz
to **prove** 110 beweisen
to **provide** 100, 183 liefern, bieten
province 10t Provinz
psychological 191 psychologisch
psychology 186 Psychologie
public 44 öffentlich
public, in ~ 48 öffentlich
to **pump** 58 pumpen
Purchasing 14 Einkauf(sabteilung)
purchasing assistant 85 Assistent/in im Einkauf
purple 9 purpur, lila
purpose 142 Zweck
purse 15p Handtasche *(AE)*, Portemonnaie *(BE)*
to **push** 57 schieben, drücken, drängen; 100 treiben; 104t stoßen
to **put** 90 formulieren, sagen
to **put sb down** 30 jdn demütigen, jdn herabsetzen
to **put sb through** 118 *(Telefon:)* jdn durchstellen
to **put an end to sth** 197 unter etw einen Schlussstrich ziehen
to **put pressure on sb** 48 auf jdn Druck ausüben
puzzled 38 verwirrt
pyramid 143t, 193 Pyramide
pyrotechnics 142 Feuerwerk

Q

qualification 88, 187 Abschluss, Qualifikation
quality, to **be high ~** 26 von hoher Qualität sein
quantity 121 Menge
questionnaire 67 Fragebogen
quotation 181 Zitat
quote 100 Zitat

R

race 79p, 184 Rennen; 87 Rasse
race track 79p Rennstrecke
racer 196 Schnellboot
racing 79p Rennsport, Rennen
racing driver 102t Rennfahrer/in
racism 92 Rassismus
radio 144t Funkgerät, Funk
radio operator 197 Funker/in
rail tunnel 100 Eisenbahntunnel
railway 58 Eisenbahn
to **raise** 182 erhöhen
to **raise funds** 162t Spenden sammeln
ramp 115t Rampe
range 108t Reihe, Auswahl; 113 Sortiment, Palette
to **rank** 67 einstufen, (an-, ein) ordnen
rarely 37, 182 (nur) selten, kaum
Rastafarian 8 Rastafari, Rasta-
rate 195 Quote
rather 71 ziemlich, ganz schön
to **reach** 62 erreichen
to **react** 141 reagieren
reaction 105 Reaktion
ready, to **get ~ for sth** 22 sich auf etw vorbereiten, sich für etw fertig machen
to **realise** 94, 180 klar werden, bewusst werden
realistic 63 realistisch
reason 12 Grund
reasonable 24 vernünftig, angemessen
rebel 19 Rebell
receipt 106 Quittung
to **receive** 25 erhalten, bekommen
recent 108t jüngst; 181 aktuell
recently 42 neulich
reception 14 Empfang
receptionist 14 Empfangsmitarbeiter/in
recession 108t Rezession
recipe 76t (Koch-)Rezept
to **recognise** 46 erkennen, wiedererkennen
recommendation 72 Empfehlung
to **record** 51 aufnehmen; 59 aufzeichnen
record 28 Schallplatte
record player 28 Schallplattenspieler
recording studio 58 Tonstudio
to **recover** 168t sich erholen
to **recruit** 88 anwerben
Red Cross 94 Rotes Kreuz
to **reduce** 90 reduzieren, senken
to **reform** 56 reformieren, (grundsätzlich) ändern
reference 64 Referenz
reference information 142 *etwa:* relevante Angaben, Zusatzinformationen
refugee 18 Flüchtling
region 12 Region
to **regret** 81 bereuen; 131t bedauern
rehab 47 Entzug
to **reinforce** 194 verstärken, bestärken
to **relate sth to sth** 160 etw zu etw in Beziehung setzen
relation 168t, 180 Angehörige/r
relationship 76t, 183 Beziehung
relationship, romantic ~ 76t Liebesbeziehung
relative 18 Verwandte/r
relatively 150 verhältnismäßig, relativ
relaxation 150 Entspannung
relaxed 84 entspannt
relaxing 36 erholsam
relentless 194 unbarmherzig, schonungslos
relevant 22 relevant
reliable 75 zuverlässig
religion 8 Religion
religious 52 Religions-; 68 religiös
religious leader 181 Religionsführer/in
to **relocate** 80t umsiedeln, umziehen
to **rely on sb** 197 sich auf jdn verlassen
to **remain** 108t bleiben
remarkable 61 bemerkenswert, erstaunlich
remote 144t entlegen, abgelegen
to **remove** 44 entfernen
rent 83 Miete
to **rent** 190 mieten
to **replace** 22 ersetzen, austauschen
reply 114 Antwort
to **reply** 37, 180 antworten
report 153 Reportage
to **report** 41 berichten, Bericht erstatten
to **represent** 31 vertreten, repräsentieren
to **reproduce** 45 abdrucken, reproduzieren
republic 18 Republik
reputation 44 Ruf, Ansehen
request 64 Bitte, Wunsch
to **require** 25 wünschen, benötigen; 99 erfordern
requirement 25 Wunsch, Bedürfnis
to **research sth** 70t recherchieren, Nachforschungen anstellen
research 29 Nachforschungen, Recherche
research, to **do ~** 70t recherchieren, Nachforschungen anstellen
Research & Development (R&D) 14 Forschung(s-) und Entwicklung(sabteilung)
researcher 108t Forscher/in
reservation 25 Reservierung
to **reserve** 24 reservieren
resident 150 Bewohner, Einwohner
to **resist** 99 widerstehen
resort 168t Ferienort
resource 19 Ressource, Bodenschatz
respect 181 Respekt
to **respect** 74, 181 respektieren
respectful 156 respektvoll
to **respond (to sb/sth)** 106 (jdm) antworten, (auf etw) reagieren
responsibility 67 Verantwortung, Verantwortlichkeit
responsibility, to **take ~** 120 Verantwortung übernehmen
responsible 75 verantwortungsbewusst
rest 150 Erholung, Pause, Ruhe
restaurant car 54 Speisewagen
result 32 Ergebnis, Folge
résumé (AE) 63 Lebenslauf
retail 112 Einzelhandel
retail outlet 112 (Einzelhandels-) Geschäft
retailer 157 Einzelhändler
to **retire** 134 sich zur Ruhe setzen
retired 156 im Ruhestand, pensioniert
reusable 162t wiederverwendbar
to **re-use** 163 wiederverwenden
to **return** 58 zurückkehren
to **reverse** 170 rückgängig machen, umkehren
to **review** 143 überprüfen, überdenken, Revue passieren lassen
to **revolve around sth** 157 sich um etw drehen
reward 73 Lohn
to **rewrite** 22 neu schreiben, neu formulieren
rickshaw 136 Rikscha
rid, to **get ~ of sth** 66p etw loswerden
ride 99 Fahrgeschäft, Karussel
to **ride (a bike)** 99 (Fahrrad) fahren
rider 100 (Motorrad-)Fahrer/in
right away 70t sofort
to **ring** 105 läuten, schellen
to **rise** 81 steigen, ansteigen
to **rise above sth** 58 über etw hinausgehen, etw überwinden
risk 58 Risiko
risk, to **take a ~** 58 ein Risiko eingehen
risk-taker 99 risikobereite Person
risky 99 riskant
rival 88 rivalisierend, Rivale
rivalry 88 Rivalität
road, dirt ~ 144t unbefestigte Straße, Sandpiste
to **roast** 154 braten
roasted 150 geröstet, gebraten
robot 112 Roboter
role 15p Rolle
role model 135, 186 Vorbild
to **role-play** 14 mit verteilten Rollen spielen
roll 112 Ballen, Rolle
romantic relationship 76t Liebesbeziehung
roof 160 Dach

root 180 Wurzel
rough 144t rau, holprig, einfach
round-the-world sailor 110 Weltumsegler/in
route 166 Weg, Route
rubbish 115t Abfall, Müll
rubbish bin (BE) 15p Mülleimer
rude 38, 181 unhöflich, unverschämt
ruin 123 Ruine
to **ruin** 100 zugrunde richten, ruinieren
rule 69 Regel, Vorschrift
to **run sth** 88 etw anbieten, durchführen
to **run sb over** 100 jdn überfahren
to **run (a business)** 74 (ein Geschäft) leiten, führen
runner 49 Läufer/in
running water 58 fließendes Wasser, Trinkwasser
rupee 194 Rupie
rural 19 ländlich
to **rush** 38 eilen

S

safe, to **play it** ~ 99 auf Nummer sicher gehen
safely 55 sicher
safety, health and ~ 108t Arbeitsschutz, Arbeitssicherheit
safety gear 99 Sicherheitskleidung, -ausrüstung
safety guard 112 Schutzblende, Sicherheitsabdeckung
to **sail** 104 segeln
sailing boat 59 Segelboot
sailor 110 Segler/in
salary 167 Lohn, Gehalt
sale 117 Schlussverkauf; 157 Verkauf
sales 14 Vertrieb, Verkauf(sabteilung); 159 Absatz
sales assistant 34 Verkäufer/in
sales manager 122 Verkaufsleiter/in, Vertriebsleiter/in
salesperson 64 Verkäufer/in
salmon 147 Lachs
same-sex 17 gleichgeschlechtlich
sand blasting 120 Sandstrahlen
satellite 144t Satellit
satisfaction 73t Genugtuung
satisfied 63 zufrieden
saturated 148 gesättigt
sauce 154 Soße
sausage 7 Wurst, Würstchen
to **save** 57 retten
to **save sth** 28 etw sparen
say 121 zum Beispiel
to **say sth to sb's face** 90 jdm etw ins Gesicht sagen
scale 130t Waage; 147 (Fisch-) Schuppe
to **scan** 66 absuchen, durchsuchen, *(Text)* überfliegen
scandal 47 Skandal
to **scare sb** 41 jdm Angst einjagen, jdn verängstigen
scene 117 Szene, Vorfall, Anblick
scenery 168t Landschaft, Kulisse
scheduling 142 Zeitplan, Zeitplanung
scholarship 52 Stipendium
school leaving certificate 85 Schulabgangszeugnis
school-leaver 68 Schulabgänger/in
scientist 49 (Natur-) Wissenschaftler/in
to **score** 89 *(Tore, Punkte etc.)* erzielen, schießen
screen 143t Leinwand
scuba diving 124 Gerätetauchen
seal 196 Robbe
search 46 Suche
to **search for sth** 24 etw suchen
seaside 34 am Meer, Küsten-
seat 55 Platz, Sitz
Second World War 28 der Zweite Weltkrieg
second-largest 7 zweitgrößte/r/s
secondary school (BE) 64 Hauptschule/Realschule
secretly 47 heimlich
security 44 Sicherheit; 130t Sicherheitskontrollen, Sicherheitspersonal
security guard 99 Wachmann/-frau
to **seek** 74 suchen
to **seem** 29 scheinen
selection 80 Auswahl
self-control 181 Selbstbeherrschung
self-reliance 66p Selbstständigkeit
selfishness 139t Egoismus, Selbstsucht
semi-finals 153t Halbfinale
sensation 30 Sensation
sense 112 Sinn
sensible 139t vernünftig
sentence 11 Satz
to **separate** 58 sich trennen
separate(ly) 112 getrennt
series 193 Reihe
serious 33 ernst, ernsthaft
seriously, to **take sb/sth** ~ 76 jdn/etw ernst nehmen
session 88 Sitzung, Stunde
set 70t Reihe, Menge, Gruppe
to **set** 58 setzen
to **set up** 58 aufbauen, gründen, einrichten; 74 aufstellen; 78 sich niederlassen
setting 26t Landschaft; 37 Einstellung; 73 Umgebung, Rahmen, Umfeld
to **settle down** 28 sesshaft werden, zur Ruhe kommen, es sich bequem machen
several 26t mehrere
to **sew** 112 nähen
sewing machine 112 Nähmaschine
sexuality 48 Sexualität
shadow 138 Schatten
shape 70t Form
share 182 Anteil, Teil
to **share sth** 24 (sich) etw teilen
sharp 112 scharf, spitz
sheep, sheep 26t Schaf, Schafe
sheet (of paper) 113 Blatt (Papier)
shelf, shelves 50 Regal, Regale
shell 160 Schneckenhaus
shepherd 196 Schäfer
to **shift** 104t verlagern
to **shine** 138 scheinen, glänzen
shipbuilding 7 Schiffbau
shirt 27 Hemd
shock 28 Schock
shocked 38 schockiert
shocking 48 schockierend
to **shoot** 73 (Film-, Foto-) Aufnahmen machen; 160 *(Foto, Video etc.)* aufnehmen
to **shoot sb** 91 auf jdn schießen, jdn erschießen
shooting 88 Schießerei
shoplifting 100 Ladendiebstahl
shopper 115 Käufer/in
shoulder 106 Schulter
to **shout at sb** 38 jdn anschreien
to **show up** 156 auftauchen, sichtbar werden
shrimp 150 Garnele
to **shut sb out** 115 jdn aussperren
shy 160 schüchtern
shyness 160 Schüchternheit
siblings 17 Geschwister
sick leave 80 Krankheitsurlaub, Krankschreibung
side dish 150 Beilage
side-effect 106 Nebenwirkung
sight 123 Sehenswürdigkeit
sign 83 Schild; 181 Zeichen, Anzeichen
to **sign sb** 58 jdn unter Vertrag nehmen
to **sign up** 88 sich anmelden, sich einschreiben
signed 46 unterzeichnet
significance 66 Bedeutung
significant 157 erheblich, bedeutend
silicosis 120 Silikose, Staublunge
silly 33 albern, dumm
similar 74 ähnlich
since 10t seit
since, ever ~ 76t seitdem
since then 38 seitdem
single 25 Einzel-
single parent 17 Alleinerziehende/r
to **sink sth** 196 etw versenken
site 40 Website; 108t Baustelle; 125 Stätte, Platz, Schauplatz
size 19 Größe
skier 105 Skifahrer/in
skill 51 Fähigkeit, Fertigkeit
skilled trade 185 Handwerksberuf
to **skim** 66 *(Text)* überfliegen
skin 92 Haut
skyscraper 70t Wolkenkratzer, Hochhaus
sliced 158 in Scheiben
slightly 80 ein bisschen, etwas
slim 144t schlank
slope 100 Piste
to **slow down** 104t bremsen, langsamer werden
smart 28 clever, schick; 51 intelligent
to **smoke** 33 rauchen
so far 34 bis jetzt, so weit
to **soak sth** 148 etw einweichen (lassen)
social 37 sozial, gesellschaftlich
social(ly) 103 sozial, gesellschaftlich
society 191 Gesellschaft
soft 112 weich
to **soften** 120 weicher machen
solar panel 160 Solarzelle
soldier 188 Soldat/in
solution 93 Lösung
to **solve** 57 lösen
sorry, to **feel** ~ 39 Leid tun
to **sort sth out** 139t etw in Ordnung bringen
to **sound** 35 klingen
source 148 Quelle
space 37 Raum, Platz; 58 Weltraum
to **specialise in sth** 72t sich auf etw spezialisieren
species 197 Art
specific 31 speziell
specifically 80t speziell
spectacular 52 spektakulär
speed 99 Geschwindigkeit
to **speed up** 104t beschleunigen
to **spend** 24 *(Zeit)* verbringen
spicy 154 würzig, scharf
spiky 32 stachelig
spillage 83 Verschütten
spinach 148 Spinat
to **split** 157 teilen, aufteilen; 189 spalten
to **spoil** 157 verderben
spokesperson 186 Sprecher/in
spontaneous 71 spontan
spotlight 183 Rampenlicht
square kilometre 7 Quadratkilometer
stadium 153t Stadion
staff 95p Mitarbeiter, Personal
stage 143t Bühne
stairs 15p Treppe
stamina 66p Durchhaltevermögen, Ausdauer
stand, to **make a** ~ 92 für etw eintreten
to **stand out** 74 hervorstechen, herausragen
star 26t Stern
starchy 147 stärkehaltig
to **start a company** 58 ein Unternehmen gründen
starter 154 Vorspeise
starved 139t ausgehungert
state 184 Zustand
to **state** 63 sagen, erklären, angeben
statement 10 Aussage, Behauptung
station 162t (Radio-, Fernseh-) Sender
stationery 50 Schreibwaren, Briefpapier
statistic 76 Statistik
statue 193 Statue
stay 25 Aufenthalt
to **steal** 41t stehlen, *hier:* ausspannen
steam, to **let off** ~ 66p Dampf ablassen
steep 193 steil, *(Tal:)* eng
to **steer** 104t steuern
step 33 Schritt
stepmother 17 Stiefmutter
stereo 192 Stereoanlage

to **stick sth** 28 etw stecken, stechen
sticky notes 16 Klebezettel
to **stitch sth together** 112 zusammennähen
stomach 88 Bauch; 154t Magen
stop 109 Haltestelle
store 115t Laden, Geschäft
to **store** 191 lagern
straight on 14t geradeaus
stranger 37 Fremde/r
strategy 153 Strategie
stream 62 Strom
strength 85 Stärke
to **strengthen** 148 stärken
to **stress sb out** 70t jdn stressen, jdn fertig machen
stressful 78 anstrengend, stressig
strict 69 streng
to **structure** 76 strukturieren
study 64 Studium; 121 Untersuchung, Studie
to **study** 84, 180 studieren; 180 etw genau ansehen
stuff 181 Zeug(s)
stupid 41t dumm, doof
stylistical 56 stilistisch
subsidiary 78 Niederlassung
substitute 82 Ersatz, Ersetzung
subtitle 13 Untertitel
to **succeed** 139t Erfolg haben, erfolgreich sein
success 57 Erfolg
successful 51 erfolgreich
suddenly 38 plötzlich
to **suffer** 183 leiden
to **suffer sth** 120 etw erleiden
suffering 184 Leid, Leiden
to **suggest** 46 vorschlagen
to **suggest sth** 157 auf etw hindeuten, etw erkennen lassen
suggestion 70t Vorschlag
suicide 66p Selbstmord
suit 27 Anzug
to **suit** 95 passen
suitable 26 geeignet
to **sum up** 63 zusammenfassen
to **summarize** 63 zusammenfassen
summit 160 Gipfel
sunburn 125 Sonnenbrand
sunflower 147 Sonnenblume
sunglasses 27 Sonnenbrille
sunlight 138 Sonnenlicht
superior 195 Vorgesetzte/r
to **supervise** 190 leiten, führen, beaufsichtigen
supervisor 166 Vorgesetzte/r
supplement 148 Zusatz; 187 Ergänzung
supplier 73t Zulieferer, Lieferant/in; 157 Anbieter
supplies 144t Vorräte
support 66p Unterstützung; 85 Hilfe
to **support** 31 unterstützen, untermauern
to **suppose** 144t annehmen, glauben
supposed, to **be ~ to do sth** 38 (eigentlich) etw tun sollen
surface 163 Oberfläche
surname 25 Nachname
to **surround** 192 umgeben, umzingeln
survey 80 Umfrage, Gutachten; 179 Untersuchung
to **survey sb** 80t jdn befragen
to **survive** 166, 194 überleben
suspicious, to **be ~ of sb/sth** 87 gegenüber jdm/etw misstrauisch/argwöhnisch sein
sustainable 159 nachhaltig
to **swap** 95 tauschen
to **sweat** 153t schwitzen
sweater 117 Pullover
swimsuit 127 Badehose, -anzug, Bikini
to **switch** 15p tauschen
to **switch off** 163 ausschalten, ausmachen
synonym 16 Synonym
synthetic 112 synthetisch, künstlich hergestellt
systems thinking 160 Systemdenken

T

table tennis 88 Tischtennis
tablet 106 Tablette
tabloid journalism 183 Boulevardpresse
to **take sth out on sb** 66p etw an jdm auslassen
to **take sth up** 110 mit etw anfangen, etw annehmen
to **take off** 104t abheben, starten
to **take off your clothes** 48 sich ausziehen
to **take sb/sth seriously** 76 jdn/etw ernst nehmen
to **take care of sb/sth** 71 sich um jdn/etw kümmern
to **take part in sth** 12 an etw teilnehmen
to **take place** 20 stattfinden
to **take a break from sth** 26t etw hinter sich lassen, einer Sache entkommen
to **take a message** 118 *(Telefon:)* jdm etw ausrichten
to **take a risk** 58 ein Risiko eingehen
to **take a turn at the controls** 190 das Steuer übernehmen
to **take action** 160 tätig werden, Maßnahmen ergreifen
to **take it in turns** 14 sich abwechseln
to **take responsibility** 120 Verantwortung übernehmen
talent agent 48 (Schauspiel-)Agent/in, (Künstler-)Vermittler/in
talented 135 talentiert
tap water 170 Leitungswasser
task 23 Aufgabe
taste 139t Geschmack
to **taste** 36 schmecken
tasty 158 schmackhaft, lecker
tax 166 Steuer
team mate 188 Mannschaftskamerad/in
to **tear** 92 zerreißen
technical 57 technisch
technically minded 75 technikinteressiert
technician 143 Techniker/in
technique 192 Methode, Technik
technology 29 Technologie, Technik
telecommunications industry 79p Telekommunikationsbranche
to **telephone** 18 telefonieren
to **tell lies** 48 Lügen verbreiten
temple 193 Tempel
temporary 78 *(Stelle:)* befristet
term 73 Begriff; 187 Trimester, Semester
terrace 128 Terrasse
terrible 24 furchtbar
terrifying 110 schrecklich, furchterregend
text message 41t SMS
thank God 44 Gott sei Dank
to **think about sth** 56 sich über etw Gedanken machen
thought 70t Gedanke
thousand 20 tausend, Tausend
thread 40 Faden
threat 41 Drohung
to **threaten** 41t drohen
thrill 100 Nervenkitzel
to **throw sb out** 88 jdn hinauswerfen
to **throw sth away** 36 etw wegwerfen
ticket machine 54 Fahrkartenautomat
tie 88 Krawatte
tied up 95 beschäftigt, verhindert
tight 27, 190 eng, knapp
time, all the ~ 37 ständig, andauernd
timeline 91 Zeitachse, Zeitstrahl
timetable 167t Fahrplan
tiny 136 winzig
tipping point 88 der Tropfen, der das Fass zum Überlaufen bringt
tired 91 müde
title 44 Titel
to conclude 56 abschließend
to **tolerate** 141 tolerieren
tomb 181 Grabkammer
tongue, mother ~ 179 Muttersprache
tonne 112 Tonne
Too bad. 76t Pech gehabt!
too good to be true 99 zu schön, um wahr zu sein
tool 46 Werkzeug
tooth 32 Zahn, Zähne
top 62 Spitze, Gipfel
top, on ~ of 51t auf
to **top** 150 *(eine Speise mit Soße)* überziehen, übergießen
to **touch** 138 berühren
touch, to **get out of ~ with sb** 65 den Kontakt zu jdm verlieren
touch, to **keep in ~** 38 in Verbindung bleiben
tough 66p hart
tour guide 70t Reiseführer/in, Reiseleiter/in
tourism 58 Tourismus
tournament 153 Turnier
track 54 Gleis
track and field 153 Leichtathletik
tracksuit 27 Trainingsanzug
tractor 58 Traktor
trade 157 Handel, Branche
tradition 18 Tradition
traditional 18 traditionell
traffic lights 86 Ampel
tragedy 38 Tragödie
tragic 48 tragisch
to **train (as ...)** 66p, 185 eine Ausbildung (zum/zur ...) machen
train, to **change ~s** 54 umsteigen
trainee 52 Auszubildende/r
training 66p Ausbildung
translation 16 Übersetzung
transportation 136 Beförderung
to **trash sth** 139t etw kaputtschlagen
travel arrangements 24 Reisepläne
traveller 125 Reisende/r
treat, It's my ~. 154 Das geht auf mich. Du bist eingeladen.
treatment 108t Behandlung
trial run 167t Probelauf
tribe 180 Stamm
trip 52, 180 Reise
trouble 58 Ärger, Schwierigkeiten, Probleme
trouble, to **get in ~** 91 Ärger/Schwierigkeiten bekommen
trouble, to **keep sb out of ~** 182 jdm Ärger ersparen
truck driver 182 LKW-Fahrer/in
true 39 wahr
true, to **come ~** 63 wahr werden, sich verwirklichen
to **trust** 38, 190 vertrauen
truth 138 Wahrheit
to **try one's hand at sth** 135 sich in etw versuchen
the Tube 86 *die Londoner U-Bahn*
turbine 58 Turbine
turbulent 139t turbulent
turn, It's your ~. 65 Du bist dran.
turn, to **take a ~ at the controls** 190 das Steuer übernehmen
turn, to **take it in ~s** 14 sich abwechseln
to **turn sth off** 38 etw ausschalten
to **turn up** 166 kommen, auftauchen
to **turn right/left** 14 rechts/links abbiegen
turning point 66p Wendepunkt
tutor 156 (Betreuungs-)Lehrer/in
to **tutor** 156 unterrichten
TV series 13 Fernsehserie
TV set 28 Fernsehgerät, -apparat
TV show 56 Fernsehsendung, -serie
twice 61 zweimal
to **type** 46 tippen, eingeben

U

ultimate 48 größte/r/s, endgültig
unaware, to **be ~ of sth** 191 sich einer Sache nicht bewusst sein
unbelievable 19 unglaublich
uncle 17 Onkel
uncomfortable, to **feel ~** 87 sich unwohl fühlen
uncountable 146 unzählbar
to **uncover** 168t aufdecken
underground (train) 86 U-Bahn
underlined 93 unterstrichen

to **undress** 48 sich ausziehen
unemployment 108t Arbeitslosigkeit
unemployment benefit 141 Arbeitslosengeld
unfamiliar 79 unbekannt
unfortunately 48 leider, unglücklicherweise
unfriendly 35 unfreundlich
unhealthy 56 ungesund
unification 10 Vereinigung
unified 77 vereint, vereinigt
to **unify** 10t vereinigen
unimportant 30 unwichtig, unbedeutend
unit 16 Lektion; 121 Einheit
unity 88 Einheit
universe 100 Universum
unknown 36 unbekannt
unless 146 außer wenn, es sei denn
unlimited 156 unbegrenzt
unlucky, to **be** ~ 88 kein Glück haben
unnecessary 165 unnötig
unnoticed, to **go** ~ 138 nicht beachtet werden
unprepared 76 unvorbereitet
unprofessional 44 unprofessionell
unprotected 103 ungeschützt
unsaturated 148 ungesättigt
unsettled 195 turbulent, stürmisch
unspoilt 168t unverdorben, unverbaut
unsuitable 44 ungeeignet, unpassend
unsure 70 unsicher
unsustainable 197 nicht nachhaltig
unusual 17p ungewöhnlich
up till now 42 bis jetzt
update 37 Aktualisierung
to **upload** 37 hochladen
upset 38 bestürzt, aufgeregt, aus der Fassung
to **upset sb** 41 jdn ärgern, aufregen, aus der Fassung bringen
upstairs 38 oben, nach oben
upwards 185 aufwärts
urban 19 städtisch, Stadt-
use 44 Gebrauch, Benutzung
to **use sth up** 191 etw aufbrauchen, etw verbrauchen
user 37 Benutzer/in
usually 13 gewöhnlich, normalerweise

V

valley 193 Tal
value 139t Wert, Wertvorstellung
van 112 Lieferwagen
to **vandalize** 102 verwüsten, mutwillig beschädigen, zerstören
vanilla 154 Vanille
various 114 verschiedene/r/s
to **vary** 179 variieren
vegetarian 23 Vegetarier/in
vending machine 15p Automat
venue 143 Veranstaltungsort
verse 30 Strophe
versus (vs.) 142 gegenüber, im Gegensatz zu
veterinary clinic 64 Tierklinik
via 130t über
vicious 66p brutal, bissig
victim 41 Opfer
video projector 15p Beamer
view 45 Ansicht, Meinung
to **view** 185 betrachten, sehen
village 58 Dorf
violence 89 Gewalt
violent 47, 181 brutal, gewalttätig
virtual 157 virtuell
virus 148 Virus
vision 92 Vision
visit, to **pay a** ~ **to sth** 180 etw besuchen
visitor 14 Besucher/in
to **visualize sth** 99 sich etw bildlich vorstellen
vitamin 106t Vitamin
vocabulary 37, 179 Wortschatz
vocabulary book 16 Vokabelheft
vocational college 64 Berufsfachschule
vocational school 166 Berufsschule
vocational training 80t Berufsausbildung
voice 13 Stimme
voicemail 51 Anrufbeantworter
volcanic stone 112 Vulkangestein, Vulkansteine
voluntary 64 freiwillig, ehrenamtlich
to **volunteer** 68 ehrenamtlich/unentgeltlich arbeiten
to **vote** 10t abstimmen, wählen

W

wage 113 Lohn
wages 81 Lohn, Gehalt
to **wait in line** 150 sich in einer Warteschlange anstellen
walk, to **go for a** ~ 22, 109 spazieren gehen
wall 21 Wand
walls 123 Stadtmauer
to **wander** 70 wandern, schlendern
war 18 Krieg
war, civil ~ 156 Bürgerkrieg
War, the Gulf ~ 28 der Golfkrieg
War, Second World ~ 28 der Zweite Weltkrieg
war, to **be at** ~ 19 im Krieg sein
warcraft 157 Kriegshandwerk
ward 190 Station, Abteilung (im Krankenhaus)
warehouse 112 Lager, Lagerhalle
warm-up 7 Vorbereitung, Aufwärmen
to **warn** 164 (davor) warnen
warrior 197 Krieger/in
to **waste** 63 verschwenden, vergeuden
waste 163 Abfall
waste, electronic ~ 159 Elektronikschrott
waste of time 81 Zeitverschwendung
wastebasket 50 Papierkorb
water conservation 162t Wassersparen, Wasserreinhaltung
water polo 184 Wasserball
way, by the ~ 34 übrigens
weak 93 schwach
weakness 85 Schwäche
wealthy 58, 189 wohlhabend, reich
to **wear** 27 *(Kleidung:)* tragen
to **weave** 112 weben
to **weep** 180 weinen
weight 104t Gewicht
weight loss 120 Gewichtsverlust
weird 40 seltsam, verrückt
welcome, You're ~. 14t Bitte (sehr).
to **welcome sb** 20 jdn willkommen heißen
well, as ~ **as** 183 ebenso wie
well, to **do** ~ 108t (es) gut gehen
wet 126 feucht, nass
whale 196 Wal
whale catcher 196 Walfänger
(steering) wheel 102t Lenkrad, Steuer
wheelchair 92 Rollstuhl
wheeled, three-~ 136 dreirädrig
whether 39 ob
while 32 während
white water 100 Wildwasser
whole grain 147 Vollkorn
wide 65 breit, weit
wife 17 Ehefrau
wild 9 wild
wildlife 74 Tierwelt, Tier-
willing 80t, 186 bereit, willens
to **win the lottery** 105 im Lotto gewinnen
windmill 58, 193 Windmühle
wing 104t Flügel, Tragfläche
winner 52 Gewinner/in
wise 44 klug
wish 70t Wunsch
to **wish** 25 wünschen
within 92 innen
womanly 193 weiblich, fraulich
wonderful 24 wunderbar
to **work out** 26t trainieren; 76t klappen, funktionieren
to **work sth out** 36 etw herausbekommen
to **work overtime** 83 Überstunden machen
work environment 80 Arbeitsumfeld
work experience 34 Praktikum; 64 Berufserfahrung
work placement 64 Praktikum
working hours 80 Arbeitszeiten
workmate 80 Arbeitskollege/-in
workplace 169 Arbeitsplatz
works 116 Werk
worksheet 144t Arbeitsblatt
world record 58 Weltrekord
worn 120 abgenutzt, abgetragen
to **worry** 99 beunruhigen
to **worry about sth** 28 sich um etw Sorgen machen
to **worship** 193 anbeten, verehren
worth 58, 182 wert
wrestler 51 Ringer/in
wrestling 51 Ringen
to **write sth out** 15 etw aufschreiben
to **write a cheque** 190 einen Scheck ausstellen

Y

yacht 110 Yacht
yet 42 schon, bereits
yoghurt 147 Joghurt
You're welcome. 14t Bitte (sehr).
Yours faithfully 25 *(Brief:)* Mit freundlichen Grüßen
Yours sincerely 75 Mit freundlichen Grüßen
youth 41 Jugend; 100 Jugendliche/r
youth worker 139 Sozialpädagoge/-in, Erzieher/in, Jugendarbeiter/in

Z

zebra 9 Zebra
zinc 112 Zink
zip 112 Reißverschluss

Basic word list

Diese Liste enthält ca. 650 Grundwörter, die in **Work with English** als bekannt vorausgesetzt werden. Nicht aufgeführt, jedoch sind international Wörter (*taxi*, *email* usw.) und einige sehr elementare Wörter wie Pronomen, Zahlen und Tage.

above *über, oben*
according to *zufolge, gemäß, nach, laut*
actual(ly) *tatsächlich*
address *Adresse*
adjective *Adjektiv*
adventure *Abenteuer*
afternoon *Nachmittag*
afterwards *danach*
again *wieder*
against *gegen*
age *Zeitalter, Alter*
air *Luft*
airport *Flughafen*
alcohol *Alkohol*
almost *fast, beinahe*
already *schon, bereits*
always *immer*
angry *wütend, verärgert*
animal *Tier*
another *noch eine*
answer *Antwort, Lösung; (be) antworten*
anybody *jemand, jede/r*
anyone *jemand, jede/r*
anything *etwas, alles*
around *herum*
arrive *ankommen*
ask *fragen, bitten*
autumn *Herbst*
available *verfügbar*
away *weg, entfernt*
back *zurück*
bad *schlecht, schlimm*
bag *Tasche, Beutel*
bathroom *Badezimmer, Bad*
be *sein*
beach *Strand*
bean *Bohne*
beautiful *schön*
because *weil*
bed *Bett*
bedroom *Schlafzimmer*
beef *Rindfleisch*
beer *Bier*
before *vor, vorher*
begin *anfangen, beginnen*
beginning *Anfang*
believe *glauben*
belong *gehören*
below *unter, unten*
best *beste/r/s, am besten*
better *besser*
between *zwischen*
bicycle *Fahrrad*
big *groß*
bike *(Motor-)Rad*
biker *(Motor-)Radfahrer/in*
biography *Biographie*
birthday *Geburtstag*
bit *(ein) bisschen*
black *schwarz*
blue *blau*
body *Körper*
book *Buch; buchen, bestellen*
bored *gelangweilt*
boring *langweilig*
born *geboren*
both *beide*
bottle *Flasche*
box *Kasten, Kästchen, Schachtel*
boyfriend *Freund*
bread *Brot*
break *Pause; brechen*
breakfast *Frühstück*
bring *bringen, holen*
brother *Bruder*
brown *braun*
building *Gebäude*
bus *(Linien-)Bus*
business *Geschäft, Firma*
busy *beschäftigt, besetzt*
buy *kaufen*
by *durch, mit, bei*
cake *Kuchen, Torte*
call, be ~ed *heißen*
called *namens, mit dem Namen*
caller *Anrufer/in*
can *dürfen, können*
car *Auto*
card *Karte*
careful *vorsichtig, sorgfältig*
carrot *Karotte, Möhre*
carry *tragen*
cat *Katze*
central *zentral*
centre *Zentrum*
chair *Stuhl, Sessel*
change *(Ver-)Änderung, Wechsel; (aus)wechseln, (sich) ändern, verändern*
character *Charakter*
chat *Unterhaltung; sich unterhalten*
cheese *Käse*
child *Kind*
children *Kinder*
chocolate *Schokolade*
choose *(aus)wählen*
Christmas *Weihnachten*
church *Kirche*
cigarette *Zigarette*
city *(Groß-)Stadt*
class *Klasse*
classmate *Klassenkamerad/-in*
classroom *Klassenzimmer*
clean *reinigen, säubern; sauber*
climb *klettern, (be-, ein)steigen*
clock *Uhr*
close *schließen, abschließen*
close (to) *nahe (bei)*
clothes *Kleidung, Kleider*
coast *Küste*
coat *Mantel*
coffee *Kaffee*
cold *kalt*
collect *sammeln*
college *Fachhochschule*
colour *Farbe*
come *kommen*
comedy *Komödie*
complain *sich beklagen, (sich) beschweren, reklamieren*
complete *vollständig; vervollständigen, ausfüllen*
concert *Konzert*
continent *Erdteil, Kontinent*
continue *fortfahren, fortsetzen*
cook *kochen, zubereiten; Koch/Köchin*
cooking *Kochen*
copy *Kopie; abschreiben, kopieren*
cost *Kosten; kosten*
country *Land, Staat*
course *Kurs, Lehrgang, Gang*
course, of ~ *natürlich, selbstverständlich*
crazy *verrückt*
cup *Tasse*
cut *schneiden*
damage *Schaden; beschädigen*
dance *tanzen; Tanz*
dancer *Tänzer/in*
danger *Gefahr*
dangerous *gefährlich*
dark *Dunkelheit; dunkel*
date *Datum*
daughter *Tochter*
day *Tag*
dead *tot*
death *Tod, Todesfall*
decide *(sich) entscheiden, beschließen*
decision *Entscheidung*
describe *beschreiben*
description *Beschreibung, Schilderung*
desk *(Schreib-)Tisch*
diagram *Grafik, Diagramm, Abbildung*
die *sterben*
diet *Diät*
difference *Unterschied*
different *anders, verschieden*
difficult *schwer, schwierig*
dinner *(Abend-)Essen*
dislike *nicht mögen*
do *tun, machen*
document *Dokument, Papier*
dog *Hund*
door *Tür*
double *doppelt*
down *unten, hinunter*
drawing *Zeichnung*
dream *Traum; träumen*
dress *Kleid*
drink *Getränk; trinken*
drive *(Auto) fahren*
drug *Droge*
dry *trocken; trocknen*
each *jede/r/s*
ear *Ohr*
early *früh*
east *Osten*
Easter *Ostern*
easy *leicht, einfach*
eat *essen*
egg *Ei*
either *entweder*
empty *leer*
end *Ende, Schluss; (be)enden*
ending *Ende*
enjoy *genießen, gefallen*
enough *ausreichend, genug*
even *sogar (noch)*
evening *Abend*
ever *je(mals)*
every *jede/r/s*
everybody *jede/r*
everyone *jede/r/s, alle*
everything *alles*
everywhere *überall*
exam *Examen, Prüfung*
exercise *Übung*
expensive *teuer*
explain *erklären, erläutern*
expression *Ausdruck*
eye *Auge*
fact *Tatsache, Fakt*
factory *Fabrik, Werk*
fall *fallen*
false *falsch*
family *Familie*
famous *berühmt*
far *weit (entfernt)*
farm *Bauernhof*
farmer *Bauer/Bäuerin*
fast *schnell*
fat *Fett; dick, fett*
favourite *Lieblings-*
feel *(sich) fühlen*
female *weiblich, Frauen-*
few *ein paar, wenig/e*
fight *(be)kämpfen: Kampf, Streit*
file *Ordner, Datei*
find *finden, suchen*
fine *gut, schön, fein*
finish *Ende; (be)enden, fertig werden, erledigen*
fire *Feuer*
firm *Firma*
first *erste/r/s, zuerst*
first name *Vorname*
floor *Fußboden*
fly *fliegen*
follow *(be)folgen*
following *folgende*
food *Essen, Nahrung*
foot *Fuß*
football *Fußball*
forever *für immer*
forget *vergessen*
form *Form, Formular*
free *kostenlos, frei*
friend *Freund/in*
friendly *freund(schaft)lich*
from *von*
fruit *Obst, Frucht, Früchte*
full *voll*
fun *Spaß, Vergnügen*
fun *Spaß*
funny *lustig, komisch, merkwürdig*
future *Zukunft; (zu)künftig*
game *Spiel*
gift *Geschenk*
girl *Mädchen*
girlfriend *Freundin*
give *geben*
glass *Glas*
go *gehen, fahren*
go away *weggehen*
good *gut*
goods *Güter, Waren*
grade *Note*
granddad/-father *Großvater*
grandma/-mother *Großmutter*
great *groß(artig), toll*
green *grün*
grey *grau*
group *Gruppe*
guess *Annahme; raten, schätzen*
guitar *Gitarre*
hair *Haar(e)*
half *Hälfte; halb*
ham *Schinken*
hand *Hand*

happiness *Glück*
happy *glücklich, froh, zufrieden*
hard *schwer, hart*
hat *Hut*
hate *hassen, nicht mögen*
have fun *sich amüsieren*
head *Kopf*
hear *hören*
heart *Herz*
help *Hilfe; helfen*
here *hier*
high *hoch, groß; äußerst*
holiday *Ferien, Urlaub*
home *Zuhause, Heim; nach Hause*
home, at ~ *zu Hause, daheim*
homework *Hausaufgaben*
hope *hoffen; Hoffnung*
hospital *Krankenhaus*
hot *heiß, warm; scharf*
hour *Stunde*
house *Haus*
how *wie*
huge *riesig*
hungry *hungrig*
husband *(Ehe-)Mann*
idea *Idee, Gedanke*
ill *krank*
important *wichtig*
include *enthalten, umfassen*
including *einschließlich*
indoors *innen*
information *Angaben, Information(en), Auskunft*
inside *innerhalb, drinnen*
interview *Interview, Vorstellungsgespräch; interviewen*
into *in … hinein*
invite *einladen*
job *Arbeit, Stelle, Aufgabe*
joke *Witz*
jump *springen*
just *einfach, nur, genau*
key *Schlüssel, Taste*
kilometre *Kilometer*
kiss *küssen; Kuss*
kitchen *Küche*
know *kennen, wissen*
language *Sprache*
large *groß, umfangreich*
last *letzte/r/s, zuletzt*
late *spät*
latest *neueste/r/s*
laugh *lachen*
leader *Leiter/in, Anführer*
learn *lernen, erfahren*
least *wenigstens*
leave *(ver)lassen*
left *linke/r/s, links; übrig*
leg *Bein*
lesson *Lektion, Unterrichtsstunde*
letter *Brief, Buchstabe*
life *Leben*
lift *Fahrstuhl, Aufzug*
like *(ähnlich) wie; mögen, gern tun*
line *Leitung, Linie, Zeile*
lipstick *Lippenstift*
list *Liste; auflisten, notieren*
listen *zuhören*
little *klein, wenig*
live *wohnen, leben*
long *lang*
look *Blick; (aus)sehen, blicken*
lose *verlieren*
lost *verloren*
lot (of), a ~ *viel, sehr*
loud *laut*
love *Liebe; lieben, sehr gern mögen*
lovely *schön, hübsch, reizend*
low *niedrig*
luck *Glück*
lucky *glücklich*
lunch *Mittagessen*
machine *Maschine*
mad *verrückt, toll*
main *Haupt-*
make *machen*
male *männlich*
man *Mann, Mensch*
mark *markieren*
market *Markt*
math(ematic)s *Mathe(matik)*
maybe *vielleicht*
meal *Essen, Mahlzeit*
meat *Fleisch*
meet *(zusammen)treffen, begegnen, kennen lernen*
message *Mitteilung, Nachricht*
metre *Meter*
milk *Milch*
miss *verpassen, vermissen*
money *Geld*
month *Monat*
more *mehr*
morning *Morgen*
most *meist*
motorbike *Motorrad*
mountain *Berg*
move *(sich) bewegen, umziehen*
much *viel*
mushroom *Pilz*
music *Musik*
name *Name*
nationality *Staatsangehörigkeit, Nationalität*
need *Bedarf, Bedürfnis; brauchen, benötigen*
negative *negativ*
nervous *nervös*
nice(ly) *schön, nett*
night *Nacht*
nightlife *Nachtleben*
no-one *niemand, keine/r/s*
nobody *niemand*
noise *Geräusch, Lärm*
noisy *laut, geräuschvoll*
north *Nord(en)*
northern *nördlich*
nose *Nase*
note *Notiz; beachten, notieren*
notes *Notizen*
nothing *nichts*
now *nun, jetzt*
number *Zahl, Anzahl, Nummer*
nurse *Krankenschwester/-pfleger*
nut *Nuss*
office *Büro, Amt*
old *alt*
onion *Zwiebel*
only *nur, einzige/r/s*
open *öffnen; offen*
opinion *Meinung, Einschätzung*
orange *orange*
organize *organisieren*
other *andere/r/s*
outdoors *draußen*
outside *außer(halb)*
over *(vor)über*
page *Seite*
pairwork *Partnerarbeit*
paper *Papier, Zeitung*
parents *Eltern*
part *Teil, Rolle*
past *vorbei, nach; Vergangenheit*
pay *(be)zahlen*
pea *Erbse*
peanut *Erdnuss*
people *Personen, Menschen*
per *pro*
perhaps *vielleicht, eventuell*
phone *Telefon; anrufen*
phone call *(Telefon-)Anruf*
phone number *Telefonnummer*
piano *Klavier*
picture *Bild*
piece *Stück*
pink *rosa*
place *Stelle, Platz; setzen, stellen*
plan *Plan; planen*
plant *Pflanze*
play *spielen*
please *bitte*
pleased *erfreut, froh*
plenty of *viel(e)*
point *Punkt; Komma*
police *Polizei*
policeman *Polizist*
poor *arm, schlecht, mangelhaft*
portion *Portion, Menge, Anteil*
positive *positiv*
postcard *Postkarte*
poster *Plakat*
potato *Kartoffel*
practice *Übung*
prefer *vorziehen, bevorzugen*
pretty *hübsch; ziemlich*
prince *Prinz*
probably *wahrscheinlich*
problem *Problem*
program *(Computer-)Programm*
programme *(Radio-, TV-) Sendung, Programm*
project *Projekt*
pub *Kneipe, Gaststätte*
pull *ziehen*
pupil *Schüler/in*
push *schieben, drücken, drängen*
put *setzen, stellen, legen*
question *Frage*
quick *schnell*
quiet *still, ruhig*
quite *ziemlich, ganz*
rain *Regen; regnen*
read *lesen*
ready *bereit, fertig*
real *echt, wirklich*
reality *Realität, Wirklichkeit*
really *wirklich, eigentlich, tatsächlich*
reason *Grund, Vernunft*
recognize *erkennen, wiedererkennen, anerkennen*
red *rot*
relax *(sich) erholen*
remember *sich erinnern, daran denken*
repeat *wiederholen*
reponsible *verantwortlich, zuständig*
restaurant *Restaurant*
rice *Reis*
rich *reich*
right *rechts, rechte/r/s, richtig; Recht*
ring *Ring; klingeln, anrufen*
road *(Land-)Straße*
room *Zimmer, Raum*
round *Runde; rund*
run *laufen, rennen*
sad *traurig*
salt *Salz*
same *gleiche/r/s, der-, die-, dasselbe*
school *Schule*
science *Naturwissenschaft*
scissors *Schere*
sea *Meer, (die) See*
second *zweite/r/s; Sekunde*
secret *Geheimnis*
secretary *Sekretär/in*
section *Abschnitt*
see *sehen*
seem *scheinen*
sell *(sich) verkaufen*
send *senden, schicken*
serve *dienen, bedienen, servieren*
set *setzen*
several *etliche, einige, mehrere*
ship *Schiff*
shock *Schock*
shoe *Schuh*
shop *Laden, Geschäft; einkaufen*
shopping mall *Einkaufsstraße, Kaufhauspassage*
short *kurz, klein*
should *solle/n, sollte/n*
shout *schreien, rufen*
show *zeigen*
sick *krank*
side *Seite*
silent *still*
silly *dumm, doof, albern, lächerlich*
sing *singen*
singer *Sänger/in*
sister *Schwester*
sit *sitzen, sich setzen*
ski *Ski; Ski fahren*
sky *Himmel*
sleep *Schlaf; schlafen*
slow(ly) *langsam*
small *klein*
smile *lächeln; Lächeln*
snow *Schnee; schneien*
soft *weich*
some *einige, etwas*
someone *jemand*
something *etwas*
sometimes *manchmal*
son *Sohn*
soon *bald*
sort *Sorte, Art*
soup *Suppe*
south *Süden*
speak *sprechen, reden*
speaker *Redner/in, Sprecher/in*
special *besonders*
spell *buchstabieren, schreiben*
stand *stehen*
start *Beginn; anfangen, starten, beginnen*
station *Bahnhof*
stay *Aufenthalt; bleiben, übernachten*

stop *Halt; (an)halten, aufhören (mit)*
store *Laden, Geschäft*
story *Geschichte*
strange *fremd, seltsam*
street *Straße*
strong *stark, kräftig*
student *Student/in, Schüler/in, Lernende/r*
stupid *dumm*
subject *(Schul-)Fach, Thema*
sugar *Zucker*
summer *Sommer*
sun *Sonne*
supermarket *Supermarkt*
sure *sicher*
sure *sicher(lich), freilich*
surname *Nachname, Familienname*
surprise *Überraschung; überraschen*
swim *schwimmen*
table *Tisch, Tabelle*
take *nehmen, bringen, dauern*
talk *Gespräch, Unterhaltung; sprechen, reden*
tea *Tee*
teach *unterrichten, lehren*
teacher *Lehrer/in*
tell *sagen, erzählen*
than *als*
these *diese*
thin *dünn*
thing *Sache, Ding, Gegenstand*
think *denken, meinen, finden, glauben*
though *obwohl, doch*
throw *werfen*
ticket *Karte, Fahrschein*
time *Zeit, Mal*
today *heute*
together *zusammen*
tomato *Tomate*
tomorrow *morgen*
tonight *heute Abend/Nacht*
top *Spitze, Gipfel; Spitzen-*
topic *Thema*
total(ly) *völlig, (ins)gesamt*
tourism *Tourismus*
town *Stadt*
toy *Spielzeug*
train *Zug; ausbilden*
trainee *Auszubildende/r, Praktikant/in*
training *Ausbildung, Übung, Training*
translate *übersetzen, übertragen*
transport *Transport, Verkehr*
travel *Reisen; reisen, fahren*
tree *Baum*
trousers *Hose*
true *richtig, wahr*
truth *Wahrheit*
try *versuchen, probieren*
turn into *einbiegen in*
type *Art, Typ; erfassen, tippen*
typical *typisch*
understand *verstehen, begreifen*
unhappy *unglücklich, unzufrieden*
university *Universität*
until *bis*
use *benutzen, verwenden; Verwendung*
useful *nützlich*
usual(ly) *normalerweise, gewöhnlich, meistens*
vegetable *Gemüse*
village *Dorf*
visit *Besuch; besuchen, besichtigen*
waiter *Kellner*
wash *waschen*
way *Methode, Mittel*
weather *Wetter*
white *weiß*
window *Fenster*
wine *Wein*
wood *Holz*
world *Welt*
yoghurt *Joghurt*
zoo *Zoo*

Geographical word list

Africa ['æfrɪkə] *Afrika*
African ['æfrɪkən] *afrikanisch, Afrikaner/in*
Alps [ælps] *Alpen*
Amazon ['æməzən] *Amazonas*
American [ə'merɪkən] *amerikanisch*
Arab ['ærəb] *arabisch, Arabisch, Araber/in*
Arabic ['ærəbɪk] *arabisch, Arabisch*
Arctic ['ɑ:ktɪk] *Arktis, arktisch*
Asia ['eɪʃə] *Asien*
Asian ['eɪʃn] *asiatisch, Asiat/in*
Atlantic [ət'læntɪk] *Atlantik, atlantisch*
Australia [ɒ'streɪliə] *Australien*
Australian [ɒ'streɪliən] *australisch, Australier/in*
Austria ['ɒstriə] *Österreich*
Austrian ['ɒstriən] *östereichisch, Österreicher/in*
Baltic ['bɔ:ltɪk] *baltisch*
Baltic Sea [ˌbɔ:ltɪk 'si:] *Ostsee*
Bangladesh [ˌbæŋglə'deʃ] *Bangladesch*
Bangladeshi [ˌbæŋglə'deʃi] *aus/Bewohner von Bangladesch*
Beijing [ˌbeɪ'dʒɪŋ] *Beijing, Peking*
Belgium ['beldʒəm] *Belgien*
Belize [bə'li:z] *Belize*
Bengal ['beŋgl] *Bengalen*
Benin [be'ni:n] *Benin*
Botswana [bɒt'swɑ:nə] *Botswana*
British ['brɪtɪʃ] *britisch*
Briton ['brɪtn] *Brite/Britin*
Cameroon [ˌkæmə'ru:n] *Kamerun*
Canada ['kænədə] *Kanada*
Canary Islands [kə'næri aɪləndz] *Kanarische Inseln*
Caribbean [ˌkærə'bi:ən] *Karibik*
Channel ['tʃænl] *Ärmelkanal*
Channel Islands ['tʃænl aɪləndz] *Kanalinseln*
China ['tʃaɪnə] *China*
Chinese [tʃaɪ'ni:z] *chinesisch, Chinesisch, Chinese/-in*
Congo, Democratic Republic of the ~ ['kɒŋgəʊ] *Kongo, demokratische Republik*
Congolese [ˌkɒŋgə'li:z] *kongolesisch, Kongolese/-in*
Cyprus ['saɪprəs] *Zypern*
Czech [tʃek] *tschechisch, Tschechisch*
Czech Republic [ˌtʃek rɪ'pʌblɪk] *Tschechische Republik*
Denmark ['denmɑ:k] *Dänemark*
Earth [ɜ:θ] *Erde*
Egypt ['i:dʒɪpt] *Ägypten*
Europe ['jʊərəp] *Europa*
European [ˌjʊərə'pi:ən] *europäisch, Europäer/in*
Finland ['fɪnlənd] *Finnland*
French [frentʃ] *französisch*
Geneva [dʒə'ni:və] *Genf*
German ['dʒɜ:mən] *deutsch, Deutsch, Deutsche/r*
Germany ['dʒɜ:məni] *Deutschland*
Ghana ['gɑ:nə] *Ghana*
Greece [gri:s] *Griechenland*
Greek [gri:k] *griechisch, Griechisch, Grieche/-in*
Guyana [gaɪ'ænə] *Guyana*
Hungary ['hʌŋgəri] *Ungarn*
India ['ɪndiə] *Indien*
Indian ['ɪndiən] *indisch, Inder/in*
Indonesia [ˌɪndəʊ'ni:ziə] *Indonesien*
Ireland ['aɪələnd] *Irland*
Irish ['aɪrɪʃ] *irisch, Ire/Irin*
Italian [ɪ'tæljən] *italienisch, Italienisch, Italiener/in*
Italy ['ɪtəli] *Italien*
Jamaica [dʒə'meɪkə] *Jamaika*
Japan [dʒə'pæn] *Japan*
Japanese [ˌdʒæpə'ni:z] *japanisch, Japanisch, Japaner/in*
Kenya ['kenjə] *Kenia*
Korea [kə'rɪə] *Korea*
Latvia ['lætviə] *Lettland*
Madagascar [ˌmædə'gæskə] *Madagaskar*
Malawi [mə'lɑ:wi] *Malawi*
Malawian [mə'lɑ:wiən] *malawisch, Malawer/in*
Malaysia [mə'leɪziə] *Malaysia*
Malta ['mɔ:ltə] *Malta*
Maltese [ˌmɔ:l'ti:z] *maltesisch, Maltesisch, Maltese/r*
Mecca ['mekə] *Mekka*
Mediterranean [ˌmedɪtə'reɪniən] *Mittelmeer-*
Mediterranean Sea [medɪtəˌreɪniən 'si:] *Mittelmeer*
Milan [mɪ'læn] *Mailand*
Monaco ['mɒnəkəʊ] *Monaco*
Moscow ['mɒskəʊ] *Moskau*
Munich ['mju:nɪk] *München*
Namibia [nə'mɪbiə] *Namibia*
New South Wales [ˌnju: saʊθ 'weɪlz] *Neusüdwales (australischer Bundesstaat)*
New Zealand [ˌnju: 'zi:lənd] *Neuseeland*
North America [ˌnɔ:θ ə'merɪkə] *Nordamerika*
Pakistan [ˌpækɪ'stɑ:n] *Pakistan*
Papua New Guinea [ˌpæpuə nju: 'gɪni:] *Papua Neu-Guinea*
Philippines ['fɪləpi:nz] *Philippinen*
Poland ['pəʊlənd] *Polen*
Polish ['pɒlɪʃ] *polnisch, Polnisch*
Portugal ['pɔ:tʃʊgl] *Portugal*
Prague [prɑ:g] *Prag*
Puerto Rico [ˌpwɜ:təʊ 'ri:kəʊ] *Puerto Rico*
Rome [rəʊm] *Rom*
Russia ['rʌʃə] *Russland*
Rwanda [ru'ændə] *Ruanda*
Scotland ['skɒtlənd] *Schottland*
Sicily ['sɪsəli] *Sizilien*
Singapore [ˌsɪŋə'pɔ:] *Singapur*
Singaporean [ˌsɪŋə'pɔ:riən] *singapurisch, Singapurer/in*
Somalia [sə'mɑ:liə] *Somalia*
South Africa [ˌsaʊθ 'æfrɪkə] *Südafrika*
South America [ˌsaʊθ ə'merɪkə] *Südamerika*
Soviet Union [ˌsəʊviət 'ju:niən] *Sowjetunion*
Spain [speɪn] *Spanien*
Spanish ['spænɪʃ] *spanisch, Spanish, Spanier/in*
Sudan [su'dɑ:n] *Sudan*
Sweden ['swi:dn] *Schweden*
Swedish ['swi:dɪʃ] *schwedisch, Schwedisch*
Tanzania [ˌtænzə'ni:ə] *Tansania*
Tenerife [ˌtenə'ri:f] *Teneriffa*
Tunisia [tju'nɪziə] *Tunesien*
Turkey ['tɜ:ki] *Türkei*
Turkish ['tɜ:kɪʃ] *türkisch, Türkisch*
Uganda [ju'gændə] *Uganda*
United Kingdom (UK) [juˌnaɪtɪd 'kɪŋdəm] *Vereinigtes Königreich*
USA [ˌju: es 'eɪ] *Vereinigte Staaten von Amerika*
Vatican City [ˌvætɪkən 'sɪti] *Vatikanstadt*
Vietnam [ˌvi:et'næm] *Vietnam*
Vietnamese [viˌetnə'mi:z] *vietnamesisch, Vietnamesisch*
Warsaw ['wɔ:sɔ:] *Warschau*
Zambia ['zæmbiə] *Sambia*
Zimbabwe [zɪm'bɑ:bwi] *Simbabwe*

Irregular verbs

be	was/were	been	*sein*
beat	beat	beaten	*schlagen, besiegen*
become	became	become	*werden*
begin	began	begun	*anfangen, beginnen*
break	broke	broken	*brechen*
build	built	built	*bauen*
burn	burnt/ burned	burnt/ burned	*(ver)brennen*
buy	bought	bought	*kaufen*
come	came	come	*kommen*
cut	cut	cut	*schneiden*
do	did	done	*tun, machen*
draw	drew	drawn	*zeichnen*
dream	dreamt	dreamt	*träumen*
drink	drank	drunk	*trinken*
drive	drove	driven	*fahren*
eat	ate	eaten	*essen*
fall	fell	fallen	*fallen*
feed	fed	fed	*füttern, ernähren*
feel	felt	felt	*(sich) fühlen, empfinden*
fight	fought	fought	*kämpfen*
find	found	found	*finden*
fit	fit/fitted	fitted	*passen, sitzen; anbringen*
fly	flew	flown	*fliegen*
forget	forgot	forgotten	*vergessen*
get	got	got (AE gotten)	*bekommen*
give	gave	given	*geben*
go	went	gone	*gehen, fahren*
grow	grew	grown	*wachsen*
hang	hung	hung	*hängen*
have	had	had	*haben*
hear	heard	heard	*hören*
hide	hid	hidden	*(sich) verstecken*
hit	hit	hit	*schlagen*
hold	held	held	*halten, festhalten*
keep	kept	kept	*behalten*
know	knew	known	*kennen, wissen*
lay	laid	laid	*legen*
learn	learnt/ learned	learnt/ learned	*lernen*
leave	left	left	*abfahren, verlassen, weggehen*
let	let	let	*lassen*
lie	lay	lain	*liegen*
light	lit	lit	*anzünden, beleuchten, anmachen*
lose	lost	lost	*verlieren*
make	made	made	*machen*
mean	meant	meant	*meinen, bedeuten*
meet	met	met	*treffen*
pay	paid	paid	*bezahlen*
put	put	put	*setzen, stellen, legen*
quit	quit/ quitted	quit/ quitted	*verlassen, aufhören*
read	read	read	*lesen*
ride	rode	ridden	*reiten, fahren*
rise	rose	risen	*(an)steigen*
run	ran	run	*laufen, rennen*
say	said	said	*sagen*
see	saw	seen	*sehen*
sell	sold	sold	*verkaufen*
send	sent	sent	*senden, schicken*
set	set	set	*setzen, stellen*
show	showed	shown	*zeigen*
sit	sat	sat	*sitzen*
sleep	slept	slept	*schlafen*
smell	smelt/ smelled	smelt/ smelled	*riechen*
speak	spoke	spoken	*sprechen*
spell	spelt/ spelled	spelt/ spelled	*buchstabieren*
spend	spent	spent	*ausgeben, verbringen*
shut	shut	shut	*schließen*
sing	sang	sung	*singen*
stand	stood	stood	*stehen*
steal	stole	stolen	*stehlen*
swim	swam	swum	*schwimmen*
take	took	taken	*nehmen*
teach	taught	taught	*unterrichten, beibringen*
tell	told	told	*sagen, erzählen*
think	thought	thought	*denken*
throw	threw	thrown	*werfen*
understand	understood	understood	*verstehen*
wear	wore	worn	*tragen*
win	won	won	*gewinnen*
write	wrote	written	*schreiben*

Bildquellenverzeichnis

S. 8 / 1 / Shutterstock / Galyna Andrushko, S. 8 / 2 / Shutterstock / Randall Stevens, S. 8 / 3 / Shutterstock / Caleb Foster, S. 8 / 4 / Alamy / Ken Welsh, S. 8 / 5 / Shutterstock / Regien Paassen, S. 9 / 6 / Fotofinder / Bildagentur-online / TIPS-Images S. 9 / 7 / Shutterstock / covenant, S. 9 / 8 / Alamy / Tom Gilks, S. 9 / 9 / Picture-Alliance / WILDLIFE / M.Harvey, S. 12 / Shutterstock / Yuri Arcurs, S. 16 / V. Maly, S. 17 / oben / Picture-Alliance / WHITE_HOUSE / epa Annie Leibowitz, S. 17 / mitte-links / Alamy / Golden Pixels LLC / Kablonk, S. 17 / unten-li / Alamy / vikki martin, S. 17 / unten-mi / Alamy / Image Source / IS-200508, S. 17 / unten-re / Alamy / Image Source / IE080, S. 18 / oben / fotolia / Monart Design, S. 18 / mitte / Alamy / dbimages / Marcia Chambers, s. 18 / unten / Alamy / Oleksiy Maksymenko Photography, S. 19 / Corbis / Pascal Deloche, S. 20 / links / V. Maly, S. 20 / rechts / Shutterstock / Reda, S. 21 / 1 / Shutterstock / Yuri Arcurs, S. 21 / 2 / shutterstock / Sonya etchison, S. 21 / 3 / Shutterstock / Viaceslav K., S. 21 / 4 / shutterstock / Edyta Pawlowska, S. 21 / unten / Shutterstock, S. 24 / 1 / Shutterstock / Alexzel, S. 24 / 2 / Shutterstock / Rob Wilson, S. 24 / 3.1 / Shutterstock / Rihardzz, S. 24 / 3.2 / Shutterstock / Shebeko, S. 24 / 3.3 / Shutterstock / Kiselev Andrey Valerevich, S. 24 / 4 / Shutterstock / Feichka, S. 24 / 5 / Shutterstock / Leigh Prather, S. 26 / Picture-Alliance / Lonely Planet Images / Jean-Bernard Carillet, S. 28 / 1 / Picture-Alliance / k09, S. 28 / 2 / Corbis / Peter Turnley, S. 28 / 3 / Picture-Alliance / dpa / Photoshot, S. 30 / Alamy / Pictorial Press Ltd, S. 31 / 1 / Alamy / AF archive, S. 31 / 2 / Alamy / Pictorial Press Ltd, S. 31 / 3 / Alamy / Trinity Mirror / Mirrorpix, S. 31 / 4 / Alamy / Keystone Pictures USA, S. 34 / shutterstock / mangostock, S. 36 / shutterstock / Martin Lehmann, S. 37 / 1 / Shutterstock / waynehowes, S. 37 / 2 / Shutterstock / Nihat Dursun, S. 38 / Alamy / MARKA / jader alto, S. 47 / 1 / Picture-Alliance / Elizabeth Pantaleo, S. 47 / 2 / Photoshot / Retna Pictures / Starface, S. 47 / 3 / Picture-Alliance / dpa / Hubert Boesl, S. 47 / 4 / Picture-Alliance / Landmark Media / Can Nguyen, S47 / 5 / Photoshot / Xinhua / Agencia Estado, S. 47 / 6 / Picture-Alliance / Abaca Khayat, S. 47 / 7 / Picture-Alliance / Tass / Sindeyev Vladimir, S. 47 / 8 / Picture-Allianz / Abaca Khayat, S. 48 / 1 / Picture-Alliance / Landov Barrett 2893612, S. 48 / 2 / Picture-Alliance / epa Sullivan Pool, S. 48 / 3 / Picture-Alliance / dpa / Fabian Bimmer, S. 48 / 4 / Picture-Alliance / dpa-Zentralbild / Jens Kalaene, S. 48 / 5 / Picture-Alliance / Nancy Kaszerman, S. 52 / 1 / Picture-Alliance / newscom / DVS, S. 52 / 2 / Picture-Alliance / dpa / Astro, S. 52 / 3 / Alamy / 67photo, S. 57 / 1 / Shutterstock / Martin Allinger, S. 57 / 2 / Alamy / IS2 Image Source, S. 57 / 3 / Shutterstock / shooarts, S. 57 / 4 / Shutterstock / Konstantin Chagin, S. 57 / 5 / Picture-Alliance / dpa-Zentralbild / Arno Burgi, S. 57 / 6 / Shutterstock / corepics, S. 57 / 7 / Picture-Alliancd / beyond foto, S. 57 / 8 / Shutterstock / hektoR, S. 57 / 9 / Alamy / Karen Spencer, S. 58 / 1 / Picture-Alliance / dpa / Kay Nietfeld, S. 58 / 2 / Picture-Alliance / Frank Hoermann / SVEN SIMON, S. 58 / 3 / Picture-Alliance / dpa / Keystone Rena Durham - Kpa, S. 61 / John Deputy, S. 62 / Picture-Alliance / Jazz Archiv / Markus Lubitz, S. 64 / Picture-Alliance / Wildlife / M.Hamblin, S. 65 / Alamy / David Cole, S. 67 / 1 / Shutterstock / Alex Staroseltsev, S. 67 / 2 / Shutterstock / luxorphoto, S. 67 / 3 / Shutterstock / Liv friis-larsen, S. 67 / 4 / Shutterstock / Goodluz, S. 68 / Shutterstock / Stephen Coburn, S. 70 / 1 / Shutterstock / liseykina, S. 70 / 2 / Shutterstock / maxstockphoto, S. 70 / 3 / Shutterstock / lakov Kalinin, S. 70 / 4 / Shutterstock / Fesus Robert, S. 73 / 1 / Picture-Alliance / dpa / Achim Scheidemann, S. 73 / 2 / Picture-Alliance / g90, S. 73 / 3 / Alamy / Picture Contact BV / jochem wijnands, S. 76 / Shutterstock / Deklofenak, S. 77+78oben / Shutterstock / corepics, S. 78 / 1 / Alamy / Profimedia International s.r.o. / S / PX1M / Lukáš Cetera, S. 78 / 2 / Alamy / Peter Widmann, S. 78 / 3 / Alamy / Adrian Muttitt, S. 80 / Shutterstock / Yuri Arcurs, S. 83 / 1 / Shutterstock / Fejas, S. 83 / 2 / Shutterstock / zenks22, S. 83 / 3 / Shutterstock / wolfmaster13, S. 83 / 4 / Shutterstock / Carsten Reisinger, S. 83 / 5 / Shutterstock / Creation, S. 87 / 1 / Picture-Alliance / J.W. Alker, S. 87 / 2 / Alamy / Stacy Walsh Rosenstock, S. 87 / 3 / Shutterstock / Monkey Business Images, S. 87 / 4 / Alamy / ACE STOCK LIMITED / acestock, S. 87 / 5 / Alamy / PYMCA / TED POLHEMUS, S. 87 / 6 / Shutterstock / R. Gino Santa Maria, S. 87 / 7 / Alamy / Jochen Tack, S. 88 / Guardian / David Silitoe, S. 92 / Shutterstock / olly, S. 93 / 1.1 / Shutterstock / Kripke, S. 93 / 1.2 / Shutterstock / zirconicusso, S. 93 / 2 / Shutterstock / Gerard Koudenburg, S. 93 / 3 / Shutterstock / Howard Sandler, S. 93 / 4 / Picture-Alliance / Wolfgang Kluge, S. 94 / Picture-Alliance / dpa / Bernd Settnik, S. 96 / a / Shutterstock / ahmet urkac, S. 96 / b / Shutterstock / Alex Mit, S. 96 / c / Shutterstock / scusi0-9 S. 96 / d / Shutterstock / foxy cat, S. 96 / e / Shutterstock / Yobidaba, S. 96 / unten / Alamy / Sport In Pictures, S. 102 / 1 / Shutterstock / Gary Paul Lewis, S. 102 / 2 / Shutterstock / Piotr Marcinski, S. 102 / 3 / Shutterstock / Foto011, S. 102 / 4 / Shutterstock / Steve Lovegrove, S. 102 / 5 / Shutterstock, S. 102 / 6 / Shutterstock, S. 103 / oben_links / Fotolia / Dean Moriarty, S. 103 / oben_rechts / Fotolia / BlueOrange Studio, S. 103 / mitte / Shutterstock / auremar, S. 103 / unten_links / Shutterstock / Chuck Rausin, S. 103 / unten_rechts / Shutterstock / Miroslaw Dziadkowiec, S. 104 / Picture-Alliance / bildagentur-online, S. 106 / Alamy / Russell Mills Architectural, S. 111 / AdverstArchive, S. 112 / Shutterstock / nito, S. 118 / Shutterstock / Minerva Studio, S. 121 / Alamy / Northern Ireland / Stephen Barnes, S. 123 / 1 / Fotofinder / Your_Photo_Today, S. 123 / 2 / Shutterstock / Kanwarjit Singh Boparai, S. 123 / 3-8 / viewingmalta.com, S. 124 / 1 / Shutterstock / Monkey Business Images, S. 124 / 2 / Picture-Alliance / Uwe Gerig, S. 124 / 3 / Shutterstock / Dmitriy Shironosov, S. 125 / Shutterstock / Koshevnyk, S. 129 / 1 / Shutterstock / Koshevnyk, S. 129 / 2 / Shutterstock / Anthony Worsdell, S. 130 / 1 / Shutterstock / Iurii Osadchi, S. 130 / 2 / Alamy / Inspirestock Inc., S. 131 / 1 / Picture-Alliance / Holger Hollemann, S. 131 / 2 / Fotofinder / Keystone / Volkmar Schulz, S. 131 / 3.1 / Shutterstock / Djordje Radivojevic, S. 131 / 3.2 / Shutterstock / Donald Sawvel, S. 131 / 3.3 / Shutterstock / Donald Sawvel, S. 131 / 3.4 / Shutterstock / Radoman Durkovic, S. 131 / 3.5 / Shutterstock / Radoman Durkovic, S. 131 / 3.6 / Shutterstock / Donald Sawvel, S. 132 / 1 / Shutterstock / koteus, S. 132 / 2 / Shutterstock / Axel Wolf, S. 132 / 3 / Shutterstock / dslaven, S. 135 / 1 / Picture-Allianz / PA Gareth Fuller 6132884, S. 135 / 2 / Picture-Alliance / Maxppp / Patrick Clemente, S. 135 / 3 / Picture-Alliance / dpa / Ronald Wittek, S. 135 / 4 / Picture-Alliance / epa / Michael Reynolds, S. 135 / 5 / Picture-Alliance / Maxppp / Philippe De Poulpiquet, S. 135 / 6 / Picture-Alliance / dpa / Photoshot, S. 136 / 1 / Babar Ali, S. 136 / 2 / Babar Ali, S. 138 / Shutterstock / Steve Bower, S. 142 / Shutterstock / rozbyshaka, S. 143 / 1 / Shutterstock / lithian, S. 143 / 2 / Shutterstock / Goodluz, S. 143 / 3 / Shutterstock / StockLite, S. 144 / Shutterstock / Ralph Loesche, S. 145 / 1 / Fotolia / Monkey Business, S. 145 / 2 / Fotolia / mema, S. 149 / 1 / Shutterstock / Petar Ivanov Ishmiriev, S. 149 / 2 S. 149 / 1 / Shutterstock / FotoFinder / vario images, S. 150 / 1 / Alamy / Travelscape Images, S. 150 / 2 / 123rf / Olga Chernetskaya, S. 150 / 3 / 123rf / bedolaga, S. 150 / 4 / 123rf / Engin Korkmaz, S. 152 / Shutterstock / auremar, S. 153 / 1 / Shutterstock / CLS Design, S. 153 / 2 / Shutterstock / auremar, S. 153 / 3 / 123rf / designpics, S. 153 / 4 / Shutterstock / Galina Barskaya, S. 153 / 5 / Shutterstock / Aleksandr Markin, S. 155 / Shutterstock / corepics, S. 156 / 1 / Alamy / ImagesBazaar, S. 156 / 2 / Alamy / GoGo Images Corporation, S. 157 / Picture-Alliance / Imaginechina Liu Lu, S. 159 / 1 / Picture-Alliance / WILDLIFE / J.Mallwitz, S. 159 / 2 / Picture-Alliance / Ton Koene, S. 159 / 3 / Picture-Alliance / WILDLIFE / P.Oxford, S. 159 / 4 / Picture-Alliance / WILDLIFE / D.J.Cox, S. 159 / 5 / Shutterstock / froxx, S. 159 / 6 / Shutterstock / ssuaphotos, S. 160 / 1 / Alamy / Frances Roberts, S. 160 / 2 / Alamy / Juice Images, S. 160 / 3 / Alamy / christian kober, S. 169 / 1 / Shutterstock / SVLuma, S. 169 / 2 / Alamy / Travelshots, S. 174 / Picture-Alliance / dpa / Michael Kappeler

Wir danken allen Rechteinhabern für die Abdruckgenehmigung. Da es uns leider nicht möglich war, alle Rechteinhaber zu ermitteln, bitten wir, sich gegebenenfalls an den Verlag zu wenden.

European Union

Donau Auen

Robert Petermann

DONAU AUEN

ROBERT PETERMANN

lwmedia VERLAG

IMPRESSUM

ISBN 978-3-9502275-4-3

Bilder und Texte: Robert Petermann
Redaktion: Oliver Lehmann
Artdirektion: Patrick Püribauer
Projektleitung: Prok. Alexandra Salvinetti

Karte: Nationalpark Donau-Auen

Druck und Bindung: Druckerei Janetschek Gmbh, Heidenreichstein
Vertrieb: Residenz Verlag

INHALT

EINSTIMMUNG

DIE AU – ein Lebensraum der Superlative

Eine natürliche Au ist ein Mosaik höchst unterschiedlicher Teil-Ökosysteme, wie beispielsweise dem Auwald, den verschiedenartigen Augewässern, Schotterbänken, dem Flussufer und den Inseln im Strom. Flussauen sind überaus komplexe und vielgestaltige Lebensräume und somit Ökosysteme eines höheren Ranges. Alle diese Lebensräume, so stark sie sich auch voneinander unterscheiden, finden sich auf relativ engem Raum nebeneinander. Die dadurch entstehende Dichte des Angebots ans Lebensräumen ist ein entscheidender Grund für die enorme Artenvielfalt in den Auen. Rund 100 Vogelarten brüten in den Donauauen, 30 Säugetierspezies leben hier, ebenso wie 8 Arten von Reptilien und 60 verschiedene Fischarten. Somit sind die Auen entlang der Donau eines der artenreichsten Ökosysteme Mitteleuropas.

Ein Teil dieser Artenvielfalt wird auf den folgenden Seiten präsentiert. Viele der beschriebenen Tiere sind allgemein bekannt und gelten als Charakterarten oder *flagship species* der Au, wie Biber, Eisvogel, Sumpfschildkröte oder die Reiher. Diese sind, zumindest aus einiger Entfernung, relativ häufig zu beobachten. Andere hingegen, wie die meisten Amphibien, unter ihnen Knoblauchkröte und Kammmolch leben sehr versteckt, und sind dementsprechend selten zu sehen. Es sind aber gerade die Amphibien, die so typisch für die Auen sind, und für die die natürlichen Ausysteme ein unersetzliches Refugium darstellen. Diese doppellebigen Tiere, die das Land ebenso zum Leben brauchen wie das Wasser, stehen gleichnishaft für die amphibische Au, die ebenfalls nur durch das Zusammenspiel von Land und Wasser existieren kann. Insgesamt leben 13 Amphibienarten in den niederösterreichischen Donauauen, darunter die ursprüngliche Rotbauchunke, welche die Strategie der perfekten Tarnung ihrer Oberseite mit der auffälligen Warnfärbung ihrer Unterseite verbindet. Moorfrösche, die – braun gefleckt – das Jahr hindurch sich kaum vom Waldboden unterscheiden, die Männchen in der Paarungszeit jedoch ein intensiv blaues Kleid anlegen. Oder Laubfrösche, die je nach Stimmung und Untergrund grau oder braun gefärbt sind, meist jedoch in kräftigem Grün hoch oben in den Bäumen leben.

Hinzu kommen noch die Eisvögel, deren prächtige Färbung man nur von der tropischen Vogelwelt kennt; Raupen, die an unsichtbaren Fäden zwischen den Bäumen zu schweben scheinen; Spinnen, die auf und unter der Wasseroberfläche jagen; Schlangen, die behände Schwimmer sind und Fischen und Fröschen nachstellen. An Land finden sich Pflanzen, die in ihren Kesselfallen Insekten fangen, um sie erst nach der Bestäubung wieder frei zu lassen. All diese faszinierenden Lebewesen, und Tausende mehr, bevölkern das schmale grüne Band der Donauauen zwischen den Metropolen Wien und Bratislava.

Bereits die große Vielfalt, die der kleine Flecken unberührter Natur vor unserer Haustüre hervorbringt, lässt den Beobachter ins Schwärmen geraten. Ihm ergeht es dabei ein wenig wie dem nüchternen Denker Charles Darwin bei der Betrachtung der verschiedenen Lebewesen und der Art ihrer Entstehung; so schreibt er im letzten Kapitel seines bahnbrechenden Werkes über die Entstehung der Arten:

„Es ist anziehend beim Anblick eines Stückes Erde bedeckt mit blühenden Pflanzen aller Art, mit singenden Vögeln in den Büschen, mit schaukelnden Faltern in der Luft, mit kriechenden Würmern im feuchten Boden sich zu denken, dass alle diese Lebensformen so vollkommen in ihrer Art, so abweichend unter sich und in allen Richtungen so abhängig von einander, durch Gesetze hervorgebracht sind, welche noch fort und fort um uns wirken.“

Kein anderer Lebensraum unserer Breiten ändert sein Erscheinungsbild so häufig und so grundlegend wie Flussauen. Neben der Vielfalt an Lebensräumen und deren Bewohnern findet sich ein weiteres Charakteristikum, das die Auen prägt: der ständige Wandel, dem sie unterworfen sind. Im Hochsommer erinnert das undurchdringliche Dickicht der Wälder an tropische Dschungel: Konrad Lorenz verglich die Altarme in den Donauauen mit denen des Orinoko. Im Winter hingegen wirkt die Au kahl und unbelebt. Zwar verkriechen sich Reptilien, Amphibien und Wirbellose im Boden, um den Winter zu überleben; viele Vögel ziehen in wärmere Gefilde, im Gegenzug kommen dafür unzählige Vögel aus dem Norden, um entlang der eisfreien Donau zu überwintern. Im Frühling kehrt wieder vermehrt Leben in die Auen ein, Frösche, Kröten und Molche bevölkern in Scharen die Gewässer, um sich zu paaren, die Luft wird wieder von unzähligen Insekten erobert, und den Waldboden überzieht der Bärlauch mit einem Meer an zarten weißen Blüten.

Der wohl wichtigste Faktor, der die Auen gestaltet und verändert, ist jedoch das Wasser. Mit den wechselnden Pegelständen der Donau ändert sich auch der Wasserstand der Augewässer. Diese stehen entweder direkt mit dem Fluss in Verbindung oder werden über das Grundwasser gespeist. Bei Niedrigwasser fallen weite Teile der Gewässer trocken, und es bilden sich entlang des Flussufers und an den großen Nebenarmen ausgedehnte Schotterflächen. Diese dienen Kiesbrütern, wie Flussuferläufer und Flussregenpfeifer als Brutrevier. Steigt das Wasser der Donau, durchströmt es wieder die Neben- und Altarme, und sie werden selbst wieder ein Teil des Stromes.

Hochwässer verändern die Au am eindrücklichsten. Die Donau tritt über ihre Ufer, ergießt sich in Altarme und in den Auwald. In den, zum Teil meterhohen, Fluten ertrinken viele Tiere, andere versuchen sich auf Bäume zu retten oder klammern sich an Treibholz und versuchen so dem Tod zu entkommen. Die Hochwässer sind die wesentliche Kraft, die zwar Zerstörung bringt, aber auch neuen Lebensraum schafft.

Analog zu den jährlichen Überschwemmungen des Nils, dessen Wasser und nährstoffreiche Schlammfracht eine höchst produktive Landwirtschaft ermöglichten, und somit die Grundlage der Hochkultur des alten Ägyptens legte, sind auch die Hochwässer der Donau die Basis fast allen Lebens in der Au. Hochwasserereignisse verjüngen die Au, sie tragen Inseln und Schotterbänke ab, um sie wo anders als neues Land wieder abzulagern. Bäume werden umgerissen und mit anderem Treibholz oft zu riesigen Haufen zusammengeschwemmt. Diese großen Mengen an totem Holz bieten unzähligen Arten von Insekten und anderen Wirbellosen Nahrung und Lebensraum.

Wo Hochwässer noch (oder wieder) durch die Altarme strömen können, schwemmen sie auch die Sedimente aus und verhindern somit ihr Verlanden. Durch die ständige Umgestaltung erreicht eine natürliche Au nie den Zustand eines statischen Gleichgewichtes, es ist eine permanente Sukzession, die selbst über lange Zeiträume ihr Endstadium, die Klimax, nie erreicht.

Dieser Vielfalt des Lebens und der Lebensräume sowie dem ständigen Wandel der Au geht dieses Buch nach. Die Bilder zeigen die Au im Laufe der Jahreszeiten, bei Tag und bei Nacht, unter Wasser oder von hoch oben aus der Luft. Den besten Überblick über die ebene Aulandschaft erhält man von oben, wenn man sich mit einem Flugzeug über den Boden erhebt. Aus dieser Perspektive wird die Mannigfaltigkeit der Lebensräume sichtbar, die auf kleinem Raum nebeneinander existieren. Es wird aber auch deutlich, wie schmal und verletzlich das grüne Band des Lebens entlang der Donau ist. Die Auen sind umgeben von intensiv genutzten Agrarsteppen, der Nationalpark liegt mitten in der boomenden Centrope-Region und ist permanent den Begehrlichkeiten der Menschen ausgesetzt.

Taucht man hingegen unter die Oberfläche der Altarme, erschließt sich einem eine neue Welt. Den meisten von uns sind bunte tropische Korallenriffe vertrauter als die Unterwasserwelt der Augewässer. Besonders geeignet, um den amphibischen Charakter der Au darzustellen, sind Aufnahmen, die die Landschaft teils über, teils unter Wasser einfangen. Nachtaufnahmen zeichnen ein fremdes, verklärtes Bild der Au, das jedoch nicht die Wirklichkeit abbildet, sondern aus den technischen Limitierungen der Fotografie heraus entsteht. Langzeitbelichtungen zeigen die Au nur beschienen vom schwachen Licht des Mondes, Sterne zeichnen ihre Bahnen in den Nachthimmel, Wolken werden vom Wind durch das Bild getrieben, die Oberfläche der Donau verschwimmt zu einem glatten Wasserspiegel.

KAPITEL 1

DIE DONAU

DIE LEBENSADER DER AU

AUWÄLDER SÄUMEN DEN STROM

Die Donau ist die Lebensader der Auen. Vor der großen Flussregulierung im 19. Jahrhundert war der Strom in den Donauniederungen reich verzweigt. Ein dichtes Netz von Haupt-, Neben- und Altarmen durchzog die Landschaft und war fortwährender Veränderung unterworfen. Das Flussbett verlagerte sich, Altarme verlandeten und neue entstanden; Inseln wurden aufgeschüttet und später wieder abgetragen, Waldflächen bildeten sich und wurden anschließend von Hochwässern vernichtet.

Freie Fließstrecken der Donau finden sich außerhalb des Nationalparks Donau-Auen nur noch im engen Tal der Wachau. Auf der gesamten übrigen Strecke sind die Ufer verbaut und bieten einen trostlosen Anblick. Die Kraft der Donau, die sie umgebende Landschaft zu gestalten und zu verändern, ist teilweise noch im Nationalpark am Werk und wird heute durch flussbauliche Maßnahmen weiter gefördert.

1

DIE DONAU – EIN GEBIRGSFLUSS

Im Bereich der österreichischen Donauauen ist die Donau ein Gebirgsfluss. Diese Definition scheint dem ersten Anschein der ruhig und gemächlich dahinfließenden Donau zu widersprechen. Dennoch ist sie ein machtvoller Strom, der auf der Strecke durch den Nationalpark jährlich 350.000 Kubikmeter Geschiebe transportiert und durch die hohe Feinsediment-Fracht von mehreren Millionen Tonnen im Jahr sein Wasser graugrün färbt. Wenn man sich in die Donau begibt, wird die Kraft der starken Strömung unmittelbar erlebbar. Und unter Wasser hört man das charakteristische Singen des transportierten Geschiebes.

UFER DER DONAU

Natürliche Ufer an der Donau sind überaus selten geworden. Nur wenige Uferabschnitte lassen erahnen, wie der Strom vor der nahezu völligen Verbauung ausgesehen hat: Weite Schotterflächen lagern vor dem Auwald und werden von den Wellen der Donau umspielt. Die Uferbereiche sind ein extremer Lebensraum, der am häufigsten dem Wechsel zwischen Überflutung und Trockenfallen ausgesetzt ist. Dennoch sind es gerade diese Ufer, welche so wertvollen Tieren wie den Flussuferläufern Raum zum Brüten bieten.

Reich strukturierte Ufer mit ruhigen Buchten und Schotterbänken sind auch für die Fortpflanzung vieler Donaufische von großer Bedeutung. Buchten bieten Fischlarven und Jungfischen reichlich Nahrung und einen sicheren Ort zum Heranwachsen, bis sie groß und kräftig genug sind, auch in der rauen Umgebung des offenen Stromes zu überleben. Viele der gut 60 Fischarten, die im Bereich der Donauauen leben, benötigen diese Flachwasserbereiche zur Fortpflanzung.

DIE INSELN BEI ORTH

Inseln, wie hier bei Orth an der Donau, erstrecken sich mancherorts in den Strom. Sie entstehen in strömungsgeschützten Flussabschnitten, wo im Laufe der Zeit größere Schotterbänke entstehen. Nach der weiteren Ablagerung von feineren Sedimenten, wie Sand und Schlamm, fassen Weiden und Pappeln Fuß, verfestigen mit ihren Wurzeln den Boden und ermöglichen es der jungen Insel, sich im ständigen Kampf gegen die erodierende Kraft der Donau zu behaupten.

Durch das Mondlicht, das die dünne Bewölkung durchdringt,

INSEL IM STROM

Der niedrige Wasserstand der Donau lässt das Schotterufer deutlich erkennen, welches die Insel wie ein Gürtel umschließt. Auf dieser so kleinen Insel, die nur von einer Handvoll Bäumen bestanden ist, zeigt sich, auf welch kleinem Raum eine Vielzahl von Lebensräumen existieren kann: Hoch aufragender Wald, Bereiche, die von niedrigen Strauchweiden bewachsen sind, angeschwemmtes Totholz, alles vom Schotterfeld des Ufers eingefasst und von der Donau umgeben.

Aber nicht nur räumlich sind die Inseln sehr vielgestaltig, auch im Lauf eines Jahres, besser gesagt, abhängig vom Wasserstand der Donau, ändert sich ihr Erscheinungsbild. Bei Niedrigwasser sind sie direkt mit dem Auwald verbunden, steigt der Pegel, werden sie gänzlich von Wasser umgeben; bei Hochwasser gehen sie völlig in der Donau unter.

1

GELEGE DES FLUSSREGENPFEIFERS *(Charadrius dubius)*

Tarnen und Täuschen sind die Strategien, mit denen der Flussregenpfeifer seinen Nachwuchs schützt. Die Eier legt er völlig ungeschützt auf den nackten Schotterboden, wo sie dank ihrer perfekten Tarnung nahezu unsichtbar sind. Kommt dennoch ein Räuber zu nahe an das Nest, zeigt das Weibchen das faszinierende Verhalten des Verleitens. Es erweckt durch Hinken und Hängenlassen eines Flügels den Eindruck, verletzt zu sein, und gaukelt so dem potenziellen Nesträuber eine leichte Beute vor. Dabei entfernt sich der Vogel, den Feind im Schlepptau, immer weiter vom Gelege, und fliegt abschließend einfach davon. Der irritierte Feind hat nun sowohl das Gelege als auch den vermeintlich flügellahmen Altvogel aus den Augen verloren.

Aber nicht nur Fressfeinde stellen eine Gefahr für die Nachkommen des Flussregenpfeifers dar. Allein das Anlegen des Nestes auf den Schotterflächen entlang der Donau und der Nebenarme stellt eine ständige Bedrohung dar. Denn diese Flächen sind nur deshalb frei und vegetationslos, weil sie häufig von Hochwässern, die eben auch zur Brutzeit auftreten können, überflutet werden. An diesen Umstand haben sich die Vögel im Laufe ihrer Evolution angepasst und sind in der Lage, den Verlust eines Geleges mit bis zu drei neuen Gelegen in einer Brutsaison auszugleichen.

Obschon sich der Flussregenpfeifer an seine unstete und gefahrvolle Umgebung anzupassen vermochte, dem zerstörerischen Einfluss des Menschen hat er wenig entgegenzusetzen. Flussregulierungen nahmen ihm den Großteil seiner Brutreviere, und an den wenigen verbliebenen Inseln, Sand- und Schotterbänken wird er nur allzu häufig durch Menschen vom Gelege verscheucht.

Dunkle Gewitterwolken kündigen an, dass sich eine Regenfront der Au nähert. Heftige Regenfälle sind auch im riesigen Einzugsgebiet der Donau niedergegangen und lassen ihren Wasserstand nun steigen. Der Strom tritt über seine Ufer und fließt durch seine Seitenarme.

WASSER DER DONAU DURCHSTRÖMT EINEN NEBENARM

Dieses Bild zeigt denselben Seitenarm wie die folgenden Seiten und macht deutlich, wie rasch und drastisch sich das Erscheinungsbild der dynamischen Augewässer ändern kann. Aus unbewegten, seichten Lacken werden reißende Bäche, die bei großen Hochwasserereignissen selbst zu riesigen Strömen anwachsen können. Diesen Kräften haben Wasserpflanzen oder Schilfflächen an den Ufern nichts entgegenzusetzen, sie werden von den Fluten entwurzelt und fortgetragen.

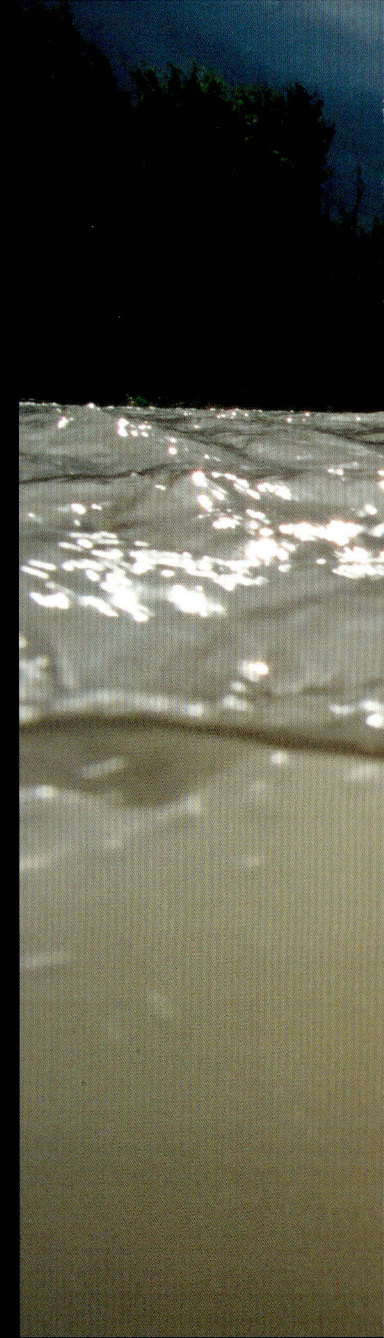

FREIE SCHOTTERFLÄCHE ENTLANG EINES NEBENARMES

Der Mitterhaufen bei Haslau ist wohl die wildeste und ursprünglichste Region der Donauauen. Eine Reihe von Seitenarmen, die mit der Donau in Verbindung stehen, durchzieht die Au wie ein Netz. Diese werden bei steigendem Wasserstand unmittelbar in das Fließgeschehen der Donau eingebunden und stellen gleichsam die Nabelschnur dar, durch die das Ökosystem Au mit dem Strom in Verbindung steht.

Bei Überschwemmungen gerät der Gewässergrund in Bewegung, Sande und Schotter werden abgetragen und anderorts wieder abgelagert; an den Prallhängen entstehen steile Uferböschungen, in denen der Eisvogel seine Bruthöhlen gräbt. Fallen diese Seitenarme bei Niedrigwasser trocken, entstehen ausgedehnte, vegetationslose Schotterfelder, die ebenso wie die natürlichen Donauufer, einen seltenen und überaus wertvollen Lebensraum bilden.

1

1

SCHWIMMENDER BIBER
(Castor fiber)

Selbst Tiere, die sich bestens im Wasser zurecht finden wie der Biber, sind vom Hochwasser beeinträchtigt. Da ihre Bauten überschwemmt sind und sie keine Rückzugmöglichkeiten haben, sind die ansonst sehr scheuen, nacht- und dämmerungsaktiven Tiere im überfluteten Auwald auch tagsüber häufig zu beobachten.

HOCHWASSER IM AUWALD

So katastrophal diese Ereignisse auch für viele Individuen sind, so wichtig sind sie für das Ökosystem Au. Natürliche Flussauen sind keine ruhigen Laubwälder, die von einigen Gewässern durchzogen werden. Es sind vielmehr stark veränderliche Lebensräume, die ihre Einzigartigkeit durch die enge Verbindung mit dem Strom gewinnen.

AULANDSCHAFT IM MONDLICHT

Augewässer mit unbewachsenen Ufern und Schotterbänken sind typisch für natürliche Ausysteme. Ständig wechselnde Wasserstände und regelmäßige Hochwässer verändern laufend und dynamisch die Uferzonen der Altarme.

DIE FLUT DES FRÜHJAHRS

Schmilzt im Frühling der Schnee in den Alpen, führen die großen Zubringer, wie Inn, Enns und Salzach, der Donau enorme Wassermassen zu.

Erst aus dem Flugzeug wird ersichtlich, wie weiträumig die Au unter Wasser steht; oft geht das gesamte Gebiet zwischen Marchfelddamm und Strom in den eisigen Fluten unter.

1

1

ÜBERFLUTETER AUWALD

Weite Teile der Au stehen nach Hochwasserereignissen oft tagelang unter Wasser. Die Fluten bringen Unmengen an nährstoffreichem Sediment in die Au und tragen zur enormen Produktivität der Auwälder bei.

Die aus egoistischer Sicht wohl unangenehmste Begleiterscheinung von Hochwässern ist der Umstand, dass Gelsen nun schier unbegrenzte Fortpflanzungsmöglichkeiten finden. In den Tagen und Wochen nach solchen Fluten wird die Zuneigung zum Lebensraum Au durch diese Blutsauger auf eine harte Probe gestellt. Für das Ökosystem Donauauen sind sie aber ein unverzichtbarer Bestandteil seiner Funktionsfähigkeit.

NACH DER FLUT

Nach dem Schrecken des Hochwassers kehrt wieder Ruhe in die Au ein. Auf einer neu aufgeschichteten Schotterbank lässt sich ein Biber nieder, um sein Fell zu putzen. Im Hintergrund sind noch Wasserpflanzen zu erkennen, die vom Hochwasser ausgeris-

ALTARMUFER BEI NIEDRIGWASSER

Im Herbst weist die Donau oft sehr niedrige Pegel auf. Dann sinkt auch der Wasserstand in den Altarmen, und diese fallen teilweise trocken. Die kleinen Inseln und Teile des vormaligen Gewässergrundes können nun zu Fuß erreicht werden.

1

WECHSELNDE WASSERSTÄNDE – EIN CHARAKTERISTIKUM DER NEBENARME

Zieht sich das Wasser aus den Altarmen zurück, bleibt angeschwemmtes Holz am Ufer zurück. Auch die Muscheln, die dem zurückweichenden Wasser nicht folgen konnten, liegen auf dem Trockenen und bieten eine willkommene Nahrungsquelle für Landbewohner.

WALD UND WASSER
– DIE PRÄGENDEN FAKTOREN DER AU

Beide Bilder illustrieren das Zusammenwirken von Wald und Wasser, sie scheinen auf den ersten Blick ähnlich, in der Dimension trennen sie jedoch zwei Größenordnungen. Links zu sehen ist eine Luftaufnahme eines ausgewachsenen Pappelwaldes, der unter Wasser steht. Das Bild zur Rechten zeigt wenige Zentimeter große, junge Weiden, die auf frisch aufgeschüttetem Sandboden keimen und diesen wie einen Rasen bedecken.

Weiden und Pappeln sind die Pioniere unter den Aubäumen. Millionenfach treiben ihre Flugsamen im Frühjahr durch die Luft, bereit neue, vegetationslose Flächen zu besiedeln. Gehen sie auf geeigneten Stellen nieder, bilden sich bald dichte Bestände junger Bäume, die auch imstande sind, längere Überflutungen zu überleben. Mit ihren Wurzeln verfestigen sie den neuen Boden, und ihre oberirdischen Teile begünstigen bei Überschwemmungen die Ablagerung feiner Sedimente. Somit trotzen sie dem Fluss wieder ein Stück Land a und lassen es zu Auwald werden.

KAPITEL 2

ALTARME

LEBEN AN DEN GEWÄSSERN DER AU

DAS KÜHWÖRTHERWASSER

Die Gewässer der Au sind sehr vielgestaltig, ihre Entstehung verdanken sie jedoch alle der Donau. Das Ausmaß, in dem sie noch mit dem Strom und dessen Grundwasserregime in Verbindung stehen, charakterisiert die verschiedenen Typen von Augewässern. Die dynamischen Nebenarme werden bei hohen Pegelständen von Wasser durchströmt und bei Niedrigwasser zu kahlen Schotterflächen. Entfernt man sich vom Strom, so ändert sich auch die Erscheinung der Augewässer. Röhrichtgürtel und Sumpfpflanzen bewachsen die Ufer und ein Dickicht von Wasser- und Schwimmpflanzen besiedeln den Wasserkörper.
Diese dicht verwachsenen Altarme und Autümpel sind Lebensraum einer Unzahl von Amphibien, Reptilien, Fischen, Insekten und anderer wirbelloser Tiere.
Sie tragen trotz ihrer Reichhaltigkeit an Leben aber bereits den Keim des Todes in sich: Augewässer, die nicht mehr in das Fließgeschehen der Donau eingebunden werden, beginnen zu verlanden. Im Laufe der Zeit bilden sich dicke Sedimentschichten am Grund, Röhricht und Holzgewächse dringen immer weiter vor, bis schließlich nur noch ein feuchter Graben zurückbleibt.

TEICHROSE *(Nuphar lutea)*

Die Donauauen sind ein Kontinuum verschiedener Lebensräume, über wie auch unter Wasser - dieser Vielfalt verdanken sie ihre enorme Biodiversität.

Das Kühwörtherwasser war vor der großen Donauregulierung Teil des verzweigten Flussbettes der Donau. Heute zeigt es die charakteristischen Eigenschaften eines, vom Strom abgeschnittenen, Altwassers. Seine Wasserführung ist hauptsächlich durch den Grundwasserspiegel bestimmt. Aber auch diese Schwankungen werden durch die mächtigen Schichten von feinen Sedimenten am Grund gebremst, wodurch der Wasserstand relativ konstant bleibt. Seine Ufer sind zum Teil von ausgedehnten Schilfflächen bestanden, die Oberfläche bedecken Teich- und Seerosen.

VON HOCHWASSER DURCHSTRÖMTER NEBENARM

Augewässer sind nicht immer idyllisch und ruhig, bei höheren Pegelständen der Donau werden aus den stillen Nebenarmen fließende Gewässer. Die periodische Ausschwemmung des Beckengrundes ist von hoher Bedeutung, denn sie verhindert die Ablagerung feiner Sedimente und das Aufkommen von höheren Wasserpflanzen. Dadurch wird das sonst schrittweise erfolgende Verlanden dieser Gewässer verhindert.

LUFTAUFNAHME EINES ALTARMES

Fliegt man über die Auen, wird deutlich, wie reich strukturiert dieser Lebensraum ist. Die Wasserflächen der Altarme sind von Teichrosen bedeckt, vereinzelt finden sich kleinere Schilfbestände, Treibholzhaufen wurden an den Ufern angeschwemmt, am festen Land wachsen hohe Weiden. Nur erahnen kann man die Diversität unter Wasser.

EINE JAGDSPINNE *(Dolomedes fimbriatus)* AUF DER WASSEROBERFLÄCHE

Jagdspinnen sind perfekt an das Leben an Gewässern angepasst. Sie können unter Wasser tauchen und sind auch, dank ihrer Behaarung an den Beinen, in der Lage, über das freie Wasser zu laufen. Beide Fähigkeiten nutzen sie, um vor Feinden zu fliehen und um ihre Beute zu jagen. Diese besteht zumeist aus Wasserinsekten oder Kaulquappen, die sie durch die Wasseroberfläche hindurch ergreifen und mit einem Giftbiss binnen Sekunden töten. Große Weibchen, die besonders viel Energie zur Reifung ihrer Eier benötigen, können sogar kleine Fische bis zur Größe von Stichlingen überwältigen.

SCHWIMMENDE **RINGELNATTER**
(Natrix natrix)

Die Ringelnatter ist die häufigste Schlangenart in den Auen. Sie ist hervorragend an das Leben am Wasser angepasst. Als gute Schwimmerin und Taucherin kann sie neben ihrer Hauptnahrung - den Amphibien - auch Fische erbeuten.

DER EISVOGEL *(Alcedo atthis)*

Der Eisvogel ist der einzige heimische Vertreter einer überaus großen Familie von Vögeln, die vor allem die Tropen der Alten Welt und Australasiens besiedelt und sich durch ihr farbenprächtiges Gefieder auszeichnet. Er ist eine charakteristische Art natürlicher, dynamischer Fließgewässer und durch seine Ansprüche hinsichtlich Brutraum und Jagdrevier an diese Lebensräume gebunden. Demzufolge ist er hierzulande in seinem Bestand stark gefährdet, in den Donauauen findet man noch den größten geschlossenen Eisvogelbestand Österreichs.

Seine Nisthöhlen gräbt er in steile Uferböschungen, die sich meist an den Prallhängen von durchströmten Nebenarmen befinden. In Frühjahr gräbt das Weibchen die bis zu drei Meter lange Brutröhre, während das Männchen mit seinen Füßen den Abraum aus der Höhle befördert. Dort ist das Gelege vor Räubern wie Dachs oder Fuchs zwar sicher, jedoch besteht die Gefahr, dass bei starkem Hochwasser die gesamte Böschung abgetragen und das Nest zerstört wird. Als Anpassung an diese Risiken brüten Eisvögel in günstigen Jahren bis zu dreimal. Die sehr hohe Reproduktionsfähigkeit ist auch deshalb vonnöten, da in strengen Wintern, in denen viele Gewässer zufrieren, die Eisvögel von ihrer Nahrungsquelle - Fischen - abgeschnitten werden und nicht selten ein Großteil des Bestandes durch Hunger zugrunde geht.

Oft kann man Eisvögel auf ihren Sitzwarten, meist Ästen, die über das Wasser ragen, beobachten. Dort halten sie nach Fischen Ausschau, die sie durch einen gezielten Tauchstoß erbeuten. Die Fische werden auf dem Ast totgeschlagen und mit dem Kopf voran verschlungen.

SEEFROSCH *(Rana ridibunda)* IN EINEM STARK VERWACHSENEM ALTARM

Vor allem für die heimische Amphibienfauna sind natürliche Auen von essenzieller Bedeutung. Die Doppellebigkeit der Amphibien, das Leben im Wasser und an Land, ihre auffällige Metamorphose von der Larve zum adulten Tier macht sie zu Sinnbildern der Au, die ihrerseits die Verbindung zwischen Wasser und Land darstellt. In den Donauauen finden sich fast alle heimischen Amphibien, insgesamt leben hier - wenn man den aus dem See- und Kleinen Wasserfrosch entstandenen Hybriden Teichfrosch als Art ansieht - 13 Arten von Fröschen, Unken, Kröten und Molchen.

Selbst die kleine Zahl der bei uns lebenden Amphibien umfasst faszinierende Arten, und man kann nur erahnen, wie groß die Vielfalt an Farben, Formen und Verhalten der tropischen Arten sein mag. Daher ist es verwunderlich, dass Carl von Linné die Lurche als „schreckliche und widerwärtige Tiere" beschrieb, die wegen ihres Gestankes und des schrecklichen Giftes verhasst seien, weshalb „der Schöpfer kaum Kraft verwendet hat, um viele von ihnen zu schaffen". Es fällt schwer, einem so Großen der Naturgeschichte zu widersprechen, in diesem Fall aber hat sich Linné gründlich geirrt.

Im Laufe der Evolution von Amphibien war die Eroberung des Landes eine fundamentale Entwicklungsrichtung. Dieser entscheidende Schritt war es, der die Entstehung aller Landwirbeltiere, der Reptilien, der Vögel, der Säugetiere - und somit auch von uns Menschen - ermöglichte. Im Gegensatz zu uns, haben fast alle Amphibien die endgültige Trennung vom Wasser aber nie vollzogen. Bis heute sind sie bei ihrer Fortpflanzung an das Wasser gebunden. Dort legen sie die Eier, aus denen wasserlebende Larven schlüpfen, die über Kiemen atmen. Erst während der Metamorphose entwickeln sie ihre Extremitäten, verlieren die Flossen und bilden Lungen aus. Im übertragenen Sinn kann man daher den evolutionären Durchbruch im Erdaltertum jedes Jahr in unseren Auen nachempfinden, wenn ehedem kiemenatmende, flossentragende Tiere das Festland erobern.

Kaum ein Zitat trifft so passend auf die Metamorphose der Amphibien zu, wie der Essaytitel des berühmten Evolutionsbiologen T. G. Dobzhanski, der sagt: „Nichts in der Biologie ergibt einen Sinn außer im Licht der Evolution."

SCHWIMMENDER SEEFROSCH
(Rana ridibunda)

Auch unter Wasser sind Grünfrösche gut getarnt. Die dunklen, grünen und braunen Flecken lösen die Form des Frosches auf; das macht ihn zwischen den Wasserpflanzen schwer erkennbar. Die Frösche zeigen auch eine helle Bauchseite, welche sie den nach oben gerichteten Blicken von Raubfischen entzieht.

TEICHMUSCHEL IM UNTERLAUF DES ROSSKOPFARMES

Eine Teichmuschel durchpflügt den Grund eines Altarmes. Deutlich erkennt man, dass dieser Altarm noch zeitweise von Hochwasser durchströmt wird. Der grobe Schotterboden ist nur von einer dünnen Schicht feiner Sedimente bedeckt und Wasserpflanzen fehlen fast völlig. Auch existieren entlang der Ufer kaum Röhricht- oder Sumpfpflanzengesellschaften, wie sie für Altwässer typisch sind, die vom Strom kaum noch beeinflusst werden.

Für die heimischen Wassermollusken sind Auensysteme im Allgemeinen von existenzieller Bedeutung. Sie sind Refugien, in welchen die Tiere vor Lebensraumverlust und Umweltverschmutzung einigermaßen sicher sind, und von denen aus ihre Larven die Fließgewässer wieder besiedeln können. Man nimmt an, dass etwa die Hälfte der wasserbewohnenden Weichtierarten aussterben würde, gingen die dynamischen Augewässer verloren.

SILBERREIHER *(Egretta alba)*

Das bevorzugte Jagdrevier des Silberreihers sind die seichten Uferregionen der Altarme, durch die er mit seinen langen Beinen schreitet und durch schnelles Zustoßen mit dem langen, spitzen Schnabel seine Beute aus dem Wasser fängt. Er stellt vor allem Fischen und Amphibien nach. Zu seinem Nahrungsspektrum gehören aber auch Wirbellose wie Insekten, Würmer und Wasserschnecken.

Der Silberreiher zählt zu den wohl schönsten Aubewohnern – diese Schönheit war es aber auch, die ihn an den Rand der Ausrottung drängte. Die Schmuckfedern der Männchen waren im neunzehnten Jahrhundert in der Damenmode so begehrt, dass die Vögel zu Tausenden abgeschossen wurden. Aber noch bis in die heutige Zeit wird ihm, als vermeintlichem Fischereischädling, nachgestellt. Dieses Schicksal teilt er mit seinem Verwandten dem Graureiher und auch mit den Kormoranen. Der permanente Jagddruck ließ den Silberreiher überaus scheu werden; seine Fluchtdistanz beträgt Hunderte von Metern und nötigt dem Fotografen ein hohes Maß an Beharrlichkeit ab.

In den Donauauen sind diese eleganten Vögel das ganze Jahr hindurch anzutreffen, sie brüten jedoch in den ausgedehnten Schilfbeständen um den Neusiedlersee.

Zu sehen ist die letzte Phase im Dasein eines Altarmes. Das Gewässer wurde vollständig von der Donau abgeschnitten, und im Laufe der Zeit lagerten sich große Mengen an Sediment auf seinem Grund ab. Der Wald rückt unaufhaltsam vor und wird sich in wenigen Jahren gänzlich über das ehemalige Gewässer ausbreiten.

ALTARM IN AGONIE

In einem dynamischen Auensystem ist die Verlandung von Gewässern ein völlig natürlicher Vorgang, denn gleichzeitig werden durch die Umlagerungen von Nebenarmen laufend neue Gewässer gebildet. Nur wenn die Dynamik der Au verloren geht und keine neuen Altarme entstehen, führt das Verlanden allmählich zu einem Verlust der Altwässer und zu einer Monotonisierung des Lebensraumes.

ROTBAUCHUNKE
(Bombina bombina)

Das auffälligste Merkmal der Rotbauchunken ist die namensgebende Warnfärbung ihrer Körperunterseite. Den besten Schutz bietet ihnen jedoch ihre grau-braun marmorierte Oberseite, wodurch die Tiere kaum in den verkrauteten Gewässern oder am Uferboden ausgemacht werden können. Bedroht sie dennoch ein Feind, und eine Flucht ist zwecklos, zeigen sie den sogenannten Unkenreflex: sie nehmen die Kahnstellung ein, wobei sie den Rücken durchbiegen, den Kopf und die Extremitäten anheben, um so ihre rot-schwarze Warnfarbe zu präsentieren. Diese Warnung signalisiert dem Feind, dass die Unke in ihren Hautdrüsen ein giftiges Sekret produziert: Der Feind möge erst gar nicht versuchen, sie zu fressen. Die Kombination aus getarnter Oberseite und warnender Unterseite ist eine faszinierende Manifestation dieser beiden so unterschiedlichen Überlebensstrategien.

ALTARM
IN DER ABENDDÄMMERUNG

Vom letzten Hochwasser noch etwas mitgenommen wirkt das Rohrglanzgras, das am Ufer der Altarme wächst. Es überlebt auch an Gewässern, die häufig von Hochwasser betroffen sind, und wo sich kein Binsen- oder Schilfröhricht ausbreiten kann. Durch sein dichtes Wurzelgeflecht verfestigt es die Uferbereiche und schützt diese somit vor der erodierenden Kraft des Wassers.

BIBER *(Castor fiber)*
BEI NACHT

Der hauptsächlich dämmerungs- und nachtaktive Biber ist mit seinem dichten Fell und den verschließbaren Nasen- und Ohrenöffnungen bestens an das Leben im Wasser angepasst. Es sind überaus scheue Tiere, die bei der geringsten Störung, mit lautem Klatschen des Schwanzes, abtauchen.

Alle heute in den Auen lebenden Biber gehen auf Wiedereinbürgerung zurück, denn bereits Mitte des 19. Jahrhunderts wurden die großen Nager in Mitteleuropa ausgerottet. Die Biber wurden wegen ihres Pelzes und Fleisches gejagt. Besonders begehrt aber war das Bibergeil. Bibergeil oder Castoreum wurde aus den Drüsensäcken gewonnen, die beide Geschlechter besitzen, um Duftmarken zu setzen. Bereits seit der Antike wurde dieser Substanz eine Heilwirkung bei diversen neurologischen Leiden nachgesagt, und sie blieb bis zum Verschwinden des Bibers gefragt.

ALTARM BEI NACHT

Nur vom Mondlicht beschienen, zeichnen einige Wolken ihre Bahnen über den Himmel.

Wenn die Nacht über die Au hereinbricht, werden unzählige Tiere aktiv. Wasserfledermäuse fliegen dicht über der Wasseroberfläche und suchen mit ihrem Echolot nach Insekten. Auch viele Amphibien gehen lieber in den kühlen, feuchten Nachtstunden auf Jagd, von den Gelsen ganz abgesehen. An Sommerabenden kann man die Männchen der Glühwürmchen beobachten, die auf der Suche nach Weibchen Leuchtspuren durch den Auwald ziehen.

FLIEGENDE KORMORANE
(Phalacrocorax carbo)

Spätestens bei Einbruch der Dunkelheit kehren die letzten Kormorane auf ihre Schlafbäume zurück. Die Bewegung der Flügel verschwimmt im schwachen Mondlicht, und die Vögel erinnern am Foto beinahe an Flughörnchen.

VON EINEM BIBER BENAGTER BAUM

Seitdem im Nationalpark die forstwirtschaftliche Nutzung des Auwaldes ausgesetzt wurde, ist der Biber das Säugetier, das den Wald am auffälligsten gestaltet. Entlang der Donau und der Altwässer fällt er Pappeln und Weiden von teilweise beachtlicher Größe. Diese stürzen zumeist ins Wasser, wo die Biber sich an der Rinde junger Zweige gütlich tun. Somit trägt er wesentlich zur Bildung

TOTER BAUM

Sie sind selten geworden: Wälder, in denen abgestorbene Bäume stehen. Totes Holz ist jedoch ein überaus wichtiger Bestandteil des Waldes und stellt Lebensraum und Nahrung für eine Vielzahl von Tierarten dar. Die Baumhöhlen werden von Mardern, Fledermäusen, Eulen und vielen anderen Tieren bewohnt. Besonders wertvoll sind abgestorbene, aber noch stehende Bäume. Diese Dürrlinge sind dem prallen Sonnenlicht ausgesetzt und wichtige Brutstätte unzähliger Insekten.

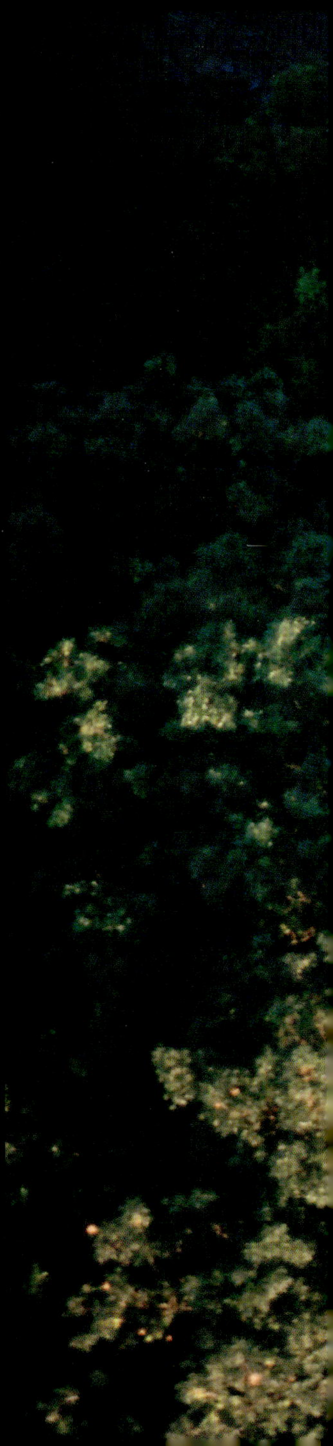

SCHWEFELPORLING
(Laetiporus sulphureus)

Von den rund 1500 Pilzarten, die in der Au absterbendes oder totes Holz besiedeln, ist der Schwefelporling zweifelsfrei der schönste. Er besiedelt überwiegend absterbende Silberweiden und lebt dann noch einige Zeit auf dem toten Baum. Seine intensiv gelb oder orange gefärbten Fruchtkörper findet man das ganze Jahr hindurch.

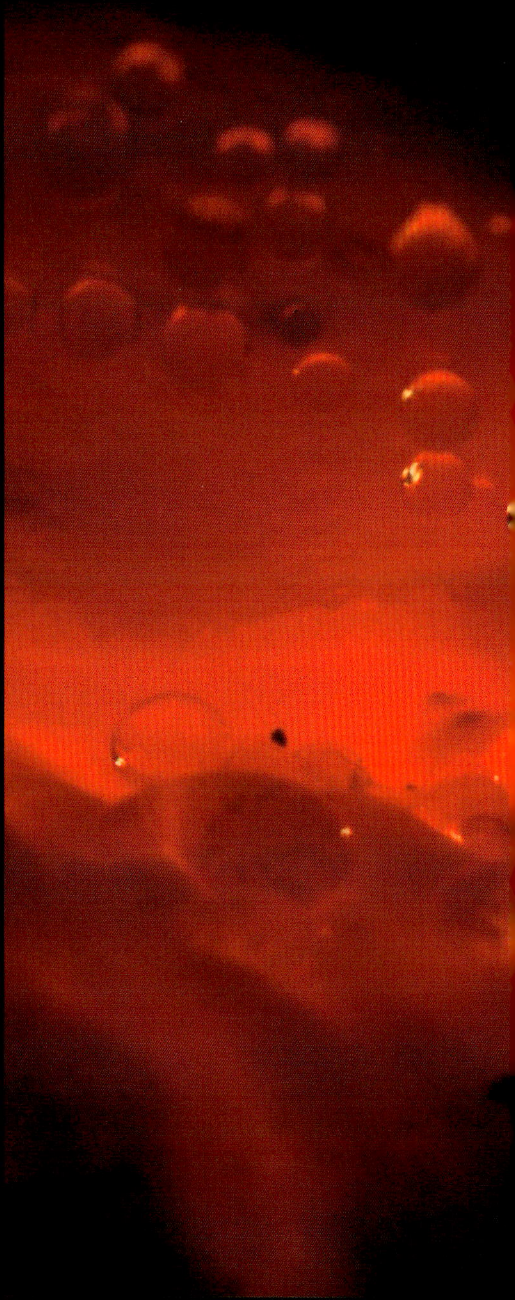

TAUTROPFEN AN EINEM SCHWEFELPORLING

Über Nacht sammeln sich Tautropfen zwischen den Konsolen des Schwefelporlings. Das Blitzgerät wurde bei dieser Aufnahme direkt auf den Pilz gesetzt, das Licht durchdringt den Fruchtkörper und bringt ihn von innen her zum Leuchten.

RAUPE DES SCHWAMMSPINNERS
(Lymantria dispar)

Als ob sie schwebte, hängt die Raupe des Schwammspinners an einem unsichtbaren Seidenfaden aus den Baumkronen. Es ist ein waghalsiges Unterfangen, bietet sie sich doch förmlich den Vögeln als Nahrung an. Die Raupe verlässt sich allein auf ihre langen Borsten, die sie für Fressfeinde unattraktiv machen.

LAUBFROSCH
(Hyla arborea)

Der Laubfrosch gehört zu einer überaus artenreichen Familie von Fröschen, die weltweit verbreitet ist, mit der größten Vielfalt jedoch die Tropen besiedelt. In unseren Breiten ist er die einzige Froschart, die auf Bäumen lebt. Mit Haftscheiben an seinen Fingern und Zehen sowie der klebrigen Bauchhaut ist er ein hervorragender Kletterer, der sich bis in Höhen von zehn Metern vorwagt.

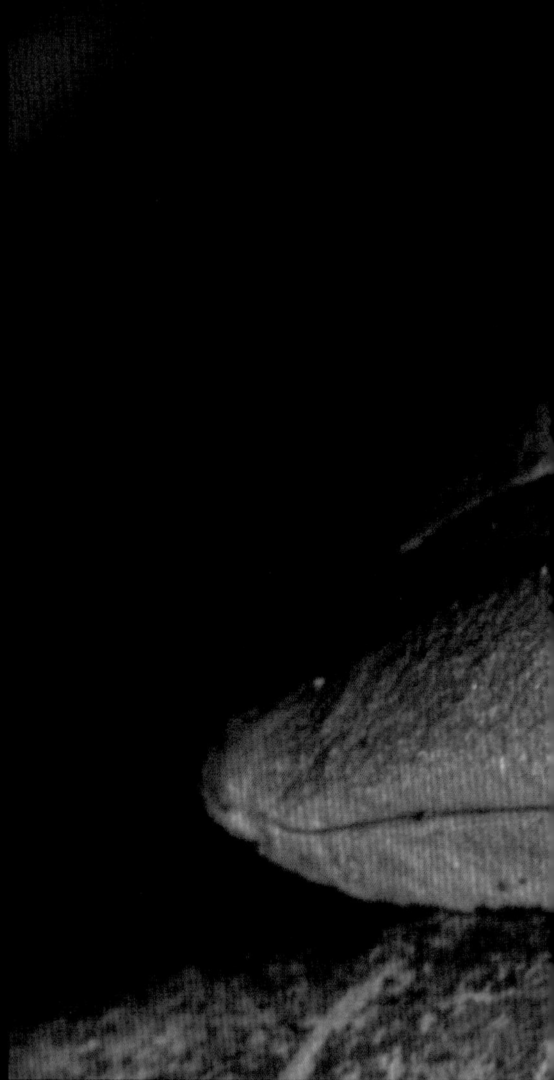

DER AUWALD STEHT UNTER WASSER

Bei starken Hochwässern steht der Auwald metertief unter Wasser. Sträucher, selbst junge Bäume werden zur Gänze überflutet. Der überflutete Wald ist für uns beinahe undurchdringlich, begibt man sich dennoch in das Chaos, bekommt man eine Vorstellung, welch ein einschneidendes Ereignis eine Überschwemmung für die Bewohner des Auwaldes sein kann.

OSTERLUZEI
(Aristolochia clematitis)

Nicht von ungefähr erinnern die Blüten der Osterluzei an die Form der Kelche tropischer Kannenpflanzen, denn auch die Osterluzei fängt Insekten. Diese werden nicht verdaut, dienen als Stickstoffquelle und sollen die Blüten bestäuben. Ähnlich wie beim Aronstab werden Insekten in die Kesselfalle gelockt, durch Reusenhaare an der Flucht gehindert und erst nach deren Verwelken pollenbeladen wieder entlassen, um in die nächste Falle zu tappen.

Wichtig ist die Osterluzei auch als Futterpflanze für die Raupen des Osterluzeifalters. Die Donauauen sind wichtige Refugien für beide, die Osterluzei und deren Falter.

ARONSTAB *(Arum alpinum)*

Der Aronstab ist ein heimischer Vertreter einer Pflanzenfamilie, die überwiegend in den Tropen beheimatet ist. Er zeigt eine untypische Strategie, sich von Insekten befruchten zu lassen: diese werden nicht durch intensive Färbung, verlockenden Duft oder nahrhaften Nektar angelockt, sondern die Blütenröhren erzeugen Wärme. Insekten, welche die erwärmten Blüten aufsuchen, werden in der Kesselfalle gefangen, und Borstenkränze hindern die Tiere daran, wieder ins Freie zu gelangen. Die Blüte ist so konstruiert, dass Tiere, die bereits Pollen eines anderen Aronstabs mitbringen, diesen zuerst an der Narbe abstreifen. Danach reifen die männlichen Staubblätter und beladen das Insekt erneut mit Pollen. Nach einer Nacht in Gefangenschaft kann das Tier, über die nun verwelkten Borstenhaare, ins Freie klettern, um am kommenden Abend erneut in einer erwärmten Blüte Zuflucht zu suchen.

MOORFROSCH *(Rana arvalis)*

Außerhalb der Fortpflanzungszeit lebt der Moorfrosch, wie die meisten Amphibien der Au, an Land. Aufgrund seiner typischen Marmorierung an Flanken und anderen Merkmalen kann man ihn vom häufigen Springfrosch unterscheiden. In der dynamischen Aulandschaft des Nationalparks ist der Moorfrosch selten, man findet ihn nur vereinzelt in den Randbereichen. Größere Bestände kommen in den Auen nordwestlich von Wien vor.

In der Paarungszeit zeigt der Moorfrosch einen spektakulären Farbwechsel: wie auf Seite 148 zu sehen, legen die Männchen dann ihr intensiv blaues Balzkleid an.

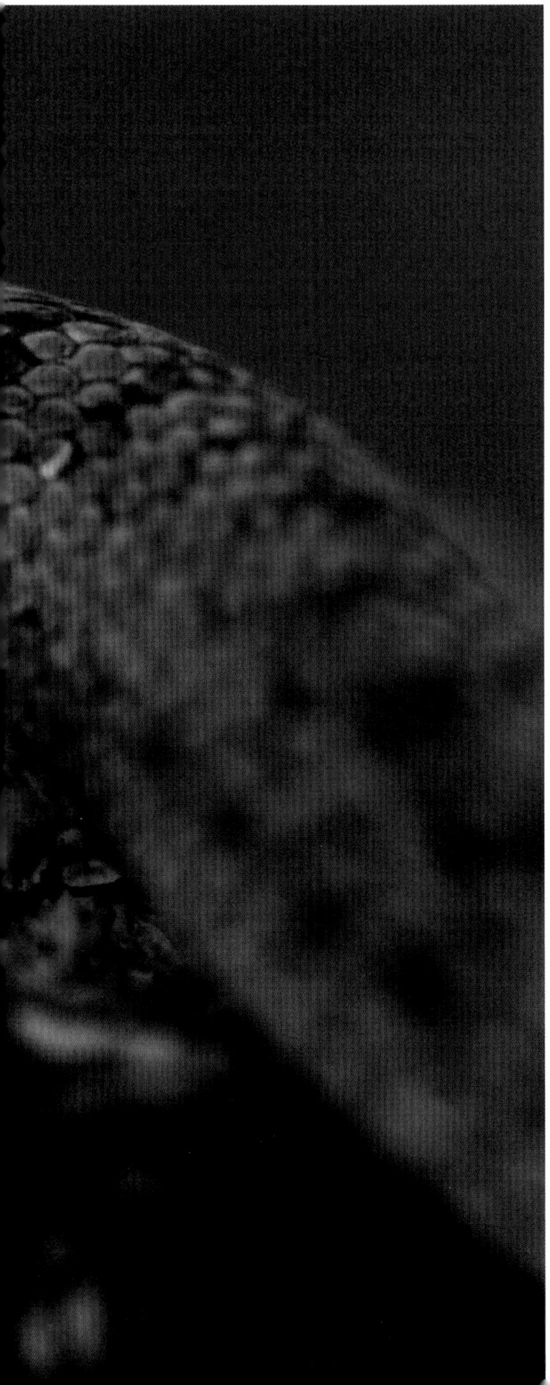

SCHLINGNATTER
(Coronella austriaca)

Die Schlingnatter ist eine besonders wärmeliebende Schlangenart. Sie besiedelt offene und trockene Regionen der Au und ist häufig in der Nähe von Heißländen zu finden. Sie ist eine sehr geschmeidige Schlange, die sich hauptsächlich am Boden bewegt, gelegentlich aber auch in die unteren Etagen von Sträuchern klettert. Ihre Nahrung besteht großteils aus jungen Schlangen, Eidechsen und Blindschleichen, gelegentlich raubt sie auch Nester von Mäusen oder Spitzmäusen aus. Sie tötet ihre Beutetiere, indem sie diese fest umschlingt und dadurch erdrückt. Wird die Schlingnatter selbst von einem Feind bedroht, setzt sie sich mit Bissen zur Wehr.

Wie die Kreuzotter ist auch die Schlingnatter lebendgebärend. Die jungen Schlangen sind bei ihrer Geburt lediglich von dünnen transparenten Schleimhüllen umgeben, aus denen sie sich rasch befreien.

HEISSLÄNDE IM MONDSCHEIN

Vom Licht des untergehenden Mondes beschienen liegt eine karge Heißlände wie eine Insel in den üppigen Wäldern der unteren Lobau. Heißländen bilden sich an Stellen mächtiger Schotterpakete, die später nicht durch Anschüttung feinerer Sedimente bedeckt wurden. Die geringe Bodenauflage und der sehr wasserdurchlässige Untergrund ist daher zu trocken, um Bäumen oder Sträuchern das Wachstum zu ermöglichen. Dafür bildet sich eine savannenähnliche Landschaft mit wunderbaren Trockenrasen, die vor allem im Frühjahr durch die Blüten einer Vielzahl von Orchideenarten besticht. Diese trockenen Standorte stehen in starkem Kontrast zur vom Wasser geprägten Aulandschaft, und bilden Lebensräume für Tiere, die an heiße, trockene Bedingungen angepasst sind. Smaragdeidechse und Gottesanbeterin, welche man üblicherweise gar nicht in feuchten Auen erwarten würde, sind typische Bewohner dieser Landstriche. Somit stellen die Heißländen einen weiteren, fremdartigen Baustein im Mosaik unterschiedlicher Biotope dar, dem Flussauen ihren Artenreichtum verdanken.

Das Vorkommen der sehr seltenen Smaragdeidechsen ist ausschließlich der Existenz der Heißländen zu verdanken. Sie siedeln an warmen aber deckungsreichen Orten und finden in den exotisch trockenen Heißländen, die vom üppig wuchernden Auwald umgeben sind, einen idealen Lebensraum.

MÄNNLICHE SMARAGDEIDECHSE
(Lacerta viridis)

Die Männchen der Smaragdeidechse zeigen ritualisierte Kommentkämpfe. Bevor es zu einer tatsächlichen Auseinandersetzung kommt, versuchen die Tiere den Gegner durch rituelles Heben und Senken des Kopfes und Hin- und Herschlagen des Schwanzes zu beeindrucken. Fühlt sich nach diesem zur Schau stellen der Kräfte keiner der beiden Kontrahenten unterlegen, kommt es zum Kampf. Hierbei wird versucht den Gegner in den Nacken oder in die Extremitäten zu beißen. Smaragdeidechsen sind sehr kräftige Tiere, und es besteht dabei die Gefahr, dass sich die Tiere ernsthaft verletzen. Erkennt einer der Kontrahenten seine drohende Niederlage, beginnt er zu „treteln": Er tritt mit den Vorderbeinen auf der Stelle und hebt und senkt dabei den Kopf. Damit signalisiert er, dass er die Überlegenheit des Gegners anerkennt. Dieser stellt danach den Angriff ein, der Revierkampf ist entschieden und die Verletzungsgefahr minimiert.

KAPITEL 4

JAHRESZEITEN

DIE MACHT DES SAISONALEN WANDELS

VERLANDENDER ALTARM IM HERBST

Dieses Bild zeigt denselben verlandenden Altarm, wie auf Seite 72. Jetzt im Herbst, wenn die abgefallenen Blätter den Boden bedecken, wird deutlich, woher ein Teil des Materials kommt, das Gewässer verlanden lässt. Pflanzliche Überreste, Laub der Bäume, abgebroche ne Äste, abgestorbene Wasserpflanzen sammeln sich am Grund an und werden zu Schlamm zersetzt, der langsam den Altarm auffüllt. Ist das Gewässer nicht mehr mit der Donau in Verbindung, schwemmen keine Hochwässer die Sedimente mehr aus, führt dieser Prozess unweigerlich zum Verschwinden des Altarmes.

SPÄTHERBST AM ALTARM

Im November fallen die letzten Blätter von den Bäumen, die Au ist in feuchten Nebel gehüllt und erscheint trist und leblos. Die Amphibien und Reptilien haben ihre Winterquartiere bezogen, und viele der Singvögel haben schon vor geraumer Zeit den Zug in wärmere Gefilde angetreten.

Die Au ist aber längst nicht ganz ohne Leben, an den Altarmen zeugen gefällte Bäume und abgenagte Äste vom nächtlichen Treiben der Biber.

DIE AU IM HERBST

Wenn sich im Herbst die Blätter der Bäume gelb verfärben, bietet die Au für kurze Zeit einen farbenprächtigen Anblick.

LAUFENDER BIBER *(Castor fiber)*

Ein Biber läuft mit einem Weidenast im Maul über ein Schotterufer. Biber halten keinen Winterschlaf und müssen daher auch in der kalten Jahreszeit genügend pflanzliche Nahrung finden. Die Hauptnahrungsquelle sind jetzt die Äste und Stämme von Weiden und Pappeln, wobei die Tiere aber nicht die Rinde oder das Holz fressen, sondern nur das zwischen Holz und Rinde gelegene, nährstoffreiche Gewebe nutzen. Um an dieses zu gelangen, fällen sie nun vermehrt Bäume entlang der Ufer. Stürzen die Bäume ins Wasser, bleiben sie nicht nur länger genießbar, sie sind für die Tiere auch unter Wasser zugänglich, falls die Gewässer völlig zufrieren.

SONNENUNTERGANG ÜBER DER DONAU

Ein Wintertag neigt sich seinem Ende zu, und eine bitterkalte Nacht bricht über die Au herein. An diesen Tagen ist das Rot der untergehenden Sonne oft die einzige Farbe, die den fahlen, graubraunen Auwald ziert.

EISSCHOLLEN BEDECKEN DIE DONAU

Selten kommt es vor, dass in besonders kalten Wintern die Donau völlig zufriert. Üblicherweise bewirkt die Strömung, dass der Strom größtenteils eisfrei bleibt, vereinzelt treiben dann kleinere Eisschollen im Wasser, und lediglich entlang der Ufer und in seichten, geschützten Buchten bilden sich im Winter kleinere Eisdecken. Bleiben aber über Wochen die Temperaturen weit unter Null, nehmen Zahl und Größe der Eisschollen zu, bis sie sich verbinden und zu einer geschlossenen Eisdecke werden. Das völlige Zufrieren der Donau vertreibt die Tausenden Wasservögel, die im Winter aus Nordeuropa zu Gast sind. Diese wandern nach Süden, wenn die Gewässer ihrer Heimat von Eis bedeckt sind und ihnen somit der Zugang zur Nahrung genommen wird. Friert auch bei uns der Strom zu, müssen diese Vögel weiterziehen.

Große Gefahr droht, wenn die Eisdecke der Donau unvermittelt aufbricht. Dann kann es vorkommen, dass die Eisschollen von der Strömung zu mächtigen Barrieren aufgetürmt werden. Solche Eisstöße haben in der Vergangenheit katastrophale Fluten verursacht, wenn die Eisdämme den Strom zwangen sich ein neues Bett zu suchen, oder plötzlich zerbrachen und sich zerstörerische Flutwellen über das Land ergossen. Einer der Hauptgründe für die Donauregulierung war auch der Gedanke, dass sich im begradigten und konzentrierten Gerinne Eisstöße nicht mehr so leicht bilden können - was auch eingetreten ist.

LACHMÖWE IM WINTERKLEID
(Larus ridibundus)

Im Winter finden sich große Schwärme von Lachmöwen an der Donau ein. Sie weichen dem Eis auf ihren nördlichen Heimatgewässern aus. Lachmöwen sind äußerst geschickte Flieger, die oft ihre Nahrung im Flug von der Wasseroberfläche aufnehmen.

EISDECKE ÜBER EINEM ALTARM

Bleibt die Temperatur längere Zeit unter dem Gefrierpunkt, bedecken dicke Eisschichten die Augewässer. Tiere und Pflanzen haben verschiedenste Strategien entwickelt, um diese extreme Zeit zu überstehen.

AULANDSCHAFT VOR SONNENAUFGANG

Kurz bevor sich die Sonne am Morgen zeigt, erreichen die Temperaturen ihren Tiefpunkt. Die Au erstarrt in der Kälte des Winters, und über den offenen Wasserflächen bildet sich dünner Nebel.

WINTERLICHER ALTARM BEI NACHT

Still und unbewegt liegt ein Altarm in einer kalten Winternacht. Doch Schotterfelder, Steilufer und umgestürzte Bäume zeigen, dass es sich um einen sehr dynamischen Bereich handelt. Dieser Altarm wird häufig von der über die Ufer tretenden Donau durchströmt, Schotterbänke werden abgetragen und an anderen Stellen wieder aufgehäuft, sein Verlauf ändert sich unaufhörlich.

DIE AU BEI KÄLTE UND FINSTERNIS

Selbst in Winternächten zeigt die Au wunderbare Ansichten, wenn sie nur vom Licht des aufgehenden Mondes erhellt wird.

KORMORAN *(Phalacrocorax carbo)*

Der gelbe Kehlsack des Kormorans lässt seine Verwandtschaft mit den Pelikanen erahnen, gemeinsam mit den Tölpeln gehören sie der Ordnung der Ruderfüßer an.

Kormorane ernähren sich von Fischen, denen sie unter Wasser tauchend nachstellen. Im Gegensatz zu den meisten anderen Wasservögeln ist daher ihr Gefieder nicht durch eine Fettschicht wasserabweisend, sondern lässt die Luft bei den Tauchgängen aus dem Federkleid entweichen. Dadurch vermindert sich der Auftrieb der Vögel unter Wasser, und sie können in größere Tiefen tauchen. Der Nachteil dieser Strategie ist jedoch, dass die Vögel nach jedem Tauchgang triefend nass sind und ihr Gefieder trocknen müssen. Häufig sieht man daher Kormorane mit ausgespreizten Flügeln am Flussufer oder auf Bäumen sitzen.

Tagsüber findet man die Kormorane meist beim Fischen an der Donau oder an großen Nebenarmen. Am Abend ziehen sie in Gruppen zu ihren Schlafbäumen. Im Flug nehmen Kormorane eine deutliche Keilformation ein, die an den Zug von Gänsen erinnert.

Heutzutage sind Kormorane fast nur noch Wintergäste in den Donauauen, nur Jungtiere bleiben auch den Sommer über hier. Früher jedoch lebten sie das ganze Jahr hindurch hier und bildeten große Brutkolonien, die letzte wurde in den 1960-er Jahren von Fischern zerstört. Recht verwunderlich ist jedoch, dass auch heutzutage Kormorane noch legal abgeschossen werden dürfen. Durch seine Jagd nach Fischen kommt er in Konflikt mit den Interessen des Menschen, der scheinbar fürchtet, durch die Nahrungskonkurrenz der Kormorane in Bedrängnis zu geraten.

KRONENDACH DES WINTERLICHEN AUWALDES

Nachdem die Blätter abgefallen sind, wird das feine Muster der verzweigten Baumkronen sichtbar. Auch noch in der Starre des Winters wird die Vielfalt des Waldes deutlich, die Rinden der unterschiedlichen Baum- und Straucharten variieren in verschiedenen Braun-, Grau- und Rottönen.

Kahl ragen die Aubäume in den winterlichen Himmel. An der monotonen Regelmäßigkeit ist zu erkennen, dass es sich hier nicht um natürlich entstandenen Auwald handelt, sondern um Pflanzungen von Hybridpappeln. Mit diesen rasch wachsenden Bäumen wurden große

DIE AU IM WINTER

Bereiche der Au aufgeforstet, um den forstwirtschaftlichen Ertrag zu steigern. Diese Zeit ist zumindest in einigen Bereichen der Donauauen vorbei, und in die Pappelmonokulturen kehrt nach und nach die Vielfalt zurück. Da sich die Hybridpappeln mit der Schwarzpappel kreuzen, sind sie eine große Gefahr für die einheimischen Schwarzpappel-Bestände. Rechts des Altarmes, der das Bild durchzieht, ist der ursprüngliche Auwald mit seinen vielen verschiedenen Gehölzarten zu erkennen.

GRAUREIHER *(Ardea cinerea)*

Ein Graureiher sitzt auf einem umgestürzten Baum. Diese Reiherart findet sich überall in der Au. Ein Teil der Tiere bleibt auch den Winter über seinem Standort treu, solange die Gewässer nicht zufrieren. Im Gegensatz zu ihren Verwandten, den Silberreihern, brüten Graureiher in Kolonien hoch in alten Bäumen. In den östlichen Donauauen gibt es insgesamt drei solcher Brutkolonien. Sie erfüllen auch für andere, gefährdete Vogelarten eine wichtige Funktion. Nachtreiher, Würgfalken, Seeadler oder Milane siedeln sich häufig innerhalb oder am Rande dieser Brutkolonien an.

MOORFROSCH *(Rana arvalis)* IN SEINEM BLAUEN BALZKLEID

Im Frühling bringen die intensiv blau gefärbten Moorfrösche die erste Farbe in die Augewässer. Außerhalb der Paarungszeit sind beide Geschlechter farblich nicht voneinander zu unterscheiden, während der Balz sind die Männchen aber oft intensiv blau gefärbt.

LAUBFROSCH *(Hyla arborea)*
IM FRÜHLING

Im Frühling kehrt langsam wieder das Grün als dominierende Farbe in die Au zurück, und auch die Laubfrösche erwachen nach ihrer Monate dauernden Winterstarre.

BLÜTEN DES BÄRLAUCHS
(Allium ursinum)

Zeitig im Frühjahr bedecken die jungen, saftig grünen Blätter des Bärlauchs oft große Flächen des Aubodens. Diese Zeit zählt kulinarisch zweifelsfrei zu den besten, die die Au zu bieten hat. Steht Wochen später der Bärlauch in voller Blüte, wird der Waldboden von einem weißen Blütenmeer überzogen.

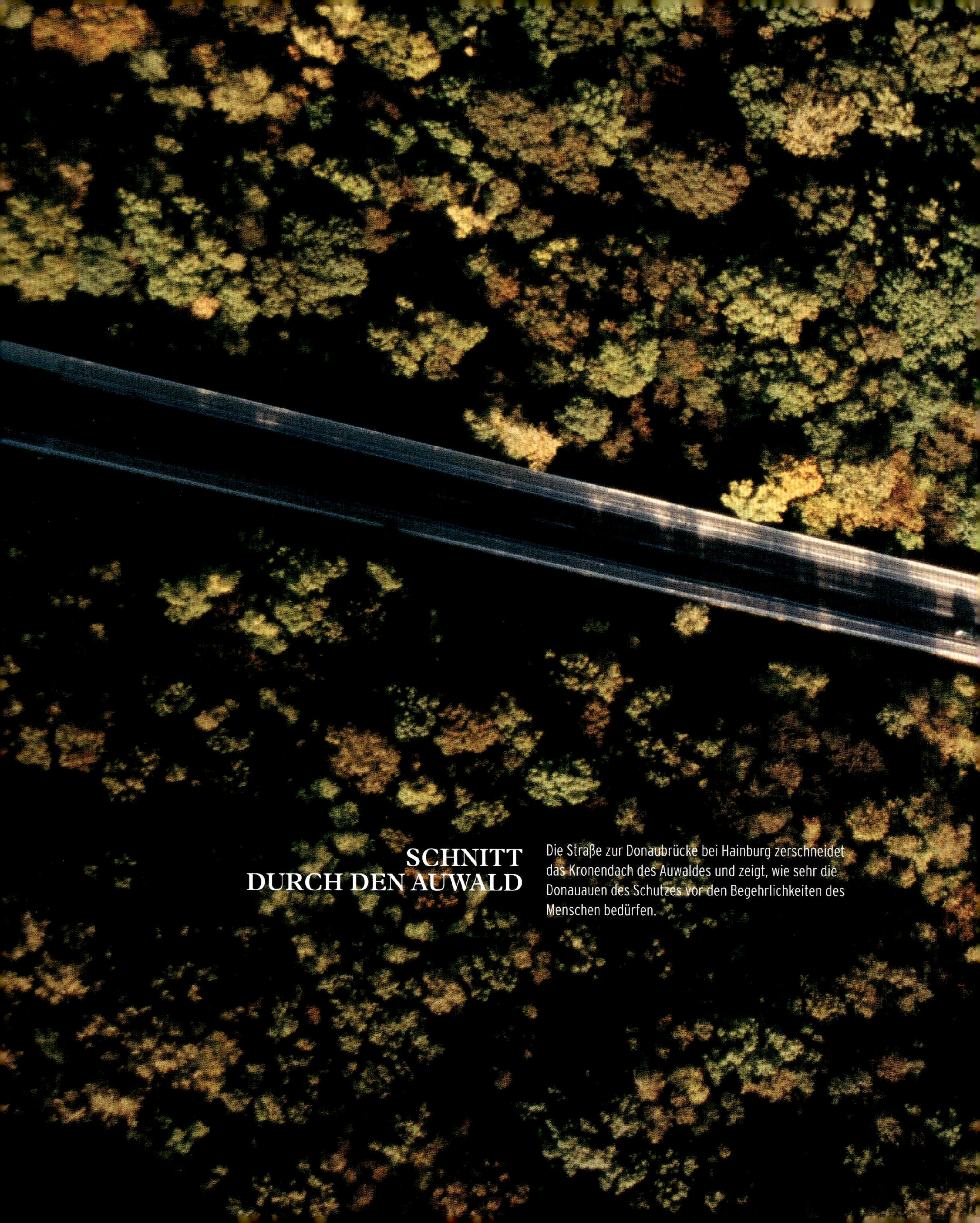

SCHNITT DURCH DEN AUWALD

Die Straße zur Donaubrücke bei Hainburg zerschneidet das Kronendach des Auwaldes und zeigt, wie sehr die Donauauen des Schutzes vor den Begehrlichkeiten des Menschen bedürfen.

AUSKLANG

ABFLUG EINER LACHMÖWE
(Larus ridibundus)

NATIONALPARK DONAU-AUEN

Der Nationalpark Donau-Auen liegt zwischen den europäischen Hauptstädten Wien und Bratislava, in den Bundesländern Wien und Niederösterreich. Er schützt auf über 9.300 ha Fläche eine der letzten großen Flussauen Mitteleuropas. Weit über die Grenzen Österreichs bekannt wurden die Donau-Auen in den 1980er Jahren: Die Hainburger Au-Besetzung verhinderte das geplante Donaukraftwerk. Mit der Gründung des Nationalpark Donau-Auen in Wien und Niederösterreich im Jahr 1996 wurde das Gebiet nachhaltig unter internationalen Schutz gestellt. Die Auwälder stehen außer Nutzung, damit sich die Natur möglichst frei entfalten kann. Innovative Wasserbauprojekte erhalten und verbessern die Dynamik. Mit einem bunten Spektrum an Exkursionen und attraktiven Einrichtungen ist der Nationalpark Donau-Auen ein Zentrum der Umweltbildung. Das Besucherzentrum mit Nationalpark-Ausstellung und Au-Erlebnisgelände Schlossinsel befindet sich im revitalisierten Schloss Orth.

Die hier noch auf knapp 50 km frei fließende Donau ist seine Lebensader. Ihr lebendiges Wechselspiel mit Pegelschwankungen bis zu sieben Meter gestaltet die Aulandschaft immer wieder neu. Nur unverbaute Flüsse vermögen die sie begleitende Landschaft zu gestalten. Sie nagen am Ufer, bilden durchspülte Seitenarme, Inseln können entstehen, Altwässer verlanden, Waldflächen kommen auf und werden wieder abgetragen. Die Flüsse bringen Nährstoffe ein und tragen Sedimente aus. Der Rhythmus von Hoch- und Niederwasserphasen tut sein Übriges. Dieses Auf und Ab macht das Bestehen einer Aulandschaft erst möglich. Damit entsteht eine dynamisch vernetzte Flusslandschaft, die sich ständig ändert und somit eine Fülle

an Lebensräumen für zahllose teils seltene und bedrohte Tier- und Pflanzenarten bietet.

Die Natur sich selbst zu überlassen, genügt nicht immer – der Nationalpark braucht die Rücknahme alter Eingriffe, insbesondere überzogener Flussregulierungen. Seit der Gründung des Nationalparks konnten die ökologischen Verhältnisse der Donau-Auen bereits in wichtigen Teilbereichen verbessert werden. Ein Hauptziel ist, die Donau wieder besser mit den Altarmen zu vernetzen. Denn die Au benötigt regelmäßige Überschwemmungen, um zu bestehen. Diese Gewässervernetzungen sind zukunftsweisend und finden internationale Beachtung. Durch Uferrückbau werden wieder natürliche Flachufer und Schotterbänke geschaffen – als Lebensraum und Kinderstube für bedrohte Wasservögel und Flussfische. Große Projekte und internationale Kooperationen werden in den kommenden Jahren die ökologische Situation der Donau-Auen östlich von Wien weiter verbessern.

In den Wäldern des Nationalparks wird die Anreicherung mit Altholz angestrebt. Dieses sichert zahlreichen spezialisierten Lebewesen das Überleben. Die Wandlung der Arten- und Alterszusammensetzung der Baumbestände zurück zum Naturwald ist ein langsamer, stetiger Prozess.

Im Nationalpark Donau-Auen wird Arten- und Biodiversitätsschutz primär durch Erhalt und Entwicklung der Abläufe gesichert. Für besonders gefährdete Arten werden jedoch unterstützende Forschungs- und Schutzprogramme entwickelt, wie zum Beispiel für den Seeadler, den Europäischen Hundsfisch und die Europäische Sumpfschildkröte.

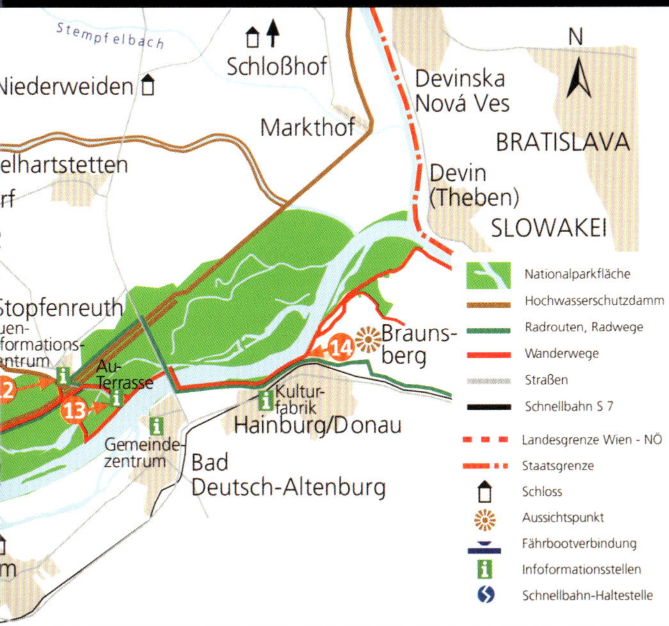

Treffpunkte für Exkursionen

1. nationalparkhaus wien-lobAU
2. Saltenstraße, Lobaubrücke
3. Lobaumuseum/Vorwerk
4. Panozzalacke, Parkplatz
5. Groß-Enzersdorf, Endstat. Bus 26A
6. Schönau, Imbiss-Stube bei Schutzdamm
7. Maria Ellend, Bahnhof
8. schlossORTH Nationalpark-Zentrum
9. Orth/Donau, GH Uferhaus
10. Haslau, Haltestelle S7 od. Parkplatz (Sportpl.)
11. Schloss Eckartsau, NP-Infostelle
12. Stopfenreuth, Auen-Info-Zentrum
13. Stopfenreuth, Au-Terrasse, Uferstraße
14. Hainburg, Parkplatz bei Donaulände

DER AUTOR

Dr. Robert Petermann, aufgewachsen in der Steiermark, zog zum Studium der Molekularbiologie nach Wien. Nach mehreren Jahren in der Grundlagenforschung verließ er die Forschungslabors, absolvierte ein Wirtschaftsstudium und wechselte in die Pharmazeutische Industrie.

Der Versuch biologische Phänomene zu verstehen, war stets Teil seiner Tätigkeiten und bildet auch die Grundlage des vorliegenden Buches. Darüber hinaus war es aber auch die Ästhetik der Aulandschaft und ihrer Bewohner, welche den Ausschlag dafür gab, diesen Lebensraum in Fotografien zu beschreiben.

DANKSAGUNG

Dieses Buch entstand durch die Unterstützung zahlreicher Personen, von denen ich folgenden zu besonderem Dank verpflichtet bin:

WISSENSCHAFTLICHE BERATUNG:
Dr. Josef Trauttmannsdorff, Forschungsgemeinschaft Wilhelminenberg; Dr. Manfred Pintar, Universität für Bodenkultur; Mag. Heimo Schedl, Universität für Bodenkultur; Dr. Christian Baumgartner, Nationalpark Donau-Auen; Mag. Georg Frank, Nationalpark Donau-Auen; Mag. Matthias Schmidt, BirdLife Österreich

DESIGN- UND LAYOUTENTWURF:
Mag. Beate Hecher, Wien

TECHNISCHE UNTERSTÜTZUNG:
Mag. Christoph Erhart, Graz
Bill Lorenz, BSc, Altenberg

PILOT/FLUGKOORDINATION:
Harald Ullmann, Wiener Neustadt

Sehr verbunden bin ich auch Dr. Jürgen Hatzenbichler, Chefredakteur des Universum Magazins, der von Beginn an dieses Projekt unterstützt hat.

ZUR FOTOGRAFIE:
Die Aufnahmen entstanden über einen Zeitraum von nahezu drei Jahren in den Auen bei Stockerau und im Nationalpark Donau-Auen. Die Bilder aus dem Nationalpark entstanden in öffentlich zugänglichen Bereichen bzw. in Absprache mit der Nationalpark-Verwaltung.